Collins

500 QUIZZES

PUB·QUIZ

10,000 QUESTIONS

?

Published by Collins
An imprint of HarperCollins Publishers
Westerhill Road
Bishopbriggs
Glasgow G64 2QT

www.harpercollins.co.uk

First Edition 2018

10 9 8 7 6 5 4 3 2 1

ISBN 978-0-00-829027-6

www.harpercollins.co.uk

Typeset by Puzzler Media

Printed and bound by CPI Group (UK) Ltd, Croydon, CR0 4YY

A catalogue record for this book is available from the British Library.

If you would like to comment on any aspect of this book, please contact us at the above address or online.
E-mail: puzzles@harpercollins.co.uk

Introduction

What makes a good quiz? A witty and amusing host and a choice of interesting categories are good places to start.

You could combine the hosting talents of Alexander Armstrong and Jeremy Paxman but you need a great set of questions too.

That's where *Collins Pub Quiz* comes in. We've taken the hassle out of creating the perfect quiz by providing 10,000 questions on all manner of subjects in an easy-to-use format.

There's something on offer for everyone, too, from easy questions for those taking their first tentative steps from quizzing base camp right up to super-tricky testers for those experienced trivia travellers heading for the highest peaks of general knowledge.

Let's get going.

The quizzes

The book is divided into two parts, each with 250 quizzes. Half of the quizzes are based on themes ranging from biology to buildings, money to mythology, nature to numbers and a whole host of subjects in between. The rest of the quizzes are pot luck and contain a little bit of everything.

The quizzes in each part of the book are grouped together depending on how tricky we think they are. The easy ones come first, followed by medium and finally hard.

Easy

With a wide range of themes on offer in our easy section, you're bound to find some questions and quizzes easy and others a bit harder. It's not all straightforward in this section though: watch out for a few themes that aren't quite as obvious as the title suggests. Quiz 251 marks the start of the second easy section.

Medium

You'll get a good general knowledge workout when you tackle our medium quizzes. Classic themes that appeared in the easy section are repeated here, but you'll most likely need some extra thinking time to complete the quizzes at this level. The second medium section starts at Quiz 401.

Hard

You'll really need to work those little grey cells when you venture into our hard quiz section, so set aside plenty of time. An enthusiast's knowledge would be a definite advantage on some of the themed quizzes. When you've toiled your way through the first section, the second hard section begins at Quiz 476.

The answers

Each quiz header tells you where the answers are printed. They're mostly just a couple of pages away, for example the answers to Quiz 1 appear at the bottom of Quiz 3. The exceptions are the last two quizzes in each part of the book, which appear at the bottom of the first two quizzes in that part.

Running a quiz

When you're running a quiz, there's a great sense of satisfaction to be had in doing a job well, and a little bit of effort beforehand will go a long way to making sure that your quiz goes without a hitch.

❖ Plan: consider how many questions you want to ask in the time available, making sure you leave enough thinking time between questions. Once you've done that, pick a good range of subjects so that there's something for everyone.

❖ Rehearse: Go through all the questions you're going to be asking beforehand, checking any potentially tricky pronunciations and making sure your timings work. Note down all the questions (notes look better in a quiz environment than reading from a book) and answers. Every effort has been made to ensure that all the answers in *Collins Pub Quiz* are correct. Despite our best endeavours, mistakes may still appear. If you see an answer you're not sure is right, or if you think there's more than one possible answer, then do check.

❖ Paper and writing implements: make sure you prepare enough sheets of paper for everyone to write on, including scrap paper, and have plenty of pens to hand for those who need them.

❖ Prizes: everyone likes a prize. No matter how small, it's best to have one on offer.

Good luck! We hope you enjoy *Collins Pub Quiz*.

Contents

Easy Quizzes

1. Pot Luck
2. Sport
3. Pot Luck
4. 1980s Music
5. Pot Luck
6. Art
7. Pot Luck
8. Geography
9. Pot Luck
10. History
11. Pot Luck
12. Out and About
13. Pot Luck
14. Nursery Rhymes
15. Pot Luck
16. Fictional Couples
17. Pot Luck
18. Africa
19. Pot Luck
20. Sea Creatures
21. Pot Luck
22. Film
23. Pot Luck
24. Human Biology
25. Pot Luck
26. Myth and Legend
27. Pot Luck
28. The UK
29. Pot Luck
30. Rugby
31. Pot Luck
32. Television
33. Pot Luck
34. Vegetarian Food
35. Pot Luck
36. Board Games
37. Pot Luck
38. Animal World
39. Pot Luck
40. Italy
41. Pot Luck
42. Gold and Silver
43. Pot Luck
44. Disney Films
45. Pot Luck
46. Numbers
47. Pot Luck
48. Politics
49. Pot Luck
50. Theatre
51. Pot Luck
52. Clothing and Fabric
53. Pot Luck
54. Literature
55. Pot Luck
56. Over and Out
57. Pot Luck
58. Natural World
59. Pot Luck
60. On the Road
61. Pot Luck
62. 1960s Music
63. Pot Luck
64. Food and Drink
65. Pot Luck
66. Orange
67. Pot Luck
68. Science
69. Pot Luck
70. Snooker
71. Pot Luck
72. Words
73. Pot Luck
74. Three Letters
75. Pot Luck
76. The USA
77. Pot Luck
78. Leisure
79. Pot Luck
80. Engineering
81. Pot Luck
82. Classical Music
83. Pot Luck
84. Paul
85. Pot Luck
86. 21st-Century Film
87. Pot Luck
88. Q & I
89. Pot Luck
90. Pop Music
91. Pot Luck
92. Buildings
93. Pot Luck
94. Planet Earth
95. Pot Luck
96. Classic Sitcoms
97. Pot Luck
98. Sporting Venues
99. Pot Luck
100. World History
101. Pot Luck
102. Russia
103. Pot Luck
104. Blue
105. Pot Luck
106. On the Water
107. Pot Luck
108. Drinks
109. Pot Luck
110. Duos
111. Pot Luck
112. London
113. Pot Luck
114. Night and Day
115. Pot Luck
116. Technology
117. Pot Luck
118. Team Sports
119. Pot Luck
120. South America
121. Pot Luck
122. 21st-Century Music
123. Pot Luck
124. Education
125. Pot Luck
126. Musicals
127. Pot Luck
128. Famous Gardens
129. Pot Luck

130. Cookery
131. Pot Luck
132. Sun
133. Pot Luck
134. Harry Potter
135. Pot Luck
136. Money
137. Pot Luck
138. Colours
139. Pot Luck
140. Europe
141. Pot Luck
142. Cartoons
143. Pot Luck
144. To a T
145. Pot Luck
146. Lines
147. Pot Luck
148. Mr and Mrs
149. Pot Luck
150. TV Scientists

Medium Quizzes

151. Pot Luck
152. UK Politics
153. Pot Luck
154. At the Double
155. Pot Luck
156. Sport
157. Pot Luck
158. 1960s Music
159. Pot Luck
160. Europe
161. Pot Luck
162. Film
163. Pot Luck
164. History
165. Pot Luck
166. Classic Novels
167. Pot Luck
168. Makers and Collectors
169. Pot Luck

170. Food and Drink
171. Pot Luck
172. Georges
173. Pot Luck
174. Science
175. Pot Luck
176. Geography
177. Pot Luck
178. Tennis
179. Pot Luck
180. Television Costume Drama
181. Pot Luck
182. Art and Music
183. Pot Luck
184. Communications
185. Pot Luck
186. Tourist Attractions
187. Pot Luck
188. Animal World
189. Pot Luck
190. Queen Victoria
191. Pot Luck
192. On the Move
193. Pot Luck
194. France
195. Pot Luck
196. Space
197. Pot Luck
198. Rock Music
199. Pot Luck
200. ABC
201. Pot Luck
202. The 1970s
203. Pot Luck
204. Kate
205. Pot Luck
206. In the Garden
207. Pot Luck
208. Spies on Television
209. Pot Luck
210. Planet Earth
211. Pot Luck
212. War Films

213. Pot Luck
214. Technology and Inventions
215. Pot Luck
216. Modern Fiction
217. Pot Luck
218. Words
219. Pot Luck
220. Numbers
221. Pot Luck
222. Royalty
223. Pot Luck
224. Chemistry
225. Pot Luck

Hard Quizzes

226. Music
227. Pot Luck
228. Third Place
229. Pot Luck
230. Geography
231. Pot Luck
232. Art
233. Pot Luck
234. History
235. Pot Luck
236. Buildings
237. Pot Luck
238. Film
239. Pot Luck
240. Natural World
241. Pot Luck
242. Science
243. Pot Luck
244. Literature
245. Pot Luck
246. Sport
247. Pot Luck
248. Words
249. Pot Luck
250. Europe

Easy Quizzes

251. Pot Luck
252. Science
253. Pot Luck
254. Food and Drink
255. Pot Luck
256. Literature
257. Pot Luck
258. Animal World
259. Pot Luck
260. Television Satire
261. Pot Luck
262. Sport
263. Pot Luck
264. Black
265. Pot Luck
266. Politics
267. Pot Luck
268. Numbers
269. Pot Luck
270. Germany
271. Pot Luck
272. Planet Earth
273. Pot Luck
274. 1970s Music
275. Pot Luck
276. Hats
277. Pot Luck
278. Animal Inspiration
279. Pot Luck
280. The UK
281. Pot Luck
282. Children's Literature
283. Pot Luck
284. Film
285. Pot Luck
286. Private Investigations
287. Pot Luck
288. Solar System
289. Pot Luck
290. Geography
291. Pot Luck
292. Occupations

293. Pot Luck
294. Television
295. Pot Luck
296. History
297. Pot Luck
298. Jazz and Blues
299. Pot Luck
300. Science Fiction
301. Pot Luck
302. Shapes
303. Pot Luck
304. Words
305. Pot Luck
306. Pop Music
307. Pot Luck
308. Technology
309. Pot Luck
310. France
311. Pot Luck
312. On Stage
313. Pot Luck
314. Hard Times
315. Pot Luck
316. Stately Homes
317. Pot Luck
318. Sporting Equipment
319. Pot Luck
320. White
321. Pot Luck
322. Long-Running Televison Series
323. Pot Luck
324. Dead or Alive
325. Pot Luck
326. Europe
327. Pot Luck
328. Art
329. Pot Luck
330. Fruit and Vegetables
331. Pot Luck
332. Human Biology
333. Pot Luck
334. Fighting Talk

335. Pot Luck
336. Winter Sports
337. Pot Luck
338. Classical Music
339. Pot Luck
340. Travelling Around
341. Pot Luck
342. Heads Up
343. Pot Luck
344. Eating Out
345. Pot Luck
346. Seasons
347. Pot Luck
348. Superheroes
349. Pot Luck
350. Weather
351. Pot Luck
352. On Wheels
353. Pot Luck
354. Colours
355. Pot Luck
356. Romantic Comedies
357. Pot Luck
358. Leisure
359. Pot Luck
360. Dance
361. Pot Luck
362. 1950s
363. Pot Luck
364. To And Fro
365. Pot Luck
366. Four-legged Friends
367. Pot Luck
368. Sweet Things
369. Pot Luck
370. Money
371. Pot Luck
372. Celebrity
373. Pot Luck
374. In the Garden
375. Pot Luck
376. Indoor Sports
377. Pot Luck

378. Musicals
379. Pot Luck
380. Inventors And Inventions
381. Pot Luck
382. Mythology
383. Pot Luck
384. Two-word Terms
385. Pot Luck
386. Musicians
387. Pot Luck
388. Poetry
389. Pot Luck
390. It Figures
391. Pot Luck
392. Bars
393. Pot Luck
394. London
395. Pot Luck
396. Names
397. Pot Luck
398. Lands
399. Pot Luck
400. Birds

Medium Quizzes

401. Pot Luck
402. Sport
403. Pot Luck
404. Prequels and Sequels
405. Pot Luck
406. The UK
407. Pot Luck
408. Food and Drink
409. Pot Luck
410. World Politics
411. Pot Luck
412. Geography
413. Pot Luck
414. Pop Music
415. Pot Luck
416. Crime
417. Pot Luck
418. Sitcoms

419. Pot Luck
420. Literature
421. Pot Luck
422. History
423. Pot Luck
424. Mathematics
425. Pot Luck
426. The USA
427. Pot Luck
428. Film
429. Pot Luck
430. Green
431. Pot Luck
432. Money
433. Pot Luck
434. Animal World
435. Pot Luck
436. Television
437. Pot Luck
438. A & E
439. Pot Luck
440. The 1980s
441. Pot Luck
442. Science
443. Pot Luck
444. Europe
445. Pot Luck
446. Team Sports
447. Pot Luck
448. Art and Music
449. Pot Luck
450. Around the House
451. Pot Luck
452. 1990s Music
453. Pot Luck
454. Leisure
455. Pot Luck
456. Performing Arts
457. Pot Luck
458. Fiction
459. Pot Luck
460. Planet Earth
461. Pot Luck

462. Scotland
463. Pot Luck
464. The Tudors
465. Pot Luck
466. Cricket
467. Pot Luck
468. Musicians and Songwriters
469. Pot Luck
470. Words
471. Pot Luck
472. Landmarks
473. Pot Luck
474. XYZ
475. Pot Luck

Hard Quizzes

476. Natural World
477. Pot Luck
478. Names
479. Pot Luck
480. Food and Drink
481. Pot Luck
482. Literature
483. Pot Luck
484. Entertainment
485. Pot Luck
486. Geography
487. Pot Luck
488. Language
489. Pot Luck
490. Music
491. Pot Luck
492. Inovations
493. Pot Luck
494. Sport
495. Pot Luck
496. The Arts
497. Pot Luck
498. History
499. Pot Luck
500. Photography

1 The study of fungi is given what name?

2 What is meant by the American expression "from soup to nuts"?

3 What crisp biscuit made from unleavened bread is traditionally eaten at Passover?

4 The children's book *The Witches* (1983) was written by which author?

5 What does the "A" stand for in the abbreviation CIA?

6 In a track race, what do sprinters start from?

7 What term is given to a writ demanding attendance at court?

8 Which long-running drama series features the pub The Dog in the Pond?

9 Who changed the royal family name from Saxe-Coburg-Gotha to Windsor?

10 On the Swedish flag what is the colour of the cross?

11 Who is the author of *The Da Vinci Code*?

12 Which radio code word is between Quebec and Sierra?

13 From which occupation do the four Teenage Mutant Ninja Turtles take their names?

14 To which group of birds does the capercaillie belong?

15 To what does paediatric medicine relate?

16 Which British monarch succeeded Queen Victoria?

17 Nat King Cole was famous for playing which instrument?

18 Which of the Seven Dwarfs was always feeling tired?

19 What is a rotunda?

20 Which day of the week is named after the god Saturn?

Easy

Medium

Hard

Answers to QUIZ 249 – Pot Luck

1	Spanish	11	Sir Charlie Chaplin
2	Trinidad	12	A space
3	*Northanger Abbey*	13	1920s
4	Ukraine	14	1804
5	Pall Mall	15	Sir Rod Stewart
6	*A Tale Of Two Cities*	16	AP McCoy
7	Tyrrhenian	17	Marne
8	Corunna	18	Hymn book
9	Max Frisch	19	Belgium
10	Ian Dury	20	An architect

Easy

1 What was the original name of boxer Muhammad Ali?

2 How many players are in a cricket team?

3 Which country won the FIFA World Cup in 1982 and 2006?

4 How many points does a try score in rugby union?

5 What is the nickname of the South African rugby union team?

6 What is a sword with a three-sided blade used in fencing?

7 Which team won both the men's and the women's Boat Races in 2018?

8 Which racecourse is home to the Scottish Grand National?

9 In snooker, what is the name of the rest which supports the cue above ball height?

10 Catcher and shortstop are positions in which sport?

11 Which New York district has the eponymous Globetrotters for a basketball team?

12 Who won his fourth Formula 1 World Championship in 2017?

13 St Moritz is home to which famous bobsled track?

14 Which tennis player won her first grand slam singles title at the 2018 Australian Open?

Medium

15 In the 1970s, which horse won the Grand National three times?

16 What is the American name for Association Football?

17 Which equestrian discipline involves deportment and control?

18 At which venue is the US Open tennis tournament played?

19 In which sport are there madisons and pursuits?

20 How many walls surround a squash court?

Hard

Answers to QUIZ 250 – Europe

1	Draco	11	Trondheim
2	Valois	12	The Seine
3	Lysander	13	Gulf of Gabès, Mediterranean Sea
4	Naples	14	Gluck
5	Israel	15	1821
6	Henri Cartier-Bresson	16	Cremona
7	Abraham Ortelius	17	Delos
8	Lisbon	18	Saint Kevin
9	Hungarian	19	Costa del Sol
10	1886	20	Herman Hesse

ANSWERS ON PAGE 5

1 What is the science and study of drawing maps known as?

2 Key Largo and Key West are off the coast of which US state?

3 What is the name of the line which can be found on world maps which divides the Earth into Northern and Southern hemispheres?

4 What astrological term describes a person born on St George's Day?

5 In which modern country was the capital of the Incan empire?

6 What kind of animal is a Russian Blue?

7 If you were watching someone on a PGA tour what would you be watching?

8 What type of knife can also describe a thin heel on a shoe?

9 What is the Latin name for Scotland?

10 In which century was Botticelli born?

11 What is a quarter of 180?

12 Which model was known as "The Shrimp"?

13 What item of clothing do Americans call a vest?

14 Ash Wednesday is the first day of which period of fasting?

15 What is the fifth book of the New Testament?

16 In which comedy series did Ruth Madoc play Gladys Pugh?

17 By what name was Aragorn first known to Frodo in *The Lord of the Rings*?

18 In the TV series *Thunderbirds*, who was the pilot of the underwater rescue missions?

19 Which twilled cotton fabric is used to make jeans?

20 What colour is the paint cobalt?

Answers to QUIZ 1 – Pot Luck

1	Mycology	11	Dan Brown
2	From start to finish	12	Romeo
3	Matzo	13	Artists
4	Roald Dahl	14	The grouse family
5	Agency	15	Children
6	Blocks	16	Edward VII
7	Subpoena	17	Piano
8	*Hollyoaks*	18	Sleepy
9	King George V	19	A round building
10	Yellow or gold	20	Saturday

Easy

Medium

Hard

ANSWERS ON PAGE **6**

Easy

1   Who had a hit in 1981 with *Tainted Love*?

2   How were Mike Nolan, Bobby G, Jay Aston and Cheryl Baker collectively known in the 1980s?

3   Twin brothers Charlie and Craig Reid form which Scottish duo, who had their first hit in 1987?

4   Which group had a 1986 hit with *Hunting High and Low*?

5   What was the title of the 1980 album by Adam and the Ants?

6   Which group had a hit in 1988 with *Don't Turn Around*?

7   Which female singer joined UB40 for their 1985 hit *I Got You Babe*?

8   *Caravan of Love* was a 1986 hit for which group?

9   *Nothing's Gonna Stop Us Now* by Starship featured in which 1987 film?

10   Who was the only person to appear in both the London and Philadelphia Live Aid concerts?

Medium

11   Which band's first hit was 1981's *Planet Earth*?

12   *Only You*, a 1983 hit for the Flying Pickets, was originally recorded by which duo?

13   *Use It Up and Wear It Out* was a 1980 hit for which group?

14   What was the last single issued by Wham!?

15   Which duo had a 1988 hit with *I Owe You Nothing*?

16   In which year was Michael Jackson's *Thriller* album released?

17   Who wrote Roxy Music's 1981 chart-topper *Jealous Guy*?

18   *The Tide Is High* was a 1980 single by which group?

19   In which year did the Human League top the charts with *Don't You Want Me*?

20   What colour door did Shakin' Stevens sing about in 1981?

Hard

Answers to QUIZ 2 – Sport

1	Cassius Clay	11	Harlem
2	11	12	Lewis Hamilton
3	Italy	13	Cresta Run
4	Five	14	Caroline Wozniacki
5	Springboks	15	Red Rum
6	Épée	16	Soccer
7	Cambridge	17	Dressage
8	Ayr	18	Flushing Meadow
9	Spider	19	Cycling
10	Baseball	20	Four

1   In which *Carry On* film did Phil Silvers feature?

2   The Weird Sisters appear in which Shakespeare play?

3   Which Greek maiden became the personification of the soul?

4   Who won an Oscar for her role in the 2008 film *The Reader*?

5   What number is represented by the Roman numeral D?

6   On mobile phones with a keypad on the handset, which letters appear on the number 6 key?

7   Which imperial liquid measure is equal to two pints?

8   Is France ahead of or behind Greenwich Mean Time?

9   Which musical is based on a short story entitled *The Idyll of Miss Sarah Brown*?

10 Who played Grant Mitchell in *EastEnders*?

11 At what degree Celsius does water freeze?

12 Is a pollack a freshwater or seawater fish?

13 Who publish a magazine called *The Watchtower*?

14 On what part of your body would you wear a stole?

15 Bruce Wayne is the real name of which comic-book hero?

16 Which ancient Greek author wrote the fable of *The Tortoise and the Hare*?

17 What name is given to the stiff slender leaf of a conifer?

18 Which canal runs between London and Birmingham?

19 Captain Haddock is which fictional character's best friend?

20 Which is the southernmost capital city in the world?

Easy

Medium

Hard

Answers to QUIZ 3 – Pot Luck

1	Cartography	11	45
2	Florida	12	Jean Shrimpton
3	The equator	13	Waistcoat
4	Taurean	14	Lent
5	Peru	15	Acts
6	Cat	16	*Hi-de-Hi!*
7	Golf	17	Strider
8	Stiletto	18	Gordon Tracy
9	Caledonia	19	Denim
10	15th century	20	Blue

Easy

1   Which famous painting was stolen from the Louvre art gallery on 20th August 1911?

2   Which Spanish painter's name comes from his having been born on Crete?

3   Picasso and Braque established which 20th-century art movement?

4   Timothy Spall portrayed which English artist in a 2014 film?

5   Which representative body of artists was founded in 1768?

6   Who painted *The Singing Butler* (1992)?

7   *The Monarch of the Glen* by Edwin Landseer features which male animal?

8   Which English artist painted *The Blue Boy* (1779)?

9   What was the first name of Surrealist painter Magritte?

10 *Girl with a Pearl Earring* was painted by which artist?

11 Which potter won the 2003 Turner Prize?

12 What is the name of the board on which an artist mixes paint?

13 Who was the 17th-century Dutch portrait painter of *The Laughing Cavalier*?

14 *The Scream* (1893) was painted by which Norwegian artist?

Medium

15 In which city is the Prado Museum of art?

16 With what instrument of martyrdom is St Catherine of Alexandria depicted in art?

17 Which painter was famous for his "matchstick" figures?

18 *La Primavera* was painted by which Italian artist?

19 What was Rembrandt's nationality?

20 What term is given to a painting on three separate panels joined by hinges?

Hard

Answers to QUIZ 4 – 1980s Music

1	Soft Cell	11	Duran Duran
2	Bucks Fizz	12	Yazoo
3	The Proclaimers	13	Odyssey
4	A-ha	14	*The Edge of Heaven*
5	*Kings of the Wild Frontier*	15	Bros
6	Aswad	16	1982
7	Chrissie Hynde	17	John Lennon
8	The Housemartins	18	Blondie
9	*Mannequin*	19	1981
10	Phil Collins	20	Green

1   *Country House* and *Girls and Boys* were hits for which band?

2   What was buried with Qin Shi Huang, the first Emperor of China, to protect him in the afterlife?

3   Near which Kent port is the English opening of the Channel Tunnel?

4   Which town is the location of the University of Surrey?

5   On an archery target, how many colours are there?

6   What are the Southern Lights also called?

7   What is an accompanied vocal solo in a cantata?

8   Who invented the phonograph?

9   Which fictional character had a diary published at the age of $13\frac{3}{4}$?

10   In which county is Colchester, Britain's oldest recorded town?

11   What type of creature is cartoon character Yogi?

12   Who sang the 1971 hit version of *Without You*, a 1994 hit for Mariah Carey?

13   Who played the title role in the film *Elizabeth: The Golden Age*?

14   Is Zambia ahead of or behind Greenwich Mean Time?

15   Which type of cloth is made from flax?

16   What is the name for the part of a willow tree that bears pollen and nectar?

17   In the 1968 film *Oliver!*, which actor played the role of Fagin?

18   What part of the body would be affected if you suffered from myopia?

19   What is the official language of Morocco?

20   In a pack of cards, how many eyes can be seen on the Jacks?

Easy

Medium

Hard

Answers to QUIZ 5 – Pot Luck

1	*Carry On Follow That Camel*	11	0
2	*Macbeth*	12	Sea fish
3	Psyche	13	Jehovah's Witnesses
4	Kate Winslet	14	Shoulders
5	500	15	Batman
6	MNO	16	Aesop
7	Quart	17	Needle
8	Ahead	18	Grand Union
9	*Guys and Dolls*	19	Tintin
10	Ross Kemp	20	Wellington, New Zealand

Easy

1. What name is given to the line of rocks off the western point of the Isle of Wight?
2. Queensland is a state in which country?
3. Kirkcaldy is in which historic county of Scotland?
4. Which Scottish island was linked to the mainland by a bridge in 1995?
5. ATL is the international airport code for which US city?
6. Which Italian city is said to be built on seven hills?
7. What name is given to the series of lakes mainly found in Norfolk?
8. Which is the southernmost US state?
9. Dover lies opposite which French port?
10. Spain and Portugal comprise part of which peninsula?
11. In which mountain range is Ben Nevis?
12. Nassau is the capital of which Caribbean island group?
13. Which is the world's deepest ocean?
14. In which county is Royal Tunbridge Wells?

Medium

15. What is the Spanish name for Spain?
16. The river Liffey flows into which sea?
17. In which English county is the town of Bromsgrove?
18. What is the form of address for an Italian married woman?
19. What is the capital of New York State?
20. Of what are there 100 in a US dollar?

Answers to QUIZ 6 – Art

1	*Mona Lisa*	11	Grayson Perry
2	El Greco	12	Palette
3	Cubism	13	Frans Hals
4	JMW Turner	14	Edvard Munch
5	Royal Academy	15	Madrid
6	Jack Vettriano	16	Wheel
7	Stag	17	LS Lowry
8	Thomas Gainsborough	18	Botticelli
9	René	19	Dutch
10	Johannes Vermeer	20	Triptych

Hard

QUIZ 9 – Pot Luck

ANSWERS ON PAGE 11

1. What term is given for lines that run from the centre to the edge of a circle?
2. Tenerife is part of which island group?
3. What collective name is given to foods such as fusilli and linguine?
4. With which city is the Sally Lunn bun associated?
5. How many stomachs has a cow?
6. In 2011, which band had a hit with *Paradise*?
7. What is the chemical symbol for iodine?
8. Who wrote the novel *2001: A Space Odyssey*?
9. In the English alphabet, what is the 13th letter?
10. What is a sheepshank?
11. On which part of your body would you wear a homburg?
12. If you betray your country what crime do you commit?
13. In the Bible, who was the father of Shem, Ham and Japheth?
14. What was Elvis Presley's first chart hit in the UK?
15. Cape Canaveral was formerly known by what name?
16. Who directed the 1966 thriller *Torn Curtain*?
17. Which orchestra was founded in Manchester in 1858?
18. What term is given to the young of a whale?
19. Who played the title role in the 2013 film *Mandela: Long Walk to Freedom*?
20. Who was the first woman to win a Nobel Prize?

Easy

Medium

Hard

Answers to QUIZ 7 – Pot Luck

1	Blur	11	Bear
2	The Terracotta Army	12	Nilsson
3	Folkestone	13	Cate Blanchett
4	Guildford	14	Ahead
5	Five	15	Linen
6	Aurora Australis	16	Catkin
7	Aria	17	Ron Moody
8	Thomas Edison	18	Eyes
9	Adrian Mole	19	Arabic
10	Essex	20	12

Easy

1 What was an old five-shilling piece called?

2 In 1913, what make and model of car became the first to be mass-produced on an assembly line?

3 To which island was Napoleon first exiled?

4 What was the surname of Henry VIII's sixth wife?

5 Which religious movement in the Christian church was founded by brothers Charles and John Wesley?

6 Ukraine and Belarus were a part of which country until 1991?

7 Which WWII battleship shared its name with a 19th-century German statesman?

8 Which "metallic" period occurred around 1000BC?

9 During which war did the Battle of Marston Moor take place?

10 Which November 11, 1918 event is marked every year on that date?

11 What name is given to a member of the pre-conquest population of Mexico?

12 During which war did Operation Desert Storm take place?

Medium

13 What nationality was explorer Vasco da Gama?

14 William of Orange was married to which queen?

15 Who was the longest-reigning British king?

16 In which century was Christopher Columbus born?

17 What was East Germany's official name?

18 The Getty family made their fortune from which commodity?

19 Who was victorious at the battle of Bannockburn in 1314?

20 Which was the first complete motorway to be built in Britain?

Hard

1   What is the currency of Australia?

2   In 2010, who took over the Radio 2 breakfast show from Sir Terry Wogan?

3   Which Christmas food has the Latin name *Brassica oleracea var. gemmifera*?

4   Who was the author of the second Gospel?

5   Which strategy game is played on a board in the shape of a six-pointed star?

6   In which century was Leonardo da Vinci born?

7   Who topped the charts in 2000 with *Life Is a Rollercoaster*?

8   In Scrabble®, how many points is the letter J worth?

9   Which African country lies immediately north of Sudan and east of Libya?

10   The zodiac sign Virgo covers which two calendar months?

11   Which colour of snooker ball has the second highest points value?

12   How many feet are there in a dozen yards?

13   Of what is graphology the study?

14   Who starred as Caractacus Potts in the 1968 film *Chitty Chitty Bang Bang*?

15   Which TV quiz show is hosted by Jeremy Vine?

16   Hibernia was the Roman name for which country?

17   Who was the last viceroy of India?

18   What is an ampersand used to mean?

19   Which biblical character demanded the head of John the Baptist as a reward for her dancing?

20   What type of creature is a sika?

Easy

Medium

Hard

Answers to QUIZ 9 – Pot Luck

1	Radii	11	Head
2	Canaries	12	Treason
3	Pasta	13	Noah
4	Bath	14	*Heartbreak Hotel*
5	Four	15	Cape Kennedy
6	Coldplay	16	Sir Alfred Hitchcock
7	I	17	Hallé
8	Arthur C Clarke	18	Calf
9	M	19	Idris Elba
10	A knot	20	Marie Curie

1 Maastricht airport is in which country?

2 Which French phrase in English means a road closed at one end?

3 What do Americans call a sidewalk?

4 What is the name given to the key of a map?

5 If you were arriving at Piccadilly mainline railway station, where would you be?

6 How is a footpath indicated on a map?

7 The Clacket Lane services are on which motorway?

8 El Al is the national airline of which country?

9 What nationality was the airline entrepreneur Sir Freddie Laker?

10 Which American train service connects many US states and several Canadian cities?

11 What is the nickname of London's public transport system which is mostly underground?

12 A juggernaut is what type of vehicle?

13 Which railway service makes exclusive use of the Channel Tunnel?

14 What name is given to the noisy line that warns a driver of the edge of the road?

15 What term describes a stretch of road where stopping is not allowed?

16 In internal combustion engines, which device produces the mix of air and petrol?

17 Which country does a car come from if it has the international registration letter D?

18 What would you be travelling in if you were in a Pullman?

19 Which car company has the Corolla range?

20 Galileo Galilei airport is in which country?

Answers to QUIZ 10 – History

1	Crown	11	Aztec
2	Ford Model T	12	The Gulf War
3	Elba	13	Portuguese
4	Parr	14	Queen Mary II
5	Methodism	15	George III
6	USSR	16	15th century
7	*Bismarck*	17	German Democratic Republic
8	Iron Age	18	Oil
9	First English Civil War	19	Robert the Bruce
10	Armistice	20	M1

1 Which German bacteriologist gave his name to a dish used in laboratories?

2 In the radio phonetic alphabet, what is the code word for the first vowel?

3 What is the capital of Tasmania?

4 How is the midwinter described in the title of a well-known carol?

5 What is the former name of Vietnam's Ho Chi Minh City?

6 Whom did Muhammad Ali beat in the "Rumble in the Jungle"?

7 Which ten-letter word for a colour combines two words to do with water?

8 *My Sweet Lord* was a 1971 hit for which member of the Beatles?

9 In which century was Abraham Lincoln born?

10 What kind of creature is an anchovy?

11 What does the initial "E" in E-number stand for?

12 In the painting *The Birth of Venus* by Botticelli, what is the goddess standing on?

13 Which ship was crushed by pack ice in Antarctica's Weddell Sea in 1915?

14 Which former name of an Israeli port is spelt like a land measurement?

15 How many tricks make up a grand slam in bridge?

16 Which actor starred in the 1980 film *Raging Bull*?

17 After whom were teddy bears named?

18 Which duo topped the charts in 1984 with *Freedom*?

19 Which side of a ship is on the right as you face forward?

20 Sir Laurence Olivier and Sir Michael Caine starred in which 1972 film?

Easy

Medium

Hard

Answers to QUIZ 11 – Pot Luck

1	The Australian Dollar	11	Pink
2	Chris Evans	12	36
3	Brussels sprouts	13	Handwriting
4	Mark	14	Dick Van Dyke
5	Chinese Checkers	15	*Eggheads*
6	15th	16	Ireland
7	Ronan Keating	17	Lord Louis Mountbatten
8	Eight	18	And
9	Egypt	19	Salome
10	August and September	20	Deer

Easy

1   Where did the little boy live in *Baa Baa Black Sheep*?

2   Where did Miss Muffet eat her curds and whey?

3   Who marched ten thousand men up and down a hill?

4   Tom the piper's son stole which animal before running away?

5   Which profession follows tinker, tailor and soldier in a nursery rhyme?

6   In the rhyme *This Little Piggy*, what did the third little piggy eat?

7   Who stole the tarts made by the Queen of Hearts?

8   Who cut off the tails of the three blind mice?

9   What did the Incy Wincy Spider climb up?

10 Little girls are made of which substances, according to the traditional rhyme?

11 After Humpty Dumpty fell off the wall, who tried but failed to put him back together?

12 Who was told to "put the kettle on"?

13 Which musical instrument is mentioned in *Little Boy Blue*?

14 Where does the Muffin Man live?

Medium

15 In *Sing a Song of Sixpence*, what was the Queen eating in her parlour?

16 What did Little Jack Horner pull out of his pie after he stuck his thumb in it?

17 In *Hickory, Dickory, Dock*, which creature ran up the clock?

18 When Jack and Jill went up the hill to fetch water, what did Jack break when he fell down?

19 After Little Bo Peep lost her sheep, what was she advised to do?

20 What did the girls do when Georgie Porgie kissed them?

Hard

Answers to QUIZ 12 – Out and About

1	The Netherlands	11	The Tube
2	Cul-de-sac	12	Lorry
3	Pavement	13	Eurostar
4	A legend	14	Rumble strip
5	Manchester	15	Clearway
6	A dotted line	16	Carburettor
7	M25	17	Germany
8	Israel	18	Train
9	English	19	Toyota
10	Amtrak	20	Italy

ANSWERS ON PAGE 17

1 An image of which Australian animal can be found on the tail of a Qantas aeroplane?

2 Who became leader of the Soviet Union in 1985?

3 Which group were *Rockin' All Over the World* in 1977?

4 What are the first and last planets in our solar system, listed in order of their distance from the Sun?

5 Which "ology" is concerned with the study and treatment of crime?

6 In films what do the letters PG stand for ?

7 Which actor played Frank Drebin in *Police Squad!* and the *Naked Gun* films?

8 In the 15th century, which teenage girl led the French army against the English?

9 What number is represented by the Roman numeral M?

10 The programme *Any Answers* gave listeners the chance to comment on which programme?

11 Who played Vito Corleone in the 1972 film *The Godfather*?

12 Guiseppe Verdi is most famous for which type of musical work?

13 What is the name of the rocky headland at the southern tip of South America?

14 In which year was *Ashes to Ashes* a hit for David Bowie?

15 Who was the brother of Cain in the Bible?

16 What colour is Noddy's hat?

17 Murray Walker commentated on which sport?

18 Where is a cummerbund worn?

19 Fountains Abbey is in which county?

20 Which Dutch cheese is famously round and red?

Easy

Medium

Hard

Answers to QUIZ 13 – Pot Luck

1	Petri	11	Europe
2	Alpha	12	A shell
3	Hobart	13	*Endurance*
4	Bleak	14	Acre
5	Saigon	15	13
6	George Foreman	16	Robert De Niro
7	Aquamarine	17	Theodore Roosevelt
8	George Harrison	18	Wham!
9	19th century	19	Starboard
10	A fish	20	*Sleuth*

QUIZ 16 – Fictional Couples

ANSWERS ON PAGE 18

Easy

1 Dawn and Tim finally become a couple at a Christmas party in which UK mockumentary sitcom?

2 Ken and Barbie® dolls were made by which American toy manufacturing company?

3 Clark Kent and Lois Lane worked for which newspaper?

4 What are the first names of Fred and Wilma Flintstone's neighbours, Mr and Mrs Rubble?

5 Whom did Princess Leia marry in *Star Wars*?

6 How many children do Homer and Marge Simpson have?

7 Which princess did Shrek fall in love with?

8 In which city did Romeo and Juliet live?

9 Where in Essex did Gavin from *Gavin & Stacey* live?

10 In which Jane Austen novel did Elizabeth Bennet and Mr Darcy fall in love?

Medium

11 In the TV show *The Big Bang Theory*, who dates Sheldon Cooper?

12 What were Lady and the Tramp eating when they shared their first kiss?

13 Pongo and Perdita are a couple in which Disney film?

14 What is the surname of Morticia and Gomez?

15 What was the name of Ross and Rachel's baby in the TV series *Friends*?

16 Edward Cullen and Bella Swan became a couple in which film series?

17 Which Hogwarts house were both Ron and Hermione sorted into?

18 Jack and Vera Duckworth were a couple in which TV soap?

19 Who is the primary on-and-off love interest for Carrie Bradshaw in *Sex in the City*?

20 Mary Jane Watson and Gwen Stacy were both girlfriends of which character?

Hard

Answers to QUIZ 14 – Nursery Rhymes

1	Down the lane	11	The king's horses and king's men
2	On a tuffet	12	Polly
3	The Grand Old Duke of York	13	Horn
4	Pig	14	Drury Lane
5	Sailor	15	Bread and honey
6	Roast beef	16	A plum
7	The Knave of Hearts	17	Mouse
8	The farmer's wife	18	His crown
9	A water spout	19	Leave them alone
10	Sugar and spice and all things nice	20	Cry

1   Which was the first National Park to be established in Britain?

2   Which two Australian animals are featured on the country's coat of arms?

3   Kingston is the capital city of which country?

4   Who features in the title of a Wagner opera along with Tristan?

5   Which character is played by Deborah Kerr in the 1956 film *The King and I*?

6   How many minutes are there in two and a half hours?

7   In which sport are stones and a broom used?

8   Which battle was fought on June 18, 1815?

9   In *Absolutely Fabulous*, who played Patsy Stone?

10   Who is the heroine of Philip Pullman's *His Dark Materials* trilogy?

11   The Sugar Plum Fairy appears in which ballet?

12   What is a pack made up of cups, swords, wands and pentacles called?

13   Ni is the chemical symbol for which element?

14   Which poet wrote *A Red, Red Rose* (1794)?

15   Which army rank is the higher, colonel or brigadier?

16   How many atoms of oxygen are there in one molecule of water?

17   Who, in the nursery rhyme, was born on Monday and buried on Sunday?

18   Who was queen for nine days in 1553?

19   During which British monarch's reign was the Penny Post instituted?

20   How many sides has a heptagon?

Easy

Medium

Hard

Answers to QUIZ 15 – Pot Luck

1	Kangaroo	11	Marlon Brando
2	Mikhail Gorbachev	12	Opera
3	Status Quo	13	Cape Horn
4	Mercury and Neptune	14	1980
5	Criminology	15	Abel
6	Parental Guidance	16	Blue
7	Leslie Nielsen	17	Motor racing
8	Joan of Arc	18	Around the waist
9	1000	19	North Yorkshire
10	*Any Questions*	20	Edam

ANSWERS ON PAGE **20**

Easy

1   Which South African conflict lasted from 1899 to 1902?

2   Which African dictator did Forest Whitaker portray in the 2006 film *The Last King of Scotland*?

3   Which waters lie between Africa and Australia?

4   What is the name of the small kingdom that lies wholly within South Africa?

5   Which African country lies between Algeria and Libya?

6   Which Tanzanian mountain is the highest in Africa?

7   *Death on the Nile* is a novel by which crime writer?

8   What is biltong?

9   What is the official language of Libya?

10 Afrikaans is a variety of which European language?

Medium

11 How many continents are larger than Africa?

12 From what is the North African staple food couscous made?

13 What is the capital of Kenya?

14 In 1984, which South African clergyman was awarded the Nobel Peace Prize?

15 Which African fly transmits sleeping sickness?

16 Which precious stone is associated with the South African city of Kimberley?

17 Humphrey Bogart and Ingrid Bergman starred in which classic 1942 film?

18 What country was known as "the Gift of the Nile"?

19 Which band had a hit with *Africa* in 1983?

20 Which island is known for being the place where former South African president Nelson Mandela was jailed?

Hard

Answers to QUIZ 16 – Fictional Couples

1	*The Office*	11	Amy Farrah Fowler
2	Mattel	12	Spaghetti
3	*The Daily Planet*	13	*101 Dalmatians*
4	Barney and Betty	14	Addams
5	Han Solo	15	Emma
6	Three (Bart, Lisa and Maggie)	16	*Twilight*
7	Fiona	17	Gryffindor
8	Verona, Italy	18	*Coronation Street*
9	Billericay	19	Mr Big
10	*Pride and Prejudice*	20	Peter Parker/Spider-man

ANSWERS ON PAGE **21**

1   Which part of an insect bears the legs and wings?

2   Who played the character of Charlene Robinson in the Australian series *Neighbours*?

3   Which duo had a 1992 hit with *Stay*?

4   With how many pieces does a chess player start a game?

5   Is Turkey ahead of or behind Greenwich Mean Time?

6   What is the capital of the Baltic state of Latvia?

7   Which large mammal was ridden by Hannibal over the Alps?

8   In the Bible, which book immediately follows the Acts of the Apostles?

9   For which film did Dame Helen Mirren win an Oscar in 2006?

10   Astigmatism is a condition affecting which part of the body?

11   What are dried plums called?

12   In which county is Land's End?

13   What is the first name of Miss Doolittle, the heroine of George Bernard Shaw's *Pygmalion*?

14   What does the Q stand for in IQ?

15   In which country did Bob Hawke win four elections in a row before being ousted by Paul Keating?

16   What is Marshal Cogburn's nickname in the John Wayne film *True Grit*?

17   Which actress starred in the TV series *Cheers* and the *Look Who's Talking* films?

18   What is the middle colour of the Italian flag?

19   In which decade of the 20th century was Che Guevara born?

20   Which spirit is flavoured with juniper berries?

Easy

Medium

Hard

Answers to QUIZ 17 – Pot Luck

1	Peak District	11	The Nutcracker
2	Kangaroo and Emu	12	Tarot cards
3	Jamaica	13	Nickel
4	Isolde	14	Robert Burns
5	Anna	15	Brigadier
6	150	16	One
7	Curling	17	Solomon Grundy
8	Waterloo	18	Jane Grey
9	Joanna Lumley	19	Queen Victoria
10	Lyra	20	Seven

QUIZ 20 – Sea Creatures

1   Which of the whale species is the largest?

2   Where do turtles lay their eggs?

3   The Portuguese man-of-war employs what as a defence?

4   Which pigment is obtained from the inky secretion of the cuttlefish?

5   What is the name for an adult female whale?

6   A starfish has how many arms?

7   Which class of animals includes crabs and lobsters?

8   Which mammal has blue and killer varieties?

9   A periwinkle is what type of creature?

10   A creature such as a mussel that has two shells is described by what term?

11   Which marine gastropod is famed for its immovability?

12   What is the alternative name for the king crab?

13   How many tentacles does an octopus have?

14   What term is given to creatures such as sole and halibut that live on the sea bed?

15   Chowder is traditionally made using which shellfish?

16   What term is used to describe a marine mammal such as a whale or porpoise?

17   What is krill?

18   What type of sea creature is a lion's mane?

19   Which mollusc has a fan-shaped shell?

20   How do male humpback whales communicate?

Answers to QUIZ 18 – Africa

1	Second Boer War	11	One (Asia)
2	Idi Amin	12	Semolina
3	Indian Ocean	13	Nairobi
4	Lesotho	14	Desmond Tutu
5	Tunisia	15	Tsetse
6	Kilimanjaro	16	Diamond
7	Dame Agatha Christie	17	*Casablanca*
8	Dried and cured meat	18	Egypt
9	Arabic	19	Toto
10	Dutch	20	Robben Island

ANSWERS ON PAGE 23

1   Which radio code word comes before Quebec?

2   What is the surname of *White Wedding* singer Billy?

3   How many railway stations are there on a Monopoly™ board?

4   *Don't Cry For Me, Argentina* features in which musical?

5   Which 1970s band had hits with *Needles and Pins* and *Living Next Door to Alice*?

6   What is the unit of currency in Canada?

7   Which Australian bird is famous for laughing?

8   A concierge does what job?

9   Who topped the UK singles chart in 2006 with *Irreplaceable*?

10 From which politician did policemen get the nickname "Peelers"?

11 For what purpose was the Leaning Tower of Pisa built?

12 Of what is palaeontology the study?

13 Which geographical group includes Lanzarote?

14 What is the English equivalent of the French name Pierre?

15 What name was given to a two-wheeled Roman racing vehicle?

16 What is a female chicken called?

17 Which game is also the name of a gourd-like vegetable?

18 Which cultivated moth lays its eggs on mulberry plants?

19 In which country is Benfica a leading football club?

20 William Hartnell was the first actor to play the main character in which TV series?

Easy | **Medium** | **Hard**

Answers to QUIZ 19 – Pot Luck

1   Thorax
2   Kylie Minogue
3   Shakespears Sister
4   16
5   Ahead
6   Riga
7   Elephant
8   Romans
9   *The Queen*
10 The eye
11 Prunes
12 Cornwall
13 Eliza
14 Quotient
15 Australia
16 Rooster
17 Kirstie Alley
18 White
19 1920s
20 Gin

Easy

1 Which 1952 film featured the song *Do Not Forsake Me*?

2 Who played the title role in the 2016 film *Florence Foster Jenkins*?

3 What is the surname of actor Sean, Sam in the *Lord of the Rings* films?

4 In the 1997 film *Batman & Robin*, who played Mr Freeze?

5 Which actor uttered the immortal line: "Infamy, infamy – they've all got it in for me!"?

6 "It's a big building with patients – but that's not important right now" is a line from which 1980 film?

7 In which country is the 2003 film *Lost in Translation* set?

8 Which film won the Academy Award for Best Picture in 2017?

9 Who directed the 2013 film *The Wolf of Wall Street*?

10 Who played Mr Darcy in the 2005 film *Pride and Prejudice*?

Medium

11 In which of his films did Quentin Tarantino appear as Mr Brown?

12 Which actress starred as Viola de Lesseps in the 1998 film *Shakespeare in Love*?

13 The 1993 film *Shadowlands* tells the story of which writer?

14 *The Power of Love* was a hit song from which 1985 film?

15 Who starred in the 1967 film *Half a Sixpence*?

16 The song *Moon River* is from which 1961 film?

17 Which 1964 film was subtitled *How I Learned to Stop Worrying and Love the Bomb*?

18 Who played Private Ryan in the 1998 film *Saving Private Ryan*?

19 Which disaster movie was inspired by a 1999 book entitled *The Coming Global Superstorm*?

20 In which film did the following appear: "It was beauty killed the beast"?

Hard

Answers to QUIZ 20 – Sea Creatures

1	Blue whale	11	Limpet
2	On a beach	12	Horseshoe crab
3	Sting	13	Eight
4	Sepia	14	Flatfish
5	Cow	15	Clam
6	Five	16	Cetacean
7	Crustacea	17	Plankton
8	Whale	18	Jellyfish
9	Sea snail	19	Scallop
10	Bivalve	20	Singing

1   In which leisure pursuit might you do a Turkey Trot or a Bunny Hug?

2   Which group sang *Shang-a-Lang* in the 1970s?

3   Who played Norma in the TV series *The Royle Family*?

4   In which country is the port of Livorno?

5   What was the first name of *The Goon Show* character Seagoon?

6   Which car company manufactures the Focus?

7   Which Roman fountain featured in Fellini's *La Dolce Vita*?

8   Other than plasma, what matter is neither solid nor liquid?

9   On which Caribbean island is the Bay of Pigs?

10 Which band released the 1997 hit single *Tubthumping*?

11 The adjective caprine relates to which type of animal?

12 What was the name of Lacey's partner in the title of a 1980s detective series?

13 What is the British equivalent of the American realtor?

14 The precious stone sapphire is usually what colour?

15 Pyrophobia is a fear of what?

16 Which Amateur Association has the abbreviation AAA?

17 In which county is Beachy Head?

18 What is a scout rally called?

19 In bungee-jumping, what is a bungee?

20 Which fruit provides the basis for Cumberland sauce?

Easy

Medium

Hard

Answers to QUIZ 21 – Pot Luck

1	Papa	11	As a bell tower (campanile)
2	Idol	12	Fossils
3	Four	13	Canary Islands
4	*Evita*	14	Peter
5	Smokie	15	Chariot
6	Canadian dollar	16	Hen
7	Kookaburra	17	Squash
8	Caretaker	18	Silk moth
9	Beyoncé	19	Portugal
10	Sir Robert Peel	20	*Doctor Who*

QUIZ 24 – Human Biology

ANSWERS ON PAGE 26

Easy

1 What term is given to the removal of a sample of tissue from the body for diagnostic examination?

2 What is the medical name for dizziness due to heights?

3 Which part of the body is affected by glaucoma?

4 What colour blood cells do lymph glands produce?

5 Encephalitis causes inflammation in which part of the body?

6 By what name is the illness rubella more commonly known?

7 The acoustic nerve serves which part of the body?

8 What is the outer layer of skin called?

9 Where in the body is the thyroid gland?

10 How many teeth do adult humans have?

Medium

11 The tibia is a bone in which part of the body?

12 What is the medical term for pain in the lower back muscles?

13 Of what is pharmacology the study?

14 Which is the longest bone in the human body?

15 Which two types of cord connect muscle to bone?

16 Bile is produced by which organ in the body?

17 Which part of the human tongue is most sensitive to sweet things?

18 Which vessel in the neck carries blood from the head and face?

19 Where are the clavicles?

20 Which tissue links the heel to the calf muscles?

Hard

Answers to QUIZ 22 – Film

1	*High Noon*	11	*Reservoir Dogs*
2	Meryl Streep	12	Gwyneth Paltrow
3	Astin	13	CS Lewis
4	Arnold Schwarzenegger	14	*Back to the Future*
5	Kenneth Williams (*Carry On Cleo*)	15	Tommy Steele
6	*Airplane!*	16	*Breakfast at Tiffany's*
7	Japan	17	*Dr Strangelove*
8	*Moonlight*	18	Matt Damon
9	Martin Scorsese	19	*The Day after Tomorrow*
10	Matthew MacFadyen	20	*King Kong*

24

1   What is the code word between kilo and Mike used in radio communications?

2   The 1954 novel *Lord of the Flies* was written by which author?

3   Who is the patron saint of Venice?

4   Which brass instrument is used for military signals?

5   In 1944, in which country did the Battle of Arnhem take place?

6   Who ordered the building of the Pavilion at Brighton?

7   Which exercises are designed to increase oxygen consumption and speed blood circulation?

8   Plymouth has what postcode area code?

9   Which large endocrine gland is situated at the base of the neck?

10   What is a young fox called?

11   A clouded agaric is what type of organism?

12   Which motorway service station on the M1 takes its name from a nearby motor racing circuit in Leicestershire?

13   How many terms did Sir Winston Churchill serve as British prime minister?

14   Tom Hanks starred in which 1993 film, the name of a US city?

15   What is Mull's chief town?

16   What did the 1948 Marshall Plan provide?

17   Who played James Bond in *Octopussy*?

18   The 1844 novel *The Count of Monte Cristo* was written by which author?

19   What was George Michael's first solo single?

20   Who played Angie Watts in *EastEnders*?

Easy

Medium

Hard

Answers to QUIZ 23 – Pot Luck

1	Ballroom dancing	11	Goat
2	Bay City Rollers	12	Cagney
3	Liz Smith	13	Estate agent
4	Italy	14	Blue
5	Ned	15	Fire
6	Ford	16	Athletics
7	Trevi	17	East Sussex
8	Gas	18	Jamboree
9	Cuba	19	A rope
10	Chumbawamba	20	Redcurrant

Easy

1   What is the name of the island in Arthurian legend that is sometimes identified with Glastonbury Tor?

2   What was the riddle-setting creature of Greek mythology with a human head and a lion's body?

3   In Greek mythology, what is the name of the underworld?

4   Which fabled sea monster is said to appear off the coast of Norway?

5   Which mythical creature is a symbol of Wales?

6   In Roman mythology, who is the god of the sea?

7   Who was the Norse god of thunder?

8   Who was the ancient Egyptian sun god, usually depicted as having the head of a hawk?

9   Which legendary siren lured Rhine boatmen to their death?

10   In Greek mythology, who was the divine messenger of the gods?

11   Which legendary king wished that all he touched would turn to gold?

12   Who was King Arthur's father?

13   Which legendary bird was said to have risen from its own ashes?

Medium

14   Who was the Greek god of love?

15   What was the name of Romulus' brother, one of the twin founders of Rome?

16   Will Scarlett was a friend of which legendary outlaw?

17   What was left in Pandora's box once it was opened and emptied of all evils?

18   Whose face was said to have launched 1000 ships?

19   In Roman mythology, which rural deity had a man's body and a goat's horns, ears, tail and hind legs?

20   Which word is another name for the Abominable Snowman?

Hard

ANSWERS ON PAGE 29

1   By what first name was music-hall comedian Mr Flanagan known?

2   In which county would you find Poole and Swanage?

3   What is the name of the inlet between Norfolk and Lincolnshire?

4   Of which people was Ghengis Khan the leader?

5   Which ruler referred to the English as a nation of shopkeepers?

6   Which motorway connects London and Swansea?

7   In the Bible, which Book immediately follows Matthew?

8   The warmth rating of what is measured in togs?

9   Which city in North Queensland is the gateway to the Great Barrier Reef?

10   What was David Bowie's real surname?

11   Who played the lead role in the 1962 film *Lawrence of Arabia*?

12   A Persian Blue is what kind of animal?

13   What is the word for a condiment container?

14   What is the name of Tintin's dog?

15   What were the names of the three tunnels dug by POWs in the film *The Great Escape*?

16   What is the title of the theme song from the film *Titanic*?

17   "Unlucky for some" is the traditional bingo call for which number?

18   In tennis, what name is given to a score of 40-40?

19   The zodiac sign Scorpio covers which two calendar months?

20   What substance can be sulphuric or hydrochloric?

Easy

Medium

Hard

Answers to QUIZ 25 – Pot Luck

1	Lima	11	Fungus
2	William Golding	12	Donington Park
3	Saint Mark	13	Two
4	Bugle	14	*Philadelphia*
5	Netherlands	15	Tobermory
6	George IV, as Prince Regent	16	US aid to Europe
7	Aerobics	17	Sir Roger Moore
8	PL	18	Alexandre Dumas
9	Thyroid	19	*Careless Whisper*
10	Cub	20	Anita Dobson

ANSWERS ON PAGE 30

Easy

1. In which county is Gatwick airport?

2. What is the military rank below sergeant?

3. Which isle is the largest of the Inner Hebrides?

4. Which animal accompanies the unicorn in the Royal arms?

5. The Old Bailey figure of justice holds a sword and what else?

6. In which street is London's Savoy Theatre?

7. What does BSI stand for?

8. In which month of 2011 were the Census forms filled in?

9. In which National Park is Kinder Scout?

10. Which famous prehistoric monument is found on Salisbury Plain?

11. What are the initials of the Cheltenham-based spy centre?

12. Who founded the National Viewers and Listeners Association in 1965?

13. What is the Viking Centre in York called?

14. In which county is the town of Macclesfield?

Medium

15. Which town is the easternmost point of Britain?

16. Which Royal Corps is nicknamed the "Sappers"?

17. In which year were parts of Buckingham Palace opened for the general public to view?

18. Tintern Abbey stands in which river valley?

19. Where in London is Nelson's Column?

20. In which Scottish city is an annual arts festival held along with its popular Fringe?

Hard

Answers to QUIZ 26 – Myth and Legend

1	Avalon	11	Midas
2	Sphinx	12	Uther Pendragon
3	Hades	13	Phoenix
4	Kraken	14	Eros
5	Dragon	15	Remus
6	Neptune	16	Robin Hood
7	Thor	17	Hope
8	Ra	18	Helen of Troy
9	Lorelei	19	Faun
10	Hermes	20	Yeti

QUIZ 29 – Pot Luck

ANSWERS ON PAGE 31

1   With which meat is apple sauce traditionally served?

2   The character of Scout Finch features in which 1960 novel?

3   Which sport includes sculls, strokes and slides?

4   Which part of the body has an external, middle and inner section?

5   In a Shakespeare play, who kills Desdemona?

6   How many Commandments feature in the title of a Charlton Heston film?

7   What is the sixth sign of the zodiac?

8   In which century was Elizabeth I born?

9   What is the capital of Syria?

10 Which comic writer created the fictional Blandings Castle?

11 What is the dialling code for Liverpool?

12 In which country was the Bayeux Tapestry created?

13 What were the first names of Nureyev and Fonteyn?

14 Which instrument measures the height of an aircraft above sea level?

15 What may be described as O negative, for example?

16 Mount Parnassus is in which country?

17 How often is golf's US Masters held?

18 Which famous US soul record label is based in Detroit?

19 In which country is All Nippon Airways based?

20 Where does Enid Blyton's character of Noddy live?

Easy

Medium

Hard

Answers to QUIZ 27 – Pot Luck

1	Bud	11	Peter O'Toole
2	Dorset	12	Cat
3	The Wash	13	Cruet
4	Mongols	14	Snowy
5	Napoleon Bonaparte	15	Tom, Dick and Harry
6	M4	16	*My Heart Will Go On*
7	Mark	17	13
8	Duvets	18	Deuce
9	Cairns	19	October & November
10	Jones	20	Acid

Easy

1   What number shirt is worn by a fullback in Rugby Union?

2   Who was 22 years old when he first captained England in 1988?

3   Where would you watch the Rhinos playing rugby?

4   Newlands Stadium is located in which city?

5   Which player scored the winning drop goal in the last minute of extra time against Australia in the 2003 Rugby World Cup Final?

6   Who was the first English player to play in 50 internationals?

7   Who is credited with inventing Rugby Union?

8   The club Wasps is based in which city?

9   What is the nickname of the Australian Rugby League side?

10 In which colours do Bath play?

11 How many players are in a Rugby League team?

12 Which New Zealand winger scored four tries against England in the 1995 World Cup?

13 Which stadium is home to Scottish Rugby Union?

14 How long is a Rugby Union match?

Medium

15 Who won the first Rugby Union World Cup, held in 1987?

16 In which year did Rugby Union become professional?

17 What is the English Rugby Union team's emblem?

18 Which Welsh player was a regular captain on A Question of Sport from 1978 to 1981?

19 The Varsity Match is associated with which ground?

20 Which player, often ranked as Scotland's greatest, was nicknamed the "Border Terrier"?

Hard

Answers to QUIZ 28 – The UK

1	West Sussex	11	GCHQ
2	Corporal	12	Mary Whitehouse
3	Skye	13	Jorvik
4	Lion	14	Cheshire
5	Scales	15	Lowestoft
6	The Strand	16	Royal Engineers
7	British Standards Institute	17	1993
8	March	18	Wye Valley
9	Peak District	19	Trafalgar Square
10	Stonehenge	20	Edinburgh

1   Which Russian title was first formally assumed by Ivan the Terrible?

2   On a Monopoly™ board, what colour is Piccadilly?

3   Which Gilbert and Sullivan opera is set in the town of Titipu?

4   Whose first album was entitled *Voice of an Angel*?

5   Which vegetable has Jerusalem and globe varieties?

6   Dipsophobia is the fear of what?

7   Which cocktail of rum and lime juice is named after a beach in Cuba?

8   Which major competition was first won by Uruguay in 1930?

9   In which country is the town of Alice Springs?

10   What sea lies between Turkey and Russia?

11   Which evergreen tree is associated with the country of Lebanon?

12   In the *Guardians of the Galaxy* film franchise, who stars as Peter Quill?

13   Who was the drummer with Nirvana who went on to found Foo Fighters?

14   Sutton Coldfield is a suburb of which city?

15   What are sheepshank and surgeon's examples of?

16   In which Canadian province is Calgary?

17   How many yards are there in a mile?

18   Which hairdresser pioneered the geometric haircut in the 1960s?

19   What is the name of Jeeves' employer in the PG Wodehouse stories?

20   Ricotta is a cheese from which country?

Answers to QUIZ 29 – Pot Luck

1	Pork	11	0151
2	*To Kill a Mockingbird*	12	France
3	Rowing	13	Rudolph, Margot
4	Ear	14	The altimeter
5	Othello	15	Blood group
6	Ten	16	Greece
7	Virgo	17	Annually
8	16th	18	Motown
9	Damascus	19	Japan
10	PG Wodehouse	20	Toyland

Easy

1   Which actor portrayed Rowdy Yates in the series *Rawhide?*

2   Who played Inspector Morse in the original series?

3   In which long-running series did Howard Keel play the character of Clayton Farlow?

4   In which city was *The Royle Family* set?

5   Which TV show made Pamela Anderson famous?

6   In which series did a dog called Rowf play the piano?

7   In which decade was *Birds of a Feather* screened for the first time?

8   Who was Doyle's colleague in *The Professionals?*

9   Who would you expect to hear shouting "Yabba-dabba-doo"?

10   In the series *New Tricks*, who played Gerry Standing?

Medium

11   What was the name of the *Neighbours* character played by Ian Smith?

12   Who was crowned the first "King of the Jungle" in *I'm a Celebrity...Get Me Out of Here!?*

13   What was Corporal Jones' day job in *Dad's Army?*

14   On which quiz show are the number of passes taken into account in the event of a tie?

15   Which series was based at Sun Hill police station?

16   What was the name of the chief engineer in the original *Star Trek* series?

17   Which professor presented *The Wonders of the Solar System* and *The Wonders of the Universe?*

18   Who was Stimpy's cartoon pal?

19   In which decade of the 20th century was Phillip Schofield born?

20   In which series did Ant and Dec play PJ and Duncan?

Hard

Answers to QUIZ 30 – Rugby

1	15	11	13
2	Will Carling	12	Jonah Lomu
3	Leeds	13	Murrayfield
4	Cape Town	14	80 minutes
5	Jonny Wilkinson	15	New Zealand
6	Rory Underwood	16	1995
7	William Webb Ellis	17	Red rose
8	Coventry	18	Gareth Edwards
9	Kangaroos	19	Twickenham
10	Blue, Black and White	20	Gary Armstrong

QUIZ 33 – Pot Luck

ANSWERS ON PAGE 35

1   What name is given to a brooch that contains a raised figure or design?

2   In the nursery rhyme, what is Humpty Dumpty assumed to be?

3   What term describes instruments that produce sound when struck?

4   The Renault car company was founded in which country?

5   Which drink was created when Indian army officers added quinine to soda water to help fight malaria?

6   Who had an 1986 no.1 with *Take My Breath Away*?

7   According to legend, in what environment would a Kraken be found?

8   How many signs of the zodiac are there?

9   Which sauce did Henry Heinz begin to manufacture in 1876?

10   The radio observatory Jodrell Bank is near which major Cheshire town?

11   Which region of the Earth contains the South Pole?

12   Who is Sherlock Holmes' arch-enemy?

13   In darts, what is the lowest score from three different trebles?

14   Who starred in the 1994 film *The Mask*?

15   What does a snorkel help you do?

16   Which London building is nicknamed "Ally Pally"?

17   What is the second lightest chemical element?

18   0131 is the dialling code for which city?

19   In which month is the longest day in Britain?

20   Who is R2-D2's robot companion in *Star Wars*?

Easy

Medium

Hard

Answers to QUIZ 31 – Pot Luck

1	Tsar	11	Cedar
2	Yellow	12	Chris Pratt
3	*The Mikado*	13	Dave Grohl
4	Charlotte Church	14	Birmingham
5	Artichoke	15	Knots
6	Drinking alcohol	16	Alberta
7	Daiquiri	17	1760
8	FIFA World Cup	18	Vidal Sassoon
9	Australia	19	Wooster
10	Black Sea	20	Italy

1 What are grissini?

2 Which cheese shares its name with a famous West Country gorge?

3 Kale belongs to which family of vegetables?

4 What is the main herb in pesto sauce?

5 What type of fruit is dried to produce a sultana?

6 Which lettuce shares its name with a mass of floating frozen water?

7 A British variant of cheese on toast made with a cheese sauce is known by what name?

8 What type of food is nori?

9 What is a traditional British food made from the leftover vegetables of a roast dinner?

10 "Buddha's Delight" is a dish originating from which country?

11 Miso soup is made from the paste of which bean?

12 A burrito is usually made with what type of flatbread?

13 Soy bean curd is also known by what name?

14 Which flower's petals are steeped in water to create the traditional flavouring for Turkish delight?

15 Glamorgan sausages are traditionally made from cheese, breadcrumbs and which vegetable?

16 What type of bean is used to make baked beans?

17 For what do the letters TVP stand in the meat substitute?

18 Gnocchi is a food from which country?

19 What is the main ingredient in a chow mein?

20 Basmati and pilaf are varieties of what?

Answers to QUIZ 32 – Television

1	Clint Eastwood	11	Harold Bishop
2	John Thaw	12	Tony Blackburn
3	*Dallas*	13	A butcher
4	Manchester	14	*Mastermind*
5	*Baywatch*	15	*The Bill*
6	*The Muppets*	16	Scotty
7	1980s	17	Brian Cox
8	Bodie	18	Ren
9	Fred Flintstone	19	1960s
10	Dennis Waterman	20	*Byker Grove*

QUIZ 35 – Pot Luck

1   What term is given to a voluntary renunciation of the throne of a country?

2   In the 1939 film *Gone with the Wind*, who played Rhett Butler?

3   What is the English meaning of the phrase *Anno Domini*?

4   What is the mathematical method of calculating by symbols?

5   In greyhound racing, what colour jacket is worn by the dog in trap three?

6   If three is on the top side of a die, what number is on the hidden side?

7   In Cockney rhyming slang, what are "plates of meat"?

8   Who or what is Sweet William?

9   Who had hits with *Passengers* and *I'm Still Standing*?

10 From which country do Volkswagen cars originate?

11 In which county is Blackpool?

12 Who is the TV cartoon son of Marge and Homer?

13 Which island is located south of Turkey and northwest of Israel?

14 In the rhyme, who went with Christopher Robin to Buckingham Palace?

15 What well-known dinosaur species' name includes the word "king" in Latin?

16 Which ABBA hit inspired the name for a 1990s Steve Coogan show?

17 The Pittsburgh Steelers play which sport?

18 Which brothers wrote the music and lyrics for *Crazy for You*?

19 Which liquid measure is equivalent to a quarter of a pint?

20 On which Cornish moor is Jamaica Inn located?

Easy
Medium
Hard

Answers to QUIZ 33 – Pot Luck

1	Cameo	11	Antarctic
2	An egg	12	Moriarty
3	Percussion	13	18
4	France	14	Jim Carrey
5	Tonic water	15	Breathe under water
6	Berlin	16	Alexandra Palace
7	In the sea	17	Helium
8	12	18	Edinburgh
9	Tomato ketchup	19	June
10	Macclesfield	20	C-3PO

Easy

1 In which board game does the player act as a doctor removing plastic ailments from a patient?
2 In which two-player game do players take turns placing coloured disks in a vertical grid?
3 What is the full name of the game often referred to as D&D?
4 Which board game takes its name from an apology?
5 The American game Parcheesi is similar to which game played in the UK?
6 Which board game includes the characters of Colonel Mustard and Miss Scarlet?
7 In which popular board game can players choose to play as a Scottish terrier and racing car, amongst others?
8 In which general knowledge game released in 1981 do players collect "wedges" of different colours?
9 What two-player game shares its name with a Shakespeare play?
10 In which classic game must the player travel from the bottom left of the board to the top right by rolling dice and avoiding hazards?

Medium

11 In which game must players guess the word drawn by their team-mates?
12 Which game involves a spinner and a plastic mat with red, yellow, green and blue circles?
13 What is the name of the game in which players are represented by rodent-shaped game pieces?
14 In which game must the player roll five dice in certain combinations to win?
15 What is the name of the board game in which up to four players must construct words to win points?
16 Which two chess pieces are involved in the move "castling"?
17 In which strategy board game must a player conquer the earth through conflict or diplomacy?
18 Which board game issued in 1992 gives players 30 seconds to describe words to their team?
19 Which board game is played by two players who must guess the positions of the opposing player's pieces to win?
20 In which board game must players move 15 pieces across and off the board to win?

Hard

Answers to QUIZ 34 – Vegetarian Food

1	Breadsticks	11	Soy bean
2	Cheddar	12	Tortilla
3	Cabbage	13	Tofu
4	Basil	14	Rose
5	Grape	15	Leeks
6	Iceberg	16	Haricot
7	Welsh rarebit	17	Textured Vegetable Protein
8	Seaweed	18	Italy
9	Bubble and squeak	19	Noodles
10	China	20	Rice

ANSWERS ON PAGE **39**

1   Which monarch is credited with writing *Greensleeves*?

2   Hg is the symbol for which chemical element?

3   What was the first name of Mr Packer, the Australian entrepreneur who died in 2005?

4   Which word means "related to the moon"?

5   What is the meaning of the name of the Spanish lottery *El Gordo*?

6   In which country is the city of São Paulo?

7   Which is the alternative term for the playing card the Jack?

8   What is the traditional colour for Aran wool?

9   In which century was Hans Christian Andersen born?

10   London and Southampton are connected by which motorway?

11   Which fruit's varieties include Mirabelle and Yellowgage?

12   Which girl group had a 1983 hit with *Cruel Summer*?

13   What was the nationality of the mathematician, philosopher and scientist Aristotle?

14   What is New York's Metropolitan Opera more popularly called?

15   Captain Hastings is the sidekick of which fictional detective?

16   Who released the hit 1987 single *You Win Again*?

17   In which US state is Lubbock?

18   What is caviar?

19   Which green salad vegetable belongs to the same family as the squash?

20   What is ten cubed?

Easy

Medium

Hard

Answers to QUIZ 35 – Pot Luck

1	Abdication	11	Lancashire
2	Clark Gable	12	Bart
3	In the year of Our Lord	13	Cyprus
4	Algebra	14	Alice
5	White	15	Tyrannosaurus Rex
6	Four	16	*Knowing Me, Knowing You*
7	Feet	17	American Football
8	A plant	18	George and Ira Gershwin
9	Sir Elton John	19	Gill
10	Germany	20	Bodmin

Easy

1 What is the term for a male wild pig?

2 Is a bass a freshwater or sea fish?

3 A chameleon can change the colour of which part of its body?

4 Which creature leaves "hills" on lawns?

5 What is a female horse called, up to the age of four years?

6 For which marsupial is "mob" a collective noun?

7 How many legs has a cranefly?

8 What name is given to an adult male seal?

9 What is the body of a penguin covered with?

10 A baby elephant is known by what name?

11 Which is the smallest bird in the world?

12 Army, weaver and leafcutter are types of which insect?

13 What is another name for the prairie wolf?

14 What is Britain's largest land mammal?

Medium

15 A glow-worm is not a worm: what type of creature is it?

16 What kind of animal is a pipistrelle?

17 A seahorse is what type of creature?

18 What term describes a black and white horse?

19 Grizzly bears are what colour?

20 What name is given to the larva of a fly?

Hard

1 Which actress starred in the film *Sliding Doors*?

2 Golders Green is a suburb of which UK city?

3 Where is the Sea of Showers?

4 How much did the wedding ring of the Owl and the Pussycat cost?

5 Zak and Marlon are members of which *Emmerdale* family?

6 "On a dark desert highway, cool wind in my hair, Warm smell of colitas, rising up through the air" is a lyric from which song?

7 Who starred as John Merrick in the 1980 film *The Elephant Man*?

8 In which year did man first set foot on the moon?

9 In which month does Royal Ascot take place?

10 Where in Scotland is an old blacksmith's shop a tourist attraction?

11 What is a worshipper of Brahma, Vishnu and Shiva?

12 Which DJ created the character of Captain Kremmen?

13 In which county is Whipsnade Zoo?

14 Which type of 1950s music used a washboard?

15 What name is given in law to a person who makes a will?

16 Merlin counselled which legendary king?

17 In which country was Sir Alexander Fleming born?

18 What type of creatures were dinosaurs?

19 Which bodily organ gives its name to a variety of bean?

20 How many lanes are usually used for racing in an Olympic swimming pool?

Easy

Medium

Hard

Answers to QUIZ 37 – Pot Luck

1	Henry VIII	11	Plums
2	Mercury	12	Bananarama
3	Kerry	13	Greek
4	Lunar	14	The Met
5	The Fat One	15	Hercule Poirot
6	Brazil	16	Bee Gees
7	Knave	17	Texas
8	Cream	18	Salted fish roe
9	19th century	19	Cucumber
10	M3	20	1000

1 The patron saint of animals, St Francis, was born in which Italian town?

2 A pizza Margherita has which three main toppings?

3 In the Italian language, which city is known as *Napoli*?

4 What is the name of Italy's top-flight football league?

5 Which make and model of car was popularised in the 1969 film *The Italian Job*?

6 Which Italian city is one of the world's most important fashion capitals?

7 The ceiling of the Sistine Chapel was painted by which artist?

8 Which city is known particularly for its bridges, canals and gondolas?

9 In a traditional Italian meal, what is the first course called?

10 Which Italian explorer sailed from Europe to find a route to Asia and instead landed in the Americas?

11 What animal is said to have suckled the twin brothers who founded Rome in ancient myth?

12 What does the word *grazie* mean?

13 The Italian flag has which three colours?

14 Which Roman general and politician was assassinated on the Ides of March?

15 What is the name of the small sovereign state located within Italy's capital city?

16 The ancient city of Pompeii was destroyed by which volcano?

17 What was the currency used in Italy before its adoption of the euro in 2002?

18 In which circular structure did the gladiators of Ancient Rome fight?

19 Which sea is immediately beneath the boot-shaped peninsula of Italy?

20 What is the name of Europe's tallest active volcano, located on the east coast of Sicily?

Answers to QUIZ 38 – Animal World

1	Boar	11	Bee hummingbird
2	Sea fish	12	Ant
3	Skin	13	Coyote
4	Mole	14	Red deer
5	Filly	15	A beetle
6	Kangaroo	16	A bat
7	Six	17	A fish
8	Bull	18	Piebald
9	Feathers	19	Brown
10	Calf	20	Maggot

ANSWERS ON PAGE 43

1 Which units are used to measure sound intensity?

2 In which country did chilli con carne originate?

3 What kind of plant is Lady's Slipper?

4 In which town were the band Slade formed?

5 What type of gem is The Star of Africa?

6 How many laps are completed in a speedway race?

7 On a standard keyboard, the "(" and ")" symbols share keys with which two numbers?

8 How many wheels are there on a quad bike?

9 In music, which note is written on the bottom line of the stave with a treble clef?

10 The zodiac sign Taurus covers which two calendar months?

11 In the rhyme, where does Goosey Goosey Gander wander?

12 In the initials FIFA, what does the first F stand for?

13 If a crowd is three, how many is company?

14 What type of creature is a natterjack?

15 What was the name of Mackenzie Crook's character in the TV series *The Office*?

16 In which county is Windsor Castle?

17 Romano and Desiree are varieties of which vegetable?

18 What type of animal is a Samoyed?

19 Which singer starred in the 1992 film *The Bodyguard*?

20 What is the county town of West Sussex?

Easy

Medium

Hard

Answers to QUIZ 39 – Pot Luck

1	Gwyneth Paltrow	11	Hindu
2	London	12	Kenny Everett
3	On the Moon	13	Bedfordshire
4	A shilling	14	Skiffle
5	The Dingles	15	Testator
6	*Hotel California* (Eagles)	16	King Arthur
7	John Hurt	17	Scotland
8	1969	18	Reptiles
9	June	19	Kidney
10	Gretna Green	20	Eight

Easy

1   What type of creature is a goldcrest?

2   What type of meat is silverside?

3   At which racecourse does the Gold Cup steeplechase take place every March?

4   At the end of which coloured arch is there said to be a crock of gold?

5   *The Silver Chair* is a 1953 novel by which author?

6   What is goldenrod?

7   In which 1986 horror film did Jeff Goldblum star?

8   With which English king is the Field of the Cloth of Gold associated?

9   Which band released the 1972 single *Solid Gold Easy Action*?

10   Who played M for the first time in the James Bond film *GoldenEye*?

11   In the proverb, speech is silver but what is golden?

12   What name was given to one of the legendary Greek seamen who followed Jason in search of the Golden Fleece?

13   According to the Beatles, who had a silver hammer?

Medium

14   In which year did Queen Elizabeth II celebrate her Golden Jubilee?

15   Who performed the theme song to the Bond film *Goldfinger*?

16   A Golden Delicious is what type of fruit?

17   What is the chemical symbol for gold?

18   What term is given to an older person who is computer literate?

19   How many years of marriage are marked by a silver wedding anniversary?

20   What is "black gold"?

Hard

Answers to QUIZ 40 – Italy

1	Assisi	11	She-wolf
2	Tomato, mozzarella and basil	12	Thank you
3	Naples	13	Green, white and red
4	Serie A	14	Julius Caesar
5	Mini Cooper S	15	Vatican City
6	Milan	16	Mount Vesuvius
7	Michelangelo	17	Italian Lira
8	Venice	18	Amphitheatre
9	Antipasto	19	Mediterranean Sea
10	Christopher Columbus	20	Mount Etna

1 What is the capital of Poland?

2 What is chervil?

3 "Key of the door" is the traditional bingo call for which number?

4 Who was Dick Grayson's original alter ego?

5 Who wanted to ask the Wizard of Oz for courage?

6 In 2013 which singer released the song *Wrecking Ball*?

7 An amoeba has how many cells?

8 Which birthstone is linked to May?

9 Which 1987 Steve Martin film was based on *Cyrano de Bergerac* (1897)?

10 Which French monarch was known as the "Sun King"?

11 What was the title of Frankie Goes to Hollywood's second chart-topper?

12 Thermophobia is the fear of what?

13 What is the log thrown in the Highland Games called?

14 Moving anticlockwise on a dartboard, what number is next to 5?

15 Which fruit has a Victoria variety?

16 In which US city is the Grand Ole Opry?

17 Whose real name was Georgios Panayiotou?

18 Back, blanket and buttonhole are all types of what?

19 Which TV comedy series was a spoof on the 1970s series *Secret Army*?

20 What is H_2SO_4?

Easy

Medium

Hard

Answers to QUIZ 41 – Pot Luck

1	Decibels	11	Upstairs and downstairs and in my lady's chamber
2	Mexico	12	Fédération
3	Orchid	13	Two
4	Wolverhampton	14	Toad
5	Diamond	15	Gareth Keenan
6	Four	16	Berkshire
7	Nine and zero	17	Potato
8	Four	18	Dog
9	E	19	Whitney Houston
10	April and May	20	Chichester

Easy

1 Who plays Captain Jack Sparrow in the *Pirates of the Caribbean* films?

2 Which character has the catchphrase "To infinity and beyond"?

3 The title character of which 1941 animated film never speaks?

4 In which US state was the 2002 film *Lilo & Stitch* set?

5 Which film was filmed at East High School in Salt Lake City, Utah?

6 In which film would you find the trio Shenzi, Banzai and Ed?

7 Which 1995 film features the song *Colors of the Wind*?

8 In which 2015 film do the characters Joy, Sadness, Fear and Disgust appear?

9 In *Snow White and the Seven Dwarfs*, what poisoned food item did the Queen give to Snow White?

10 What is the name of Amy Adams' princess in the 2007 film *Enchanted*?

Medium

11 Which character in *Frozen* (2013) was voiced by Idina Menzel?

12 Which 2004 film followed the lives of a family of undercover superheroes?

13 In *The Jungle Book*, what type of animal is Shere Khan?

14 Lightning McQueen features in which series of films?

15 In the 2008 film, what type of animal is Bolt?

16 To which creature did Peter Pan feed Captain Hook's hand?

17 In the 1991 animated film *Beauty and the Beast*, what enchanted item is hidden in the west wing of the castle?

18 In *The Little Mermaid* (1989), what type of creature is Sebastian?

19 What is the surname of the family in *Mary Poppins*?

20 What is the name of Sleeping Beauty?

Hard

1 Which song, originally released in 1975, was a posthumous no.1 single for John Lennon?

2 Lombardy is a region of which country?

3 Whose diary had its last entry on 1st August 1944?

4 Who encouraged us to *Meet the Romans* in a BBC series?

5 In which country was Roger Federer born?

6 From 1714 to 1830 all British monarchs shared what name?

7 What name is given to an imaginary line around the globe parallel with the Equator?

8 Who played Basil Fawlty in the classic TV series?

9 What is the first army rank held by soldiers who are not officers?

10 What instrument can be bass, electric or Spanish?

11 The 1972 novel *Watership Down* was written by which author?

12 Which 1995 film featured a talking pig?

13 What is the square root of 9?

14 In which area of Los Angeles is the exclusive shopping street Rodeo Drive?

15 The 2006 film *The Good Shepherd* is about the early history of which organisation?

16 In which English county is Basildon?

17 The tears of which creature are said to be a sign of insincere grief?

18 Which car company has the Lexus as its luxury brand?

19 The McLaren Formula 1 team has its headquarters in which Surrey town?

20 What are substitutes in cricket not normally allowed to do?

Easy

Medium

Hard

Answers to QUIZ 43 – Pot Luck

1	Warsaw	11	*Two Tribes*
2	A herb	12	Heat
3	21	13	Caber
4	Robin	14	12
5	Lion	15	Plum
6	Miley Cyrus	16	Nashville
7	One	17	George Michael
8	Emerald	18	Stitches
9	*Roxanne*	19	*'Allo, 'Allo!*
10	Louis XIV	20	Sulphuric acid

1   Which numerical system is based on tens?

2   What is the total number of sides on three rectangles?

3   How many millimetres are there in three centimetres?

4   What is 75% of 200?

5   What is the second month of the year to have exactly 31 days?

6   How many square inches in a square foot?

7   Approximately how many whole ounces are equivalent to 170 grammes?

8   "Dancing Queen" is a traditional bingo call for which number?

9   If a million is written in digits, how many zeros are there?

10 What number is opposite a one on a dice?

11 How many hours are there in four days?

12 What number is between 6 and 15 on a dartboard?

13 After seven which is the next highest prime number?

14 What is the square root of 36?

15 How many edges are there on a cube?

16 What is 80% of 400?

17 How many are there in a baker's dozen?

18 How many leaves are there on a lucky clover?

19 What number is cubed to give an answer of eight?

20 Paper with a size of 210mm x 297mm is known by which A number?

Answers to QUIZ 44 – Disney Films

1	Johnny Depp	11	Elsa
2	Buzz Lightyear (*Toy Story*)	12	*The Incredibles*
3	Dumbo	13	Tiger
4	Hawaii	14	*Cars*
5	*High School Musical*	15	A dog
6	*The Lion King*	16	Crocodile
7	*Pocahontas*	17	A rose
8	*Inside Out*	18	Crab
9	Apple	19	Banks
10	Giselle	20	Aurora

Easy

Medium

Hard

QUIZ 47 – Pot Luck

ANSWERS ON PAGE 49

1 A London terminus and Underground line are both named after which monarch?

2 How many cards of the same suit are needed for a flush in poker?

3 In which month does Cowes Week take place?

4 In *Cinderella*, what did the fairy godmother use to create her coach?

5 Each episode of the TV series *The Rockford Files* began with what type of message?

6 In which country is the city of Toulouse?

7 Who loads his van "Early in the morning, just as day is dawning"?

8 What was the denomination of the crooked coin which the crooked man found beside a crooked stile?

9 The "Shift" key on a standard keyboard often features an arrow pointing in which direction?

10 On an Ordnance Survey map, what is indicated by a light blue area?

11 Which South American country is nearest to Africa?

12 Which element is found in bones, shells and teeth?

13 Which dog show was first held in Islington in 1891?

14 A lion represents which zodiac sign?

15 What is a fossilised yellowish-brown resin?

16 In which century was Charles Darwin born?

17 How many athletes are there in an Olympic relay team?

18 Who wrote the comic opera *Trial by Jury*?

19 What is 1/4 expressed as a percentage?

20 In the Bible, who was the son of Isaac and Rebecca and the brother of Jacob?

Answers to QUIZ 45 – Pot Luck

1	*Imagine*	11	Richard Adams
2	Italy	12	*Babe*
3	Anne Frank	13	Three
4	Dame Mary Beard	14	Beverly Hills
5	Switzerland	15	CIA
6	George	16	Essex
7	Line of Latitude	17	Crocodile
8	John Cleese	18	Toyota
9	Private	19	Woking
10	Guitar	20	Bat, bowl or captain the side

Easy

1   With which politicial group is the Fabian Society associated?

2   Privy Counsellors and government ministers are given what title?

3   Who preceded Tony Blair as UK Prime Minister?

4   Which is the UK's lower parliamentary chamber?

5   Which building is located at 1600 Pennsylvania Avenue in Washington DC?

6   What is the name of the elected chamber of the Tynwald on the Isle of Man?

7   In January 2017, who became US Vice President?

8   Which committee is formed from the backbench Conservative MPs?

9   *Time* Magazine named which politician as Person of the Year in 2016?

10 Which former MP was nicknamed "Tarzan"?

Medium

11 Who was British PM from 1908 to 1916?

12 Which dam, constructed in the 1930s, was named after the 31st President of the United States?

13 In which building was Sir Winston Churchill born?

14 Nelson Mandela became president of South Africa in which year?

15 Who was David Cameron's predecessor as Prime Minister?

16 How many general elections did Baroness Margaret Thatcher win in the 1980s?

17 Which US statesman was credited with inventing both the lightning conductor and bifocal lenses?

18 In 1988 François Mitterrand was re-elected president of which country?

19 Which future US president did Jacqueline Bouvier marry in 1953?

20 Which former MP has presented many TV series based on the *Bradshaw's Guides* to the railways?

Hard

Answers to QUIZ 46 – Numbers

1	Decimal	11	96
2	12	12	10
3	30	13	11
4	150	14	Six
5	March	15	12
6	144	16	320
7	Six	17	13
8	17	18	Four
9	Six	19	Two
10	Six	20	A4

ANSWERS ON PAGE 51

1   What is the collective name for a group of rhinoceroses?

2   In which ocean are the Azores?

3   How would 71 be shown in Roman numerals?

4   Who hosted the TV programme *The Golden Shot* from 1967 to 1972 and 1974 to 1975?

5   Which sport featured in the film *White Men Can't Jump* (1992)?

6   What name is given to the number below the line in a fraction?

7   How many furlongs are there in a mile?

8   In the rhyme *Jack Be Nimble*, what did Jack jump over?

9   Which mountain overlooks the Swiss town of Zermatt?

10 Moving anticlockwise on a dartboard, what number is next to 19?

11 Which letter is to the right of the letter G on a standard keyboard?

12 In music, what is a note if it is neither sharp nor flat?

13 What are pieces of grain husk separated from flour after milling?

14 Of which US state is Juneau the capital?

15 Who created the characters of Tom Bombadil?

16 Who designed Elizabeth Hurley's famous "safety pin" dress?

17 Pattaya is a resort in which country?

18 Which stimulant is found in tea and coffee?

19 Which airport has the code IST?

20 On an Ordnance Survey map, what is indicated by the abbreviation BR?

Easy

Medium

Hard

Answers to QUIZ 47 – Pot Luck

1	Victoria	11	Brazil
2	Five	12	Calcium
3	August	13	Crufts
4	A pumpkin	14	Leo
5	An answerphone message	15	Amber
6	France	16	19th century
7	Postman Pat	17	Four
8	Sixpence	18	Gilbert and Sullivan
9	Up	19	25%
10	Water	20	Esau

1 Who wrote the stage show *The Rocky Horror Show* and played Riff Raff in the film adaptation?

2 In 1984 The Society of West End Theatre Awards were renamed in honour of whom?

3 How many sisters were in the title of the play by Chekhov?

4 In which musical are the songs *Mr. Cellophane* and *Razzle Dazzle* sung?

5 Who wrote the play *The History Boys*?

6 In which country are Tony awards presented?

7 Who wrote *The Birthday Party* and *The Caretaker*?

8 In which London borough is the Globe Theatre?

9 What is the title of the British weekly newspaper and website for people involved in the performing arts?

10 Who wrote the play *How the Other Half Loves*?

11 Algernon Moncrieff and Cecily Cardew feature in which play?

12 What word taken from the French describes an afternoon show?

13 In which city is the Bolshoi Theatre?

14 Which stage direction indicates that an actor should leave the stage?

15 Who wrote the play *Cat on a Hot Tin Roof*?

16 What do you wish a performer when you say "break a leg"?

17 *Jumpers* and *Arcadia* are plays by which Czech-born playwright?

18 Who first produced *Les Misérables* in London?

19 In the farce, where did Charley's Aunt come from?

20 Which king is killed in Act Two of Shakespeare's *Macbeth*?

Answers to QUIZ 48 – Politics

1	The Labour Party	11	HH Asquith
2	Right Honourable	12	Hoover Dam
3	Sir John Major	13	Blenheim Palace
4	House of Commons	14	1994
5	The White House	15	Gordon Brown
6	House of Keys	16	Two
7	Mike Pence	17	Benjamin Franklin
8	1922 Committee	18	France
9	Donald Trump	19	John F Kennedy
10	Baron Michael Heseltine	20	Michael Portillo

1   On a standard roulette wheel which numbers appear on the black?

2   What is a quesadilla traditionally filled with?

3   Which US city is the setting for the 1976 film *Assault on Precinct 13*?

4   What is the only astrological sign not named after a living creature?

5   In an adaptation of which Jane Austen novel did Hugh Grant play Edward Ferrars?

6   Mitsubishi has its headquarters in which country?

7   In which county is Chartwell, the former home of Sir Winston Churchill?

8   In which decade was the Cold War officially declared over?

9   How many floors are there on a double-decker bus?

10   What do Americans call a see-saw?

11   What is the name of the sprite in Shakespeare's *The Tempest*?

12   Which legendary character has been played on screen by Russell Crowe and Kevin Costner, amongst others?

13   In which century was Al Capone born?

14   Which actress starred in the 2010 film *Eat Pray Love*?

15   In which country would you find airports with the codes BCN, MAD and PMI?

16   Which singer had a backing band called The Crickets?

17   On an Ordnance Survey map, what is indicated by crossed swords?

18   From which country does the song *Waltzing Matilda* originate?

19   In which country was comedian Katherine Ryan born?

20   With which group did Sir Paul McCartney have the 1977 hit *Mull of Kintyre*?

Easy

Medium

Hard

Answers to QUIZ 49 – Pot Luck

1	A crash	11	H
2	Atlantic Ocean	12	Natural
3	LXXI	13	Bran
4	Bob Monkhouse	14	Alaska
5	Basketball	15	JRR Tolkien
6	Denominator	16	Versace
7	Eight	17	Thailand
8	The candlestick	18	Caffeine
9	Matterhorn	19	Istanbul
10	Three	20	Bridge

1 Which biblical character made a coat of many colours for his son Joseph?

2 In which decade did jeans become popular after James Dean wore them in *Rebel Without a Cause*?

3 What is the name of the process which combines fibres to form yarn?

4 Which fabric derives its name from the capital of the Syrian Arab Republic?

5 What part of an outfit might be described as "leg-of-mutton"?

6 From which country did the cotton cloth nankeen originate?

7 Which fabric derives its name from the French *serge de Nîmes*?

8 The worm known as *Bombyx mori* produces what type of fibre?

9 What type of hat is associated with Sherlock Holmes?

10 What machine is used to weave cloth?

11 On a clothing label, what is indicated by a triangle with a cross through it?

12 The duffel coat and bag were invented in which country?

13 What is a tabard?

14 What type of fabric shares its name with a light cake of US origin?

15 Which item of clothing goes with "tails" to indicate a formal outfit?

16 Which nickname for a US detective derives from footwear?

17 Called braces in the UK, what is the American name for straps used to hold up trousers?

18 Which type of hat shares its name with a cover used in the garden?

19 What is a crinoline?

20 Where would a gaiter be worn?

Answers to QUIZ 50 – Theatre

1	Richard O'Brien	11	*The Importance of Being Earnest*
2	Sir Laurence Olivier	12	Matinée
3	Three	13	Moscow
4	*Chicago*	14	Exit
5	Alan Bennett	15	Tennessee Williams
6	USA	16	Good luck
7	Harold Pinter	17	Sir Tom Stoppard
8	Southwark	18	Sir Cameron Mackintosh
9	*The Stage*	19	Brazil
10	Sir Alan Ayckbourn	20	Duncan

ANSWERS ON PAGE 55

1   How many stripes does a police sergeant have on his arm?

2   What is the unit of currency in Estonia?

3   In a game of bezique, what is the minimum number of players required?

4   What is the capital of the Czech Republic?

5   How many official languages are there in Switzerland?

6   What type of horse racing does not include fences and obstacles?

7   What is the square root of 25?

8   Which Black Sea peninsula was the location of a war in the 19th century?

9   Which Lancashire seaside resort has a famous Pleasure Beach?

10 Rory Bremner and Chris Barrie were among the people providing voices on which satirical show of the 1980s and 1990s?

11 Edinburgh has what postcode area code?

12 Where did Joan of Arc win her famous victory against the English?

13 What is the term for an irrational fear of enclosed spaces?

14 What is organza?

15 Paddington, Marylebone and Waterloo are linked by which London Underground line?

16 What metallic element is mixed with tin to form the alloy bronze?

17 In which decade did Channel 4 start?

18 What do the letters PS stand for at the end of a letter?

19 Which fictional sleuth featured in the mystery *Death on the Nile*?

20 Who hosted the 2006 FIFA World Cup?

Easy

Medium

Hard

Answers to QUIZ 51 – Pot Luck

1	Even numbers	11	Ariel
2	Cheese	12	Robin Hood
3	Los Angeles	13	19th century
4	Libra	14	Julia Roberts
5	*Sense and Sensibility*	15	Spain
6	Japan	16	Buddy Holly
7	Kent	17	Site of a battle
8	1990s	18	Australia
9	Two	19	Canada
10	Teeter-totter	20	Wings

Easy

1 Who wrote the 1968 novel *Airport*?

2 Which famous children's author and artist lived and worked in the Lake District for much of her life?

3 Who was the dictator of Oceania in George Orwell's *Nineteen Eighty-Four*?

4 In *The Jungle Book*, what is the name of the bear?

5 Who wrote *The Hobbit*?

6 "Water, water everywhere" are words from which Coleridge poem?

7 Who wrote the fable *The Fox and the Grapes*?

8 Who wrote the 1938 novel *Rebecca*?

9 Which book includes the words "All for one and one for all"?

10 Who created the character of Huckleberry Finn?

11 From which country does Hercule Poirot hail?

12 Which famous novel begins "It is a truth universally acknowledged that a single man in possession of a good fortune must be in want of a wife"?

Medium

13 Which classic book features Mole, Rat, Badger and Toad?

14 Who wrote the novel *Brighton Rock* (1938)?

15 Why was Tweedledum cross with Tweedledee?

16 Passepartout is Phileas Fogg's manservant in which 1873 novel?

17 Lee Child has written about which fictional character since 1997?

18 What is the surname of Arthur, the main character in *The Hitch-Hiker's Guide to the Galaxy*?

19 *The Casual Vacancy* was the first foray into adult fiction for which children's author?

20 In what country are Jo Nesbo's books set?

Hard

Answers to QUIZ 52 – Clothing and Fabric

1	Jacob	11	Do not bleach
2	1950s	12	Belgium
3	Spinning	13	Sleeveless tunic
4	Damask	14	Chiffon
5	Sleeve	15	Top hat
6	China	16	Gumshoe
7	Denim	17	Suspenders
8	Silk	18	Cloche
9	Deerstalker	19	Hooped petticoat
10	Loom	20	On the lower leg

ANSWERS ON PAGE 57

1 Who played James Bond in *The World Is Not Enough*?

2 He is the chemical symbol for which element?

3 The letter D is on which row of a computer keyboard?

4 In cricket how many balls are there in an over?

5 What is the next highest prime number above 31?

6 Who hosted the UK game show, *Deal or No Deal*?

7 Which character "stole a pig and away did run"?

8 Which tragic Shakespearean king had three daughters?

9 What is a cheroot?

10 On a dartboard, what number is to the immediate left of 20?

11 What source of light is used in producing a hologram?

12 What type of animal is a springbok?

13 In which county is Kidderminster?

14 What is the surname of the central gangster family in *Peaky Blinders*?

15 Who created the sculpture *The Angel of the North*?

16 What is the hardest gemstone?

17 In Scrabble®, what colour are the triple-word score squares?

18 Which mountain range runs through Peru and Chile?

19 In *Dad's Army*, what did Pike's mother always try to make him wear?

20 The 1985 event Live Aid was organised to provide aid to which country?

Answers to QUIZ 53 – Pot Luck

1	Three	11	EH
2	Euro	12	Orleans
3	Two	13	Claustrophobia
4	Prague	14	Fabric
5	Four	15	Bakerloo
6	Flat	16	Copper
7	Five	17	1980s
8	Crimea	18	Postscript
9	Blackpool	19	Hercule Poirot
10	*Spitting Image*	20	Germany

ANSWERS ON PAGE 58

Easy

1 Who starred in the 1987 film *Over the Top*?

2 *Out of the Blue* was a 1977 album by which group?

3 Who starred as RP McMurphy in the 1975 film *One Flew Over the Cuckoo's Nest*?

4 Barra and Benbecula are part of which island chain?

5 Which English football club did Marc Overmars play for from 1997 to 2000?

6 Who released the 2004 single *Left Outside Alone*?

7 What colour is used to describe the situation of being overdrawn in terms of funds?

8 In which sport might a ball end up out of bounds?

9 What do the initials PTO indicate at the bottom of a page?

10 Which outlaw did Clint Eastwood play in a 1976 film?

Medium

11 In which game might a player end up with an overtrick?

12 What do the initials OB stand for in relation to television?

13 Who composed the *William Tell Overture* (1829)?

14 According to the saying, what is something out of if it is out of sight?

15 In the rhyme *Hey Diddle Diddle*, what jumped over the Moon?

16 Which sport featured in the 1979 play *Outside Edge*?

17 Which character in *The Wizard of Oz* sings *Over the Rainbow*?

18 In which part-improvised TV series did Hugh Dennis and Claire Skinner play the parents of three children?

19 What do the initials OHP stand for?

20 Which band released the 1991 album *Out of Time*?

Hard

Answers to QUIZ 54 – Literature

1 Arthur Hailey
2 Beatrix Potter
3 Big Brother
4 Baloo
5 JRR Tolkien
6 *Rime of the Ancient Mariner*
7 Aesop
8 Dame Daphne du Maurier
9 *The Three Musketeers*
10 Mark Twain
11 Belgium
12 *Pride and Prejudice*
13 *The Wind in the Willows*
14 Graham Greene
15 He had spoiled his new rattle
16 *Around the World in Eighty Days*
17 Jack Reacher
18 Dent
19 JK Rowling
20 Norway

QUIZ 57 – Pot Luck

1   Which car company manufactures the Cayenne?

2   What was American MR Bissell's dust-collecting invention?

3   What term describes a way of representing a number as a fraction of 100?

4   Which 1707 law joined England and Scotland?

5   Which actor was married twice to Elizabeth Taylor?

6   Sting, Andy Summers and Stewart Copeland made up which group?

7   Which section of an orchestra includes trumpets and trombones?

8   On UK roads, what shape is a road sign that gives an order?

9   Who had a hit in 1984 with *Girls Just Want to Have Fun*?

10 What is the traditional bingo call for the number 76?

11 Which is the southernmost of North America's Great Lakes?

12 Who was King Henry VIII's fifth wife?

13 In the nursery rhyme, what was the monotonous diet of the children of the Old Lady who lived in a shoe?

14 Which army rank is immediately above private?

15 Is volleyball normally played indoors or outdoors?

16 What is the science and study of the measurement of time known as?

17 In which county would you visit Sissinghurst Gardens?

18 To which family does the chive belong?

19 On a radio tuning dial, for what do the letters FM stand?

20 The 1981 song *Endless Love* was a hit for which duo?

Easy · **Medium** · **Hard**

Answers to QUIZ 55 – Pot Luck

1	Pierce Brosnan	11	Laser
2	Helium	12	Antelope
3	Middle row of letters	13	Worcestershire
4	Six	14	Shelby
5	37	15	Sir Antony Gormley
6	Noel Edmonds	16	Diamond
7	Tom the piper's son	17	Red
8	Lear	18	Andes
9	Cigar	19	His scarf
10	Five	20	Ethiopia

Easy

1 What is a young goat called?

2 A muscovy is what sort of bird?

3 Dates grow on what type of tree?

4 What is an acanthus?

5 What word is used to describe a group of dolphins?

6 Hawthorn traditionally blooms in which month?

7 What is the collective name for a group of crows?

8 Which insects communicate with one another by dancing?

9 How is the climber *Hedera helix* better known?

10 How many legs has a crab?

11 What is the green colouring matter in plants called?

12 Mountain ash is another name for which tree?

13 Conkers come from which tree?

14 What general term is given to a creature that does not have a backbone?

15 From what is the horn of a rhinoceros formed?

16 Which is the world's fastest land mammal?

17 Is a sole a freshwater or sea fish?

18 What is the term for a male badger?

19 Which Christmas decoration is a parasite of the apple tree?

20 Which tree is named after a UK capital city?

Medium

Hard

Answers to QUIZ 56 – Over and Out

1	Sylvester Stallone	11	Bridge
2	Electric Light Orchestra	12	Outside broadcast
3	Jack Nicholson	13	Rossini
4	Outer Hebrides	14	Out of mind
5	Arsenal	15	The cow
6	Anastacia	16	Cricket
7	Red (In the red)	17	Dorothy
8	Golf	18	*Outnumbered*
9	Please turn over	19	Overhead projector
10	Josey Wales	20	REM

1   Before the invention of the clock what was anticlockwise known as?

2   On a Monopoly™ board, what colour is Leicester Square?

3   How many balls are used in a game of billiards?

4   Who wrote the novel *Little Women* (1868)?

5   Which sitcom starred Lenny Henry as Gareth Blackstock?

6   0114 is the dialling code for which city?

7   Of which country was Juan Carlos king?

8   How many million dollars did the *Man* cost in the title of a 1970s TV series?

9   Which waterfall comprises the Horseshoe Falls and American Falls, separated by Goat Island?

10   In which year did Michael Jackson have a hit with *Billie Jean*?

11   Which French phrase used in English means each dish individually priced?

12   Which 1960 film starred Kirk Douglas and Jean Simmons?

13   Florence is the capital of which region of Italy?

14   What term is given to artistic handwriting, usually produced with a special pen?

15   What type of fruit is Packham's Triumph?

16   Where on the body could a cataract form?

17   In which decade of the 20th century was Michaela Strachan born?

18   Billingsgate Market was famous for what sort of food?

19   Which Romantic poet was described as "mad, bad and dangerous to know"?

20   What term is given to a positive electrode?

Easy

Medium

Hard

Answers to QUIZ 57 – Pot Luck

1	Porsche	11	Erie
2	Carpet sweeper	12	Katherine Howard
3	Percentage	13	Broth without bread
4	Act of Union	14	Lance Corporal
5	Richard Burton	15	Indoors
6	The Police	16	Horology
7	Brass	17	Kent
8	Round	18	Alliums
9	Cyndi Lauper	19	Frequency Modulation
10	Trombones	20	Diana Ross and Lionel Richie

Easy

1   On UK roads, what shape is the STOP sign that has white writing on a red background?

2   Which major UK road stretches from Edinburgh to London?

3   Which A road passes Chelmsford, Colchester and Ipswich?

4   On UK roads, what is the standard national speed limit for a car in a built-up area?

5   Carlisle and Rugby are connected by which motorway?

6   *Road to Hell* was a hit single and album for whom in 1989?

7   The Primera was a model produced by which Japanese car manufacturer?

8   On UK roads, the sign indicating a roundabout shows a circle divided into how many parts?

9   What is the number of the Manchester Orbital motorway?

10 Who had a 1991 no. 1 hit with *End of the Road*?

11 What colour of cat's-eyes are used to mark the edge of the carriageway of lay-bys and slip roads in the UK?

12 What does MPV stand for in relation to cars?

13 The Clubman is a variety of which car model?

Medium

14 What name is given to a car which has a soft roof that can be removed or folded down?

15 Which French term is applied to a two-door car with a sloping rear?

16 On an Ordnance Survey map, what is indicated by a rectangle containing "P&R"?

17 On UK roads, what shape is the Give Way sign?

18 What essential car part do Pirelli and Firestone manufacture?

19 What name is given to the speed pedal of a motor vehicle?

20 *Hit the Road, Jack* was the first UK top ten hit for which singer?

Hard

Answers to QUIZ 58 – Natural World

1	Kid	11	Chlorophyll
2	Duck	12	Rowan
3	Palm	13	Horse chestnut
4	Flower	14	Invertebrate
5	Pod	15	Keratin
6	May	16	Cheetah
7	Murder	17	Sea fish
8	Bees	18	Boar
9	Ivy	19	Mistletoe
10	Ten	20	London plane

1 What name was shared by all the kings from the House of Lancaster?

2 What military rank did Elvis Presley's manager, Tom Parker adopt?

3 What type of mythical creature did Daryl Hannah play in the film *Splash*?

4 Of which US state is Nashville the capital?

5 Which body of water is sometimes referred to as "The Pond"?

6 Sherlock Holmes played which musical instrument?

7 Which bird lays the largest egg?

8 Which country has Ankara as its capital city?

9 In which county is Newcastle-under-Lyme?

10 What is the national religion of Japan?

11 Who wrote *The Lord of the Rings* trilogy?

12 The Royal Opera House in London is home to which branch of the arts other than opera?

13 In which century was Michelangelo born?

14 The sitcom *Frasier* was set in which US city?

15 In the books by WE Johns, who is the fictional flying ace?

16 What is the traditional bingo call for the number 89?

17 What is hit with a racket in badminton?

18 Which book of the Bible tells of the birth of Moses?

19 In the 1993 film *Carlito's Way*, which actor played Carlito?

20 What kind of animal is a Cornish Rex?

Easy

Medium

Hard

Answers to QUIZ 59 – Pot Luck

1	Widdershins	11	*À la carte*
2	Yellow	12	*Spartacus*
3	Three	13	Tuscany
4	Louisa May Alcott	14	Calligraphy
5	*Chef*	15	Pear
6	Sheffield	16	The eye
7	Spain	17	1960s
8	Six million	18	Fish
9	Niagara	19	Lord Byron
10	1983	20	Anode

Easy

1. *Sunny Afternoon* was a hit in 1966 for which group?

2. Who topped the charts in 1967 with *Release Me* and *The Last Waltz*?

3. Who had a 1964 hit with *Baby Love*?

4. In which song did Desmond have a barrow in the marketplace?

5. Which singer had hits with *I Say a Little Prayer* and *Respect*?

6. What was the first UK no.1 hit for the Beach Boys?

7. *Where Do You Go To (My Lovely)?* was a 1969 hit for which singer?

8. *Those Were the Days* was a 1968 hit for which Welsh singer?

9. Which group had a 1963 hit with *You'll Never Walk Alone*?

10. Which singer starred in the 1968 film *Funny Girl*?

Medium

11. What was the first UK no.1 hit for the Monkees?

12. *Get Off of My Cloud* was a 1965 hit for which band?

13. What was the title of the Beatles' first feature film, released in 1964?

14. Who had a hit in 1960 with *Tell Laura I Love Her*?

15. What was the title of Procol Harum's chart-topping hit of 1967?

16. Which group had a 1966 hit with *I'll Be There*?

17. *Nights in White Satin* topped the UK charts in 1967 for which group?

18. Who sang about the *Green, Green Grass of Home* in 1966?

19. On which Isle was there a 1969 rock festival featuring Bob Dylan?

20. Who had a hit in 1964 with *Shout*?

Hard

QUIZ 63 – Pot Luck

ANSWERS ON PAGE 65

1 What is three cubed?

2 What nationality is Graham Norton?

3 What is the highest UK peak south of the Scottish border?

4 Excluding jokers, how many cards are there in a standard pack?

5 On what date is St George's Day celebrated?

6 In which country is the city of Nice?

7 Which progressive rock band was fronted by Fish in the 1980s?

8 In the TV series *This Is Your Life*, what colour was the famous big book?

9 Which *Finding Nemo* character was voiced by Ellen DeGeneres?

10 What is the name of Postman Pat's cat?

11 What name is given to the longest side of a right-angled triangle?

12 In the name of the Ferrari, what does *Testarossa* mean in English?

13 In *Sex and the City*, which actress played Miranda Hobbes?

14 Which country left the Commonwealth in 1961, then rejoined it in 1994?

15 On which island is *The Durrells* set?

16 Which airline company has its largest hub at Toronto Pearson International Airport?

17 In the film *Jerry Maguire*, who played Tom Cruise's love interest?

18 Who was the sixth actor to play the starring role in *Doctor Who* on television?

19 What name is given to the bluish-green coating sometimes seen on brass and copper?

20 What is a dotterel?

Easy

Medium

Hard

Answers to QUIZ 61 – Pot Luck

1	Henry	11	JRR Tolkien
2	Colonel	12	Ballet
3	Mermaid	13	15th century
4	Tennessee	14	Seattle
5	Atlantic Ocean	15	Biggles
6	Violin	16	Nearly there
7	Ostrich	17	Shuttlecock
8	Turkey	18	Exodus
9	Staffordshire	19	Al Pacino
10	Shintoism	20	Cat

Easy

1 Which small Russian buckwheat pancakes are traditionally served with soured cream?

2 What name is given to a preserved, sweetened cherry, often soaked in a suspension of food colouring?

3 Beauty of Bath and Discovery are types of which fruit?

4 How is wine described as "*chambré*" served?

5 A nectarine is a smooth-skinned variety of which fruit?

6 Which part of the mint plant is used to make mint sauce?

7 How is beef prepared to turn it into Beef Wellington?

8 What is the flavour of Grand Marnier®?

9 The kumquat belongs to which family of fruit?

10 What is the flavour of aioli sauce?

Medium

11 Which term meaning "out of date" is also a cocktail made from whisky, bitters, water and sugar?

12 Which Italian pasta sauce is made with a variety of spring vegetables?

13 What is converted into alcohol during brewing?

14 Mulligatawny is what type of food?

15 In the abbreviation VSOP that appears on some bottles of alcohol, for what do the letters OP stand?

16 Which ingredient of beer is made by steeping barley in water?

17 Rollmops are made from which fish?

18 What are the main ingredients of colcannon?

19 Which country does Tokay come from?

20 Which almond-flavoured paste is used to coat a Christmas cake?

Hard

Answers to QUIZ 62 – 1960s Music

1	Kinks	11	*I'm a Believer*
2	Engelbert Humperdinck	12	Rolling Stones
3	Supremes	13	*A Hard Day's Night*
4	*Ob-La-Di, Ob-La-Da*	14	Ricky Valance
5	Aretha Franklin	15	*A Whiter Shade of Pale*
6	*Good Vibrations*	16	Four Tops
7	Peter Sarstedt	17	Moody Blues
8	Mary Hopkin	18	Sir Tom Jones
9	Gerry and the Pacemakers	19	Wight
10	Barbra Streisand	20	Lulu

1 Who starred as Fitz in the TV series *Cracker*?

2 Which king is supposed to have hidden in a tree after the Battle of Worcester?

3 Which is the most common human blood group?

4 If something is described as Cantonese, from which country does it originate?

5 Which song begins, "They asked me how I knew, my true love was true"?

6 How many wheels are there normally on a skateboard?

7 Alphabetically, which is the last of the calendar months?

8 The Battle of Waterloo was fought in which country?

9 In Morse Code, what letter is represented by three dashes?

10 From which country does the cheese Camembert originate?

11 What was the title of the first *Lassie* film?

12 Sine, cosine and tangent are words associated with which branch of mathematics?

13 Which 20th-century novelist used a Suffolk river as a pen name?

14 In which country do the rulers sit on the Chrysanthemum Throne?

15 Which country, capital Sofia, is bordered by Turkey, Romania and Macedonia?

16 In which US state is JFK airport?

17 Which American rodent builds dams and fells trees?

18 What term is given to an inactive element such as neon or argon?

19 What type of nut is a marron glacé?

20 In the TV series *Casualty*, what is the name of the hospital?

Easy

Medium

Hard

Answers to QUIZ 63 – Pot Luck

1	27	11	Hypotenuse
2	Irish	12	Redhead
3	Snowdon	13	Cynthia Nixon
4	52	14	South Africa
5	23rd April	15	Corfu
6	France	16	Air Canada
7	Marillion	17	Renée Zellweger
8	Red	18	Colin Baker
9	Dory	19	Verdigris
10	Jess	20	Bird

Easy

1. In greyhound racing, what is the number of the trap corresponding to the orange jacket?

2. In a standard edition of Trivial Pursuit™, what subject is coloured orange?

3. Which airline company's logo is white on an orange background?

4. Which type of Japanese porcelain shares its name with a citrus fruit?

5. The House of Orange-Nassau rules which country?

6. What orange variety is also a language of Asia?

7. Orange and lemon make what flavouring?

8. The Orange Revolution took place in which European country in 2004-05?

9. In classic cuisine, what is served *a l'orange*?

10. Which orange-coloured mild cheese is named after a city in the East Midlands?

Medium

11. What does an amber traffic light mean?

12. Which famous cookware brand's signature colour is "flame"?

13. What was the first name of Sir Winston Churchill's wife?

14. Dame Judi Dench, Celia Imrie and Dame Penelope Wilton starred in which 2011 film about pensioners retiring to India?

15. Which two paint colours are mixed to obtain orange?

16. On a colour wheel, what colour is opposite orange?

17. On a standard Monopoly™ board, the orange properties are Bow Street, Vine Street and which other street?

18. Which fruit is named after a major city in north-west Morocco?

19. To what is orange juice added to make Buck's Fizz?

20. Amber Riley played Mercedes Jones in which TV series?

Hard

Answers to QUIZ 64 – Food and Drink

1	Blini	11	Old Fashioned
2	Maraschino	12	Primavera
3	Apples	13	Sugar
4	At room temperature	14	Soup
5	Peach	15	Old Pale
6	The leaves	16	Malt
7	Wrapped in pastry	17	Herrings
8	Orange	18	Cabbage and potatoes
9	Citrus	19	Hungary
10	Garlic	20	Marzipan

1   What type of bird is a gadwall?

2   The flower with the Latin name *Papaver* has what common name?

3   Which is the first month of the year to have exactly 31 days?

4   Which US state capital is the home of country and western music?

5   What is the name of Fred Flintstone's pet dinosaur?

6   In tenpin bowling, how many pins are there in the back row?

7   In which US state would you find the towns of Anchorage, Fairbanks and Moose Pass?

8   What army rank is held during initial Army training at Sandhurst Military Academy?

9   Which word describes the power generated by a water-powered turbine?

10 Which royal house preceded Stuart rule?

11 In 1981, who defeated Bjorn Borg in the men's singles at Wimbledon, halting his attempt to win a record sixth successive title there?

12 Which radio code word comes between delta and foxtrot?

13 Who provided the voice of Danger Mouse in the original cartoon series?

14 By what name is tetanus more commonly known?

15 Which pantomime features the character of Widow Twankey?

16 In which country is the city of Kathmandu?

17 What is a homburg?

18 Which group had hits in the 1990s with *No Matter What* and *When the Going Gets Tough*?

19 Which fruit has Bartlett and Conference varieties?

20 Which journalist, noted as a war correspondent, was made a CBE in the 2018 Birthday Honours?

Easy

Medium

Hard

Answers to QUIZ 65 – Pot Luck

1	Robbie Coltrane	11	*Lassie Come Home*
2	Charles II	12	Trigonometry
3	O	13	Orwell
4	China	14	Japan
5	*Smoke Gets In Your Eyes*	15	Bulgaria
6	Four	16	New York
7	September	17	Beaver
8	Belgium	18	Inert gas
9	O	19	Chestnut
10	France	20	Holby City Hospital

Easy

1 Which metallic element can be taken orally to help with X-rays?

2 Which Russian scientist is popularly known for his work with salivating dogs?

3 What is a substance made up of two or more elements?

4 What is the six-letter term for the examination of tissue to assess the presence or extent of disease?

5 In which part of the body would you find the amygdala?

6 Which hormone is secreted by cells in the pancreas?

7 What is a negatively charged particle in an atom?

8 Who famously demonstrated the electrical nature of lightning in 1752 in an experiment using a kite?

9 Ca is the symbol for which chemical element?

10 Water is made from hydrogen and which other element?

Medium

11 Which triangular bone is found at the base of the spine?

12 Ophthalmology is a branch of medicine involving which part of the body?

13 What type of substance turns litmus paper blue?

14 Which common gas is produced in respiration?

15 Al is the chemical symbol for which element?

16 In astronomy what are falling stars properly called?

17 What is a crucible used for in a laboratory?

18 Which science deals with the constituents of atoms?

19 What does a Geiger counter detect?

20 What is the science of water mechanics?

Hard

Answers to QUIZ 66 – Orange

1	Five	11	Stop if you are able to do so
2	Sports and Leisure	12	Le Creuset®
3	EasyJet	13	Clementine
4	Satsuma	14	*The Best Exotic Marigold Hotel*
5	The Netherlands	15	Red and yellow
6	Mandarin	16	Blue
7	St Clements	17	Marlborough Street
8	Ukraine	18	Tangerine
9	Duck	19	Champagne
10	Red Leicester	20	*Glee*

1   What colour are gorse flowers?

2   The Menai Strait separates which island from mainland Wales?

3   What is the name of the cold dish of poultry, mayonnaise, curry powder and apricots?

4   Which car company manufactures the Octavia?

5   What does the musical term "glissando" mean?

6   In the rhyme often quoted when magpies are seen, what is associated with five magpies?

7   What is the capital city of Albania?

8   What is Inspector Morse's first name?

9   In the *Vicar of Dibley*, what was the name of James Fleet's character?

10 Who created the series *Prime Suspect*?

11 Which actress starred in the 1983 film *Educating Rita*?

12 Where did the Pilgrim Fathers land in 1620?

13 Which is the second-largest continent?

14 For which wedding anniversary would a crystal vase be an appropriate gift?

15 Near which city is Cadbury World?

16 On UK roads, direction signs on primary routes have what colour background?

17 Which common British garden creature belongs to the locust family?

18 What is the name of the theatre cat in TS Eliot's *Old Possum's Book of Practical Cats*?

19 What fuel is used by a Bunsen burner?

20 What does BST stand for?

Answers to QUIZ 67 – Pot Luck

1	Duck	11	John McEnroe
2	Poppy	12	Echo
3	January	13	Sir David Jason
4	Nashville	14	Lockjaw
5	Dino	15	*Aladdin*
6	Four	16	Nepal
7	Alaska	17	Hat
8	Officer Cadet	18	Boyzone
9	Hydroelectric	19	Pear
10	Tudor	20	Kate Adie

Easy

1   Which of the coloured balls has the second-lowest points value?

2   What is the score achieved when making a maximum break?

3   Which retired player was famous for his large glasses?

4   "The Jester from Leicester" is the nickname of which player?

5   How many points are awarded for potting a black ball?

6   Alex Higgins was known by what nickname?

7   Which former snooker player was the co-host of the TV show *Big Break*?

8   Which Sheffield venue is famous for hosting snooker tournaments?

9   How old was Stephen Hendry when he was crowned world champion in 1990?

10   Who was the winner of the first World Championships held in 1927?

11   In which country was retired player Terry Griffiths born?

12   In which year were the first UK Snooker Championship held?

13   Neil Robertson was born in which country?

14   How many balls are there on the table at the start of a snooker match?

Medium

15   Steve Davis won how many UK Snooker Championship titles?

16   How old was Ronnie O'Sullivan when he won the UK Snooker Championship in 1993?

17   Of what material is the bed on a snooker table made?

18   How many World snooker final matches did Jimmy White lose?

19   In 2018, at the age of 43, who became the second-oldest player to win the World Championship?

20   What colour gloves does a snooker referee wear?

Hard

Answers to QUIZ 68 – Science

1	Barium	11	Coccyx
2	Pavlov	12	Eye
3	Compound	13	Alkali
4	Biopsy	14	Carbon dioxide
5	Brain	15	Aluminium
6	Insulin	16	Meteors
7	Electron	17	Heating substances
8	Benjamin Franklin	18	Nuclear physics
9	Calcium	19	Radioactivity
10	Oxygen	20	Hydraulics

QUIZ 71 – Pot Luck

1   What is the name of Chief Wiggum's son in *The Simpsons*?

2   A mukluk is worn on which part of the body?

3   What method do bottlenose dolphins use to find their prey in the sand?

4   A director utters what word to commence filming?

5   What type of dance involves moving under a low horizontal pole?

6   In which county is the town of Framlingham?

7   What is the name of Kylie Minogue's pop star sister?

8   Of which English county is Lewes the county town?

9   What is the name of the thighbone?

10 Who had a hit in 1996 with *Always Be My Baby*?

11 In rhyming slang what is a "dog and bone"?

12 Which Hollywood legend was born Archibald Leach in 1904?

13 Which Saint's Day is celebrated on 17th March?

14 A hartebeest is what type of animal?

15 Who played the Mad Hatter in the 2010 film *Alice in Wonderland*?

16 In which decade did Radio 1 start?

17 Where in the body are the adenoids?

18 What is the traditional bingo call for the number 57?

19 Which US TV series that began in 2016 features the Pearson family?

20 What type of musical instrument was invented by Laurens Hammond?

Answers to QUIZ 69 – Pot Luck

1	Yellow	11	Dame Julie Walters
2	Anglesey	12	Plymouth Rock
3	Coronation Chicken	13	Africa
4	Skoda	14	15th
5	Sliding	15	Birmingham
6	Silver	16	Green
7	Tirana	17	The grasshopper
8	Endeavour	18	Gus
9	Hugo Horton	19	Gas
10	Lynda La Plante	20	British Summer Time

Easy

1   What is the vehicle called in the UK that Americans call a trailer?

2   If someone is deliberately shunned, which English city are they said to be sent to?

3   What is an eponym?

4   What is the code-word for the ninth letter of the alphabet in radio communications?

5   According to the proverb, what do many hands make?

6   Which Latin word meaning "elsewhere" is a claim of absence from a crime scene?

7   Frigophobia is the fear of what?

8   From which language does the word "graffiti" originate?

9   What does the French word *pomme* mean?

10 According to the well-known phrase, how many words is a picture worth?

11 In Cockney rhyming slang what are "mince pies"?

12 What is a yawl?

13 Alphabetically, which is the first creature in the dictionary?

14 A piece of over-elaborate prose might be described as a passage of what colour?

Medium

15 What type of word is made from the initials of others?

16 Which word meaning "soon" is also an abbreviation meaning "not known by name"?

17 What is the more common description given to someone who is sinistral?

18 In which language is *sayonara* the word for "goodbye"?

19 What is the plural of mongoose?

20 According to the saying, on what does an army march?

Hard

Answers to QUIZ 70 – Snooker

1	Yellow	11	Wales
2	147	12	1977
3	Dennis Taylor	13	Australia
4	Mark Selby	14	21 and the cue ball
5	Seven	15	Six
6	Hurricane	16	17
7	John Virgo	17	Slate
8	The Crucible	18	Six
9	21	19	Mark Williams
10	Joe Davis	20	White

ANSWERS ON PAGE **75**

1 Which cat breed takes its name for the old name for Ethiopia?

2 Who was the original "hunter" on the 1980s TV series *Treasure Hunt*?

3 How many feet are there in ten yards?

4 Which fast food chain was founded by Colonel Sanders?

5 Who had a no.1 hit with the 1989 single *Ride on Time*?

6 What, together with time, proverbially waits for no man?

7 If something is literally petrified, what happens to it?

8 What is the sum of a century plus a gross?

9 In Greek mythology, what name was given to the food of the gods?

10 Which ocean surrounds the Maldives?

11 In which county is the town of Ashbourne?

12 Who wrote *The House at Pooh Corner*?

13 A yak is what type of creature?

14 In which country was actress Ada Nicodemou born?

15 What is the highest British civilian bravery award?

16 0117 is the dialling code for which city?

17 Who starred in the 1971 film *Get Carter*?

18 Which European leader rode a horse called Marengo?

19 What is the name of the motel in Hitchcock's *Psycho*?

20 Which element has the symbol B in the periodic table?

Easy

Medium

Hard

Answers to QUIZ 71 – Pot Luck

1	Ralph	11	Phone
2	On the foot	12	Cary Grant
3	Echolocation	13	St Patrick's Day
4	Action	14	Antelope
5	Limbo	15	Johnny Depp
6	Suffolk	16	1960s
7	Dannii	17	In the throat
8	East Sussex	18	Heinz Varieties
9	Femur	19	*This Is Us*
10	Mariah Carey	20	Organ

Easy

1 What do the initials ONO stand for in relation to selling?

2 What is the flag-carrier airline of the Netherlands?

3 Politically, what do the letters MEP stand for?

4 NSW is a state in which country?

5 Which three letters describe a product or company's exclusive appeal?

6 What do CND campaigners campaign for?

7 The SNP party operates in which part of the UK?

8 MTV launched in which decade?

9 What three letters apply to milk that has been sterilised at a high temperature?

10 Which company founded by Joseph Bamford is now a generic name for earth-moving vehicles?

Medium

11 VDU is the old term for what piece of technological equipment?

12 The BDO is the UK governing body of which sport?

13 Which group were runners-up on *The X Factor* in 2008?

14 The dog Nipper is associated with which entertainment company?

15 Who were XTC making plans for in the title of a 1979 single?

16 For what do the initials UHF stand in relation to radio broadcasts?

17 The UK's largest employer is known by which three initials?

18 The initials PLC indicate that a company has what status?

19 In which year did ABC release the original *The Lexicon of Love* album?

20 What is the full name of the disorder usually referred to as RSI?

Hard

Answers to QUIZ 72 – Words

1	Caravan	11	Eyes
2	Coventry	12	A small fishing boat
3	A word formed from a name	13	Aardvark
4	India	14	Purple
5	Light work	15	Acronym
6	Alibi	16	Anon
7	Being cold	17	Left-handed
8	Italian	18	Japanese
9	Apple	19	Mongooses
10	1000	20	Its stomach

1 The cornet belongs to which family of musical instruments?

2 What was the name of Josh Holloway's character in the TV series *Lost*?

3 What is the miraculous food described in the book of Exodus?

4 To which state do Gozo and Comino belong?

5 Who had a hit in 1960 with *Only the Lonely*?

6 What is the alcoholic ingredient of a piña colada?

7 The Roman numeral C stands for which number?

8 In which country are the Abu Simbel temples?

9 Which word means "faster than the speed of sound"?

10 Which drama series that began in 2015 features "synths"?

11 Cannelloni is what type of food?

12 Who is the only person allowed, by tradition, to consume alcohol in the chamber of the House of Commons?

13 What is the boiling point of water in Celsius?

14 What is the first name of Ada Nicodemou's *Home and Away* character?

15 How often is cycling's Tour of Spain held?

16 Which organisation produces a newspaper entitled *The War Cry*?

17 In which country were fireworks invented?

18 What does the Scottish word "swithering" mean?

19 "You talking to me?" is a line from which 1976 film?

20 What two-word term is given to the military force sent to prepare an area for operations?

Easy

Medium

Hard

Answers to QUIZ 73 – Pot Luck

1 Abyssinian
2 Anneka Rice
3 30
4 Kentucky Fried Chicken
5 Black Box
6 Tide
7 It turns to stone
8 244
9 Ambrosia
10 Indian Ocean
11 Derbyshire
12 AA Milne
13 An ox
14 Australia
15 George Cross
16 Bristol
17 Sir Michael Caine
18 Napoleon
19 Bates Motel
20 Boron

QUIZ 76 – The USA

ANSWERS ON PAGE 78

Easy

1 Which Florida national park is split by a road called Alligator Alley?

2 Baltimore is the largest city in which US state?

3 How many stripes are on the flag of the United States?

4 In which US state was Elvis Presley born in January 1935?

5 Which Massachusetts town is famous for its witch trials?

6 In which US state did the Battle of the Alamo take place?

7 The Gettysburg address was a speech given by which US president?

8 What was the name of the US mail service, started in 1860, that used horses and riders?

9 Which US city is also known as "The Big Easy"?

10 The Statue of Liberty holds what item in her right hand?

11 Which major American airline shares a name with a Greek letter?

12 The Los Angeles International airport has what three-letter code?

13 Which is the oldest national park in the USA?

14 The Dallas Cowboys play which sport?

Medium

15 Which state in America is known as the "Gambling State"?

16 What is the largest carnivore found in North America?

17 Which is America's second-largest state?

18 King George II gave his name to which American state?

19 What is the major wine producing state in the USA?

20 Who are the Democrats' chief opponents?

Hard

Answers to QUIZ 74 – Three Letters

1 Or nearest offer
2 KLM
3 Member of the European Parliament
4 Australia
5 USP (Unique selling point)
6 Nuclear Disarmament
7 Scotland
8 1980s (1981)
9 UHT
10 JCB
11 Computer monitor (visual display unit)
12 Darts
13 JLS
14 HMV
15 Nigel
16 Ultra high frequency
17 NHS
18 Issuing shares with limited liability
19 1982
20 Repetitve strain injury

76

1   On what part of your body would you wear an espadrille?

2   Who created the idea of Utopia?

3   In which county is Market Harborough?

4   Which hard black stone is a variety of lignite?

5   In the nursery rhyme, which city did the Man in the Moon enquire about how to get to?

6   In which century was Fred Astaire born?

7   Which units of measurement are used for depths at sea?

8   Which dinosaur had three horns on its head?

9   The word aural relates to which sense?

10   Which bird has short-eared and tawny species?

11   Which actress co-starred with Chris Pratt in the 2016 film *Passengers*?

12   What term is given to a mountain that could erupt at any time?

13   The 1850s novel *Little Dorrit* was written by which author?

14   Which childhood disease has the same virus as shingles?

15   Which songwriter was awarded the Nobel Prize in Literature in 2016?

16   What are dried in an oast house?

17   Joe Bugner (b.1950) was a competitor in which sport?

18   Which birthstone is linked to February?

19   What is the Latin term applied to a graduate's old university?

20   On a standard computer keyboard, which letter is between C and B?

Easy

Medium

Hard

1 If you practised callisthenics what type of activity would you be doing?

2 What nationality was Ernö Rubik, inventor of the cube that bears his name?

3 What sort of toy was a Cabbage Patch?

4 What is a workshop used for the development of light-sensitive films known as?

5 In Scrabble®, how many points is the letter E worth?

6 The core of most writing pencils is a mixture of clay and what other substance?

7 Which toy is most associated with the name Hornby?

8 What is "John Innes no. 1"?

9 Alfred Wainwright wrote books on which leisure activity?

10 Vaudeville is the American term for what type of entertainment?

11 What is the traditional term for a female Scout?

12 Which card game includes variants called stud, draw and Texas hold 'em?

13 What three colours are on a roulette wheel?

14 What would you be making if you were following the bobbin or pillow method?

15 How many cards are there in each suit?

16 How many people can you normally fit in a go-kart?

17 Which large plastic hoop became a sports craze in the 1950s?

18 What does PYO stand for?

19 How many spaces are there in a noughts-and-crosses frame?

20 What is the minimum number of people that are needed to play a game of Trivial Pursuit™?

1   What is produced by the lacrimal glands?

2   *Wild Boys* was a 1984 hit for which band?

3   Which sea lies between Italy and Croatia?

4   Which Scottish town in the Highlands was elevated to city status in December 2000?

5   On a Monopoly™ board, what colour is the Angel, Islington?

6   Where is the *Cutty Sark* moored?

7   What is a boater usually made from?

8   Who won the 2008 series of *The X Factor*?

9   As what is ferrous oxide better known?

10 When the Owl and the Pussycat went to sea, who married them?

11 How many teams compete in an individual episode of *University Challenge*?

12 Which poisonous gas is given off from a car exhaust?

13 In which county is the theme park of Drayton Manor?

14 What is 13 multiplied by 8?

15 The Whispering Gallery is in which London cathedral?

16 Which actress was the mother of Liza Minnelli?

17 Which designer did Madonna commission to design the outfits for her 1990 Blonde Ambition tour?

18 The Picanto was manufactured by which car company?

19 If you were "Sur le pont d'Avignon", which region of France would you be visiting?

20 Who was the manager of the 1966 England football team?

Answers to QUIZ 77 – Pot Luck

1	Foot	11	Jennifer Lawrence
2	Sir Thomas More	12	Active volcano
3	Leicestershire	13	Charles Dickens
4	Jet	14	Chickenpox
5	Norwich	15	Bob Dylan
6	19th century	16	Hops
7	Fathoms	17	Boxing
8	Triceratops	18	Amethyst
9	Hearing	19	*Alma mater*
10	Owl	20	V

QUIZ 80 – Engineering

1 Which supersonic form of transport was introduced in 1976 and retired in 2003?

2 Which aircraft that was first flown commercially in 1970 was nicknamed the "Jumbo Jet"?

3 The high-speed Japanese train network first introduced in 1964 is called the *Shinkansen*, but what is its more common name?

4 What was the nickname given to Robert Stephenson's steam locomotive of 1829?

5 What is the name of the record-winning fastest steam locomotive of all time?

6 Who patented the lightbulb in 1879?

7 What is the name of the Ferris wheel in London, originally built for the Millennium celebrations?

8 Opened to the public in 2013, which 95-storey building was the tallest building in the UK as at June 2018?

9 Which entrepreneur and engineer founded the company SpaceX and co-founded Tesla Inc?

10 Opened in 2010, what was the name of the tallest building in the world as at June 2018?

11 What is the name of the tallest structure in Paris, opened in 1889?

12 What is the name of the hydroelectric gravity dam in China which became fully operational in 2012?

13 Sir Christopher Cockerell invented what method of transport?

14 Which Swedish engineer, the inventor of dynamite, posthumously dedicated his fortune to establish an annual series of prizes?

15 The Bessemer process, devised in 1856, made which alloy cheaper to mass-produce?

16 Which man-made waterway in Central America links the Atlantic and Pacific Ocean?

17 For what type of construction is Glenfinnan noted?

18 The Eurostar train travels under which stretch of water?

19 In which city did the world's first underground railway open?

20 What is the name of the ancient fortification in China, said to be observable from space?

Answers to QUIZ 78 – Leisure

1	Keep-fit	11	Guide
2	Hungarian	12	Poker
3	Doll	13	Black, green, red
4	Darkroom	14	Lace
5	One	15	13
6	Graphite	16	One
7	Train sets	17	Hula hoop
8	Garden compost	18	Pick Your Own
9	Fell walking	19	Nine
10	Music Hall	20	Two

1   In which county is Stratford-upon-Avon?

2   Which English dramatist created the TV series *Boys from the Blackstuff*?

3   What two colours are on the flag waved at the end of a motor race?

4   How does 10.45 pm appear on a 24-hour clock?

5   What is the junior version of Lego® called?

6   Cotton denotes which wedding anniversary?

7   In which country would you find the Mounties?

8   Ornithophobia is the fear of what?

9   Who was the mythical son of Daedalus?

10   In which country does Alfa Romeo have its headquarters?

11   Which acid develops in milk?

12   On UK roads, what is the standard national speed limit for a car on a single carriageway when not towing a trailer?

13   Gingivitis affects which part of the body?

14   What was the first name of the owner of TV's Fawlty Towers?

15   Which group had a hit with 1986's *Manic Monday*?

16   Which moorland plant is said to bring good luck?

17   The words "Frankly, my dear, I don't give a damn" were uttered in which film?

18   Totnes and Tiverton castles are both in which county?

19   What sport is played by the San Francisco 49ers?

20   What is a fandango?

Medium

Hard

Answers to QUIZ 79 – Pot Luck

1	Tears	11	Two
2	Duran Duran	12	Carbon monoxide
3	Adriatic	13	Staffordshire
4	Inverness	14	104
5	Light blue	15	St Paul's
6	Greenwich	16	Judy Garland
7	Straw	17	Jean-Paul Gaultier
8	Alexandra Burke	18	KIA
9	Rust	19	Provence
10	The Turkey	20	Sir Alf Ramsey

1 Which musical note is equivalent in length to four quavers?

2 *Carmina Burana* was a 1930s work by which composer?

3 What was Tchaikovsky's middle name?

4 Who wrote the opera *Tosca* (1899)?

5 Who composed the *Symphonie fantastique* (1830)?

6 Which musical instrument has dampers, hammers and strings?

7 Which series of concerts is held in late summer at the Albert Hall?

8 What name is given to a composition for nine performers?

9 For which musical instrument did Chopin mostly write music?

10 What was the nationality of the composer Claude Debussy?

11 Which composer wrote the music for *Land of Hope and Glory* (1902)?

12 In which country was Antonio Vivaldi born?

13 Who wrote the 1871 opera *Aida*?

14 What fabric is often used in musical instruments to act as a sound damper?

15 Which woman is mentioned in the common title of Beethoven's *Bagatelle no. 25 in A Minor*?

16 In which Austrian city was Mozart born?

17 Which brass musical instrument shares its name with an ice cream?

18 What was the first name of the German composer Wagner?

19 What term is used to indicate that a piece of music should gradually get louder and louder?

20 Andrés Segovia was associated with which musical instrument?

Answers to QUIZ 80 – Engineering

1	Concorde	11	Eiffel Tower
2	Boeing 747	12	The Three Gorges Dam
3	The Bullet Train	13	The hovercraft
4	Stephenson's *Rocket*	14	Alfred Nobel
5	*Mallard*	15	Steel
6	Thomas Edison	16	The Panama Canal
7	The London Eye	17	Viaduct
8	The Shard	18	English Channel
9	Elon Musk	19	London
10	The Burj Khalifa	20	Great Wall of China

1   Who plays Ian Beale in *EastEnders*?

2   Who is paired with Cleopatra in the title of a Shakespeare play?

3   Which store group's slogan is "Never Knowingly Undersold"?

4   On mobile phones with a keypad on the handset, which letters appear on the number 5 key?

5   What two colours are Friesian cattle?

6   The Jazz car is manufactured by which company?

7   Villa Park is the home ground of which football team?

8   What word is ascribed to someone who holds the view that it is impossible to know whether or not God exists?

9   What is the unit of currency of Austria?

10 Where are rods and cones found in your body?

11 In a traditional song, what was the destination of Bill Brewer, Jan Stewer and Peter Gurney, amongst others?

12 Which figure symbolises the astrological sign Sagittarius?

13 Who was the lead singer of T Rex?

14 The novel *Doctor Zhivago* (1957) was written by which author?

15 Which three colours are on the flag of Australia?

16 Which American mammal is famed for its plated exterior?

17 What is the age of majority in the UK?

18 A bagel is what type of food?

19 Which gas is used in modern airships?

20 Which book title links Jules Verne and Michael Palin?

Answers to QUIZ 81 – Pot Luck

1	Warwickshire	11	Lactic acid
2	Alan Bleasdale	12	60mph
3	Black and white	13	The gums
4	22:45	14	Basil
5	Duplo®	15	The Bangles
6	Second	16	Heather
7	Canada	17	*Gone with the Wind*
8	Birds	18	Devon
9	Icarus	19	American Football
10	Italy	20	A dance

1   What was the name of Aaron Paul's character in the TV series *Breaking Bad*?

2   What is the setting for Paul O'Grady's series *For the Love of Dogs*?

3   What was the name of the retired barrister played by Paul Whitehouse on *The Fast Show*?

4   What was the real first name of Paul Hogan's character in the *Crocodile Dundee* films?

5   Which 1990 film starring Arnold Schwarzenegger was directed by Paul Verhoeven?

6   What was the title of Billy Paul's 1972 hit single?

7   For which national football team does Paul Pogba play?

8   In which 2001 film did Paul Bettany play Geoffrey Chaucer?

9   With whom did Lynsey de Paul duet on the 1977 UK Eurovision Song Contest entry *Rock Bottom*?

10 *Graceland* was a 1996 album by which musician?

11 Paul Newman played Fast Eddie Felson in which 1986 film?

12 São Paulo is the largest city in which South American country?

13 In which century was artist Paul Cézanne born?

14 Paul Giamatti played which US President in a 2008 mini-series?

15 What is Paul Merton's real surname?

16 What is the Spanish version of the name "Paul"?

17 Before becoming a TV presenter, what was Paul Hollywood's occupation?

18 Which football club did Paul Ince manage from 2013 to 2014?

19 In the New Testament, what was St Paul's original name?

20 Paul Keating (b.1944) is a former Prime Minister of which country?

Answers to QUIZ 82 – Classical Music

1	Minim	11	Sir Edward Elgar
2	Carl Orff	12	Italy
3	Ilyich	13	Verdi
4	Giacomo Puccini	14	Felt
5	Hector Berlioz	15	Elise (*Für Elise*)
6	Piano	16	Salzburg
7	The Proms	17	Cornet
8	Nonet	18	Richard
9	The piano	19	Crescendo
10	French	20	Guitar

1   Who played Lord Grantham in *Downton Abbey*?

2   Who became the permanent host of Radio 4's *Loose Ends* in 2007?

3   From which country does the dish "saltimbocca" originate?

4   What word can refer to a writing implement and an animal enclosure?

5   What are granny, reef and slip examples of?

6   In which city was John F Kennedy assassinated?

7   In which county is Robin Hood's Bay?

8   Which marine mammal has short-beaked and long-beaked species?

9   What is the crime of having two spouses?

10 In which language was *Beowulf* written?

11 Bel Air is a suburb of which US city?

12 What name is given to the part of an engine where a mixture of fuel and air are burned?

13 In an army context, what does NCO stand for ?

14 Who co-starred with Meryl Streep in the film *The French Lieutenant's Woman*?

15 What type of infection is athlete's foot?

16 Which rugby players are not involved in a scrum?

17 Eric Clapton was a member of which legendary 1960s supergroup?

18 What is notable about the phrase "Madam, I'm Adam"?

19 The Canal Turn jump is a feature of which racecourse?

20 Which 1950s singer was backed by The Comets?

Answers to QUIZ 83 – Pot Luck

1	Adam Woodyatt	11	Widecombe Fair
2	Antony	12	Archer
3	John Lewis	13	Marc Bolan
4	JKL	14	Boris Pasternak
5	Black and white	15	Blue, red and white
6	Honda	16	Armadillo
7	Aston Villa	17	18
8	Agnostic	18	Bread roll
9	Euro	19	Helium
10	Eyes	20	*Around the World in Eighty Days*

1 Who played lawyer Billy Flynn in the 2002 film *Chicago*?

2 Which real-life author did Dame Emma Thompson play in the 2013 film *Saving Mr Banks*?

3 What was the title of the 2017 *Kingsman* film?

4 In the 2004 film *Starsky & Hutch*, who played Starsky?

5 Who provided the voice of construction worker Emmet in the 2014 film *The Lego Movie*?

6 Which football manager did Michael Sheen portray in the 2009 film *The Damned United*?

7 What was the title of the 2009 Richard Curtis film about a pirate radio station?

8 Which actress starred in the 2001 film *Legally Blonde*?

9 On which planet was Matt Damon's character stranded in a 2015 film?

10 Which actress starred in the 2015 film *Far from the Madding Crowd*?

11 Which Stieg Larsson novel was filmed first in 2009 and then again in 2011?

12 What was the title of the 2016 *Bridget Jones* film?

13 Who directed the 2018 film *Solo: A Star Wars Story*?

14 In the 2018 film *Pacific Rim: Uprising*, who starred as Jake Pentecost?

15 Which town were the *Three Billboards Outside* in the title of a 2017 film?

16 Melissa McCarthy played a CIA analyst in which 2015 film?

17 In the 2001 film *Moulin Rouge!*, what was the name of Nicole Kidman's character?

18 Matthew McConaughey and Jared Leto both won Oscars for their roles in which 2013 film?

19 Which US actor starred in the 2004 film *Spanglish*?

20 Which actress played Claire Dearing in the 2018 film *Jurassic World: Fallen Kingdom*?

Answers to QUIZ 84 – Paul

1	Jesse Pinkman	11	*The Color of Money*
2	Battersea Dogs & Cats Home	12	Brazil
3	Rowley Birkin	13	19th century
4	Michael (Mike)	14	John Adams
5	*Total Recall*	15	Martin
6	*Me and Mrs Jones*	16	Pablo
7	France	17	Baker
8	*A Knight's Tale*	18	Blackpool FC
9	Mike Moran	19	Saul
10	Paul Simon	20	Australia

1   Photophobia is a fear of what?

2   Which group of people observe Hanukkah and Purim?

3   What does a practioner of the Alexander Technique aim to improve?

4   In rhyming slang what is meant by "rabbit and pork"?

5   Which comedian starred in the 1986 film *Clockwise*?

6   In which country was snooker player Judd Trump born?

7   What is one half of one quarter?

8   What word can mean both "noise" and "solid"?

9   The "£" sign appears above which number on a standard computer keyboard?

10 Which Ricky Gervais character David shares a name with a London borough?

11 Which popular children's rhyme has an association with the Black Death?

12 On which body of water are Tallinn and Riga situated?

13 A person from Antwerp has what nationality?

14 Moneymaker and Alicante are varieties of which salad fruit?

15 Which organisation in the UK regulates and certifies doctors?

16 In which decade was the Morris Minor first manufactured?

17 Which TV series was a sequel to *Life on Mars*?

18 In relation to speech and language, what do the initals RP stand for?

19 What is the distance from any point on the circumference to the centre of a circle?

20 "Slip inside the eye of your mind" is the opening line of which song?

Easy

Medium

Hard

Answers to QUIZ 85 – Pot Luck

1	Hugh Bonneville	11	Los Angeles
2	Clive Anderson	12	Combustion chamber
3	Italy	13	Non-commissioned officer
4	Pen	14	Jeremy Irons
5	Knots	15	Fungal
6	Dallas	16	Backs
7	North Yorkshire	17	Cream
8	Dolphin	18	It reads the same forwards and backwards
9	Bigamy	19	Aintree
10	Old English	20	Bill Haley

1   Queens Park Rangers football team are based at which ground?

2   *Ice Station Zebra* is a 1963 novel by which author?

3   "Que?" was the catchphrase of which 1970s sitcom character?

4   Imelda Staunton provided the voice of which character in the *Paddington* films?

5   Queen Elizabeth I was the daughter of which of Henry VIII's wives?

6   Indira Gandhi first became Prime Minister of India in which decade?

7   Quinn Fabray was a character in which musical TV series?

8   *Incommunicado* was a 1987 hit for which band?

9   Quince is a carpenter in which of Shakespeare's plays?

10 *Into the Woods* is a musical with songs written by which composer?

11 Quinsy affects which part of the body?

12 Islamabad is the capital of which country?

13 *Quartet* is a 1999 play by which writer?

14 Innsbruck is a winter sports resort in which country?

15 Quentin Tarantino directed which 2012 film?

16 *Ivor the Engine* is set in which part of the UK?

17 Quasimodo is a character created by which French writer?

18 *I'd Do Anything* is a song from which musical?

19 *Question Time* was first broadcast in which decade?

20 *Iris* (2001) starred which two actresses as Dame Iris Murdoch?

Answers to QUIZ 86 – 21st-Century Film

1	Richard Gere	11	*The Girl with the Dragon Tattoo*
2	PL Travers	12	*Bridget Jones's Baby*
3	*Kingsman: The Golden Circle*	13	Ron Howard
4	Ben Stiller	14	John Boyega
5	Chris Pratt	15	*Ebbing, Missouri*
6	Brian Clough	16	*Spy*
7	*The Boat That Rocked*	17	Satine
8	Reese Witherspoon	18	*Dallas Buyers Club*
9	Mars	19	Adam Sandler
10	Carey Mulligan	20	Bryce Dallas Howard

QUIZ 89 – Pot Luck

ANSWERS ON PAGE 91

1 The Mont Blanc tunnel links France to which country?

2 With which team did Lewis Hamilton win his first Formula 1 World Championship?

3 Which actor played Dr Benjamin Franklin "Hawkeye" Pierce in the TV series *M*A*S*H*?

4 What is an Aberdeen Angus?

5 St Stephen's Day is better known by what name?

6 In darts, what is the highest score from three different trebles?

7 BT is the postcode area code for which city?

8 Auckland is situated on which of New Zealand's islands?

9 What, in wine terminology, describes the Americas, South Africa, Australia and New Zealand?

10 The Welsh town of Caerphilly gives its name to what type of food?

11 What was the chief wolf's name in Kipling's *The Jungle Books*?

12 Which TV outdoor adventurer was made Chief Scout in 2009?

13 What word can refer to both a set of drinks bought together and a spherical shape?

14 The Kent town of Whitstable is famous for what type of seafood?

15 Which glam rock group had a hit with *Ride a White Swan* (1970)?

16 In which country is the ski resort of Davos?

17 Who is the lead singer with The Pretenders?

18 What type of creature is a nuthatch?

19 What, in military terms, was a blunderbuss?

20 "One little duck" is a traditional bingo call for which number?

Easy

Medium

Hard

Answers to QUIZ 87 – Pot Luck

1	Strong light	11	*Ring-a-ring-a Roses*
2	Jews	12	Baltic sea
3	Posture	13	Belgian
4	Talk	14	Tomato
5	John Cleese	15	General Medical Council
6	England	16	1940s
7	One eighth	17	*Ashes to Ashes*
8	Sound	18	Received Pronunciation
9	3	19	Radius
10	Brent	20	*Don't Look Back in Anger*, Oasis

89

Easy

1 *I Want to Know What Love Is* was a 1985 hit for which band?

2 Who had a 1972 hit with *Heart of Gold*?

3 Which singer released the 1984 single *Your Love Is King*?

4 *Fill Me In* was a 2000 single by which singer?

5 Which threesome sang *Robert De Niro's Waiting* in 1984?

6 What was the first no.1 hit for Adam and the Ants?

7 *The Joshua Tree* album is by which group?

8 Which group was *Hanging on the Telephone* in 1978?

9 Which singer was backed by the Heartbreakers?

10 Sir Elton John's original version of *Candle in the Wind* was written about which screen legend?

Medium

11 Who is the Corrs' lead singer?

12 Which Boyzone singer had a solo hit with *Lovin' Each Day*?

13 "Once upon a time I was falling in love, now I'm only falling apart" is a lyric from which song?

14 What was the title of the 1987 UK chart-topping hit single for the group T'Pau?

15 What did Steven Nice of Cockney Rebel change his name to?

16 *When the Going Gets Tough, the Tough Get Going* was a 1986 no. 1 for which singer?

17 Who was the lead singer of The Undertones?

18 Which song features "The girl with kaleidoscope eyes"?

19 Who had a no.1 in 1990 with *Killer*, featuring vocals by Seal?

20 Which 1960s pop group sang *He Ain't Heavy, He's My Brother*?

Hard

Answers to QUIZ 88 – Q & I

1	Loftus Road	11	Throat
2	Alistair MacLean	12	Pakistan
3	Manuel (*Fawlty Towers*)	13	Sir Ronald Harwood
4	Aunt Lucy	14	Austria
5	Anne Boleyn	15	*Django Unchained*
6	1960s (1966)	16	Wales
7	*Glee*	17	Victor Hugo
8	Marillion	18	*Oliver!*
9	*A Midsummer Night's Dream*	19	1970s (1979)
10	Stephen Sondheim	20	Dame Judi Dench and Kate Winslet

QUIZ 91 – Pot Luck

1   Who recorded the 1990 album *Listen without Prejudice Vol 1*?

2   The 205 GTi hot hatch was made by which car company?

3   Which national football team did Jack Charlton manage from 1986 to 1996?

4   In which country is Buenos Aires?

5   Which station by the River Thames on the London Underground's District Line sounds like a place to worship?

6   In which county is the ancient monument of Avebury ring?

7   Which food is called the "staff of life"?

8   On which motorway are the Knutsford and Tebay services?

9   In the children's TV series, what were the names of the Flowerpot Men?

10 What is stitchwort?

11 Which opera features the characters of Don José and Escamillo?

12 In *Rainbow*, what sort of animal was Bungle?

13 Who starred in the 1989 film *Sea of Love*?

14 In the 1957 film *Funny Face*, who is transformed into a fashion model by Fred Astaire?

15 Which Italian Renaissance painter sketched designs for both a helicopter and an aeroplane?

16 What was the ninth month of the original Roman calendar?

17 In the cartoon strip *Peanuts*, what is the name of the bird?

18 The Pacific and Atlantic Oceans are linked by which canal?

19 Which French resort is the location of an annual international film festival?

20 Which card game has the same name as a horse-racing town?

Easy

Medium

Hard

Answers to QUIZ 89 – Pot Luck

1	Italy	11	Akela
2	McLaren	12	Bear Grylls
3	Alan Alda	13	Round
4	Breed of cattle	14	Oysters
5	Boxing Day	15	T. Rex
6	171	16	Switzerland
7	Belfast	17	Chrissie Hynde
8	North Island	18	Bird
9	New World	19	A firearm
10	Cheese	20	Two

1 The Jewel House and Wakefield Tower are in which English building?

2 The Hagia Sophia museum is located in which city?

3 In which building do Chelsea Pensioners reside?

4 Which Egyptian city was the location of the Pharos lighthouse?

5 In which city is Temple Meads railway station?

6 What is the name of the BBC's London headquarters?

7 On an Ordnance Survey map, what is indicated by the abbreviation PH?

8 In Scotland, what type of building are Dryburgh, Kelso, and Melrose?

9 Until 1970, which London building held all birth, marriage and death certificates?

10 Clifford's Tower is in which English city?

11 What type of building stands on Eddystone rocks, off the Devon coast?

12 In which New York borough is the One World Trade Center located?

13 What is the world's largest art museum?

14 The Tudor fort of Portland Castle is located in which county?

15 How is the former Museum of Ornamental Art in London now known?

16 Which TV series took its title from the nickname of Christiansborg Palace, home of the Danish government?

17 St Giles' Cathedral is located in which UK city?

18 In which region of Italy are the round houses known as *trulli* found?

19 Hatfield House is in which English county?

20 For which Cardinal was Hampton Court Palace originally built?

QUIZ 93 – Pot Luck

1 Which part of the body is affected by bronchitis?

2 Which detective on TV had a bloodhound called Pedro and a Rolls-Royce called the Grey Panther?

3 In the Christian church, what term is given to the period before Christmas?

4 With which type of rock is the Welsh town of Blaenau Ffestiniog associated?

5 Which is the first month of the year to have 30 days?

6 Hoisin sauce is traditionally served with which Chinese poultry dish?

7 Which birthstone is linked to January?

8 What is the translation of the Latin phrase *Carpe diem*?

9 Which author created the character of Peter Pan?

10 Idi Amin seized power in which country in 1971?

11 Who held the position of Foreign Secretary from 2014 to 2016?

12 The fictional estate of Glenbogle was the setting for which TV series?

13 What is the capital city of Thailand?

14 Beer tankards are often made from which alloy of tin and lead?

15 What was the name of Richard III's wife?

16 The hospital department usually referred to as "Casualty" has what full name?

17 Who partnered Jennifer Warnes on the 1982 song *Up Where We Belong*?

18 Which actress was the star of the 1950 film *All about Eve*?

19 What do Americans call a pack of cards?

20 What two-word term is given to babies born from the mid-1940s to the early 1960s?

Answers to QUIZ 91 – Pot Luck

1	George Michael	11	*Carmen*
2	Peugeot	12	A bear
3	Republic of Ireland	13	Al Pacino
4	Argentina	14	Audrey Hepburn
5	Temple	15	Leonardo da Vinci
6	Wiltshire	16	November
7	Bread	17	Woodstock
8	M6	18	Panama
9	Bill and Ben	19	Cannes
10	Wild flower	20	Newmarket

ANSWERS ON PAGE **96**

Easy

1 What is the deepest land gorge in the USA?

2 What feature is described as a "beck" in the north of England?

3 Which Swiss mountain is known for its steep north face?

4 In a Welsh place name, what feature does "Aber" indicate?

5 What substance enables plants to absorb light?

6 What term is given to the wearing effect of moving water on coastal land?

7 The Seychelles are in which ocean?

8 What name is given to someone who studies the earth's structure, surface and origins?

9 In an environmental context, what does the "O" of AONB stand for?

10 Which oceanic trench is the deepest?

11 What word for a waterfall is also an eye condition?

12 The Wildfowl and Wetlands Trust was founded by which naturalist?

13 What are the loose rocks on the side of a mountain collectively described as?

14 The volcano Mount St Helens is located in which US state?

Medium

15 In the context of the UK environment, what is an NNR?

16 What is an area of water separated from the open sea by a coral reef?

17 Machair is a type of land found on the coast of which two countries?

18 What name is given to a depression in the ground surface that can appear suddenly, particularly in limestone?

19 Does a stalagmite in a cave grow upwards or downward?

20 What name is given to the Earth's outermost layer, part of the lithosphere?

Hard

Answers to QUIZ 92 – Buildings

1	Tower of London	11	Lighthouse
2	Istanbul	12	Manhattan
3	The Royal Hospital	13	The Louvre
4	Alexandria	14	Dorset
5	Bristol	15	The Victoria and Albert Museum
6	Broadcasting House	16	*Borgen*
7	Public house	17	Edinburgh
8	Abbey	18	Apulia
9	Somerset House	19	Hertfordshire
10	York	20	Thomas Wolsey

1 What is the location of the oldest university in Scotland?

2 *China Girl* was a 1983 hit for which singer?

3 What is the most common breed of guide dog?

4 Which actor starred in the 2017 film *The Greatest Showman*?

5 What is the first Greek letter?

6 Of what is olfactophobia a fear?

7 What UK airport has the code LGW?

8 What name is given to a motorway in France?

9 In which county is the picturesque village of Bourton-on-the-Water?

10 What is the term for an angle of less than 90 degrees?

11 The Tudor Rose emblem features the colours of which two royal houses?

12 Which farmer is a regular presenter on the TV series *Countryfile*?

13 Which footwear company is based in Street in Somerset?

14 What is the name of Britain and Ireland's international rugby team?

15 In *The Jungle Book*, what type of snake is Kaa?

16 Which team won the 2018 FA Cup?

17 Of what is cetology the study?

18 Brize Norton is a base used by which branch of the services?

19 In greyhound racing, what are the colours of the stripes on the jacket worn by the dog in trap six?

20 In what classic novel is Andrei Bolkonsky one of the chief characters?

Easy

Medium

Hard

Answers to QUIZ 93 – Pot Luck

1	Lungs	11	Philip Hammond
2	Sexton Blake	12	*Monarch of the Glen*
3	Advent	13	Bangkok
4	Slate	14	Pewter
5	April	15	Anne Neville
6	Peking duck	16	Accident and Emergency
7	Garnet	17	Joe Cocker
8	Seize the day	18	Bette Davis
9	JM Barrie	19	A deck
10	Uganda	20	Baby boomers

ANSWERS ON PAGE 98

Easy

1   What was the name of the fictional holiday camp where *Hi-De-Hi!* was set?

2   Which sitcom followed the escapades of the Boswell family?

3   Who played Geraldine Grainger, the Vicar of Dibley?

4   Who lived at 26 Oil Drum Lane, Shepherd's Bush?

5   In *The Royle Family*, what was the name of Denise's husband?

6   Which sitcom starred Reg Varney as Stan Butler?

7   "I have a cunning plan" was the catchphrase of which character?

8   Which sitcom featured characters including Captain Peacock and Mrs Slocombe?

9   In which sitcom did the characters of Ted Crilly, Dougal McGuire and Jack Hackett appear?

10   Rowan Atkinson played PC Fowler in which British sitcom?

Medium

11   In *To the Manor Born*, what was the name of the big house?

12   What was the name of Boycie and Marlene's son in *Only Fools and Horses*?

13   Who lived next door to Tom and Barbara in *The Good Life*?

14   In the 1970s sitcom *Rising Damp*, starring Leonard Rossiter, what was the first name of his character Rigsby?

15   What is the name of Sir David Jason's character in *Open All Hours* and its sequel?

16   Where do the ladies from *Birds of a Feather* live in the ITV version of the series?

17   In *Only Fools and Horses*, what was the name of the tower block in which the Trotters lived?

18   What was the fictional setting for the sitcom *Dad's Army*?

19   In which prison was the sitcom *Porridge* starring Ronnie Barker set?

20   What was the name of Hyacinth's hen-pecked husband in *Keeping Up Appearances*?

Hard

Answers to QUIZ 94 – Planet Earth

1	Grand Canyon	11	Cataract
2	A stream	12	Sir Peter Scott
3	Eiger	13	Scree
4	River mouth	14	Washington
5	Chlorophyll	15	National Nature Reserve
6	Erosion	16	Lagoon
7	The Indian Ocean	17	Scotland and Ireland
8	Geologist	18	Sinkhole
9	Outstanding	19	Upwards
10	The Marianas Trench	20	Crust

1   Which comedian is associated with *Carpool Karaoke*?

2   The Canal du Midi and the Canal de Garonne (Canal des Deux Mers) together split which European country?

3   In which county is Canvey Island?

4   In 1966, who painted *The Splash*?

5   What word can refer to both a waterbird and a zero score in cricket?

6   The zodiac sign Leo covers which two calendar months?

7   What is the name of the village in which Miss Marple lives?

8   How many sides has a rhombus?

9   What name is given to a member of a Nepalese armed force?

10 Which structural tissue is found in the discs between the vertebrae?

11 What is the capital of Jersey?

12 *Trigger Happy TV* and *Fool Britannia* featured which TV prankster?

13 Which actress starred in the 1998 film *The Mask of Zorro*?

14 What type of animal was TV's Skippy?

15 Which motorway connects Birmingham and Exeter?

16 In *The Owl And The Pussycat*, what was the price of the ring purchased from the Piggy-wig who stood in the wood?

17 Which spicy Cajun stew or soup contains seafood and okra?

18 What is the radio code word between sierra and uniform?

19 The men's pre-Wimbledon tennis tournament is hosted by which London club?

20 Which Oscar-winning 1981 film starred Ben Cross and Ian Charleson?

Answers to QUIZ 95 – Pot Luck

1	St Andrews	11	Lancaster and York
2	David Bowie	12	Adam Henson
3	Labrador retriever	13	Clarks
4	Hugh Jackman	14	British and Irish Lions
5	Alpha	15	Python
6	Smells	16	Chelsea FC
7	London Gatwick	17	Whales
8	Autoroute	18	RAF
9	Gloucestershire	19	Black and white
10	Acute	20	*War and Peace*

Easy

1 Which team plays rugby union at the Recreation Ground, London Road?

2 Which famous sporting venue is located in SW19?

3 The 2018 EUFA Champions League final took place in which city?

4 What is the name of the main East London site of the 2012 Olympic Games…?

5 …and which football team took up residence in the stadium in 2016?

6 Becketts is a corner on which racing circuit?

7 In which football stadium do Manchester United play all their home matches?

8 For which event was the Cardiff Millennium stadium originally built?

9 In which city is the Maracana stadium?

10 What is the name of the test cricket ground in Birmingham?

11 Which football team play their home games at the Stadium of Light?

12 Which Dorset town hosted the 2012 Olympic sailing events?

13 To which arena did the Horse of the Year Show move in 2002?

14 Which football team plays at the Emirates Stadium?

Medium

15 Which New York sporting venue, noted for hosting boxing matches, opened in 1968?

16 What was the O2 arena's temporary name during the London 2012 Olympics?

17 What is the name of the French national stadium?

18 The 2017 Open golf championship was held at which course?

19 The Lakeside Leisure Complex at Frimley Green in Surrey is home to the world championships in which indoor sport?

20 Which ground hosts the FA Cup Final?

Hard

Answers to QUIZ 96 – Classic Sitcoms

1	Maplins	11	Grantleigh Manor
2	*Bread*	12	Tyler
3	Dawn French	13	Margo and Jerry Leadbetter
4	Steptoe and Son	14	Rupert
5	Dave	15	Granville
6	*On the Buses*	16	Chigwell in Essex
7	Baldrick (*Blackadder*)	17	Nelson Mandela House
8	*Are You Being Served?*	18	Walmington-on-Sea
9	*Father Ted*	19	HMP Slade
10	*The Thin Blue Line*	20	Richard

ANSWERS ON PAGE **101**

1   Who had a hit in 1960 with *My Old Man's a Dustman*?

2   Which army rank is immediately above Major?

3   In the original TV series of *Dad's Army*, what was the name of John Le Mesurier's character?

4   Which ocean lies to the north of Russia?

5   What is a roadrunner?

6   Halle Berry and Anne Hathaway have both played which feline role on screen?

7   On UK roads, what is the standard national speed limit for a car on a single carriageway when towing a trailer?

8   The "Auld Alliance", established in the 13th century, was an agreement between which two countries?

9   Who replaced Nick Hewer as one of Lord Sugar's aides on *The Apprentice*?

10   Siena is in which region of Italy?

11   A boneshaker was an early form of which type of transport?

12   The song *Let's Go Fly a Kite* features in which musical film?

13   What is the surname of British father and son novelists, Kingsley and Martin?

14   In *Hamlet*, what is the term for the hanging tapestry behind which Polonius hides?

15   What is the French word for "beautiful"?

16   What is the religion of the Dalai Lama?

17   In which county is Penrith located?

18   In chemistry, what is a substance which cannot be split into simpler substances?

19   What is the name given to a piece of armour worn over the chest?

20   What was the first UK top ten hit for Bronski Beat?

Answers to QUIZ 97 – Pot Luck

1	James Corden	11	St Helier
2	France	12	Dom Joly
3	Essex	13	Catherine Zeta-Jones
4	David Hockney	14	Kangaroo
5	Duck	15	M5
6	July and August	16	One shilling
7	St Mary Mead	17	Gumbo
8	Four	18	Tango
9	Gurkha	19	Queen's
10	Cartilage	20	*Chariots of Fire*

1 Which captain walked out to his death from a tent during the return from the South Pole with Captain Scott in 1912?

2 Which German passenger airship was involved in the fire disaster of 1937?

3 With which country is the famous soldier Robert Clive associated?

4 Who sent the Armada against England in 1588?

5 Born in London in 1827, which surgeon was a pioneer of antiseptic surgery?

6 Who was the first Roman emperor, the adopted son and heir of Julius Caesar?

7 In which decade did George Washington become US President?

8 What colour were the shirts of Mussolini's Italian Fascists?

9 In which century AD was Hadrian's Wall built?

10 What was the nationality of WWI spy Mata Hari?

11 In which decade of the 20th century was Mikhail Gorbachev born?

12 The Battle of Bunker Hill took place during which war?

13 What was the name of the world's first nuclear-powered submarine?

14 Which world conqueror lived from 356 to 323 BC?

15 By what name was Mohandas Karamchand Gandhi more usually known?

16 Who preceded Baroness Margaret Thatcher as Prime Minister?

17 To which English ruling dynasty did Elizabeth I belong?

18 From which country did Texas gain independence in 1836?

19 In which century did the Seven Years' War take place?

20 The economic climate leading to the collapse of the British South Sea Trading Company in 1720 was given what three-word term?

Answers to QUIZ 98 – Sporting Venues

1	Bath	11	Sunderland
2	Wimbledon	12	Weymouth
3	Kiev	13	NEC, Birmingham
4	Queen Elizabeth Olympic Park	14	Arsenal FC
5	West Ham United FC	15	Madison Square Garden
6	Silverstone	16	North Greenwich Arena
7	Old Trafford	17	Stade de France
8	1999 Rugby World Cup	18	Royal Birkdale
9	Rio de Janerio	19	BDO Darts
10	Edgbaston	20	Wembley Stadium

1. What are the two main elements of the Eucharist?

2. In the context of education, for what do the initials TEFL stand?

3. Of which range is Mont Blanc the highest peak?

4. Which sport is played at Sunningdale?

5. Which British series, running for 13 episodes in 1968, featured Sir Basil and Lady Rosemary?

6. What is the first name of the clown character used by McDonald's as their primary mascot?

7. In which US state is the airport with the code DEN?

8. Which of the body's organs is affected by hepatitis?

9. What word can refer to a flying mammal and an item of sporting equipment?

10. The character of Inspector Mike Burden assisted which detective?

11. Lou Ferrigno played which "Incredible" character on TV in the 1970s?

12. During which war were Anderson shelters used?

13. Which UK city would you visit to see Roman Baths and a famous Pump Room?

14. In the novel *Oliver Twist*, what is the name of the villain who leads the gang of young thieves?

15. What colour is citrine?

16. Which animated film features the character of Jiminy Cricket?

17. What is the boiling point of water on the Fahrenheit Scale?

18. Apart from jokers, how many red cards are there in a standard pack?

19. Is a roach a freshwater or sea fish?

20. What is a bodhran?

Easy

Medium

Hard

Answers to QUIZ 99 – Pot Luck

1	Lonnie Donegan	11	Bicycle
2	Lieutenant Colonel	12	*Mary Poppins*
3	Sergeant Wilson	13	Amis
4	The Arctic Ocean	14	Arras
5	Bird	15	*Beau* or *Belle*
6	Catwoman	16	Buddhism
7	50mph	17	Cumbria
8	Scotland and France	18	Element
9	Claude Littner	19	Breastplate
10	Tuscany	20	*Smalltown Boy*

Easy

1 What is the capital of Russia?

2 What is Russia's unit of currency?

3 Which important event in Russian history occurred in 1917?

4 The name of which alcoholic Russian drink roughly translates as "water"?

5 Which complex situated in Russia's capital serves as the official residence of the President of Russia?

6 What name was given to the period of tension which existed between the East and West in the wake of WWII?

7 Do drivers in Russia drive on the right or the left-hand side of the road?

8 Which ocean lies to the east of Russia?

9 In which year of the 21st century did Russia abolish Daylight Saving Time?

10 Which plaza in Russia's capital connects to many of Russia's major roads and highways?

11 Which Russian mystic rose to power in the early 1900s by befriending the Emperor of Russia?

12 In 1957, which satellite of Russian origin became Earth's first artificial satellite?

13 What is the name given to the traditional Russian dolls of decreasing size which fit inside one another?

14 What is the name of the Russian socialist state which was dissolved in 1991?

Medium

15 What title was given to the Russian emperors?

16 In terms of landmass, is Russia the world's largest country?

17 Which Russian communist revolutionary and politician was born in 1870 and died in 1924?

18 Which sea to the south of Russia is also surrounded by, amongst other countries, Turkey, Bulgaria and the Ukraine?

19 Which animal is a widespread symbol for Russia?

20 Alaska is separated from Russia by which strait?

Hard

Answers to QUIZ 100 – World History

1	Lawrence Oates	11	1930s
2	*Hindenburg*	12	American Revolutionary War
3	India	13	USS *Nautilus*
4	Philip II	14	Alexander the Great
5	Joseph Lister (First Baron Lister)	15	Mahatma Gandhi
6	Augustus	16	James Callaghan (Baron Callaghan)
7	1780s (1789)	17	Tudor
8	Black	18	Mexico
9	Second	19	18th century
10	Dutch	20	South Sea Bubble

1 The world's first passenger train service using steam locomotives ran between which two English towns?

2 In the rhyme that starts "Two little dicky birds sitting on a wall", what were the birds called?

3 Which department store retail chain went into administration in 2016?

4 The Viva is a model of car manufactured by which company?

5 Who was leader of the Labour Party from 1992 until his death in 1994?

6 What is the name of the hill that overlooks Edinburgh?

7 In which film did Audrey Hepburn star as Holly Golightly?

8 Who was the original presenter of *Never Mind the Buzzcocks*?

9 In which sci-fi franchise do the Borg appear?

10 What name is given to an ice skating arena?

11 Puerto Rico was owned by which country before it became part of the USA?

12 What is the first name of Lucy Pargeter's *Emmerdale* character?

13 How many square feet are there in a square yard?

14 What name is given to a book in which a captain charts events on a voyage?

15 If you were using a spinnaker, what would you be doing?

16 What prefix indicates 10^{-1}

17 In which ocean is the Sargasso Sea?

18 Who is the lead singer of the band Coldplay?

19 Which pop group had a 1997 hit with *Barbie Girl*?

20 What word can refer to a sudden movement and a receptacle for rubbish?

Answers to QUIZ 101 – Pot Luck

1	Bread and wine	11	Hulk
2	Teaching English as a Foreign Language	12	WWII
3	Alps	13	Bath
4	Golf	14	Fagin
5	*The Herbs*	15	Yellow
6	Ronald	16	*Pinocchio*
7	Colorado (Denver)	17	212 degrees
8	Liver	18	26
9	Bat	19	Freshwater
10	Inspector Wexford	20	A drum

1 Who co-starred with John Belushi in the 1980 film *The Blues Brothers*?

2 Which strongly flavoured blue cheese is named after a village in northern Italy?

3 Which group had a 1979 hit with *In the Navy*?

4 On an Ordnance Survey map, what is indicated by a vertical blue line with a triangle at the top pointing to the right?

5 "Ol' Blue Eyes" was the nickname of which singer (d.1998)?

6 Which children's TV series features Zöe Salmon and Gethin Jones amongst its previous presenters?

7 What was the title of the group Blue's 2001 debut hit?

8 In which decade was the TV series *The Thin Blue Line* broadcast for the first time?

9 What is the name of the dark blue route on the map of the London Underground?

10 Which German-born actress made her name in *The Blue Angel* in 1930?

11 Who composed *Rhapsody in Blue* (1924)?

12 Which 1970s group had a hit with *Mr. Blue Sky...*?

13 ...and which 2017 sci-fi film featured the song in its opening sequence?

14 In which city is the Blue Mosque located?

15 Which national football team is known as the Azzurri?

16 In the title of a musical work by Johann Strauss the Younger, which European river was described as *Blue*?

17 Which fictional blue steam engine is best friends with another steam engine named Percy?

18 Which "blue" feature did Roy Orbison sing about in 1963?

19 In which decade was the US crime series *Hill Street Blues* first shown?

20 How is a steak cooked if it is described as "blue"?

Answers to QUIZ 102 – Russia

1	Moscow	11	Rasputin
2	Rouble	12	Sputnik
3	Russian Revolution	13	Babushka or Matryoshka dolls
4	Vodka	14	The Soviet Union (USSR)
5	Kremlin	15	Tsar
6	The Cold War	16	Yes
7	Right-hand side	17	Vladimir Lenin
8	Pacific Ocean	18	Black Sea
9	2011	19	Bear
10	Red Square	20	Bering Strait

1   In which country is the city of Vancouver?

2   On an Ordnance Survey map, what is indicated by the abbreviation Sch?

3   What do the initials COD mean in relation to commerce?

4   From which heavenly body does the chemical element helium take its name?

5   Patrick Swayze and Jennifer Grey co-starred in which 1987 film?

6   What is the first name of Nadine Mulkerrin's *Hollyoaks* character?

7   What was the first UK top ten solo hit for Randy Crawford?

8   How many sides has a parallelogram?

9   In which county is Leighton Buzzard?

10 What was the former name of the Indian city of Kolkata?

11 What does the word "potable" mean in relation to liquid?

12 Which acid builds up in the muscles during strenuous exercise?

13 Which UK car manufacturer produced the Princess?

14 In 2013, who won *The X Factor*?

15 Which short-legged dog is named after the 18th-century parson who bred them?

16 Cabot Cove, Maine, is the home of which fictional detective?

17 Which character featured in the first experimental sound cartoon, *Steamboat Willie* (1928)?

18 What was the first name of Mary Shelley's Dr Frankenstein?

19 Which cartoon character is described as "the friendly ghost"?

20 What gives red blood cells their colour?

Easy

Medium

Hard

Answers to QUIZ 103 – Pot Luck

1	Stockton and Darlington	11	Spain
2	Peter and Paul	12	Chas
3	British Home Stores (BHS)	13	Nine
4	Vauxhall	14	Log
5	John Smith	15	Sailing or yachting
6	Arthur's Seat	16	Deci
7	*Breakfast at Tiffany's*	17	Atlantic
8	Mark Lamarr	18	Chris Martin
9	*Star Trek*	19	Aqua
10	Rink	20	Skip

ANSWERS ON PAGE 108

Easy

1   In Greek mythology, what was the name of the ship on which Jason and his companions sailed?

2   Which retired ocean liner launched in 1934 is now a permanently moored tourist attraction in California?

3   What was the name of the warship launched in 1511, supposedly named after King Henry VIII's sister and the emblem of the Tudors?

4   What is the name of the mysterious American ship which was found deserted at sea in 1872?

5   If you travelled by ferry from Liverpool to the Isle of Man, at which port would you disembark?

6   What name won a 2016 online poll to name a British research vessel, but was instead given to the submersible upon the research vessel...?

7   ...and what was the research vessel actually named?

8   What is the name of the ship used by Christopher Columbus which was shipwrecked on his first voyage ?

9   From which port did the ill-fated *Titanic* sail?

10 A fast, light vessel with the hull raised slightly out of the water is given what name?

Medium

11 What is the name of Captain Jack Sparrow's ship in *Pirates of the Caribbean*?

12 Which ship is moored at The Queen's Walk, London?

13 What is the name of the ghost ship which is captained by Davy Jones in the *Pirates of the Caribbean* films?

14 On the Isle of Wight, which town is the main destination of the passenger ferry from Portsmouth?

15 In which decade was the hovercraft invented?

16 In which sport are there wild water, sprint and slalom events?

17 How many hulls does a catamaran have?

18 What term is given to the act of falling off a surfboard while riding a wave?

19 In rowing who is the person who steers a boat?

20 Which flat-bottomed boat is particularly associated with Oxford and Cambridge?

Hard

Answers to QUIZ 104 – Blue

1	Dan Aykroyd	11	George Gershwin
2	Gorgonzola	12	Electric Light Orchestra
3	Village People	13	*Guardians of the Galaxy Vol. 2*
4	Golf course	14	Istanbul
5	Frank Sinatra	15	Italy
6	*Blue Peter*	16	Danube
7	*All Rise*	17	Thomas the Tank Engine
8	1990s	18	*Blue Bayou*
9	Piccadilly Line	19	1980s
10	Marlene Dietrich	20	Very rare

ANSWERS ON PAGE **109**

Easy

1   Which Club is concerned with pedigree in the dog world?

2   What is the last month of the year to have exactly 30 days?

3   The University of Strathclyde is based in which city?

4   What is the term for the tip of a pyramid or cone?

5   *Highway to Hell* was a hit for which Australian rock group?

6   Which lunar phenomenon is used to describe something that rarely happens?

7   In which county is Devizes?

8   Which hormone regulates the amount of glucose in the blood?

9   In light opera who wanted to "let the punishment fit the crime"?

10 Which sign of the zodiac is represented by twins?

11 What is the national animal symbol of the USA?

12 Who replaced Claire Foy and Matt Smith as Queen Elizabeth II and Prince Philip in the third series of *The Crown*?

13 How many discs does each player have to start with in draughts?

14 What word can mean both "four-legged creature" and "to move quickly"?

15 During which battle was Nelson mortally wounded?

16 What is the female equivalent of a Cub Scout?

17 RIBA is the Royal Institute of British what?

18 Who had a hit in 1986 with *Chain Reaction*?

19 Which former *This Morning* presenters (1988-2001) went on to host their own show on Channel 4?

20 Which company produced the *Tom and Jerry* series of cartoons?

Medium

Hard

Answers to QUIZ 105 – Pot Luck

1	Canada	11	It's drinkable
2	School	12	Lactic acid
3	Cash (or Collect) on Delivery	13	Austin
4	The sun	14	Sam Bailey
5	*Dirty Dancing*	15	Jack Russell
6	Cleo	16	Jessica Fletcher
7	*One Day I'll Fly Away*	17	Mickey Mouse
8	Four	18	Victor
9	Bedfordshire	19	Casper
10	Calcutta	20	Haemoglobin

1 What is the name for a vodka and tomato juice cocktail?

2 Used to flavour gin, what is the fruit of the blackthorn?

3 What do the initials CAMRA stand for?

4 Which potent beverage was known in France as "the green fairy"?

5 In which country did pilsner originate?

6 Which two flavours combined make mocha?

7 What is the name for a Russian water boiler used to make tea?

8 In which month is "Beaujolais Noveau Day"?

9 Tequila comes from which country?

10 What is the main fruit used to make calvados?

11 Which drink was promoted by the song *I'd Like to Teach the World to Sing*?

12 What word is used in India for "tea"?

13 From what is the Japanese wine sake made?

14 Which aperitif has the suffix "royale" if champagne is added to crème de cassis?

15 From which country does root beer originate?

16 Which Swiss company developed the first widely used instant coffee?

17 Which popular tea variety originates from a district in West Bengal?

18 Which alcohol is used to make a daiquiri?

19 Originally launched in 1901, which bright orange soft drink is sometimes referred to as "Scotland's other national drink"?

20 If you order an *acqua frizzante* in Italy, what would you receive?

Answers to QUIZ 106 – On the Water

1	Argo	11	The Black Pearl
2	Queen Mary	12	HMS Belfast
3	Mary Rose	13	The Flying Dutchman
4	Mary Celeste	14	Ryde
5	Douglas	15	1950s
6	Boaty McBoatface	16	Canoeing
7	RRS Sir David Attenborough	17	Two
8	Santa Maria	18	Wipeout
9	Southampton	19	Cox (swain)
10	Hydrofoil	20	Punt

1   What term derived from the French language is given to the assistant to a soldier?

2   In Morse code what letter is represented by three dots?

3   What nationality was inventor James Hargreaves (b.1720)?

4   *I've Never Been in Love Before* is a song from which musical?

5   What do the initials "bhp" stand for in relation to an engine?

6   Proverbially, who tell no tales?

7   Which insect was told to "fly away home" in a children's rhyme?

8   What word is the name of a migratory bird and something that is quick?

9   Which three letters were a hit for the Jackson 5 in 1970?

10 Who became leader of the Labour Party in 2010?

11 In Scrabble®, how many points is the letter O worth?

12 Which canal is spanned by the Rialto Bridge in Venice?

13 Volvo was founded in which country?

14 Which instrument was associated with BB King?

15 Which river flows into the Tyrrhenian Sea near Pisa?

16 What animal-based fibrous protein can be injected into the skin to remove wrinkles?

17 In *A Christmas Carol*, what was the name of Scrooge's underpaid clerk?

18 What is the name of Claire Danes' *Homeland* character?

19 Who starred as James Bond in *Moonraker*?

20 What is a ragged robin?

Answers to QUIZ 107 – Pot Luck

1	Kennel Club	11	Bald eagle
2	November	12	Olivia Colman and Tobias Menzies
3	Glasgow	13	12
4	Apex	14	Hare
5	AC/DC	15	Trafalgar
6	Blue moon	16	Brownie
7	Wiltshire	17	Architects
8	Insulin	18	Diana Ross
9	The Mikado	19	Judy Finnegan and Richard Madeley
10	Gemini	20	Hanna-Barbera

Easy

1   *Scarborough Fair*, used in the film *The Graduate*, was recorded by which duo?

2   In which *Wallace and Gromit* film did the duo run a bakery called Top Bun?

3   In which trilogy of films based on a classic book did the dwarves Fili and Kili appear?

4   What was the title of Morecambe and Wise's first film?

5   Who played Peter Pascoe in the TV series *Dalziel and Pascoe*?

6   What is the name of Professor Layton's sidekick in the video games series?

7   Which pop duo consists of Neil Tennant and Chris Lowe?

8   Kirstie Allsopp presents *Location, Location, Location* with which other property expert?

9   Which 1980s duo sang *Last Christmas*?

10 Which fictional brother and sister first featured in the 2000 book *I Will Never Not Ever Eat a Tomato*?

Medium

11 Who are the Dynamic Duo?

12 Which presenting duo left *The One Show* in 2010 to join ITV's new *Daybreak* programme?

13 *(They Long to Be) Close to You* was the first hit for which duo?

14 What is the name of Clark Kent's female colleague in the *Superman* stories?

15 The TV series *Kath & Kim* was set in which country?

16 John Redmond and Kayleigh Kitson were the main characters in which TV series?

17 How are Barry and Paul Elliott better known?

18 Which duo had a 1988 hit with *I'm Gonna Be (500 Miles)*?

19 In the TV series *Mork & Mindy*, what was the name of Mork's home planet?

20 What are the first names of Agents Mulder and Scully in *The X-Files*?

Hard

Answers to QUIZ 108 – Drinks

1	Bloody Mary	11	Coca-Cola®
2	Sloe	12	Chai
3	Campaign for Real Ale	13	Rice
4	Absinthe	14	Kir
5	Czech Republic	15	USA
6	Coffee and chocolate	16	Nestlé
7	Samovar	17	Darjeeling
8	November	18	Rum
9	Mexico	19	Irn-Bru® (originally Iron Brew)
10	Apples	20	Sparkling water

QUIZ 111 – Pot Luck

ANSWERS ON PAGE 113

1 Cherish Finden and Benoit Blin are judges on which TV competition?

2 Who is the villain in Shakespeare's *Othello*?

3 What is ½ expressed as a percentage?

4 What do British stamps not have on them which most other stamps do?

5 How many *Colours in Her Hair* did McFly sing about?

6 What would you buy from a Gibbons catalogue?

7 What name is given to an indigenous person of northern Scandinavia?

8 In which American state are the Everglades?

9 By what name is sodium chloride more commonly known?

10 On UK roads, direction signs on non-primary routes have what colour background?

11 *The Model* was a 1982 UK hit for which group?

12 What is the unit of currency of Portugal?

13 What are fairy-tale giants such as Shrek called?

14 Romansch is spoken in which European country?

15 Who or what was Genevieve in the classic film of the same name?

16 Nick Heyward left which band to pursue a solo career?

17 What is the name of the modern-style keyboard that takes its name from the first six letters of the top row?

18 When did Disneyland, Paris, open?

19 In 2016, which former MP took part in *Strictly Come Dancing*?

20 Which measurement is shown first in a blood pressure reading, diastolic or systolic?

Easy

Medium

Hard

Answers to QUIZ 109 – Pot Luck

1	Aide-de-camp	11	One
2	S	12	Grand Canal
3	English	13	Sweden
4	*Guys and Dolls*	14	Guitar
5	Brake horse power	15	Arno
6	Dead men	16	Collagen
7	Ladybird	17	Bob Cratchit
8	Swift	18	Carrie Mathison
9	ABC	19	Sir Roger Moore
10	Ed Miliband	20	Wild flower

111

Easy

1 What is the name of the traditional fashion and clothing market in London's East End?

2 Which cathedral is closest to London Bridge?

3 Which London Museum has an "Imperial" name?

4 Which band released the 1979 single *London Calling*?

5 London and Cambridge are linked by which motorway?

6 Which monarch opened the Royal Albert Hall in 1871?

7 What is the name of the ceremony of sentry handover at Buckingham Palace?

8 At which Whitehall memorial does the Remembrance Service take place?

9 What colour is the Bakerloo line on a London Underground map?

10 The Serpentine boating lake is in which park?

11 What type of building is the Adelphi?

12 Which thoroughfare joins Trafalgar Square to Fleet Street?

13 Which motorway circles London?

14 In which building is the Whispering Gallery?

Medium

15 Which tourist attraction is next door to Madame Tussaud's?

16 What is the traditional colour for a London taxi?

17 Birdcage Walk is in which park?

18 Is Waterloo station south or north of the River Thames?

19 Which area of London required a passport in the title of the 1949 Ealing comedy film?

20 In which month has Open House London taken place every year since 1992?

Hard

Answers to QUIZ 110 – Duos

1	Simon and Garfunkel	11	Batman and Robin
2	*A Matter of Loaf and Death*	12	Adrian Chiles and Christine Bleakley
3	*The Hobbit*	13	The Carpenters
4	*The Intelligence Men*	14	Lois Lane
5	Colin Buchanan	15	Australia
6	Luke Triton	16	*Peter Kay's Car Share*
7	Pet Shop Boys	17	The Chuckle Brothers
8	Phil Spencer	18	The Proclaimers
9	Wham!	19	Ork
10	Charlie and Lola	20	Fox and Dana

1 What term is given to a raised road or path that crosses wet ground?

2 If you were in Germany for the Oktoberfest, what would be the main attraction?

3 What surname is shared by *TOWIE* alumni Mark and Elliott?

4 What is the nickname of Derby County FC?

5 How many minutes are there in four and three-quarter hours?

6 Cotton candy is the American term for which sweet item?

7 In which country is the port of Brindisi?

8 What word can be used to describe a setback and a boxing punch?

9 What two-word term is given to the posts taken by military personnel in readiness for battle?

10 Which airport is near the town of Bishops Stortford?

11 In grammar, what is the "object" case called?

12 What does an Australian mean by saying that something is "fair dinkum"?

13 Which monarch was the intended victim of the Gunpowder Plot?

14 Which old measures of length, also called perches or poles, were equivalent to a little more than five metres?

15 What are croutons made from?

16 The Manchester Ship Canal was opened in which century?

17 In which 1990 film did the song *King of Wishful Thinking* feature?

18 Which song from *Top Hat* begins "Heaven, I'm in heaven"?

19 Which baseball legend's nicknames included "the Bambino"?

20 Mg is the chemical symbol for which element?

Easy / Medium / Hard

Answers to QUIZ 111 – Pot Luck

1 *Bake Off: the Professionals*
2 Iago
3 50%
4 The name of the country
5 Five
6 Stamps
7 Sami
8 Florida
9 Table salt
10 White
11 Kraftwerk
12 Euro
13 Ogres
14 Switzerland
15 A car
16 Haircut 100
17 Qwerty
18 1992
19 Ed Balls
20 Systolic

1. *Phoenix Nights* stars which comedy actor as club owner Brian Potter?
2. What would your hobby be if you bought a first-day cover?
3. Which drummer and singer with a successful band had his first solo hit with *In the Air Tonight*?
4. In which month is VE Day?
5. Who had a hit with *All Night Long*?
6. In song, what did my true love send me on the second day of Christmas?
7. In which month is Burns Night celebrated?
8. Which artist painted *The Starry Night* (1889)?
9. How many days were in a working week during the 1974 power shortage?
10. Which US actor starred in *Groundhog Day*?

11. "I met a girl crazy for me, I met a boy cute as can be" is a lyric from which song?
12. Which duo had a 1973 hit with *Yesterday Once More*?
13. In which month is the shortest day in the northern hemisphere?
14. Which day of the week is named after the moon?
15. Which special day follows Shrove Tuesday?
16. For which 2007 film did Sir Daniel Day-Lewis win the Best Actor Oscar?
17. In which US state is Daytona Beach?
18. In 2016, who carried out his promise to present *Match of the Day* in his underwear if Leicester City won the Premier League?
19. On what date do Americans celebrate Independence Day?
20. In the TV series *'Allo, 'Allo!*, what code did the Resistance use to identify themselves?

Answers to QUIZ 112 – London

1	Petticoat Lane Market	11	Theatre
2	Southwark	12	Strand
3	Imperial War Museum	13	M25
4	The Clash	14	St Paul's Cathedral
5	M11	15	The Planetarium
6	Queen Victoria	16	Black
7	Changing the Guard	17	St James's Park
8	Cenotaph	18	South
9	Brown	19	Pimlico (*Passport to Pimlico*)
10	Hyde Park	20	September

QUIZ 115 – Pot Luck

ANSWERS ON PAGE 117

1   Borlotti is a variety of which type of bean?

2   What growing habit does the plant bougainvillea exhibit?

3   Which is the main deliberative body of the UN?

4   What is the value of the ace in baccarat?

5   In which century did the Duke of Marlborough win the Battle of Blenheim?

6   What word can be used to describe both a TV station and a body of water?

7   In the context of religion in England and Wales, what do the initials URC stand for?

8   Which actress was the subject of the book/film *Mommie Dearest*?

9   Who played Mick Shipman in the TV series *Gavin & Stacey*?

10 What was the occupation of Dom Pierre Perignon who developed the champagne process?

11 What does a neuroscientist study?

12 DCI Gene Hunt first appeared in which TV series?

13 "And that's all I have to say about that ..." is a line that appeared in which film?

14 What type of transport is a BMX?

15 What type of clothing is a doublet?

16 In which country did potato blight lead to a famine from 1845 to 1852?

17 What word can refer both to a building for a horse and a steady state?

18 What name is given to the theatre platform that extends in front of the curtain?

19 Which singer won the Eurovison Song Contest in 1970 with *All Kinds of Everything*?

20 Which fabric window covering that can be gathered up into ruches takes its name from a European country?

Easy

Medium

Hard

Answers to QUIZ 113 – Pot Luck

1	Causeway	11	Accusative
2	Beer	12	It's true
3	Wright	13	James I
4	The Rams	14	Rods
5	285	15	Bread
6	Candyfloss	16	19th century
7	Italy	17	*Pretty Woman*
8	Blow	18	*Cheek to Cheek*
9	Action stations	19	Babe Ruth
10	Stansted	20	Magnesium

Easy

1   Which term for a software program that translates one programming language into another can also be used to describe a crossword setter?

2   What was the name of the small magnetic storage disks that were used as external storage for personal computers?

3   Which fruit do Macintosh computers use as a logo?

4   In the Nintendo® game what is Mario's job?

5   What is the name of Amazon's virtual assistant?

6   What does GPS stand for?

7   Who was the principal founder of Microsoft®?

8   Developed by Adobe®, what is the name of the graphics editor that is now used as a verb to describe editing images?

9   What is the name of Facebook's™ communications app?

Medium

10 What term is given to part of a computer's memory that has its program permanently fixed?

11 SMS is a communication system that originated on what device?

12 What popular web mapping service was launched in February 2005?

13 What do the initials CPU stand for in relation to computers?

14 Which company managed to land and then relaunch its *Falcon 9* orbital rocket in 2017?

15 The letter S is on which row of a keyboard?

16 Which games company created Sonic the Hedgehog?

17 The binary system operates using which two digits?

18 In which decade did IBM launch their personal computer?

19 How was the early programming language Beginners All-Purpose Symbolic Instruction Code usually referred to?

20 In computing terms, what does PDF stand for?

Hard

Answers to QUIZ 114 – Night and Day

1	Peter Kay	11	*Summer Nights* (from *Grease*)
2	Stamp collecting (philately)	12	Carpenters
3	Phil Collins	13	December
4	May	14	Monday
5	Lionel Richie	15	Ash Wednesday
6	Two turtle doves	16	*There Will Be Blood*
7	January	17	Florida
8	Vincent Van Gogh	18	Gary Lineker
9	Three	19	July 4th
10	Bill Murray	20	Nighthawk

1 "I went to a party at the local county jail" are the opening words to which 10cc song?

2 What term is given to the study of viruses?

3 Whom did Henry II appoint Archbishop of Canterbury in 1162?

4 What is vitamin B2 also known as?

5 What is toasted Italian bread with olive oil and tomatoes called?

6 If you wrote down in words the digits from one to ten, which vowel would be missing?

7 What is the English translation of *Magna Carta*?

8 How is the Irish House of Deputies more commonly referred to?

9 Which painter (d.2008) was known for her pictures of portly people?

10 How many days are there in Lent?

11 What was the name of Barbara's mother in *The Royle Family*?

12 In which country would you find the Great Sandy Desert?

13 Who played Robert Baratheon in the TV series *Game of Thrones*?

14 Who is Vic Reeves' comedy partner?

15 Which family of birds do the jackdaw and magpie belong to?

16 Mike Myers created which "international man of mystery"?

17 Which Spanish author wrote *Don Quixote*?

18 With which branch of treatment is Mesmer associated?

19 What name, meaning "that can be directed", is applied to a navigable airship?

20 In which mountain range is Everest located?

Easy

Medium

Hard

Answers to QUIZ 115 – Pot Luck

1	Kidney	11	The brain
2	Climbing	12	*Life on Mars*
3	General Assembly	13	*Forrest Gump*
4	One	14	Bicycle
5	18th century	15	Jacket
6	Channel	16	Ireland
7	United Reformed Church	17	Stable
8	Joan Crawford	18	Apron stage
9	Larry Lamb	19	Dana
10	Monk	20	Austrian blind

Easy

1 In which city do Aston Villa FC play their home games?

2 How many players are there in a field hockey team?

3 From which country were the bobsleigh team immortalised in the Hollywood film *Cool Runnings*?

4 In which field event does the winning team move backwards?

5 Who was England's manager for the 1990 FIFA World Cup?

6 Which team event in men's tennis is named after an American doubles champion?

7 What is the length of a cricket pitch?

8 Which annual race between two teams was first staged in 1829?

9 Which brothers played in the England football team that won the 1966 World Cup?

10 How many riders are there in a field polo team?

11 Which rugby league team play their home matches at Headingley?

12 Which former London team earned the nickname "The Crazy Gang"?

13 In which country did ice hockey originate?

Medium

14 What is the team captain called in curling?

15 Which football team are known as the Saints?

16 Who won the FIFA World Cup in 2006?

17 In which game would you have a pitcher's mound and an outfield?

18 What is the target called in bowls?

19 What is the full name of the sport referred to as "synchro"?

20 What sport do the Buffalo Bills play?

Hard

Answers to QUIZ 116 – Technology

1	Compiler	11	Mobile phones
2	Floppy disks	12	Google Maps
3	Apple	13	Central Processing Unit
4	Plumber	14	SpaceX
5	Alexa	15	Middle row
6	Global Positioning System	16	Sega
7	Bill Gates	17	0 and 1
8	Photoshop®	18	1980s (1981)
9	Messenger	19	BASIC
10	Read Only Memory	20	Portable Document Format

1 On which river does Bath stand?

2 Who had a hit with *The First Cut Is the Deepest* in 1977?

3 The word "macho" is derived from which language?

4 Who wrote *HMS Pinafore*?

5 Which bird of prey has hen and marsh species?

6 Who starred with Dame Penelope Keith in the TV series *To the Manor Born*?

7 Who was the first leader of Russia following the 1917 revolution?

8 Is a mullet a freshwater or sea fish?

9 Who plays Fred in the TV series *Call the Midwife*?

10 What is an aconite?

11 The novel *The Wonderful Wizard of Oz* was written by which author?

12 What is the first name of Italian celebrity chef Mr Zilli (b.1956)?

13 What was the nickname of Richard Neville, 16th Earl of Warwick?

14 Which soap is set in Ramsay Street?

15 In which galaxy is Earth situated?

16 Which brand of perry is advertised with a cartoon fawn?

17 Which military unit stormed the Iranian Embassy in London in 1980?

18 What term is given to the number of white and red cells in the blood?

19 In which county is the town of Crediton?

20 If you wanted to travel to Wimbledon on the Tube, which line would you use?

Easy

Medium

Hard

Answers to QUIZ 117 – Pot Luck

1	*Rubber Bullets*	11	Norma
2	Virology	12	Australia
3	Thomas à Becket	13	Mark Addy
4	Riboflavin	14	Bob Mortimer
5	Bruschetta	15	Crows (Corvids)
6	A	16	Austin Powers
7	Great Charter	17	Cervantes
8	The Dáil	18	Hypnotism
9	Beryl Cook	19	Dirigible
10	40	20	Himalaya

Easy

1   Which Italian city inspired the name of Venezuela?

2   In 1982, Britain was at war with which South American country over the Falkland Islands?

3   Which language is used in most South American countries?

4   What is the capital and seat of government of Bolivia, which is also the highest capital city in the world?

5   What is the capital city of Brazil?

6   What is the name of the highest waterfall in the world, which is located in South America?

7   An Andrew Lloyd Webber (Baron Lloyd-Webber) and Sir Tim Rice musical was inspired by which famous First Lady of Argentina?

8   What is the name of the famous 15th-century Inca citadel in Peru?

9   Which statue on the Corcovado mountain overlooks the city of Rio de Janeiro?

10 The region of Patagonia is shared by which two countries?

11 Which city in Brazil hosted the 2016 Olympic Games?

12 What is the name of the longest river in the world, located in South America?

Medium

13 The name of an island off the west coast of Chile was inspired by which Daniel Defoe novel?

14 What is the largest country in South America?

15 Which mountain range in South America is the longest in the world?

16 Which South American country's name translates to "Equator"?

17 What type of bird is the condor?

18 Before becoming popular in Japan, in which country that colonised South America did tempura originate?

19 Montevideo is the capital of which country?

20 Which three colours appear on the Chilean flag?

Hard

1   What is a cotillion?

2   What word can mean "nearby" and "to shut"?

3   Which artist (b.1864) was famous for his posters of French dance halls and cabarets?

4   In the British army, officers of which rank hold the most senior positions?

5   Who directed the 1954 thriller *Dial M for Murder*?

6   What is the square root of 6400?

7   Mossad is the intelligence service of which country?

8   Moving clockwise on a dartboard what number is next to 9?

9   In which country did the FIFA World Cup take place in 1994?

10 Who plays Connie Beauchamp in *Casualty*?

11 What is Dick Dastardly's dog called?

12 Inner Temple, Middle Temple, Gray's Inn and Lincoln's Inn form which group?

13 Which Surrey town lies just south of Aldershot?

14 Who starred in the TV spy series *Alias*?

15 Proverbially, what can a camera not do?

16 With which "generation" was writer Jack Kerouac associated?

17 Which river flows through the city of Durham?

18 Which monarch ordered the execution of Mary, Queen of Scots?

19 What two-word term means "restrained legally"?

20 The highest mountain in Wales is in which National Park?

Easy

Medium

Hard

Answers to QUIZ 119 – Pot Luck

1	Avon	11	L Frank Baum
2	Sir Rod Stewart	12	Aldo
3	Spanish	13	Warwick the Kingmaker
4	Gilbert and Sullivan	14	*Neighbours*
5	Harrier	15	The Milky Way
6	Peter Bowles	16	Babycham
7	Lenin	17	SAS
8	Sea fish	18	Blood count
9	Cliff Parisi	19	Devon
10	Flower	20	District

Easy

1   *Hey Ya!* was a 2003 hit for which duo?

2   How many *Million Bicycles* did Katie Melua sing about in 2005?

3   Who represented the UK in the 2018 Eurovision Song Contest?

4   What was the title of Lady Gaga's debut album, released in 2008?

5   In which year did Kylie Minogue release *Can't Get You Out of My Head*?

6   Who had a hit with *Single Ladies (Put a Ring on It)* in 2008?

7   Who topped the charts in 2005 with *You're Beautiful*?

8   In 2014, which U2 album was released free of charge to all iTunes users?

9   Which US singer featured on Nelly's 2002 single *Dilemma*?

10 *In My Place* was a 2002 hit for which group?

11 What nationality is the singer Sia?

Medium

12 Which group had hits with *Rule the World* and *Shine* in 2007?

13 *Smile* was a 2006 hit for which singer?

14 Which female singer appeared as a judge for one series of *The Voice UK*, the last to be broadcast on the BBC?

15 Which girl group topped the UK singles chart in 2001 with *Whole Again* and *Eternal Flame*?

16 Who had a hit in 2001 with *Get the Party Started*?

17 *When Christmas Comes Around* was the 2013 debut single by which winner of *The X Factor*?

18 In 2012, which group won the Mercury Prize for their album *An Awesome Wave*?

19 Which former member of JLS took part in *Strictly Come Dancing* in 2017?

20 What was the name of Selena Gomez's backing band on her first three albums?

Hard

Answers to QUIZ 120 – South America

1	Venice	11	Rio de Janeiro
2	Argentina	12	Amazon
3	Spanish	13	*Robinson Crusoe* (Robinson Crusoe Island)
4	La Paz	14	Brazil
5	Brasília	15	The Andes
6	Angel Falls	16	Ecuador
7	Eva Perón	17	Vulture
8	Machu Picchu	18	Portugal
9	*Christ the Redeemer*	19	Uruguay
10	Argentina and Chile	20	Red, white and blue

QUIZ 123 – Pot Luck

1 What word can refer to both a communications device and a hanging ornament?

2 The Battle of Trafalgar took place off the coast of which country?

3 Of which Australian state is the black swan the emblem?

4 Someone taking part in a passing-out parade has completed what type of training?

5 In which century was Oliver Cromwell born?

6 What constellation is between Taurus and Pisces?

7 What is the name of the Doctor's home planet in *Doctor Who*?

8 Which is the most versatile piece on a chessboard?

9 What is a bichon frise?

10 What term is given to a narrow stretch of a road where congestion occurs?

11 In 1962, for what discovery were James Watson, Francis Crick and Maurice Wilkins awarded a Nobel Prize?

12 Which letter is to the right of the letter T on a standard keyboard?

13 Which bridge would you pass over on the M62 near Goole?

14 *Moving On Up* and *Search for the Hero* were hits for which group?

15 What is the name of the UK professional association and trade union for doctors and medical students?

16 Who directed the 2002 film *28 Days Later*?

17 Who was the US President from 1977 to 1981?

18 Which old coin was worth 21 shillings?

19 Hans Christian Andersen was what nationality?

20 What is a bandolier?

Easy

Medium

Hard

Answers to QUIZ 121 – Pot Luck

1 A dance
2 Close
3 (Henri de) Toulouse-Lautrec
4 General
5 Sir Alfred Hitchcock
6 80
7 Israel
8 12
9 USA
10 Amanda Mealing
11 Muttley
12 Inns of Court
13 Farnham
14 Jennifer Garner
15 Lie
16 The Beat Generation
17 Wear
18 Elizabeth I
19 Bound over
20 Snowdonia

1 Which author wrote about the fictional boarding school of Malory Towers?

2 In the nursery rhyme, who was followed to school by her little lamb?

3 Which TV series featured the lives of students at the fictional Manchester Medlock University?

4 Which English public school is located across the River Thames from Windsor?

5 What subject is studied at RADA?

6 What type of horses are used in the Spanish Riding School in Vienna?

7 In which high-school musical series did Matthew Morrison play Mr Schue?

8 Which British drama series set in a fictional comprehensive school ran from 1978 to 2008?

9 In Dickens' *Nicholas Nickleby*, what is the name of the poor schoolboy?

10 What is the title of the Channel 4 TV series that started in 2017 set in a fictional Yorkshire mill town?

11 "And nobody's gonna go to school today, she's going to make them stay at home" is a lyric from which song?

12 Why did London teacher Andria Zafirakou hit the headlines in March 2018?

13 Relating to teaching qualifications, for what do the initials PGCE stand?

14 Which BBC series set in a school was originally based in Rochdale then moved to Greenock?

15 Which Gilbert and Sullivan opera features the song *Three Little Maids from School Are We*?

16 What was the title of the 1980 Christmas no.1 by St Winifred's School Choir?

17 How many legs are featured in the name of a traditional school sports day event?

18 Which girls' school was created by cartoonist Ronald Searle…?

19 …and which male actor played the headmistress in the 1950s films?

20 Which future Prime Minister was Secretary of State for Education from 1970 to 1974?

Answers to QUIZ 122 – 21st-Century Music

1	OutKast	11	Australian
2	*Nine*	12	Take That
3	SuRie	13	Lily Allen
4	*The Fame*	14	Paloma Faith
5	2001	15	Atomic Kitten
6	Beyoncé	16	Pink
7	James Blunt	17	Matt Terry
8	*Songs of Innocence*	18	alt-J
9	Kelly Rowland	19	Aston Merrygold
10	Coldplay	20	The Scene

ANSWERS ON PAGE 127

1   On mobile phones with a keypad on the handset, which letters appear on the number 2 key?

2   On a Monopoly™ board, what colour is Whitechapel?

3   Who held the post of Home Secretary from 2016 to 2018?

4   Which group had a hit with *Car Wash* in 1976?

5   Which character did Connie Booth play in the TV series *Fawlty Towers*?

6   Which monarch proclaimed that she had "the heart and stomach of a king"?

7   In DIY, which type of paint is shiniest, emulsion, eggshell or gloss?

8   How many corners are there on a sugar lump?

9   What sort of vehicle is a limousine?

10 Who in zodiacal terms is the Water Bearer?

11 Which British fashion doll was introduced in the 1960s as a competitor to Barbie®?

12 Who played Mr Bumble in the 1968 film version of *Oliver!*?

13 Which Christian festival takes place on November 1?

14 What word can refer both to an intermediate state and a dance?

15 In *The House that Jack Built*, who milked the cow with the crumpled horn?

16 Andy Pandy wore a costume featuring which two colours?

17 What were the first names of 1970s crime-fighters *Starsky and Hutch*?

18 In music, what does "lento" mean?

19 The pituitary gland is at the base of which part of the body?

20 Which canal links the Atlantic Ocean and the North Sea?

Easy

Medium

Hard

Answers to QUIZ 123 – Pot Luck

1	Mobile	11	DNA structure
2	Spain	12	Y
3	Western Australia	13	The Ouse Bridge
4	Military or other service	14	M People
5	16th century	15	British Medical Association
6	Aries	16	Danny Boyle
7	Gallifrey	17	Jimmy Carter
8	Queen	18	Guinea
9	Dog	19	Danish
10	Bottleneck	20	Ammunition belt

1 The lyrics "It's just a jump to the left and a step to the right" feature in which musical?

2 Which 1978 film starred John Travolta and Olivia Newton-John?

3 Who played Marius in the 2012 film version of *Les Misérables*?

4 Which musical features the song *The Surrey with the Fringe on Top*?

5 From which musical does the song *Ol' Man River* come?

6 Glinda and Elphaba are the main characters in which musical?

7 *Jersey Boys* follows the fortunes of which real-life group?

8 *Younger than Springtime* is a song from which musical?

9 Who starred in the 1969 film musical *Sweet Charity*?

10 Who wrote the lyrics to *Jesus Christ Superstar*?

11 Which musical features the song *Shall We Dance*?

12 The English translation of *Eine Kleine Nachtmusik* by Mozart provided the title for which musical by Stephen Sondheim?

13 In *West Side Story*, what is the name of Maria's brother?

14 Catherine Zeta-Jones won the Best Supporting Actress Oscar for her role in which 2002 film musical?

15 The song *My Favourite Things* is from which musical?

16 Which 2016 film musical followed the fortunes of Sebastian and Mia?

17 The Artful Dodger is a character from which musical?

18 Who is adopted by Oliver Warbucks?

19 Which musical features the song *Sit Down, You're Rocking the Boat*?

20 Which rock musical, first performed in 2017, features the music of Jim Steinman?

Answers to QUIZ 124 – Education

1	Enid Blyton	11	*I Don't Like Mondays* (Boomtown Rats)
2	Mary	12	She won the million-dollar Global Teacher prize
3	*Fresh Meat*	13	Post-Graduate Certificate in Education
4	Eton	14	*Waterloo Road*
5	Drama	15	*The Mikado*
6	Lipizzaner	16	*There's No One Quite like Grandma*
7	*Glee*	17	Three
8	*Grange Hill*	18	St Trinian's
9	Smike	19	Alastair Sim
10	*Ackley Bridge*	20	Margaret Thatcher (Baroness Thatcher)

ANSWERS ON PAGE 129

1 Martin Fry is the frontman of which group?

2 Who wrote: "Season of mist and mellow fruitfulness"?

3 In which county is the town of King's Lynn?

4 Who is best known for playing Jack Branning in *EastEnders*?

5 What is measured using a sphygmomanometer?

6 Which two clans were involved in the 1692 Glencoe Massacre?

7 Who wrote the 2006 novel *Wicked!*?

8 Aidan O'Brien is a famous name in which sport?

9 Who was the original judge of *The Great British Bake Off* alongside Paul Hollywood?

10 Where did spies Burgess, Maclean and Philby defect to?

11 Who wrote the play *The Crucible*?

12 The Aygo is a model of car made by which car company?

13 Which group had a hit in 1978 with *Take a Chance on Me*?

14 Which town is home to Durham County Cricket Club?

15 Who does Bruce Willis play in the *Die Hard* films?

16 What is another name for the puma?

17 In rhyming slang what is a Joanna?

18 What is the square root of 81?

19 "Where can you find pleasure, search the world for treasure, learn science and technology?" is a line from which song?

20 Who directed the 2017 film *Dunkirk*?

Answers to QUIZ 125 – Pot Luck

1	ABC	11	Sindy®
2	Brown	12	Sir Harry Secombe
3	Amber Rudd	13	All Saints Day
4	Rose Royce	14	Limbo
5	Polly	15	The maiden all forlorn
6	Elizabeth I	16	Blue and white
7	Gloss	17	David and Ken
8	Eight	18	Slowly
9	A car	19	In the brain
10	Aquarius	20	Caledonian canal

Easy

1 Which estate in Wiltshire contains recreations of ruins and classical buildings such as the Pantheon and Temple of Apollo in its gardens?

2 In which London borough are the Royal Botanic Gardens at Kew?

3 Which county is usually referred to as the Garden of England?

4 What is the name of the Cornwall-based complex dominated by two large greenhouse biomes?

5 Which National Trust garden overlooks the Conwy Valley in North Wales?

6 Which biblical garden is also referred to as Paradise?

7 In which county is the RHS garden of Hyde Hall?

8 In which European city are the Boboli Gardens?

9 The Gardens by the Bay were opened in 2012 in which country?

10 Which famous landscape designer created the gardens in London's Syon Park?

Medium

11 In which part of the UK are Mount Stewart gardens located?

12 The Abbey Gardens at Tresco are located in which group of islands?

13 Are Inverewe Gardens on the east coast or west coast of Scotland?

14 Which famous garden was created by Vita Sackville-West and Harold Nicholson?

15 Which famous gardens lie approximately 14 miles south-west of Paris?

16 Which gardens in the north of England include a Poison Garden and the Grand Cascade?

17 In which county is the garden of Hidcote?

18 Studley Royal Water Gardens lie next to which abbey?

19 The Keukenhof gardens in the Netherlands are only open during which season of the year?

20 In which country is the Hellbrunn Palace, site of a famous water garden?

Hard

Answers to QUIZ 126 – Musicals

1	*The Rocky Horror Show*	11	*The King and I*
2	*Grease*	12	*A Little Night Music*
3	Eddie Redmayne	13	Bernardo
4	*Oklahoma!*	14	*Chicago*
5	*Show Boat*	15	*The Sound of Music*
6	*Wicked*	16	*La La Land*
7	The Four Seasons	17	*Oliver!*
8	*South Pacific*	18	Annie
9	Shirley MacLaine	19	*Guys and Dolls*
10	Sir Tim Rice	20	*Bat Out of Hell The Musical*

QUIZ 129 – Pot Luck

ANSWERS ON PAGE 131

1 What is the traditional bingo call for the number 70?

2 A sett provides a home for which animal?

3 What is the name of the Flintstones' home town?

4 *Too Much Too Young* was a hit for which band in 1980?

5 What tall and traditional pendulum clock design is also known as a longcase clock?

6 In the 1960s children's TV series *The Herbs*, what was the name of the dog?

7 Who played Chris Gardner in the 2006 film *The Pursuit of Happyness*?

8 What word can refer to a facial feature and the top of a hill?

9 In which county is Cerne Abbas located?

10 What is the modern name for Southern Rhodesia?

11 The Bow Street Runners were responsible for keeping order in which city?

12 What term is given to the area of a motor vehicle that is designed to give way in a crash?

13 Which Disney cartoon character was friends with Timothy Mouse?

14 On UK roads, what is the usual background colour of a sign showing tourist information?

15 Which legume is usually the main ingredient of falafel?

16 What is the study of inherited characteristics?

17 In the paso doble what is the female dancer supposed to be?

18 What term is given to a substance that causes the body to lose water?

19 *Always on My Mind* was a 1987 hit for which duo?

20 What is the study of bones called?

Easy

Medium

Hard

Answers to QUIZ 127 – Pot Luck

1	ABC	11	Arthur Miller
2	John Keats	12	Toyota
3	Norfolk	13	ABBA
4	Scott Maslen	14	Chester-le-Street
5	Blood pressure	15	John McClane
6	MacDonalds and Campbells	16	Cougar
7	Jilly Cooper	17	Piano
8	Horse racing (trainer)	18	Nine
9	Mary Berry	19	*In the Navy* (Village People)
10	USSR	20	Christopher Nolan

QUIZ 130 – Cookery

ANSWERS ON PAGE **132**

Easy

1   What is garam masala?

2   From which pulse is gram flour made?

3   What is a clear jelly of stock and gelatine called?

4   How many fluid ounces are there in a pint?

5   With what is food described as "au gratin" cooked?

6   What type of pastry is usually used to make a samosa?

7   What word that means "partly cook" can also mean "turn pale"?

8   From which country does lasagne originate?

9   How is food cooked if it is *en papillote*?

10 What is the name for a class of clarified butter often used in Indian cuisine?

11 What is the term for food that has been prepared according to the laws of Judaism?

12 Which oil is characteristically used in the cooking of South India?

13 For what is arrowroot used in cooking?

14 What French term describes a bunch of herbs in a muslin bag?

Medium

15 What is sieved to make a passata?

16 What is the basis of a sauce Béarnaise?

17 Shaoxing wine, widely used for cooking, comes from which country?

18 What French term describes a pan of hot water in which a cooking container is placed?

19 For what would you use a mandolin in the kitchen?

20 Which is darker, muscovado or demerara sugar?

Hard

Answers to QUIZ 128 – Famous Gardens

1	Stourhead	11	Northern Ireland
2	Richmond upon Thames	12	Isles of Scilly
3	Kent	13	West coast
4	The Eden Project	14	Sissinghurst
5	Bodnant	15	Versailles
6	The Garden of Eden	16	The Alnwick Garden
7	Essex	17	Gloucestershire
8	Florence	18	Fountains Abbey
9	Singapore	19	Spring
10	Capability Brown	20	Austria

1 Which tropical fruit is often made into a chutney and served with Indian food?

2 The Rosetta Stone was used to decipher which language?

3 Which chemical formula represents ice?

4 In which country is the football team Anderlecht based?

5 What is the English translation of *Fidei Defensor*, the Latin title first given to Henry VIII?

6 What word can refer to a chick's fluffy covering and a type of crossword clue?

7 In the Bible, what is the first book of the New Testament?

8 "Kelly's eye" is the traditional bingo call for which number?

9 Who is the patron saint of Ireland?

10 What word referring to a movement of water refers to a revision when read backwards?

11 Blue point and seal point are types of which cat?

12 From which country does acupuncture originate?

13 What was the name of Bryan Cranston's character in the TV series *Breaking Bad*?

14 What is the grammatical name for "the"?

15 In which county is the stately home of Petworth Park?

16 Which book and animated film featured the rabbits Bigwig and Fiver?

17 According to the proverb, what does one good turn deserve?

18 What seven-letter acronym denotes the Low Countries?

19 What type of bird is a pintail?

20 Who played the Sheriff of Nottingham in the 1991 film *Robin Hood: Prince of Thieves*?

Easy

Medium

Hard

Answers to QUIZ 129 – Pot Luck

1	Three score and ten	11	London
2	Badger	12	Crumple zone
3	Bedrock	13	Dumbo
4	The Specials	14	Brown
5	Grandfather clock	15	Chickpea
6	Dill	16	Genetics
7	Will Smith	17	The matador's cloak
8	Brow	18	Diuretic
9	Dorset	19	Pet Shop Boys
10	Zimbabwe	20	Osteology

Easy

1. Which 1960s musical included the song *Let the Sunshine In*?
2. Helios and Apollo are both identified with the Sun in which branch of mythology?
3. Which Beatles album features the song *Here Comes the Sun*?
4. Which country is known as the "Land of the Rising Sun"?
5. In which film did *Raindrops Keep Falling on My Head* appear...?
6. ...and who played the title characters?
7. *Gesundheit* is said in Germany in response to what?
8. On which continent is the capital city of Asunción?
9. Sunni is a branch of which religion?
10. What name is given to an umbrella intended to keep off the sun?

Medium

11. *Nessun Dorma* was used as the theme for the FIFA World Cup coverage in which year?
12. Norma Desmond is the main character in which film and stage musical?
13. Which artist is particularly associated with sunflowers?
14. *I Won't Let the Sun Go Down on Me* was a 1984 hit for which singer?
15. Who played Hercule Poirot in the 1982 film *Evil under the Sun*?
16. Sunderland is at the mouth of which river?
17. In which country was the Sunbeam car company founded?
18. Which duo had a 1996 no.1 with *Setting Sun*?
19. If a plant is described as a heliotrope, what does it do in reponse to the sun?
20. Which alcoholic drink precedes "Sunrise" in the name of a cocktail?

Hard

Answers to QUIZ 130 – Cookery

1	A spice mix	11	Kosher
2	Chickpea	12	Coconut oil
3	Aspic	13	Thickening sauces
4	20	14	Bouquet garni
5	Cheese	15	Tomatoes
6	Filo pastry	16	Egg yolks
7	Blanch	17	China
8	Italy	18	Bain-marie
9	In foil or paper	19	Slicing vegetables
10	Ghee	20	Muscovado

1   What was the name of the dog in *The Magic Roundabout*?

2   Who was "lost and gone forever" in the lyrics of an American folk song?

3   In the rhyme which begins "Monday's child is fair of face", which day's child has to work hard for a living?

4   In which century was Sir Walter Raleigh born?

5   President "Baby Doc" Duvalier fled from which country in 1986?

6   Who wrote the 1997 novel *Sharpe's Tiger*?

7   Where is the metatarsal arch?

8   How many *Hearts* did Phil Collins sing about in a 1988 song?

9   Which tennis player won the tournament at Queen's in June 2018?

10 In 2006, who became Britain's first female Foreign Secretary?

11 To which Florida city would you travel to visit the Epcot Center?

12 Who clashed at the Battle of Midway Island in 1942?

13 What is the name of Dennis the Menace's dog?

14 Winston Smith is the main character in which novel?

15 Between which two continents is the Red Sea located?

16 Which group had a hit in 1978 with *Picture This*?

17 Aberystwyth is located in which historic Welsh county?

18 What is Ronnie O'Sullivan's nickname?

19 The zodiac sign Cancer covers which two calendar months?

20 On which body of water is the town of Minehead?

Answers to QUIZ 131 – Pot Luck

1	Mango	11	Siamese
2	Hieroglyphics	12	China
3	H_2O	13	Walter White
4	Belgium	14	Definite article
5	Defender of the faith	15	West Sussex
6	Down	16	*Watership Down*
7	Matthew	17	Another
8	One	18	Benelux
9	St Patrick	19	Duck
10	Tide	20	Alan Rickman

QUIZ 134 – Harry Potter

ANSWERS ON PAGE **136**

Easy

1 Who played Dolores Umbridge in the *Harry Potter* films?

2 Who was the Prisoner of Azkaban?

3 In which city is the fictional street of Diagon Alley?

4 Who played Lord Voldemort in the *Harry Potter* films...?

5 ...and what was the original name of his character?

6 What type of establishment is Gringotts?

7 What is the name of the school in the *Harry Potter* books and films...?

8 ...and what is the name of the train on which students travel to it from Platform 9¾?

9 A quidditch team has Chasers, Beaters, Seekers and which other position?

10 Which house did Harry belong to?

11 Who played Professor Snape in the *Harry Potter* films?

12 Which character died in *The Goblet of Fire*?

Medium

13 Which 2016 film starring Eddie Redmayne was based on a textbook mentioned in the *Harry Potter* books?

14 In which year was the first of the *Harry Potter* novels published?

15 What is Hagrid's first name?

16 What is the name of the governing body of wizardry?

17 What was the name of the Harry Potter website launched in 2011?

18 In *Harry Potter and the Deathly Hallows*, what name was given to the objects in which Voldemort stored parts of his soul?

19 What is the name of Ron Weasley's younger sister?

20 What is the name of Draco Malfoy's father?

Hard

Answers to QUIZ 132 – Sun

|---|---|---|---|
1	*Hair*	11	1990
2	Greek	12	*Sunset Boulevard*
3	*Abbey Road*	13	Vincent Van Gogh
4	Japan	14	Nik Kershaw
5	*Butch Cassidy and the Sundance Kid*	15	Sir Peter Ustinov
6	Paul Newman and Robert Redford	16	Wear
7	A sneeze	17	England
8	South America (Paraguay)	18	The Chemical Brothers
9	Islam	19	Turns towards it
10	Parasol	20	Tequila

134

1 On a Monopoly™ board, what colour is Pentonville Road?

2 Who created the characters of Ali G, Borat and Brüno?

3 What term is given to the last stage of a relay race?

4 What is four cubed?

5 In the *Wallace and Gromit* films, what is Wallace's favourite cheese?

6 In 1800 the US government relocated to Washington from which city?

7 What relation was Edward VI to Elizabeth I?

8 Which planet is seventh in distance from the Sun?

9 Known as Venezia to the locals, what is the English name of this Italian city?

10 Who became host of *Ready Steady Cook* after Fern Britton left?

11 Which Sheffield theatre opened in 1971?

12 Which car company has the Twingo in its range?

13 Who said that "one giant leap for mankind" had been made?

14 What instrument is used to monitor heart-muscle activity?

15 In the Old Testament which book directly follows Psalms?

16 Which actress starred in the 2016 film *The Girl on the Train*?

17 What shape is fusilli pasta?

18 Who is the heroine of Disney's *Beauty and the Beast*?

19 By what initial is 007's boss known?

20 The Lorelei rock is on which river?

Easy

Medium

Hard

Answers to QUIZ 133 – Pot Luck

1	Dougal	11	Orlando
2	Clementine	12	US and Japan
3	Saturday's	13	Gnasher
4	16th century	14	*Nineteen Eighty-Four*
5	Haiti	15	Africa and Asia
6	Bernard Cornwell	16	Blondie
7	In your foot	17	Cardiganshire or Dyfed
8	Two	18	The Rocket
9	Marin Cilic	19	June and July
10	Dame Margaret Beckett	20	Bristol Channel

Easy

1. Which currency was adopted by Slovakia on January 1, 2009?

2. The tax introduced in the UK in 1989-90, commonly referred to as the the poll tax, had what actual name?

3. The phrase "In God We Trust" appears on coins from which country?

4. Which decimal coin originally had the Prince of Wales' three feathers on the reverse?

5. Which Russian coin is equivalent to 100 kopeks?

6. Who was appointed Governor of the Bank of England in 2013?

7. What is the title of the Channel 5 series following the work of High Court enforcement officers?

8. What measure is used by finance companies to assess an individual's financial reliability?

9. The initials APR stand for what?

10. What term is given to the upfront payment that an author receives to write a book?

Medium

11. In March 1988, what ceased to be legal tender in England?

12. How many sides has a 20-pence piece?

13. What is a downward adjustment to a country's official exchange rate called?

14. Who presented the 2018 series *Million Pound Menu*?

15. A period in which banks reduce their lending is given what two-word term, much used in 2008?

16. What were the first two decimal coins issued in Britain?

17. In relation to debt, for what do the initials CCJ stand?

18. What term is given to the opposite of "boom" when describing the economy?

19. Who was Martin Lewis' co-presenter on *The Martin Lewis Money Show* in 2018?

20. Which bird featured on the old coin the farthing?

Hard

Answers to QUIZ 134 – Harry Potter

1	Imelda Staunton	11	Alan Rickman
2	Sirius Black	12	Cedric Diggory
3	London	13	*Fantastic Beasts and Where to Find Them*
4	Ralph Fiennes	14	1997
5	Tom Riddle	15	Rubeus
6	A bank	16	Ministry of Magic
7	Hogwarts	17	Pottermore
8	*Hogwarts Express*	18	Horcruxes
9	Keeper	19	Ginny
10	Gryffindor	20	Lucius

1   Which series of children's stories and programmes features the Fat Controller?

2   Who sang the original version of *American Pie*?

3   The Great Fire of London happened in which year?

4   In the rhyme, where was the king while the queen was in the parlour?

5   Who wrote the 1998 novel *Evening Class*?

6   Which comedy duo's signature tune was *Bring Me Sunshine*?

7   What is a baldric?

8   The humerus is in what part of the body?

9   Which of the Vunipola brothers was the first to be signed by Saracens, Mako or Billy?

10 What word can mean both "timepiece" and "regard"?

11 Which former contestant on *The Great British Bake Off* went on to co-host *Bake Off: the Professionals* in 2018?

12 AB is the postcode of which city?

13 What is the first Army rank held on commissioning?

14 Which Russian leader was supported by the Bolsheviks?

15 "You're gonna need a bigger boat" is a famous line from which film?

16 Which Cumbrian lake is overlooked by "The Old Man"?

17 Lack of iron in the diet may contribute to which condition?

18 In which county is Cleethorpes?

19 What is the Roman numeral for five?

20 *Little Red Corvette* was a 1985 hit for which artist?

Easy

Medium

Hard

Answers to QUIZ 135 – Pot Luck

1	Light blue	11	The Crucible
2	Sacha Baron Cohen	12	Renault
3	Anchor leg	13	Neil Armstrong
4	64	14	Cardiograph
5	Wensleydale	15	Proverbs
6	Philadelphia	16	Emily Blunt
7	Half-brother	17	Spiral
8	Uranus	18	Belle
9	Venice	19	M
10	Ainsley Harriott	20	Rhine

Easy

1 Who tried to mend his head with vinegar and brown paper?

2 On the Canadian flag, what colour is the maple leaf?

3 What colour is jet?

4 What colour is *Thunderbird 4*?

5 In the TV quiz *Mastermind*, what colour is the main chair?

6 Which city of central England gave its name to a shade of green?

7 Victorian photographs are what colour?

8 What colour represents the science and nature category in a standard edition of Trivial Pursuit™?

9 Which fictional detective featured in the story *A Study in Scarlet*?

10 In heraldry, what colour is called "gules"?

Medium

11 How many visible colours has a rainbow?

12 What colour is used to describe the mood of a person who is feeling low?

13 On UK roads, what colour car is shown on the left of the sign that indicates no overtaking?

14 Which two colours are commonly used to chequer the squares of a Battenberg cake?

15 What colour hair did Elizabeth I have?

16 Ruby denotes which wedding anniversary?

17 How many points is the brown ball worth in snooker?

18 On an Ordnance Survey map, what is indicated by a plain light orange area?

19 What colour was the Trotter's Independent Trading van?

20 What three colours feature on the Irish flag?

Hard

1   Which large Mediterranean island is just south of Corsica?

2   What is the cut of beef from the lower part of the cow's leg?

3   Which is the closest Tube station to Trafalgar Square?

4   Which religion came into being after Henry VIII's break with Rome?

5   A sloop has how many masts?

6   In musical terms, what is a triad?

7   What number did the clock strike in the first verse of the nursery rhyme *Hickory Dickory Dock*?

8   What is the first book of the Old Testament?

9   Is the question mark found to the left or right on a standard computer keyboard?

10 From which country does the balalaika originate?

11 Which form of improvised jazz singing uses the voice as a musical instrument?

12 What was the first name of Dracula actor Mr Lugosi?

13 In boxing, what is a swinging blow to an opponent's chin called?

14 What is the name of the UK Girl Guiding section for five to seven year-olds?

15 Which astronomical event was depicted on The Bayeux Tapestry?

16 What title is given to the officer responsible for all of a country's armed forces?

17 In the TV series *Downton Abbey*, who played Mr Bates?

18 What was the title of the first UK top ten hit for Bow Wow Wow?

19 What word can mean searching for gold or slowly moving a camera?

20 What was the name of the plantation in the 1939 classic film *Gone with the Wind*?

Easy

Medium

Hard

Answers to QUIZ 137 – Pot Luck

1	*Thomas the Tank Engine*	11	Liam Charles
2	Don MacLean	12	Aberdeen
3	1666	13	Second Lieutenant
4	Counting house	14	Lenin
5	Maeve Binchy	15	*Jaws*
6	Morecambe and Wise	16	Coniston Water
7	Belt	17	Anaemia
8	Upper arm	18	Lincolnshire
9	Mako (2011)	19	V
10	Watch	20	Prince

1. Which river flows through Florence?
2. In which country is Lake Como?
3. Which is the most northerly capital city in Europe?
4. In which city are the tree-lined promenades called Las Ramblas?
5. The headquarters of the European Union are in which city?
6. From which country does Armagnac originate?
7. What is the capital of Switzerland?
8. The airline Lufthansa is based in which country?
9. What colour appears along with white on the Polish flag?
10. In which country is Breton a recognised language?
11. Which European capital city lies at the mouth of the River Liffey?
12. In which country is the port of St Malo?
13. The popular resort of Alicante is in which country?
14. The Simplon tunnel links Switzerland with which other country?
15. In which country was the original Legoland built?
16. Which European country's flag has green, red and white vertical bands?
17. On which island is the resort of Paphos?
18. Which river flows through Rome?
19. Valletta is the capital of which island country?
20. Which airport has the code CDG?

Answers to QUIZ 138 – Colours

1	Jack (in *Jack and Jill*)	11	Seven
2	Red	12	Blue
3	Black	13	Black
4	Yellow	14	Yellow and pink
5	Black	15	Red
6	Lincoln	16	40th
7	Sepia	17	Four
8	Green	18	Sand
9	Sherlock Holmes	19	Yellow
10	Red	20	Green, white and orange

1. What word comes before "Monica" and "Barbara" to make the names of two Californian cities?

2. Who hosted the 1980s game show *Play Your Cards Right*?

3. In which year did Elizabeth II succeed to the throne?

4. What is 60% of 3000?

5. A Chesterfield is what type of furniture item?

6. Which Cornish river shares its name with a desert animal?

7. What is a male horse kept for breeding called?

8. Karnataka is a state in which country?

9. Who played Dorothy in the TV series *Men Behaving Badly*?

10. What is a jpeg?

11. In 1976, which British driver won the Formula 1 World Championship?

12. What are the names of the two brightest stars in the constellation of Gemini?

13. Which station on the London Underground takes its name from the Lord Mayor's official residence?

14. Which area of Los Angeles has the zip code 90210?

15. In which county is Reading?

16. What do the initials YMCA stand for?

17. Which king of Israel was said to be especially wise?

18. Sciatica is pain from a nerve in which part of the body?

19. In what language was the Magna Carta written?

20. What is the square root of 144?

Answers to QUIZ 139 – Pot Luck

1	Sardinia	11	Scat
2	Shin	12	Bela
3	Charing Cross	13	Uppercut
4	Anglicanism/Church of England	14	Rainbows
5	One	15	Halley's Comet
6	A three-note chord	16	Commander-in-Chief
7	One	17	Brendan Coyle
8	Genesis	18	*Go Wild in the Country*
9	Right	19	Panning
10	Russia	20	Tara

QUIZ 142 – Cartoons

ANSWERS ON PAGE **144**

1. Which cartoon character has an anchor tattooed on his arm?
2. What type of bird is the cartoon character Foghorn Leghorn?
3. Which cartoon strip features Snoopy and Charlie Brown?
4. In the Dilbert cartoons, what is Dilbert's profession?
5. Jock and Yorky are friends of which cartoon dog?
6. Animator Simon Tofield has created a series of cartoons about which type of pet?
7. Who provides the voice of Moe in *The Simpsons*?
8. What type of creature was Mungo in the series *Mary, Mungo and Midge*?
9. "The fastest mouse in all Mexico" is the nickname of which cartoon character?
10. Which fictitious organisation featured in the *Roadrunner* cartoons?

Medium

11. In which fictitious town do Stan, Kyle, Eric and Kenny live?
12. Bugs Bunny's enemy Sam takes his first name from which National Park?
13. Which entertainment company produced the *Looney Tunes* series of cartoons?
14. In which cartoon strip does Nermal, the world's cutest kitten, appear?
15. Which cartoon bird is famous for singing I Taut I Taw a Puddy Tat?
16. Which cartoon series featured George, Jane, Judy, Elroy and a dog called Astro?
17. Professor Pat Pending took part in which competition?
18. Which series is set in the town of Quahog?
19. Ben Tennyson is the central character in which cartoon series?
20. How are Wayne and Lucien, residents of Soap City, referred to in the title of a cartoon series?

Hard

Answers to QUIZ 140 – Europe

1. Arno
2. Italy
3. Reykjavik (Iceland)
4. Barcelona
5. Brussels
6. France
7. Berne
8. Germany
9. Red
10. France
11. Dublin
12. France
13. Spain
14. Italy
15. Denmark
16. Italy
17. Cyprus
18. Tiber
19. Malta
20. Roissy Charles de Gaulle, Paris

142

1   Who wrote the 1864 novel *Journey to the Centre of the Earth*?

2   What is the chemical symbol for nitrous oxide?

3   What word describing a fastening device is also used to describe a compressed file?

4   Who was the lead singer of Culture Club?

5   How is the penultimate match in a tournament informally known?

6   What is the postcode area code for Liverpool?

7   Which Scottish river flows through the Grampian mountains into the North Sea?

8   *Bureau de change* has what English translation?

9   What is the surname of Edwin, the title character in Dickens' last unfinished novel?

10 What subject does TV presenter Joe Swift (b.1965) cover?

11 What is Rhesus positive an example of?

12 Of which martial art form is *fu jya* a style?

13 Who had a hit in 2000 with *Rock DJ*?

14 Which of these instruments is the smallest: the cello, the viola, or the violin?

15 What name is given to non-identical twins, born from two eggs?

16 What is a speech delivered from a pulpit called?

17 Who co-starred with Jack Nicholson in the 2003 film *Anger Management*?

18 From which railway station would you leave to travel directly to York from London?

19 A fulmar is what type of creature?

20 What is the centre of a cabbage called?

Easy

Medium

Hard

Answers to QUIZ 141 – Pot Luck

1	Santa	11	James Hunt
2	Sir Bruce Forsyth	12	Castor and Pollux
3	1952	13	Mansion House
4	1800	14	Beverly Hills
5	Sofa	15	Berkshire
6	Camel	16	Young Men's Christian Association
7	Stallion	17	Solomon
8	India	18	The back
9	Caroline Quentin	19	Latin
10	Image file	20	12

1 In 1965, *The Times They Are a-Changin'* was the first top ten hit for which singer/songwriter?

2 What was Terpsichore in Greek mythology?

3 The Tuileries gardens are in which European city?

4 Who played Terry McCann in the TV series *Minder*?

5 Trekkies are fans of which TV and film series?

6 In which country was Trivial Pursuit™ created?

7 Tomintoul is a village in which UK country?

8 What was the name of John Travolta's character in the film *Saturday Night Fever*?

9 Who is Titania's husband in Shakespeare's *A Midsummer Night's Dream*?

10 Who wrote the novel *Tilly Trotter*?

11 What nationality was composer Thomas Arne?

12 In which century was TS Eliot born?

13 Dame Thora Hird played which character in the TV series *Last of the Summer Wine*?

14 Taormina is on which Mediterranean island?

15 How many characters did Twitter™ allow in a tweet when the application first launched?

16 Who released a 1960 cover version of *The Twist*?

17 Which country has Tbilisi as its capital?

18 Tigger was created by which author?

19 Who wrote the 1977 novel *The Thorn Birds*?

20 Which former *Neighbours* actress had a hit with *Torn* in 1997?

1   Which Scottish engineer gave his name to the SI unit of power?

2   What does Santa traditionally travel on?

3   A salsa verde is what colour?

4   Which staff is part of the royal regalia?

5   In which clef are the lower notes on a piano usually written on a piece of music?

6   Which film studios are located at Borehamwood in Hertfordshire?

7   *Angelo* and *Figaro* were 1970s hits for which group?

8   Which 2000 Nick Park animated film was set on a farm?

9   What title is given to a graduate who studied singing or playing an instrument?

10 Founded in 1766, Christie's is what type of business?

11 What is the name given to the style of window that has a vertical sliding frame?

12 In Shakespeare's *Twelfth Night*, what is the name of Viola's twin brother?

13 Which car manufacturer produced the Panda?

14 The 1977 novel *The Shining* was written by which author?

15 What word links a bargain event with a town in Trafford?

16 On an Ordnance Survey map, what is indicated by a square containing an "i"?

17 In the TV series *Flight of the Conchords*, from what country are Bret and Jemaine?

18 In which decade was the series *'Allo 'Allo!* screened for the first time?

19 How many points is a K worth in Scrabble®?

20 Which word means both to begin and to give a jump in fright?

Answers to QUIZ 143 – Pot Luck

1	Jules Verne	11	Blood type
2	N2O	12	Kung fu
3	Zip	13	Robbie Williams
4	Boy George	14	The violin
5	Semi	15	Fraternal twins
6	L	16	Sermon
7	Spey	17	Adam Sandler
8	Office of exchange	18	King's Cross
9	Drood	19	Bird
10	Gardening	20	Heart

1 *Borderline* was a 1983 single by which singer?

2 What item of clothing can be described as A-line?

3 What does a double white line in the centre of a road indicate?

4 If someone is short of money, on what line would they be described as being?

5 Which item accompanies "hook" and "line" in a phrase meaning "completely deceived"?

6 What term is given to soldiers that are closest to the enemy?

7 What two-word term referencing a bird is sometimes given to laughter lines?

8 In which sport is play restarted with a line-out after the ball goes into touch?

9 If someone takes the easiest option, which line are they said to be taking?

10 What is a Plimsoll line used to indicate?

11 "Saline" descibes a medical solution of what compound in water?

12 What is the colour of the Jubilee Line on the London Underground map?

13 Which country built the Maginot Line in WWII?

14 Who played Secret Service agent Frank Horrigan in the 1993 film *In the Line of Fire*?

15 Kevin Federline was married to which singer from 2004 to 2006?

16 What is the American term for petrol?

17 Previously called a linesman, what is a football official at the side of the pitch now called?

18 What term is given to the chief act at a music festival?

19 Pauline Quirke is best known for playing which character in the TV series *Birds of a Feather*?

20 *I Can Do That* and *One* are songs from which 1975 musical, filmed with Michael Douglas in the starring role in 1985?

Answers to QUIZ 144 – To a T

1	Bob Dylan	11	English
2	A Muse	12	19th century
3	Paris	13	Edie
4	Dennis Waterman	14	Sicily
5	*Star Trek*	15	140
6	Canada	16	Chubby Checker
7	Scotland	17	Georgia
8	Tony Manero	18	AA Milne
9	Oberon	19	Colleen McCullough
10	Dame Catherine Cookson	20	Natalie Imbruglia

1 Which international tennis trophy did Great Britain win in 2015?

2 What was the title of Bryan Adams' first UK top twenty single?

3 What is a souk?

4 Moving clockwise on a dartboard what number is next to 15?

5 Simon Sebag Montefiore writes books on which general subject?

6 What affliction is also known as scrivener's palsy?

7 How are whiskers grown on the cheek edges referred to?

8 What form of entertainment is associated with La Scala in Milan?

9 In the Old Testament, what name was given to the chest that contained the Ten Commandments?

10 Provence and Brittany are both parts of which country?

11 How many yards are there in half a mile?

12 Which word means both a roasting device and a narrow strip of land sticking out into the sea?

13 What is a kalanchoe?

14 Jacob Marley appears in which Charles Dickens story?

15 On UK roads, what is the standard national speed limit for a car on a dual carriageway or motorway?

16 Which two countries share the world's longest frontier?

17 Which English poet wrote *Paradise Lost* (1667)?

18 Which "ology" is concerned with the human skin?

19 Edgar Rice Burroughs created which jungle hero?

20 Which South American river is the second longest in the world?

Easy

Medium

Hard

Answers to QUIZ 145 – Pot Luck

1	James Watt	11	Sash
2	Sleigh	12	Sebastian
3	Green	13	Fiat
4	Sceptre	14	Stephen King
5	Bass clef	15	Sale
6	Elstree	16	Tourist information
7	Brotherhood of Man	17	New Zealand
8	*Chicken Run*	18	1980s
9	Bachelor of music	19	Five
10	Auction house	20	Start

Easy

1   In a 1954 song, who was entreated to "Bring me a dream"?

2   Which non-existent character is said to make "Exceedingly good cakes"?

3   Who portrayed the *Star Trek* character of Mr Spock?

4   In the novel and film *Goodbye, Mr Chips*, what was Mr Chipping's profession?

5   Who played Mrs Robinson in the 1967 film *The Graduate*?

6   Winnie McGoogan is a character in which sitcom?

7   Which novel by Mrs Gaskell was adapted for TV in 2007 and starred Dame Judi Dench?

8   Who wrote the *Book of Household Management*, published in 1861?

9   Who played the starring roles in the 2005 film *Mr & Mrs Smith*?

10 In literature, who is adopted by Mr Brownlow, who is eventually revealed to be his grandfather?

Medium

11 Which instrument did Mrs Mills play?

12 Who played Mrs Hudson in the TV series *Sherlock*?

13 Which 1992 Quentin Tarantino film featured Mr Pink, Mr White and Mr Orange?

14 *Broken Wings* and *Kyrie* were 1980s hits for which group?

15 Mr Derek and Mr Roy were companions to which TV puppet?

16 Who wrote the 1925 novel *Mrs Dalloway*?

17 Who starred in the 1936 Frank Capra comedy *Mr Deeds Goes to Town*?

18 In which 1993 film did Robin Williams masquerade as a Scottish nanny?

19 Mrs Danvers is a character in which 1938 novel?

20 Which TV series introduced Mr Blobby?

Hard

Answers to QUIZ 146 – Lines

1	Madonna	11	Sodium chloride/salt
2	Skirt or dress	12	Silver
3	No overtaking	13	France
4	Breadline	14	Clint Eastwood
5	Sinker	15	Britney Spears
6	Front-line	16	Gasoline
7	Crow's-feet	17	Assistant referee
8	Rugby	18	Headline
9	Line of least resistance	19	Sharon
10	The level of loading on a ship	20	*A Chorus Line*

1 What is ¾ expressed as a percentage?

2 What word relates to both general office workers and church ministers?

3 Which group of islands off the west coast of Ireland lend their name to a thick knitwear style?

4 "Steps" is the traditional bingo call for which number?

5 What word can refer to a tree support and a storage container?

6 The sci-fi novel *Do Androids Dream of Electric Sheep?* was the basis for which film?

7 Which edible starch, used in puddings, is obtained from the palm?

8 The Welland Canal links which two Great Lakes?

9 Which army rank is between major general and general?

10 Which Scottish city is historically famous for jam, jute and journalism?

11 Who was the second wife that Henry VIII divorced?

12 In the film *Dangerous Liaisons* (1988), who played the Vicomte de Valmont?

13 Is the resort of Colwyn Bay in North Wales or South Wales?

14 What sport is played by the Chennai Super Kings?

15 How is Barbara Millicent Roberts better known?

16 What is the square root of 121?

17 Hilary Devey and Kelly Hoppen have previously been associated with which TV series?

18 Which bird has collared, stock and turtle species?

19 In the rhyme, what does the Little Star resemble in the sky?

20 In which part of the body would you find an anvil and a hammer?

Easy

Medium

Hard

Answers to QUIZ 147 – Pot Luck

1	The Davis Cup	11	880
2	*Run to You*	12	Spit
3	A marketplace	13	Plant
4	Two	14	*A Christmas Carol*
5	History	15	70 mph
6	Writer's cramp	16	The USA and Canada
7	Sideburns	17	John Milton
8	Opera	18	Dermatology
9	Ark of the Covenant	19	Tarzan
10	France	20	Amazon

1   Which comedian co-presents *Stargazing Live* with Brian Cox?

2   In the sitcom *Friends*, what was Ross' profession?

3   Who presented the 2016 series *Dangerous Earth*?

4   What was the title of the TV series in which Dr Sam Beckett was able to travel in time?

5   Who was the original presenter of *The Sky at Night...*?

6   ...and who has co-presented it with Chris Lintott since 2014?

7   Harrison Wells is the name of a scientist in which superhero TV series?

8   Which character in *The Big Bang Theory* shares his surname with a professor of science (b.1945) who has won awards for his non-fiction books?

9   Who presented the TV series *The Incredible Human Journey* and *Ice Age Giants*?

10 Professor Iain Stewart specialises in which branch of science?

11 Jem Stansfield and Dr Yan Wong were presenters of which BBC science series?

12 What was the name of the 1979-86 series presented by Professor Heinz Wolff in which teams created a mechanism to solve a challenge?

13 What nationality was scientist and broadcaster Magnus Pyke?

14 Who was Dr Bunsen Honeydew's assistant on *The Muppet Show*?

15 Professor Hubert J Farnsworth is a character in which animated series?

16 Who presented the series *Child of Our Time*?

17 In *Doctor Who*, what is the name of the Doctor's hand-held device that uses sound waves to perform various technical and mechanical functions?

18 Which TV series featured the scientists at the fictional Global Dynamics research facility?

19 Dr Mohinder Suresh was a character in which sci-fi series that ran from 2006 to 2010?

20 Professor Frink appears in which animated series?

Answers to QUIZ 148 – Mr and Mrs

1	Mr Sandman	11	Piano
2	Mr Kipling	12	Una Stubbs
3	Leonard Nimoy	13	*Reservoir Dogs*
4	Schoolteacher	14	Mr Mister
5	Anne Bancroft	15	Basil Brush
6	*Mrs Brown's Boys*	16	Virginia Woolf
7	*Cranford*	17	Gary Cooper
8	Mrs Beeton	18	*Mrs Doubtfire*
9	Brad Pitt and Angelina Jolie	19	*Rebecca*
10	Oliver (*Oliver Twist*)	20	*Noel's House Party*

1. Who sang lead vocals on the Commodores 1978 hit *Three Times a Lady*?
2. The 1997 novel *The God of Small Things* was written by which author?
3. In Morse code what letter is represented by two dashes?
4. How many pairs of walking or swimming legs has a shrimp?
5. What was the nationality of former UN Secretary General, Boutros Boutros-Ghali?
6. Of which land did Aragorn become king in *The Lord of the Rings*?
7. What is cambric?
8. What term is given to the wide sash worn with a kimono?
9. What was the first name of the sculptor Epstein, who became a British citizen in the early 1900s?
10. In which year did Giorgio Armani launch his first menswear collection?
11. Hippotherapy is a treatment involving which animal?
12. What was the first name of landscape designer "Capability" Brown?
13. What is the name of Jordan's only port?
14. Which car company produces models called Volante and Vanquish?
15. A person who is qualified to design and build roads is in which profession?
16. What is the nearest international airport to the Australian resort of Surfer's Paradise?
17. What is the capital city of Zambia?
18. Which mythical figure had repeatedly to roll a boulder up a hill?
19. The Aleutian Islands are part of which US state?
20. Which type of lizard is commonly referred to as a flying dragon?

Easy

Medium

Hard

Answers to QUIZ 149 – Pot Luck

1	75%	11	Anne of Cleves
2	Clerical	12	John Malkovich
3	Aran	13	North
4	39	14	Cricket
5	Trunk	15	Barbie®
6	*Blade Runner*	16	11
7	Sago	17	*Dragons' Den*
8	Erie and Ontario	18	Dove
9	Lieutenant general	19	A diamond
10	Dundee	20	Ear

Easy

1 What was William Gladstone's middle name?

2 Who was the inaugural First Minister of Scotland?

3 Which UK government official is ranked below a Secretary?

4 From 1997 to 2001, who was the leader of the Conservative Party?

5 Who was the UK Prime Minister during the General Strike of 1926?

6 Who was David Lloyd George's (First Earl Lloyd-George of Dwyfor's) successor as Prime Minister?

7 In which London throughfare is the main Foreign and Commonwealth office building?

8 The Gunpowder conspiracy, commemorated on November 5th, took place in which year?

9 Which former MP's memoirs include *This Boy* and *Please, Mr Postman*?

10 Who held the position of Home Secretary from 1979 to 1983?

11 At the time of the Suez crisis, who was the UK Prime Minister?

12 Who was Leader of the Labour Party from 1935 to 1955?

Medium

13 Which constituency did Gordon Brown represent before resigning in 2015?

14 In which year were proceedings in the House of Lords televised for the first time?

15 Who was Leader of the Opposition from 2003 to 2005?

16 Which government position also has the title "Second Lord of the Treasury"?

17 Who was appointed Secretary of State for Environment, Food and Rural Affairs in 2017?

18 In which year was the first UK election in which 18-21 year olds could vote?

19 Where is the Government Chief Whip's official residence?

20 Whom did Neville Chamberlain succeed as prime minister?

Answers to QUIZ 150 – TV Scientists

1	Dara Ó Briain	11	*Bang Goes the Theory*
2	Palaeontologist	12	*The Great Egg Race*
3	Helen Czerski	13	English
4	*Quantum Leap*	14	Beaker
5	Sir Patrick Moore	15	*Futurama*
6	Maggie Aderin-Pocock	16	Robert Winston (Baron Winston)
7	*The Flash*	17	Sonic screwdriver
8	Leonard Hofstadter	18	*A Town Called Eureka*
9	Alice Roberts	19	*Heroes*
10	Geology	20	*The Simpsons*

Hard

ANSWERS ON PAGE 155

1   Of which sea creature is there a variety known as Jack Sail-by-the-Wind?

2   In which US state is the city of Philadelphia?

3   Which Mexican peninsula separates the Gulf of Mexico from the Caribbean?

4   Which bird did Noah first send out of the ark?

5   In which country is Nullarbor Plain?

6   What is the name of the countess in the Shakespeare play *Twelfth Night*?

7   The Penny Black was the first adhesive stamp, but how was the Penny Red a first?

8   What is the third book of the Old Testament?

9   What type of creature is a lumpsucker?

10 What was the nickname of the American B17 bomber plane, famous for performing daylight missions during the second world war?

11 Which group had top ten hits with *Dry County* and *It's My Life*?

12 What kind of harp produces a musical sound when a current of air passes over the strings?

13 Who won *Celebrity Big Brother* in 2017?

14 Of which US state is Baton Rouge the capital?

15 Who are members of the highest of the nine orders of angels?

16 In which country is the complex of Angkor Wat?

17 What was the name of the beautiful youth in Greek mythology who spent each winter with Persephone?

18 Which artist painted *Déjeuner sur l'Herbe*?

19 Who was the Roman goddess of peace?

20 What term is given to the beam that projects from a boat's side?

Easy

Medium

Hard

Answers to QUIZ 151 – Pot Luck

1	Lionel Richie	11	Horses
2	Arundhati Roy	12	Lancelot
3	M	13	Aqaba
4	Five	14	Aston Martin
5	Egyptian	15	Civil engineering
6	Gondor	16	Gold Coast
7	A fabric	17	Lusaka
8	Obi	18	Sisyphus
9	Jacob	19	Alaska
10	1975	20	Draco lizard

Easy

1 Who played Lilith in the TV series *Cheers* and *Frasier*?

2 Which singer was born Marie McDonald McLaughlin Lawrie?

3 The disease beriberi is caused by a lack of which vitamin?

4 African bird's-eye chilli is also known by what name?

5 Which century saw the Dada art movement?

6 What is the name of the Lord High Executioner in Gilbert and Sullivan's *The Mikado*?

7 In Egyptian mythology, who was the wife of Osiris?

8 The cuscus is a variety of which type of animal?

9 From which country does the cha-cha dance originate?

10 In which year did Keke Rosberg win the Formula 1 World Championship?

Medium

11 Who released the 1980 single *Bang Bang*?

12 Which actress and singer had a 2002 hit with *Kiss Kiss*?

13 Native to Madagascar, which is the world's largest nocturnal primate?

14 What instrument is associated with Yo-Yo Ma?

15 *Pica Pica* is the Latin name for which bird?

16 Which band recorded the 1971 song *Baba O'Riley*?

17 Which reality TV star had a hit in 2002 with *Papa Don't Preach*?

18 In the TV series *Inspector Montalbano*, what is the nickname of his deputy Domenico Augello?

19 Which river flows through Northampton and Peterborough?

20 Which type of organisation was featured in the 2009 TV series *Monday Monday*?

Hard

1   What make and model of car was driven by the Duke boys in the US TV series *The Dukes of Hazzard*?

2   Chalcedony, an agate often used in cameos, is a variety of which stone?

3   What is the capital of Jordan?

4   New Hampshire has which state flower?

5   What is the alternative name for a wildebeest?

6   According to the Bible, what sort of animal did Joseph's brothers kill in order to smear his coat with blood?

7   Of which Indian state is Patna the capital...?

8   ...and to which foodstuff does it lend its name?

9   What term is given to the four principal directions of the compass?

10   Which is the second-largest city in Zimbabwe?

11   In the TV series *TJ Hooker*, who played the title role?

12   The Potala Palace is in which city?

13   Into which body of water does the Zambezi River flow?

14   What did Mary Shelley originally intend to use as a title for her novel *Frankenstein*?

15   What is the book containing the texts used in Catholic services throughout the year?

16   GK Chesterton had what first names?

17   Which medieval humour was said to cause irascibility?

18   What is a celesta?

19   In the children's TV series *The Tweenies*, what was the name of the main character who was a purple colour?

20   What type of creature is a Havana Brown?

Easy

Medium

Hard

Answers to QUIZ 153 – Pot Luck

1	Jellyfish	11	Bon Jovi
2	Pennsylvania	12	Aeolian
3	Yucatan	13	Sarah Harding
4	Raven	14	Louisiana
5	Australia	15	Seraphim
6	Olivia	16	Cambodia
7	Perforated	17	Adonis
8	Leviticus	18	Edouard Manet
9	Fish	19	Pax
10	The Flying Fortress	20	Outrigger

Easy

1 Which sport is named after the Gloucestershire seat of the Duke of Beaufort?

2 In which country was tennis player Eugenie Bouchard born?

3 Who captained the winning team at the 2014 Ryder Cup?

4 In cycle racing, what is a sag wagon?

5 Which British athlete won the Olympic long jump gold medal in 1964?

6 What do two yellow flags mean in Formula 1?

7 The winter biathlon involves skiing and which other discipline?

8 How many times was Nigel Mansell Formula 1 World Champion?

9 Where were the Summer Olympics held in 1968?

10 Why do American footballers paint black marks across their cheeks?

11 Which team won the 2018 NFL Super Bowl?

12 What was the location of the 1952 Winter Olympics?

13 What is the end of a day's play in cricket called?

14 Which cyclist turned jockey rode in the Foxhunters' Chase at Cheltenham in 2016?

Medium

15 At what sport has Ellie Simmonds won golds for Great Britain?

16 What is the opposite side to the legside in cricket?

17 What would a judo player do with a judogi?

18 Which tennis player was known as the "Rockhampton Rocket"?

19 Who won BBC Sports Personality of the Year in 2015?

20 What colour is the innermost zone in an archery target?

Hard

Answers to QUIZ 154 – At the Double

1	Bebe Neuwirth	11	BA Robertson
2	Lulu	12	Holly Valance
3	Vitamin B	13	Aye-aye
4	Piri-piri	14	Cello
5	20th century	15	Magpie
6	Koko	16	The Who
7	Isis	17	Kelly Osbourne
8	Possum	18	Mimi
9	Cuba	19	Nene
10	1982	20	Supermarket

QUIZ 157 – Pot Luck

ANSWERS ON PAGE **159**

1   Along with Gog, which Biblical giant was associated with apocalyptic prophecy?

2   Which US state is known as the "Hawkeye State"?

3   In which game does the winner "peg out"?

4   In Greek mythology, which nymph was spurned by Narcissus?

5   With what type of item is Crown Derby associated?

6   Who or what in the Old Testament is known as the Pentateuch?

7   The character of Scarpia features in which Puccini opera?

8   Which king of Thebes solved the riddle of the sphinx?

9   What term is given to the belief that everything in nature is connected in some way?

10 Which order of Greek architecture is characterised by a plain, sturdy column?

11 The lyrebird is native to which continent?

12 What is Canada's largest port on the Pacific?

13 What is the capital of Puerto Rico?

14 The millionaire Daddy Warbucks features in which musical?

15 Which soft wool cloth is named after a port on the Caspian Sea?

16 Cameroon and Chad both use which unit of currency?

17 What type of creature is an Adonis Blue?

18 Which cartoon character's brothers include Spike, Olaf and Marbles?

19 In which Shakespearean play did the line "Knock knock, who's there?" originally appear?

20 What was Tom Keating most famous for creating?

Easy

Medium

Hard

Answers to QUIZ 155 – Pot Luck

1	Dodge Charger	11	William Shatner
2	Onyx	12	Lhasa
3	Amman	13	Indian Ocean
4	Lilac	14	*The Modern Prometheus*
5	Gnu	15	Missal
6	Goat	16	Gilbert Keith
7	Bihar	17	Choler
8	Rice	18	Musical instrument
9	Cardinal points	19	Milo
10	Bulawayo	20	A cat

ANSWERS ON PAGE **160**

Easy

1   *Keep on Running* was a 1966 hit for which group?

2   Who wrote The Move's 1969 hit *Blackberry Way*?

3   Which Elvis Presley film included the song *Wooden Heart*?

4   *Tears* was a 1965 hit for which comedian?

5   *Bad Moon Rising* was a 1969 hit for which group?

6   Which singer's name was linked with the Union Gap in the name of a 1960s group?

7   Released in 1968, what was the title of Fleetwood Mac's only UK no.1 single?

8   Which actress, who later appeared in *EastEnders*, featured on the 1962 hit *Come Outside*?

9   Which band played a London rooftop concert at 3 Savile Row on January 30th 1969?

10   In which city was singer Joe Cocker born?

Medium

11   Who was hearing *Distant Drums* in 1966?

12   Who had a 1969 hit with *(If Paradise Is) Half as Nice*?

13   Whose Crazy World had a hit in 1968 with *Fire*?

14   *Sweets for My Sweet* was a 1963 hit for which group?

15   Which group topped the charts in 1969 with *Ob-La-Di, Ob-La-Da*?

16   What was the Beatles' first UK no.1 single?

17   In which year did the United Kingdom first win the Eurovision Song Contest?

18   Which group had a hit in 1968 with *Lily the Pink*?

19   *Sugar Sugar* was a 1969 hit for which group?

20   Which 1960 hit had the subtitle *Ballad of a Refuse Disposal Officer*?

Hard

Answers to QUIZ 156 – Sport

1	Badminton	11	Philadelphia Eagles
2	Canada	12	Oslo
3	Paul McGinley	13	Stumps
4	A support vehicle accompanying a bicycle	14	Victoria Pendleton
5	Lynn Davies	15	Swimming
6	Slow down and be prepared to stop	16	Offside
7	Rifle shooting	17	Wear it
8	One	18	Rod Laver
9	Mexico City	19	Sir Andy Murray
10	It helps to protect against the sun's glare	20	Gold

1   What term is given to a post for winding up a ship's cable?

2   Mars, the Roman god of battle, had which Greek counterpart?

3   What is the largest city of KwaZulu-Natal, South Africa?

4   Which US state is the official home of the Choctaw, Cherokee, Creek and Seminole tribes?

5   What is a sabot?

6   Bamako is the capital of which West African country?

7   What name is given to Beethoven's ninth symphony?

8   The Chester White is a breed of which animal?

9   Which device is used on a guitar fretboard to raise the pitch of the strings?

10   In the King James version of the Bible, what is the eighth commandment?

11   In phonetics, what do you do when you pronounce the letter "h"?

12   For which film did Michelle Pfeiffer receive her first Oscar nomination?

13   By what group name is a flock of ravens known?

14   What is a Malay dagger with a wavy-edged blade?

15   Which bay is found in the Indian Ocean, between India and Myanmar (Burma)?

16   Who wrote the autobiographies *Going to Sea in a Sieve* and *Going Off Alarming*?

17   Which fashion house did John Galliano first design for in 1997?

18   What was the name of the Israelites' "Promised Land"?

19   What expense became compulsory for cars in 1921?

20   Of what is gerontology the scientific study?

Answers to QUIZ 157 – Pot Luck

1	Magog	11	Australia
2	Iowa	12	Vancouver
3	Cribbage	13	San Juan
4	Echo	14	*Annie*
5	China	15	Astrakhan
6	The first five books	16	CFA franc
7	*Tosca*	17	Butterfly
8	Oedipus	18	Snoopy
9	Holism	19	*Macbeth*
10	Doric	20	Art forgeries

Easy

1 Which country produces "Bull's Blood" wine?

2 Which Swiss city is located where the Swiss, French and German borders meet?

3 Which French phrase is indicated by the letters RSVP?

4 The Cortes is the name of the parliament of which country?

5 Which city is served by Franz Josef Strauss airport?

6 In which Irish county is Knock?

7 Into which sea does the Po flow?

8 Which country only has borders with Switzerland and Austria?

9 Which Mediterranean island was the headquarters of the Knights of St John?

10 Which European country was unified in 1870?

Medium

11 In which district of Paris is the Sacré-Coeur?

12 Which country lies immediately south of Estonia?

13 Lëtzebuergesch is a language of what country, which adopted it as an official language in 1984?

14 In which country is the Corinth Canal?

15 Which sea lies between Italy and the Balkans?

16 What is the seventeenth letter of the Greek alphabet?

17 What is the official language of Andorra?

18 Which country sponsored the voyages of Christopher Columbus?

19 In which sea are the islands of Samos and Lesbos located?

20 Bratislava is the capital city of which country?

Hard

Answers to QUIZ 158 – 1960s Music

1	Spencer Davis Group	11	Jim Reeves
2	Roy Wood	12	Amen Corner
3	*GI Blues*	13	Arthur Brown
4	Sir Ken Dodd	14	Searchers
5	Creedence Clearwater Revival	15	Marmalade
6	Gary Puckett	16	*From Me to You*
7	*Albatross*	17	1967
8	Wendy Richard	18	Scaffold
9	Beatles	19	Archies
10	Sheffield	20	*My Old Man's a Dustman*

1   Who was the Norse god of war and poetry?

2   What is the common name of the *Felis* genus?

3   Which Canadian territory has Whitehorse as its capital?

4   Who played the title role in the 1953 western *Shane*?

5   Bogota is the capital of which South American country?

6   Which Verdi opera of 1871 is set in Egypt?

7   Which US state is nicknamed "The Granite State"?

8   On which continent is the city of Campinas?

9   Which group of stars is also known as the Seven Sisters?

10   In 1778, who became the first European to discover the Hawaiian islands?

11   In a maritime vessel's name, for what does "SS" stand?

12   Augusta is the capital of which state?

13   Of what is tachophobia a fear?

14   From which club did Manchester United sign Ruud van Nistelrooy in 2001?

15   In which forest does the River Danube rise?

16   Which Trojan king, the husband of Hecuba, was defeated by the Greeks?

17   In which year was *Coronation Street* first broadcast?

18   Who directed the 1958 film *Touch of Evil*?

19   The clarinettist Arthur Jacob Arshawsky (b.1910) was better known by which name?

20   Tony Hill and Carol Jordan are characters in books by which author?

Answers to QUIZ 159 – Pot Luck

1	Capstan	11	Aspirate
2	Ares	12	*Dangerous Liaisons*
3	Durban	13	Unkindness
4	Oklahoma	14	Kris
5	Clog	15	Bengal
6	Mali	16	Danny Baker
7	*Choral*	17	Christian Dior
8	Pig	18	Canaan
9	Capo	19	Tax discs
10	Thou shalt not steal	20	Old age

Easy

1 Which 1997 film featured the song *You Can Leave Your Hat On?*

2 In which decade of the 20th century was Sophia Loren born?

3 In which *Carry On* film did Sid James first feature?

4 Who played May Day in the Bond film *A View to a Kill?*

5 Dolly Parton and Julia Roberts starred in which 1989 film?

6 Who played Jim Graham in the 1987 film *Empire of the Sun?*

7 In *Dial M for Murder*, what sport did Ray Milland play?

8 Which star of TV's *The Avengers* featured in *A View to a Kill?*

9 Who played Meryl Streep's long-suffering assistant in the 2006 film *The Devil Wears Prada?*

10 At the 2017 Oscars, who won the Best Supporting Actor award?

Medium

11 In which film do the male and female stars go to a diner called Jack Rabbit Slim's on a date?

12 Clint Eastwood directed himself as a character called Dave Garland in which 1971 film?

13 Which comedy team first appeared in *One Night in the Tropics* (1940)?

14 Who played the title role in the 1996 film *Michael Collins?*

15 In the 1950s, which film gave Elizabeth Taylor her third successive Oscar nomination?

16 Which actress starred as Meg Altman in the 2002 film *Panic Room?*

17 Which of his films won Al Pacino the 1993 Oscar for Best Actor?

18 Who directed *The Blues Brothers?*

19 The 1996 sci-fi comedy *Mars Attacks!* featured which legendary male singer?

20 Who played the part of Billy in the 1963 film *Billy Liar?*

Hard

Answers to QUIZ 160 – Europe

1 Hungary
2 Basel
3 *Répondez s'il vous plait*
4 Spain
5 Munich
6 Mayo
7 The Adriatic
8 Liechtenstein
9 Malta
10 Italy
11 Montmartre
12 Latvia
13 Luxembourg
14 Greece
15 Adriatic
16 Rho
17 Catalan
18 Spain
19 Aegean
20 Slovakia

1 What does the musical instruction "con brio" indicate?

2 Zane Grey was famous for writing what type of book?

3 Who was Tom Cruise's first wife?

4 In which century was Venetian painter Canaletto born?

5 Who ordered the building of St Basil's Cathedral in Moscow?

6 Which pope did Francis succeed in 2013?

7 Charles Ross and Epicure are types of which fruit?

8 With what colour are Carmelite friars associated?

9 How many parts did Sir Alec Guinness play in the 1949 film *Kind Hearts and Coronets*?

10 What is the capital of the Democratic Republic of the Congo?

11 Which great English batsmen (d.2000) had the initials MCC?

12 What is the name of Claudio's beloved in Shakespeare's *Much Ado about Nothing*?

13 What word can refer to both faith and a holding fund?

14 Which poem by Keats begins "Oh what can ail thee, knight-at-arms"?

15 By what name is Beethoven's Piano Sonata No. 14 in C-sharp minor better known?

16 Which sporting activity features in the film *Touching the Void*?

17 In which decade of the 20th century was Joan Baez born?

18 What type of craft was HMS *Victorious* (1939-68)?

19 With which group did comedians Baddiel and Skinner produce the football anthem *Three Lions*?

20 Portadown and Lurgan lie in which Northern Irish county?

Answers to QUIZ 161 – Pot Luck

1	Odin	11	Steamship
2	Cat	12	Maine
3	Yukon	13	Speed
4	Alan Ladd	14	PSV Eindhoven
5	Colombia	15	Black Forest
6	*Aida*	16	Priam
7	New Hampshire	17	1960
8	South America	18	Orson Welles
9	Pleiades	19	Artie Shaw
10	James Cook	20	Val McDermid

ANSWERS ON PAGE **166**

1 Which King of England died from eating too many lampreys at a banquet in France?

2 Which Native American language was used as a code in WWII?

3 In May 1497, who sailed across the Atlantic from Bristol in the *Matthew* and landed in Newfoundland?

4 Which country was invaded by US troops in December 1989?

5 What was the name of the spacecraft that Yuri Gagarin travelled in when he became the first man in space?

6 Who was the first Soviet statesman to hold the posts of general secretary and president simultaneously?

7 In which war was the Battle of Ebro River?

8 Which major figure of Russian history was born in Ulyanovsk on the Volga?

9 In WWI which countries made up the Triple Entente?

10 Who opened the Manchester Ship Canal in 1894?

11 Where did Martin Luther nail *The 95 Theses* to a church door?

12 In which city was Checkpoint Charlie?

13 What was the name of the judge who presided over the 17th-century Bloody Assizes?

14 Which US president won a Nobel Prize in 1906?

15 At which battle in 1513 was James IV of Scotland killed?

16 What was the title formerly carried by princes and archbishops of the Holy Roman Empire, who appointed the emperor?

17 Garibaldi's followers wore what colour shirts?

18 In which year was VAT introduced in Britain?

19 Whose inaugural Presidential address stated: "Ask not what your country can do for you – ask what you can do for your country"?

20 In which century was religious reformer John Calvin born?

Answers to QUIZ 162 – Film

1	*The Full Monty*	11	*Pulp Fiction*
2	1930s	12	*Play Misty for Me*
3	*Carry On Constable*	13	Abbott and Costello
4	Grace Jones	14	Liam Neeson
5	*Steel Magnolias*	15	*Suddenly, Last Summer*
6	Christian Bale	16	Jodie Foster
7	Tennis	17	*Scent of a Woman*
8	Patrick Macnee	18	John Landis
9	Emily Blunt	19	Sir Tom Jones
10	Mahershala Ali	20	Sir Tom Courtenay

Easy

Medium

Hard

1 What number lies between 15 and 17 on a standard dartboard?

2 How many degrees Centigrade is 50 degrees Fahrenheit?

3 What are the irregularly shaped bodies in blood that help to make it clot?

4 Which is the ninth letter of the Greek alphabet?

5 Arundel Castle is the seat of which Duke?

6 Who invented corrugated iron?

7 What are latkes made from?

8 In the TV series *Family Guy*, who has provided the voice of Meg Griffin since the second series?

9 What protein is found in egg-whites?

10 What type of creature is a Scotch Argus?

11 What was the name of the fictional corporation who made RoboCop in the film of the same name?

12 In the popular Nintendo® video games franchise, what is the name of Mario's green dinosaur friend?

13 In Morse code what letter is represented by two dots?

14 How is the vegetable *Allium porrum* better known?

15 In which game might you employ the Sicilian Defence?

16 Who starred as Captain Nolan in the 1977 film *Orca*?

17 What colour is a sorrel horse?

18 What is the diameter in inches of a standard competition dartboard?

19 In the TV series Top Gear, what was the first make and model of the car used in the segment "*Star in a Reasonably Priced Car*"?

20 To which country do the Galapagos Islands belong?

Easy

Medium

Hard

Answers to QUIZ 163 – Pot Luck

1	Play vigorously	11	Colin Cowdrey (Baron Cowdrey of Tonbridge)
2	Westerns	12	Hero
3	Mimi Rogers	13	Trust
4	17th century	14	*La Belle Dame sans Merci*
5	Ivan the Terrible	15	*Moonlight*
6	Benedict XVI	16	Mountaineering
7	Apples	17	1940s
8	White (White Friars)	18	Aircraft carrier
9	Nine	19	The Lightning Seeds
10	Kinshasa	20	Armagh

ANSWERS ON PAGE **168**

Easy

1   What is the first name of Mr Marner in the title of a George Eliot novel?

2   In *Animal Farm* (1945), what type of animal is Clover?

3   Which author created the character of Horatio Hornblower?

4   Which of Wilkie Collins' novels is often considered to be the first detective novel?

5   Who is the heroine of Jane Austen's *Persuasion*?

6   Who wrote the 1961 novel *Catch-22*?

7   Clara Peggotty is a character from which Dickens novel?

8   Which Devon village is named after a Charles Kingsley novel?

9   Who is the narrator in Herman Melville's *Moby-Dick*?

10 In *The Hobbit*, what is the name of the dragon?

11 What is the name of the girl in the *Just William* stories?

12 Who wrote the novel *Tom Brown's Schooldays*?

13 Which Scottish adventurer was the inspiration for the character of Robinson Crusoe?

14 What is the surname of Henry James' heroine Isabel in the novel *The Portrait of a Lady*?

Medium

15 The 1915 novel *The Voyage Out* was written by which author?

16 From which London club in Pall Mall does Phileas Fogg set off in *Around the World in Eighty Days*?

17 What is the title of the 1886 adventure novel by Robert Louis Stevenson about a man called David Balfour?

18 Which food and drink items form the title of a Somerset Maugham novel?

19 In Charlotte Brontë's novel *Jane Eyre*, to which charitable institution is Jane sent as a child?

20 Who was the author of *The Railway Children* (1905)?

Hard

Answers to QUIZ 164 – History

1	Henry I	11	Wittenberg
2	Navajo	12	Berlin
3	John Cabot	13	Judge Jeffreys
4	Panama	14	Theodore Roosevelt
5	*Vostok I*	15	Flodden
6	Brezhnev	16	Elector
7	Spanish Civil War	17	Red
8	Lenin	18	1973
9	Germany, Austria-Hungary, Turkey	19	John F Kennedy
10	Queen Victoria	20	16th century

1   What type of bird is a garganey?

2   Alphabetically, who is the first of the New Testament apostles?

3   In which country was the French Foreign Legion founded, in 1831?

4   For which play was Arthur Miller awarded a Pulitzer Prize in 1949?

5   What is the RAF equivalent of the Royal Navy rank of vice-admiral?

6   What is the English title of the TV series *Bron/Broen*?

7   In the game of bingo, what is the traditional call for the number 61?

8   Which famous songwriting duo wrote the music and lyrics to the musical *Promises, Promises*?

9   What was Barry McGuigan's nickname?

10 The stately home of Wilton House is near which English city?

11 Who was the first player to score a maximum 147 break in World Championship snooker?

12 Bathophobia is a fear of what?

13 Which English county cricket club did Jos Buttler join in 2014?

14 Who said "A verbal contract isn't worth the paper it's written on"?

15 In Greek mythology, who was the goddess of the dawn?

16 Hydroponics is the growing of plants without what?

17 Which Roman road ran from London to York via Lincoln?

18 Of what is philology the study?

19 Which Shakespeare play includes the character of Lancelot Gobbo?

20 Who starred in the 2014 film *Noah*?

Easy

Medium

Hard

Answers to QUIZ 165 – Pot Luck

1	Two	11	Omnicorp (OCP)
2	10	12	Yoshi
3	Platelets	13	I
4	Iota	14	The leek
5	Duke of Norfolk	15	Chess
6	Henry Palmer	16	Richard Harris
7	Potatoes	17	Brown
8	Mila Kunis	18	18
9	Albumen	19	Suzuki Liana
10	Butterfly	20	Ecuador

QUIZ 168 – Makers and Collectors

ANSWERS ON PAGE **170**

Easy

1   A horologist is a maker of what items?

2   What does a phillumenist collect?

3   A cordwainer is a maker of what items?

4   What is the term for a maker of boats or ships?

5   What does a fletcher make?

6   What is the term for someone who collects stamps?

7   What does a deltiologist collect?

8   A velologist is a collector of what items?

9   What does a cartographer create?

10 What is the term for a maker of candles?

11 What does a milliner make?

12 What does a luthier make?

Medium

13 A tegestologist is a collector of what items?

14 What is the term for someone who collects coins and banknotes?

15 In what profession does a maker of fitted clothing work?

16 What does an arctophile collect?

17 What is the term for a maker of casks and barrels?

18 What does a galanthophile collect?

19 What does a scripophilist collect?

20 A bibliophile is a collector of what?

Hard

Answers to QUIZ 166 – Classic Novels

1	Silas	11	Violet Elizabeth Bott
2	Horse	12	Thomas Hughes
3	CS Forester	13	Alexander Selkirk
4	*The Moonstone*	14	Archer
5	Anne Elliot	15	Virginia Woolf
6	Joseph Heller	16	The Reform Club
7	*David Copperfield*	17	*Kidnapped*
8	Westward Ho!	18	*Cakes and Ale*
9	Ishmael	19	Lowood
10	Smaug	20	Edith Nesbit

168

1 What was the first UK top ten single for Jon and Vangelis?

2 In 1953, which statesman won the Nobel Prize in Literature?

3 What is Russia's second city, lying on the river Neva?

4 In which castle was Henry V born?

5 At the 1984 Olympics, who won the gold medal in the men's 1500 metres?

6 During which war did the Battle of Inkerman take place?

7 Which surrealist artist's works often incorporate melting watches and burning giraffes?

8 Of what is rheumatology the study?

9 In which decade of the 20th century was retired tennis player Jimmy Connors born?

10 What is baksheesh?

11 YYZ is the code for which airport?

12 What term describes the use of a word where the pronunciation of the word mimics the sound of what is named?

13 Which archipelago is linked with the Nicobar group?

14 What is the English translation of the French term *sang-froid*?

15 In the TV series *Boomers*, which actress played Joyce?

16 What type of animal is Napoleon in George Orwell's *Animal Farm*?

17 In the 1974 version of *Murder on the Orient Express*, who played Hercule Poirot?

18 What is the name for the variety of green chalcedony that contains spots of red jasper?

19 What is another name for the sharon fruit?

20 Where was Horatio Nelson (Viscount Nelson) buried?

Easy

Medium

Hard

Answers to QUIZ 167 – Pot Luck

1	Duck	11	Cliff Thorburn
2	Andrew	12	Depth
3	Algeria	13	Lancashire
4	*Death of a Salesman*	14	Samuel Goldwyn
5	Air marshal	15	Eos
6	*The Bridge*	16	Soil
7	Baker's bun	17	Ermine Street
8	Burt Bacharach and Hal David	18	Words
9	The Clones Cyclone	19	*The Merchant of Venice*
10	Salisbury	20	Russell Crowe

Easy

1   What term describes vegetables cut into thin strips?

2   Which fruit is usually used in the dessert Brown Betty?

3   What is added to hollandaise sauce to make mousseline sauce?

4   Poire belle Hélène is a classic French dessert, consisting of a poached pear in ice cream and topped with which flavour of sauce?

5   Rye whiskey, vermouth and angostura are the ingredients of which cocktail?

6   What are wrapped in bacon to make angels on horseback?

7   Which vegetable's varieties include Nantes, Mignon and Chantenay?

8   Which TV cook has written books including *At Home*, *One Step Ahead* and *Recipe for Life*?

9   What does authentic Parmesan cheese have stamped on its rind?

10 What is a savarin?

Medium

11 What drink is it considered unlucky to toast with in Germany?

12 Traditionally, mozzarella is made from the milk of which animal?

13 What is the main ingredient of the Indian dish aloo chaat?

14 Which German sausage is similar to a black pudding?

15 What is the term given to a side of unsliced bacon?

16 Madagascar produces most of the world's supply of vanilla pods. From which type of plant is vanilla obtained?

17 Appenzeller cheese comes from which country?

18 What is the literal meaning of "brandy"?

19 What type of seeds are used to make a seed cake?

20 Barolo is a wine from which Italian region?

Hard

Answers to QUIZ 168 – Makers and Collectors

1	Clocks and watches	11	Women's hats
2	Matchboxes or their labels	12	Stringed instruments
3	Shoes	13	Beer mats
4	Shipwright	14	Numismatist
5	Arrows	15	Tailoring
6	Philatelist	16	Teddy bears
7	Postcards	17	Cooper
8	Car tax discs	18	Snowdrops
9	Maps	19	Old bond and share certificates
10	Chandler	20	Books

ANSWERS ON PAGE **173**

1   In the TV series, what two items are the staple diet of *The Clangers*?

2   What is a Blenheim Orange?

3   In which year was the film *The Wizard of Oz* originally released?

4   Which Pacific island group has Suva as its capital?

5   For what are the caves at Lascaux in France famous?

6   What is the official language of Iran?

7   Which river flows through Londonderry?

8   Which 1983 Scottish comedy-drama was written by Bill Forsyth?

9   Simon de Montfort, Earl of Leicester, was killed in which battle of 1265?

10   Which Italian city is served by Marco Polo airport?

11   What term is given to a native of Monaco?

12   December 6 is the feast day of which saint?

13   What name is given to a graph showing a normal distribution?

14   What is the name for a church service held in the evening?

15   The artist Roy Lichtenstein (d.1997) was born in which country?

16   Which two of the eight main points of the compass are not used as London postcode areas?

17   Who was the father of the Grand Duchess Anastasia?

18   Euclid established the foundations of which branch of study?

19   Which band had a 1970 hit in the UK with *Make It with You*?

20   Of what is heliophobia a fear?

Easy
Medium
Hard

Answers to QUIZ 169 – Pot Luck

1	*I Hear You Now*	11	Toronto Pearson International Airport
2	Sir Winston Churchill	12	Onomatopoeia
3	St Petersburg	13	Andaman islands
4	Monmouth castle	14	Cold blood
5	Sebastian Coe (Baron Coe)	15	Alison Steadman
6	Crimean War	16	Pig
7	Salvador Dali	17	Albert Finney
8	Joints	18	Bloodstone
9	1950s	19	Persimmon
10	Money given as a tip or present	20	St Paul's Cathedral

Easy

1 Boy George made a guest appearance in which US TV series in 1986?

2 Georgetown University is in which US city?

3 Who had a 2014 hit with *Budapest*?

4 In which county is Royal St George's golf course?

5 St George's is the capital of which Caribbean island?

6 The town of Nuits-Saint-Georges is in which French wine-producing region?

7 What is the name of the scheming musician in George du Maurier's 1894 novel *Trilby*?

8 George of Denmark married which Stuart queen?

9 Which UK Prime Minister was in born in Manchester on January 17, 1863?

10 What is georgette?

11 Which US baseball legend's first names were George Herman?

12 The phrase "George, don't do that", was associated with which comedienne?

13 Who sang *The Ballad of Bonnie and Clyde* in 1967?

14 What relation was singer Rosemary Clooney to actor George Clooney?

15 George C Scott played which US general in a 1970 film of the same name?

16 Which South American country has Georgetown as its capital?

17 Who wrote the play *Arms and the Man*?

18 George W Bush was Governor of which US state before he became President in 2001?

19 Which British architect was one of the main designers of the Georges Pompidou Centre in Paris?

20 Which French writer lived with the composer Chopin?

Answers to QUIZ 170 – Food and Drink

1	Julienne	11	Water
2	Apples	12	Buffalo
3	Whipped cream	13	Potatoes
4	Chocolate	14	Blutwurst
5	Manhattan	15	A flitch
6	Oysters	16	The orchid
7	Carrot	17	Switzerland
8	Mary Berry	18	Burnt wine
9	Parmigiano-Reggiano	19	Caraway
10	A cake	20	Piedmont

ANSWERS ON PAGE 175

1   What forms the staple diet of the orang-utan?

2   Which novel is set around the events of June 16, 1904?

3   Doha is the capital of which Gulf state?

4   Which religion was called Dhamma-vinaya by its founder?

5   On a ship, what is kept in the binnacle?

6   Brixton and Euston are linked by which London Underground line?

7   Which type of butterfly can be grizzled, large or dingy?

8   In Greek mythology, who was the prophetess daughter of King Priam?

9   Are greyhounds classed as scent hounds or sighthounds?

10 Bootham Crescent is a sports stadium in which city?

11 The Simplon Pass links Italy to which country?

12 Which artist released albums titled *Face Value* and *No Jacket Required*?

13 Who wrote the 1937 play *Time and the Conways*?

14 Which group sang *I'd Like to Teach the World to Sing* in 1971?

15 Julio Iglesias played in goal for which junior Spanish team?

16 Of which southern African country is Windhoek the capital?

17 Which former champion figure skater starred as Bibi Dahl in the Bond film *For Your Eyes Only*?

18 Which singer had a 2005 hit with *Crazy Chick*?

19 The Jurassic period occurred during which geological era?

20 What part of the body would a phrenologist study?

Easy

Medium

Hard

Answers to QUIZ 171 – Pot Luck

1	Blue string pudding and green soup	11	Monégasque
2	An apple	12	St Nicholas
3	1939	13	Bell curve
4	Fiji	14	Evensong or Vespers
5	Prehistoric wall paintings	15	USA
6	Farsi	16	NE and S
7	Foyle	17	Nicholas II
8	*Local Hero*	18	Geometry
9	Battle of Evesham	19	Bread
10	Venice	20	Sunlight

Easy

1   Which US astronomer devised a classification system for galaxies in the 1920s?

2   Which essential nutrient is found in wheatgerm oil and leafy vegetables?

3   The incus bone has what common name?

4   Who was the first British woman to go into space?

5   What is the second most abundant element in the Earth's crust?

6   Which unit measures supersonic flight speed?

7   *Varicella* is the medical name for which disease?

8   Which taxonomic group ranks above "genus" and below "order"?

9   If a plant exhibits phototropism, what does it respond to?

10 What inflammation of the larynx and trachea causes a coughing illness in children?

Medium

11 Which unit of electrical current is named after a French physicist?

12 In the Earth's crust, which silvery metallic element is the most abundant metal?

13 What is the brightest star in the night sky?

14 What is the commonest gas in the atmosphere, forming 78% of the air?

15 The infectious disease rubeola is more usually known by what name?

16 Which chemical element has the symbol Rn?

17 How many moons does the planet Venus have?

18 Who was the inventor of the induction motor?

19 What is the small pear-shaped organ situated behind the liver in humans?

20 Where in the body is the supinator muscle?

Hard

Answers to QUIZ 172 – Georges

1	*The A-Team*	11	Babe Ruth
2	Washington DC	12	Joyce Grenfell
3	George Ezra	13	Georgie Fame
4	Kent	14	Aunt
5	Grenada	15	Patton
6	Burgandy	16	Guyana
7	Svengali	17	George Bernard Shaw
8	Anne	18	Texas
9	David Lloyd George (First Earl Lloyd-George of Dwyfor)	19	Richard Rogers (Baron Rogers of Riverside)
10	Fabric	20	George Sand

1   The song *Some Enchanted Evening* features in which musical?

2   Hartford is the capital of which US state?

3   From which Shakespeare play does the line "Never a lender nor a borrower be" come?

4   Which type of Formula 1 tyre is indicated by purple markings?

5   Who was king of England from 978 to 1016?

6   Which actor starred as a psychologist in the 1992 film *Final Analysis*?

7   In 1825, which British scientist discovered benzene?

8   How many inches wide should a cricket wicket be?

9   What term is used to describe any hoofed animal?

10   What is the postcode area code for Wembley Stadium?

11   Who said that he would act as an "honest broker" to deal with the 1878 Balkans crisis?

12   Which monarch bought Buckingham Palace?

13   The plant *Ananas sativus* has what common name?

14   Which horse stopped Red Rum achieving three consecutive Grand National wins?

15   Which sea is the deepest?

16   Which US director was the impetus behind the modern version of London's Globe Theatre?

17   Port Salut is what type of food?

18   What is the Underworld river of oblivion in Greek mythology?

19   Which country lies between Panama and Nicaragua?

20   What is a marionette?

Easy

Medium

Hard

Answers to QUIZ 173 – Pot Luck

1	Fruit	11	Switzerland
2	*Ulysses* (James Joyce)	12	Phil Collins
3	Qatar	13	JB Priestley
4	Buddhism	14	New Seekers
5	The compass	15	Real Madrid Castilla
6	Victoria Line	16	Namibia
7	Skipper	17	Lynn-Holly Johnson
8	Cassandra	18	Charlotte Church
9	Sighthounds	19	Mesozoic
10	York	20	The skull or head

1. Which country shares an island with Indonesia's easternmost province?
2. What is the name of the sea, situated entirely within Turkey, which separates its European and Asian parts?
3. Columbus is the capital of which US state?
4. Which river runs through Lisburn and Belfast?
5. What is the commercial capital and chief port of Yemen?
6. Which oil port of Iraq is situated on the Shatt al-Arab waterway?
7. Podgorica is the capital of which small Balkan state?
8. Which is the largest city on Bulgaria's Black Sea coast?
9. Of which country is Lusaka the capital?
10. Which geographical feature added the "Sylvania" to Pennsylvania?
11. What is the name of the stretch of water between mainland Africa and Madagascar?
12. In which US state is Mount Rushmore?
13. The Summer Isles lie at the mouth of which Scottish loch?

14. Montenegro has a coastline on which sea?
15. What is the largest city in the Middle East?
16. Eleuthera is part of which island group?
17. Which former Belgian colony lies to the south of Rwanda in central Africa?
18. What is the capital of Nepal?
19. Kibo is the highest peak of which mountain?
20. In which ocean are the Falkland Islands?

Answers to QUIZ 174 – Science

1	Hubble	11	Ampere
2	Vitamin E	12	Aluminium
3	Anvil	13	Sirius
4	Helen Sharman	14	Nitrogen
5	Silicon	15	Measles
6	Mach	16	Radon
7	Chickenpox	17	None
8	Family	18	Tesla
9	Light	19	Gall bladder
10	Croup	20	Forearm

1 Yarg cheese originated in which county?

2 Who wrote the screenplay for the film *The Madness of George III*?

3 Which sci-fi TV series was based on novels written by Blake Crouch?

4 What is the more common name for the tropical fish that is also known as rainbow fish or millionfish?

5 Which liquid is used in minimum temperature thermometers?

6 The Tijuana Brass were fronted by which musician?

7 Who directed the 1959 film *Some Like It Hot*?

8 Which group's hits include the 1984 single *I'll Fly for You*?

9 The police drama *Blue Bloods* takes place in which US city?

10 What is the lowest title of the peerage?

11 In the SI system, what is the unit of substance?

12 What is the smallest country in South America?

13 What uniform became a popular clothing choice for children after it was worn by four-year-old Albert Edward, Prince of Wales in 1846?

14 The football team Nagoya Grampus, formerly Grampus Eight, plays in which country?

15 The Clergy House, Alfriston, was the first property to be maintained by which organisation, in 1896?

16 What is an antimacassar?

17 In which county are the neolithic flint mines of Grime's Graves?

18 What is the title of Roald Dahl's book that features Mrs Silver and her pet tortoise, Alfie?

19 Who covered the Deep Purple hit *Hush* in 1996?

20 Which London museum, open from 1988 to 1999, charted the history of cinema and television?

Easy

Medium

Hard

Answers to QUIZ 175 – Pot Luck

1	*South Pacific*	11	Otto von Bismarck
2	Connecticut	12	George III
3	*Hamlet*	13	Pineapple
4	Ultrasoft	14	L'Escargot
5	Ethelred	15	The Caribbean
6	Richard Gere	16	Sam Wanamaker
7	Michael Faraday	17	Cheese
8	Nine	18	Lethe
9	Ungulate	19	Costa Rica
10	HA	20	A puppet

Easy

1 Which is the older of the Williams sisters?

2 In 1977 which controversial Romanian player used a "spaghetti string" racquet?

3 At the London 2012 Olympics who won the women's singles gold medal?

4 Which Italian player received record fines for his behaviour in 2017?

5 The tabloid press gave what nickname to Pete Sampras?

6 Which British tennis player competed in *Strictly Come Dancing* in 2008?

7 Which French player born in 1963 competed in *Celebrity MasterChef* in 2017?

8 Which player achieved the calendar-year Grand Slam in 1962 and 1969?

9 In which year was the Davis Cup founded?

10 Which Grand Slam tournament is the only one not to carry court-side advertising?

Medium

11 On which surface is the Hawk-Eye system not used?

12 Which player was disqualified during the 2012 final at Queen's?

13 Who is known as "The King of Clay"?

14 Who was the first player to win the Wimbledon mens' singles title as a wildcard entry?

15 How many Grand Slam singles titles did Martina Navratilova win?

16 As well as Swiss citizenship, which other country is Roger Federer a citizen of?

17 Who presented the winner's trophy to Virginia Wade at Wimbledon in 1977?

18 Which tennis player appeared in the James Bond film *Octopussy*?

19 Which tennis player won the women's US Open in 2017?

20 In which year was the Eastbourne International tournament first played?

Hard

Answers to QUIZ 176 – Geography

1	Papua New Guinea	11	Mozambique Channel
2	Sea of Marmara	12	South Dakota
3	Ohio	13	Loch Broom
4	Lagan	14	Adriatic
5	Aden	15	Cairo
6	Basra	16	The Bahamas
7	Montenegro	17	Burundi
8	Varna	18	Kathmandu
9	Zambia	19	Kilimanjaro
10	Forests or woods (from the Latin for "forest")	20	South Atlantic Ocean

1   What was the first UK top ten hit for the Boomtown Rats?

2   What is the medical term for a bruise?

3   Which musical trio took their name from characters in the Tintin cartoons?

4   On an Ordnance Survey map, what is indicated by the abbreviation CG?

5   In the 1950 film *Father of the Bride*, who played the bride?

6   What was the original name of Francis Drake's ship *The Golden Hind*?

7   What is the longest river entirely within Spain?

8   The Tagus, Amazon, and Orange rivers all empty into which ocean?

9   Buff Orpington and Plymouth Rock are breed of which animal?

10 The name of which famous diamond means "mountain of light"?

11 What is a pelisse?

12 What is the capital city of Oman?

13 Minervois is a wine-growing region in which country?

14 What instrument measures the current flowing in an electric circuit?

15 In the TV series *Modern Family*, what is the name of Sofia Vergara's character?

16 What is the name of the hero of the play within a play in Shakespeare's *A Midsummer Night's Dream*?

17 Which horse was National Hunt Champion of the Year four times in a row from 1987 to 1990?

18 If you saw the sign *Zimmer Frei* in Austria, what would it mean?

19 Which chef took part in *Strictly Come Dancing* in 2015?

20 What was the name of the rugby stadium in Llanelli that closed in 2008?

Easy

Medium

Hard

Answers to QUIZ 177 – Pot Luck

1	Cornwall	11	The mole
2	Alan Bennett	12	Suriname
3	*Wayward Pines*	13	Sailor suit
4	Guppy	14	Japan
5	Alcohol	15	The National Trust
6	Herb Alpert	16	A piece of cloth put over the back of a chair
7	Billy Wilder	17	Norfolk
8	Spandau Ballet	18	*Esio Trot*
9	New York	19	Kula Shaker
10	Baron	20	Museum of the Moving Image

Easy

1. Who wrote and directed the 2013 series *Dancing on the Edge*?

2. Who played the title role in the 2013 adaptation of Philippa Gregory's *The White Queen*?

3. Which US state is the setting for the series *Jamestown*?

4. What was the title of the 2009 drama series about the Pre-Raphaelite brotherhood?

5. Who played Robin Hood in the 2006 series?

6. Which writer adapted *Pride and Prejudice* for television in 1995?

7. In the series *Game of Thrones*, what is the name of John Bradley's character?

8. Who played the title role in the 2008 BBC adaptation of *Little Dorrit*?

9. In which US state was the series *Boardwalk Empire* set?

10. In the series *Ripper Street*, who played Detective Inspector Edmund Reid?

11. Romola Garai and Ben Whishaw starred in which series set in a newsroom?

Medium

12. Who played D'Artagnan in the 2014 series *The Musketeers*?

13. Uhtred of Bebbanburg is the central character of which series?

14. What was the name of Art Malik's character in the 1984 drama series *The Jewel in the Crown*?

15. In which 1990s drama series did Stella Gonet and Louise Lombard play sisters?

16. What was Mr Hudson's first name in the 1970s series *Upstairs, Downstairs*?

17. Who played Count Ilya Rostov in the 2016 TV adaptation of *War & Peace*?

18. Which actress starred in the 1980s series *The District Nurse*?

19. What is the historical setting for the TV series *Plebs*?

20. Claire Randall and Jamie Fraser are central characters in which series?

Answers to QUIZ 178 – Tennis

Hard

1	Venus	11	Clay
2	Ilie Nastase	12	David Nalbandian
3	Serena Williams	13	Rafael Nadal
4	Fabio Fognini	14	Goran Ivanišević
5	Pistol Pete	15	18
6	Andrew Castle	16	South Africa
7	Henri Leconte	17	Queen Elizabeth II
8	Rod Laver	18	Vijay Amritraj
9	1900	19	Sloane Stephens
10	Wimbledon	20	1974

QUIZ 181 – Pot Luck

ANSWERS ON PAGE **183**

1   Which song gave the Beatles their last US number one?

2   In which decade of the 20th century was Sir Sean Connery born?

3   Which racing circuit has a bend called Paddock?

4   Who was Oscar-nominated for his role as Mitch Leary in the 1993 film *In the Line of Fire*?

5   In the 1973 film, what was the name of *The Biggest Dog in the World*?

6   Which sea lies between the Aral Sea and the Black Sea?

7   Who starred as Mountie Benton Fraser in the TV series *Due South*?

8   "Knock at the door" is the traditional bingo call for which number?

9   In which sport do boys compete for the Drysdale Cup?

10 Which river runs through Preston in Lancashire?

11 What is the postcode area code for the British Forces Post Office?

12 What is an anchorite?

13 The food pipe or gullet in vertebrates is also known by what Greek word?

14 In Australian football, how many players are there on a team?

15 What is the main ingredient of food served *alle vongole*?

16 The panama hat originates from which country?

17 The skeleton of which species of dinosaur was on display in the London Natural History Museum until it was replaced in 2017?

18 Who played the title role in the TV series *Lou Grant*?

19 What is the name of the princess often saved by Mario in the video games series?

20 Whom did Edmund Ironsides succeed to the English throne?

Easy / Medium / Hard

Answers to QUIZ 179 – Pot Luck

1	*Like Clockwork*	11	A cloak
2	Contusion	12	Muscat
3	Thompson Twins	13	France
4	Cattle grid	14	Ammeter
5	Elizabeth Taylor	15	Gloria Delgado-Pritchett
6	*Pelican*	16	Pyramus
7	Ebro	17	Desert Orchid
8	Atlantic	18	Room available/vacancies
9	Chicken	19	Ainsley Harriott
10	Koh-I-noor	20	Stradey Park

1 Which Impressionist artist painted *Luncheon of the Boating Party* in 1880-81?

2 Who composed *La Mer* in the early 1900s?

3 For which instrument did Johann Sebastian Bach compose the *Goldberg Variations*?

4 What was the nationality of portrait painter John Millais (b.1829)?

5 For what is a sordino used in music?

6 What is meant by the Italian musical term "allegro molto"?

7 Who painted *The Yellow Chair* (1888)?

8 Which low-toned brass instrument's name is Latin for "trumpet"?

9 Who was employed by Charles I to paint the ceiling of the Banqueting House in London?

10 Which surrealist artist was born in Lessines, Belgium in 1898?

11 *Cavatina* by Stanley Myers was written for which instrument?

12 Which French artist painted *Still Life with Cherub* in 1895?

13 With whom did Kurt Weill collaborate on *The Threepenny Opera*?

14 Which Dutch artist (b.1872) co-founded the De Stijl art movement?

15 The 1942 piece of music entitled *Sabre Dance* was written by which composer?

16 What is the term given to a very deep operatic voice?

17 In which century was Paul Gauguin born?

18 What type of note, used as an embellishment is usually smaller than the standard notes on a stave?

19 Which Spanish artist published a series of prints called *Los Caprichos*?

20 Composed in 1868, what was Edvard Grieg's only completed concerto?

Easy

Medium

Hard

Answers to QUIZ 180 – Television Costume Drama

1	Stephen Poliakoff	11	*The Hour*
2	Rebecca Ferguson	12	Luke Pasqualino
3	Virginia	13	*The Last Kingdom*
4	*Desperate Romantics*	14	Hari Kumar
5	Jonas Armstrong	15	*The House of Eliott*
6	Andrew Davies	16	Angus
7	Samwell Tarly	17	Adrian Edmondson
8	Claire Foy	18	Nerys Hughes
9	New Jersey	19	Ancient Rome
10	Matthew Macfadyen	20	*Outlander*

1   The Winter Palace is located in which Russian city?

2   What is the lengthwise support along the base of a ship called?

3   Which West African country was formerly called French Sudan?

4   Mother Shipton's Cave is near which North Yorkshire town?

5   Why did the catfish get its name?

6   Which US peninsula, on the Atlantic coast, is shaped like a fish hook?

7   Which Greek goddess is often depicted with a greyhound at her side?

8   On which island can the remains of Knossos be found?

9   Which birthstone is linked to April?

10   Which actress starred in the BBC TV series *Sensitive Skin*?

11   Which Paul Desmond jazz composition was made famous by Dave Brubeck?

12   What was the name of the treaty that ended the War of Spanish Succession?

13   In the *Lord of the Rings*, who was killed by orcs on Amon Hen, after trying to take the ring from Frodo?

14   Which warbler shares its name with a town in the south-east of England?

15   In which decade was cricket's first World Cup Final played?

16   What were victors given in the ancient Olympics?

17   In the periodic table, which element has the atomic number 7?

18   What is another name for the belladonna lily?

19   What is the capital of the Canadian province of Alberta?

20   Which actor starred in the 2016 film *The Comedian*?

Easy

Medium

Hard

Answers to QUIZ 181 – Pot Luck

1	*The Long and Winding Road*	11	BF
2	1930s	12	A recluse
3	Brands Hatch	13	Oesophagus
4	John Malkovich	14	18
5	Digby	15	Clams
6	Caspian Sea	16	Ecuador
7	Paul Gross	17	Diplodocus
8	Four	18	Ed Asner
9	Squash	19	Princess Peach
10	Ribble	20	Ethelred the Unready

Easy

1   Which UK tabloid newspaper published its first edition in 1986 and its last in 1995?

2   What name did the Post Office Group adopt from 2001 to 2002 which was then changed to "Royal Mail PLC"?

3   What was the name of the first Russian satellite, launched in 1957?

4   From which plastic material were early phones made?

5   Which letter is between X and V on a standard keyboard?

6   What is the name of the large radiocommunications site on the Lizard peninsula in Cornwall?

7   What is the first name of the inventor of the Morse Code?

8   What did the BBC's *The Light Programme* change its name to in 1967?

9   What term, originating from compositing, is given to the spacing between lines of type on a document?

Medium

10 In which year was the Penny Post established in Britain?

11 On which network was the first mobile phone call made in Britain?

12 Which English city's public telephone boxes were originally all painted cream rather than red?

13 Who was the first director-general of the BBC, who had an annual series of lectures named after him?

14 What term is given to the title block of a newspaper or periodical?

15 In which year did John Logie Baird first transmit television in colour?

16 Radio 1 began broadcasting in which year?

17 What was the first name of radio pioneer Marconi?

18 From which building did the BBC make the first public television transmissions?

19 In which year was the first mobile phone call made in Britain?

20 In which year did ITV start broadcasting?

Hard

Answers to QUIZ 182 – Art and Music

1	Pierre-Auguste Renoir	11	Guitar
2	Claude Debussy	12	Cézanne
3	Harpsichord	13	Bertolt Brecht
4	English	14	Piet Mondrian
5	Muffling sound	15	Aram Khachaturian
6	Very fast	16	Basso profundo
7	Vincent Van Gogh	17	19th century
8	Tuba	18	Grace note
9	Rubens	19	Francisco Goya
10	René Magritte	20	*Piano Concerto in A Minor*

1   On an Ordnance Survey map, what is indicated by a blue "x" with a horizontal line joining the top two points?

2   What variety of pleasure-seeking is named for a Greek philosopher born on Samos in 341BC?

3   How many yards is the penalty spot from a soccer goal line?

4   *Barwick Green* is the signature tune to which long-running drama?

5   Which common vegetable was used by Johann Gregor Mendel to formulate his theories on genetics?

6   In which town is the Royal Agricultural University located?

7   In which city is Ben Gurion airport?

8   David Sylvian was the lead singer with which band?

9   Into which sea does the river Dnieper flow?

10   What term is given to a sculpture where the figures project slightly from the surface?

11   On which river does the city of Bordeaux stand?

12   Who starred as Janet, alongside Dame Judi Dench, in the 2004 film *Ladies in Lavender*?

13   In relation to vehicles, what is SORN?

14   In which sport did Nathan Robertson and Gail Emms win silver medals at the 2004 Olympic Games?

15   When was British Gas privatised?

16   Of which Balkan country is Ljubljana the capital?

17   Of what is ideophobia a fear?

18   What was the nickname of Viscount Townshend, who popularised crop rotation?

19   Which Canadian region is at the mouth of the St Lawrence river?

20   "Goodbye Emil, my trusted friend, We've known each other since we were nine or ten" is a lyric from which song?

Answers to QUIZ 183 – Pot Luck

1	St Petersburg	11	Take Five
2	Keel	12	Treaty of Utrecht
3	Mali	13	Boromir
4	Knaresborough	14	Dartford warbler
5	It has whiskers	15	1970s
6	Cape Cod	16	Head garland of wild olive leaves
7	Diana	17	Nitrogen
8	Crete	18	Amaryllis
9	Diamond	19	Edmonton
10	Joanna Lumley	20	Robert De Niro

1 Which landmark bears the inscription "Give me your tired, your poor, your huddled masses, yearning to breathe free"?

2 In which museum would you see Constable's *The Hay Wain*?

3 In which city are the Potemkin Steps located?

4 Which Underground line connects Marble Arch with Oxford Circus?

5 If you were at the foot of Mt Parnassus, which historic seat of the Pythia would you be visiting?

6 Which English stately home has the largest hedge maze in Britain within its gardens?

7 The Rock of Cashel is located in which Irish county?

8 A statue of which film star was unveiled in Leicester Square in 1979?

9 Which Welsh village was created by Sir Clough Williams Ellis?

10 On which thoroughfare is Grauman's Chinese Theater?

11 Which Wiltshire village is the site of an ancient stone ring?

12 Which octagonal building in Florence has sculpted bronze doors nicknamed the "Doors of Paradise"?

13 The Castle of Good Hope is a landmark in which city?

14 In which Hampshire town is there a submarine museum?

15 The Forth Rail Bridge at South Queensferry in Scotland is what type of bridge?

16 What are the Beefeaters at the Tower of London more properly called?

17 The Petrified Forest National Park is situated in which US state?

18 Opened in 1899, the Palace Pier is in which English south coast resort?

19 In which county is Buckfast Abbey?

20 Which Scottish village is nicknamed "The Osprey Village"?

Answers to QUIZ 184 – Communications

1	*Today*	11	Vodafone
2	Consignia	12	Kingston-upon-Hull
3	*Sputnik 1*	13	John Reith (Baron Reith)
4	Bakelite	14	Masthead
5	C	15	1928
6	Goonhilly	16	1967
7	Samuel	17	Guglielmo
8	Radio 2	18	Alexandra Palace
9	Leading	19	1985
10	1840	20	1955

QUIZ 187 – Pot Luck

ANSWERS ON PAGE 189

1   Which plant genus includes swede and mustard?

2   Who recorded the 1977 single *Lido Shuffle*?

3   Which letter of the alphabet is used to describe a soft lead pencil?

4   If you were holidaying in the resort of Praia da Rocha, where would you be?

5   What is the name of Gemma Chan's character in the TV series *Humans*?

6   Which country is ruled jointly by the President of France and the Bishop of Urgel?

7   Is Greenland ahead of or behind Greenwich Mean Time?

8   What type of bird is a boobook?

9   Who presented the TV series *Map Man*?

10 Which poet wrote that "In spring, a young man's fancy lightly turns to thoughts of love"?

11 What is the Scottish Gaelic name for Scotland?

12 1983's *Is There Something I Should Know?* was the first number one hit for which band?

13 Who formulated his quantum theory in 1900?

14 Named British Fashion designer of the year in 1987, who was signed up by the Givenchy label in 1995?

15 What is a carrick bend?

16 Whose backing group were The Dreamers?

17 On which river does Salisbury stand?

18 Which two Argentinian footballers were bought by Tottenham Hotspur after the 1978 FIFA World Cup?

19 In Jane Austen's *Emma*, to whom is Emma finally wed?

20 What is the state capital of Wisconsin?

Answers to QUIZ 185 – Pot Luck

1	Picnic site	11	Garonne
2	Epicureanism	12	Dame Maggie Smith
3	12	13	Statutory off-road notification
4	*The Archers*	14	Badminton
5	The pea	15	1986
6	Cirencester	16	Slovenia
7	Tel Aviv	17	Ideas
8	Japan	18	Turnip Townshend
9	Black Sea	19	Newfoundland
10	Bas-relief	20	*Seasons in the Sun*

187

ANSWERS ON PAGE 190

Easy

1 A Burmese python is usually what colour?

2 Where on a horse is the coffin joint?

3 A pangolin is what type of creature?

4 Which crab moves forward instead of sideways?

5 What type of animal is a Scottish Blackface?

6 How many chambers are there in a crocodile's heart?

7 What do frogs have in their mouths that toads do not?

8 The phalanger is another name for which marsupial?

9 What is the collective noun for a group of foxes?

10 Which is the largest land carnivore in Britain?

11 What kind of creature is a Queen Alexandra's Birdwing?

Medium

12 In October 1999, the frozen body of what kind of extinct creature was discovered in Siberia?

13 Which fish has the scientific name *Xiphias gladius*?

14 Beetles belong to which order of insect?

15 Which birds of the genus *Motacilla* have a characteristic bobbing movement?

16 What is the only variety of porpoise native to British waters?

17 What is a male alligator called?

18 The Kodiak bear is found in which US state?

19 Which non-native rodent began breeding in the wild in Britain after a number escaped from a private collection in Tring in the early 1900s?

20 In the animal kingdom, what are the four groups that make up the ape family?

Hard

Answers to QUIZ 186 – Tourist Attractions

1	Statue of Liberty	11	Avebury
2	National Gallery	12	The Baptistery
3	Odessa	13	Cape Town
4	Central Line	14	Gosport
5	The Oracle at Delphi	15	Cantilever
6	Longleat	16	Yeomen Warders
7	County Tipperary	17	Arizona
8	Sir Charlie Chaplin	18	Brighton
9	Portmeirion	19	Devon
10	Hollywood Boulevard	20	Boat of Garten

ANSWERS ON PAGE **191**

1 Which king of England was married twice, both times to countesses called Isabella?

2 Which airport is located at Yeadon?

3 Who wrote the 1994 novel *Disclosure*?

4 Who were beaten by Todd Woodbridge and Mark Woodforde in the 1996 men's Olympics doubles?

5 Which constellation is named after Andromeda's mother?

6 The character of Magwitch features in which 1861 novel?

7 What is the official language of Benin?

8 What is a simple Indian loincloth associated with Gandhi?

9 At what age did Janet Jackson release her first album?

10 Who succeeded Warren G Harding as US president?

11 What was the value of a Rugby Union try prior to 1971?

12 What is the English translation of the Italian word *vespa*?

13 In which city were the 1960 Olympic Games held?

14 Of which play did a critic once write: "this is a play in which nothing happens, twice"?

15 Who wrote the *Gormenghast* trilogy?

16 Which New Zealand city is the principal city of Otago province?

17 A Rusty Nail cocktail is a mixture of Scotch and which other alcoholic drink?

18 Who sang the theme tune to the James Bond film *GoldenEye*?

19 Which team plays at The Hawthorns?

20 Who was Prime Minister of Greece from 2009 to 2011?

Easy

Medium

Hard

Answers to QUIZ 187 – Pot Luck

1	Brassica	11	Alba
2	Boz Scaggs	12	Duran Duran
3	B	13	Max Planck
4	Portugal	14	John Galliano
5	Mia	15	Knot
6	Andorra	16	Freddie (Garrity)
7	Behind	17	Avon
8	Owl	18	Osvaldo Ardiles and Ricky Villa
9	Nicholas Crane	19	George Knightley
10	Alfred, Lord Tennyson	20	Madison

Easy

1   Which actress was Oscar-nominated for her starring role in the 1997 film *Mrs Brown*?

2   Where was Queen Victoria born...?

3   ...and in which year?

4   In which year did Queen Victoria die...?

5   ...and where was she buried?

6   What was Queen Victoria's birth name?

7   How old was Victoria when she became Queen?

8   Who was Victoria's first Prime Minister and mentor?

9   Which actress portrayed Queen Victoria in the ITV drama *Victoria*?

10 How many children did Queen Victoria have?

11 What was the name of her youngest child?

12 What was the name of her firstborn child?

Medium

13 Which Prime Minister made Victoria Empress of India...?

14 ...and in which year?

15 What was the name of the king who preceded Queen Victoria?

16 The Victoria Cross for gallantry was instituted during which war?

17 Which Prince of Saxe-Coburg and Gotha did Queen Victoria marry?

18 What was the name of her residence on the Isle of Wight?

19 Who was her eldest son and successor?

20 Which form of transport did she first use in 1842?

Hard

1. Which actress starred in the film *Baby Boom*?

2. Who is the husband of Sita, in a Hindu epic poem?

3. An unpredictable but high-impact event is given the name of which bird?

4. In which city was Robert Scott's vessel, *Discovery*, built?

5. Which decade saw the first FA Cup Final at Wembley?

6. Subtitled "a radio parlour game", which show was hosted by Stewart MacPherson, Gilbert Harding and finally Kenneth Horne?

7. What Latin name is given to a dark round room for projecting a landscape?

8. Who wrote the 1947 novel *Whisky Galore*?

9. In which city is Europe's oldest university?

10. What is the common term for calcium oxide?

11. What French term is given to a fatal blow?

12. In which English village is the Fox Talbot museum?

13. By what name is singer Stuart Goddard better known?

14. Boston Crab is a term used in which sport?

15. What is a blintze?

16. Of what is Sinology the study?

17. Who wrote the 1912 play *Androcles and the Lion*?

18. Which West African country has a name that means "land of honest men"?

19. Which body of water surrounds the island of Heligoland?

20. Who had a hit in 1983 with *Love of the Common People*?

Easy

Medium

Hard

Answers to QUIZ 189 – Pot Luck

1	King John	11	Three points
2	Leeds Bradford Airport	12	Wasp
3	Michael Crichton	13	Rome
4	Tim Henman and Neil Broad	14	*Waiting for Godot*
5	Cassiopeia	15	Mervyn Peake
6	*Great Expectations*	16	Dunedin
7	French	17	Drambuie®
8	Dhoti	18	Tina Turner
9	16	19	West Bromwich Albion
10	Calvin Coolidge	20	George Papandreou

ANSWERS ON PAGE **194**

1 What name is given to the visible electric discharge seen at a plane's wingtips or around the tops of ships' masts, caused by static electricity in the atmosphere?

2 Which UK airport was the first to have its own railway station?

3 What is the name of the junction on London's A406 North Circular Road with the A5 Edgware Road?

4 What is the name of the Australian transcontinental rail service which runs between Perth and Sydney?

5 Which airport has the code HND?

6 The navigational products company TomTom was founded in which country?

7 In relation to cars, what do the initials SUV stand for?

8 What is the name of the train which shares a similar name to a major mountain range found in America and Canada?

9 In which year did the M6 toll road open?

10 On a ship, which officer is in charge of crew and equipment?

11 What is the name of the famously luxurious South African train that runs between Pretoria and Cape Town?

12 What is the function of scuppers on ships?

13 Which car manufacturer produces the Baleno?

14 Bill Bryson described his attempts to walk which long-distance footpath in *A Walk in the Woods*?

15 What is the name of the long-distance Indian train service operated by Indian Railways?

16 The highest railway station in Europe is in which country?

17 What term is given to the fee levied on a vessel entering a port?

18 In which county is the ferry port of Heysham?

19 Which Welsh railway runs between Tywyn Wharf and Nant Gwernol?

20 Opened in 2004, what is the name of the bridge that crosses the Tarn Valley in southern France?

Answers to QUIZ 190 – Queen Victoria

1	Dame Judi Dench	11	Princess Beatrice
2	Kensington Palace, London	12	Victoria
3	1819	13	Benjamin Disraeli (First Earl of Beaconsfield)
4	1901	14	1876
5	Frogmore, Windsor	15	William IV
6	Alexandrina Victoria	16	The Crimean War
7	18	17	Prince Albert
8	Lord Melbourne	18	Osborne House
9	Jenna Coleman	19	Edward VII
10	Nine	20	Train

1 O'Hare airport serves which American city?

2 In the TV Series *Are You Being Served*, which actor played Mr Lucas?

3 Which sauce has a name that means "hunter" in French?

4 What does a lexicographer study or create?

5 In which decade was Princeton university founded?

6 On which Canadian island is the city of Victoria?

7 Who portrayed Lara Croft on screen in the 2018 film *Tomb Raider*?

8 What is the legal term for a written declaration?

9 In which decade was the first oil well discovered in the USA?

10 Who wrote the 1939 novel *Tropic of Capricorn*?

11 What term is given to the point in an orbit that is most distant from the body being orbited?

12 What is a young shark called?

13 What is the dialling code for Norwich?

14 In which Shakespeare play does a forest apparently move?

15 The Royal Society was founded during the reign of which monarch?

16 What type of bird is a pochard?

17 In which country is the Curragh racecourse?

18 What sport is featured in the 1961 film *The Hustler*?

19 In which country does Skoda have its headquarters?

20 What is copra?

Easy

Medium

Hard

Answers to QUIZ 191 – Pot Luck

1	Diane Keaton	11	*Coup de grâce*
2	Rama	12	Lacock
3	Black swan	13	Adam Ant
4	Dundee	14	Wrestling
5	1920s	15	A pancake
6	*Twenty Questions*	16	The Chinese
7	Camera obscura	17	George Bernard Shaw
8	Sir Compton Mackenzie	18	Burkina Faso
9	Bologna	19	The North Sea
10	Lime	20	Paul Young

ANSWERS ON PAGE 196

1   Who won the FIFA World Player of the Year three times between 1998 and 2003?

2   Which region of northern France has Lille as its prefecture?

3   What was the name of the rural guerrillas of the French wartime Resistance movement?

4   In which village can you visit Claude Monet's house and garden?

5   Which grape from the Languedoc-Roussillon area can be used to make dry or dessert wines?

6   In the 12th century, who was Heloise's lover?

7   Which region borders Germany and Switzerland?

8   Which variety of steak is named after a French writer and diplomat?

9   What name is given to a municipal subdivision of a large city, especially Paris?

10 Cannes and Saint-Tropez are on what shore area?

11 Which Channel port is at the mouth of the River Seine?

12 What are the initials of the French railway system?

13 The Prix de l'Arc de Triomphe takes place at which racecourse?

14 Who was Prime Minister of France from 1906 to 1909 and 1917 to 1920?

15 The dish boeuf bourguignon originates from which area of France?

16 Which of the Channel Islands is nearest to France?

17 Who was President of France from 1981 to 1995?

18 Which town of northern France is famous for its tapestry weaving?

19 On which river are Blois, Tours and Orléans?

20 Which city in Limousin is famous for its porcelain?

Answers to QUIZ 192 – On the Move

1	St Elmo's fire	11	*Blue Train*
2	Gatwick	12	To drain away water
3	Staples Corner	13	Suzuki
4	Indian Pacific	14	Appalachian Trail
5	Tokyo	15	Rajdhani Express
6	The Netherlands	16	Switzerland
7	Sport utility vehicle	17	Groundage
8	Rocky Mountaineer	18	Lancashire
9	2003	19	Talyllyn Railway
10	Boatswain/bosun	20	Millau Viaduct

1 Which 1980s-90s band sang *Martha's Harbour*?

2 Who was Odin's wife in Norse mythology?

3 Who was *Kung Fu Fighting* at the top of the charts in 1974?

4 In March 2004, which British boxer won the WBF Heavyweight title, his first professional title?

5 Which type of rock takes its name from the Latin word *granum*, meaning "grained"?

6 Which snooker player won the 2018 Masters?

7 In which Scottish city is the Citizens Theatre?

8 What is the state capital of Oregon?

9 What is the name of Adrian Mole's girlfriend?

10 Where is the harbour of the Golden Horn?

11 For which office does an MP apply to resign from the House of Commons?

12 Which actor wrote, directed and starred in the 2005 film *Good Night, and Good Luck*?

13 William of Wykeham (b.1324) was Bishop of which city before becoming Chancellor of England?

14 Who wrote *The Descent of Man* in 1871?

15 What term describes the properties of a solid object in motion?

16 Which bird of prey has a Montagu's species?

17 In which state is the ski resort of Aspen?

18 Which major road is carried by the Kessock Bridge?

19 Which book of the Bible shares its name with a book by Leon Uris?

20 Tin denotes which wedding anniversary?

Answers to QUIZ 193 – Pot Luck

1	Chicago	11	Apogee
2	Trevor Bannister	12	Pup
3	Chasseur	13	01603
4	A dictionary	14	*Macbeth*
5	1740s (1746)	15	Charles II
6	Vancouver Island	16	Duck
7	Alicia Vikander	17	Ireland
8	Affidavit	18	Pool
9	1850s (1859)	19	Czech Republic
10	Henry Miller	20	The dried kernel of the coconut

Easy

1   The Crab Nebula is situated in which constellation?

2   Which is the nearest star system to our solar system?

3   In diameter, approximately how many times larger than the Moon is the Earth?

4   Which planet is the least dense?

5   What is the name of the largest moon of Neptune?

6   In June 1983, who became the first American woman in space?

7   Which planet's rings were discovered in 1979?

8   Who was the first American to orbit the Earth?

9   For what do the letters SETI stand?

10 In relation to distance measurement in the solar system, what is an AU?

11 Which planet has moons called Europa and Ganymede amongst others?

12 Which is the second-largest planet in the solar system?

13 Since the final space shuttle mission, what has been the method of transport for astronauts travelling to and from the International Space Station?

Medium

14 What is the Russian equivalent of NASA?

15 What term is given to the science of space flight?

16 What was Tim Peake's occupation immediately before becoming an astronaut?

17 In which year was the Hubble Space Telescope launched?

18 Of which planet are Rhea and Phoebe satellites?

19 Who wrote the 2013 book *An Astronaut's Guide to Life on Earth*?

20 What feature of the night sky is also called the Via Lactea?

Hard

Answers to QUIZ 194 – France

1	Zinedine Zidane	11	Le Havre
2	Hauts-de-France	12	SNCF
3	Maquis	13	Longchamp
4	Giverny	14	Georges Clemenceau
5	Grenache	15	Burgundy
6	Abelard	16	Alderney
7	Alsace	17	François Mitterand
8	Chateaubriand	18	Arras
9	Arrondissement	19	Loire
10	Côte d'Azur (French Riviera)	20	Limoges

1 What is the basic unit of currency in China?

2 What nationality was the mathematician Leonhard Euler?

3 Sir Alex Ferguson managed which two European Cup Winners' Cup winners?

4 In which part of the human body is the hypothalamus located?

5 Which variety of Chinese is spoken in Hong Kong?

6 What is the postcode area code for Windsor Castle?

7 Of which Canadian province is Halifax the capital?

8 What is the meaning of the Japanese word "judo"?

9 What is the fourth book of the Old Testament?

10 Which actress starred as Nora Walker in the TV series *Brothers & Sisters*?

11 Apiphobia is a fear of what?

12 Which town is served by an airport that was originally opened as RAF Hurn?

13 Who wrote the music and lyrics for *Guys and Dolls*?

14 Which Swiss town is famous for its jazz festival?

15 *Lipstick, Powder and Paint* was a hit for which singer in 1985?

16 What is the traditional bingo call for the number 75?

17 What kind of acid is normally used in a car battery?

18 In which century was Sir Isaac Newton born?

19 What is mixed with cement to make concrete?

20 What Russian word, originally used in the 1980s, describes the policy of making government more open and democratic?

Easy

Medium

Hard

Answers to QUIZ 195 – Pot Luck

1	All About Eve	11	Chiltern Hundreds
2	Freya (or Frigg)	12	George Clooney
3	Carl Douglas	13	Winchester
4	Audley Harrison	14	Charles Darwin
5	Granite	15	Dynamics/kinetics
6	Mark Allen	16	Harrier
7	Glasgow	17	Colorado
8	Salem	18	A9
9	Pandora	19	Exodus
10	Istanbul	20	Tenth

Easy

1   Which girl's name was a single by Fleetwood Mac in 1976?

2   Which band's frontman is also a commercial pilot and international fencer?

3   Who sang the theme tune to the 2006 film *Casino Royale*?

4   Thom Yorke is the frontman for which band?

5   What was the birth name of Meat Loaf?

6   What are the first names of the Van Halen brothers?

7   Muse hail from which Devonshire seaside town?

8   What was the title of Stiltskin's only UK chart-topper in 1994?

9   Who is U2's drummer?

10 *A Beautiful Lie* and *This Is War* are albums by which band?

Medium

11 Who was the guitarist with Led Zeppelin?

12 What was the title of Rush's only UK top twenty single?

13 The 1998 song *Iris* was recorded by which American band?

14 Which group had a hit album in 1982 with *Love Over Gold*?

15 Which founding member of Deep Purple was the guitarist with Rainbow?

16 Brandon Flowers is the lead singer of which band?

17 Anthony Kiedis is a founder member of which rock band?

18 *Waiting for a Girl like You* was a hit for which group in 1981?

19 As of 2018, which song by Scorpions holds the record for the best-selling single by a German artist?

20 Kelly Jones is the lead singer with which band?

Hard

Answers to QUIZ 196 – Space

1	Taurus	11	Jupiter
2	Alpha Centauri	12	Saturn
3	Four	13	Soyuz rocket
4	Saturn	14	Roscosmos
5	Triton	15	Astronautics
6	Sally Ride	16	Test pilot
7	Jupiter	17	1990
8	John Glenn	18	Saturn
9	Search for Extra Terrestrial Intelligence	19	Chris Hadfield
10	Astronomical Unit	20	The Milky Way

1   What is the traditional women's outfit worn for Scottish country dancing?

2   What is the sixth letter of the Greek alphabet?

3   Opened in 1761, which was Britain's first wholly artificial canal?

4   From which island does Marsala wine originate?

5   Whose albums include *The Soul Sessions* and *Mind Body & Soul*?

6   What was the title of the 1997 thriller starring Clint Eastwood and Gene Hackman?

7   Which circuit hosted the Formula 1 German Grand Prix in 2018?

8   Which fruit is Spain's national symbol?

9   What is the English name of the walkway between the Doge's Palace and the old prisons in Venice?

10 What solid figure is defined by having every point on its surface equidistant from its centre?

11 Which name is used as a signature by the Archbishop of York?

12 How old did women have to be to vote in the UK in 1918?

13 Who recorded the 1988 single *Walk the Dinosaur*?

14 On which motorway is the highest point of the UK motorway network?

15 Which town is the administrative centre for Moray in Scotland?

16 Who was shot and killed by John Bellingham in 1812?

17 Which Manchester TV studio became a tourist attraction in the 1980s?

18 Finish and browning are used in which building trade?

19 What type of stone is the Star of India?

20 Which kind of prepared grease is used to waterproof leather?

Easy

Medium

Hard

Answers to QUIZ 197 – Pot Luck

1	Yuan	11	Bees
2	Swiss	12	Bournemouth
3	Aberdeen and Manchester United	13	Frank Loesser
4	The brain	14	Montreux
5	Cantonese	15	Shakin' Stevens
6	SL	16	Strive and strive
7	Nova Scotia	17	Sulphuric
8	Gentle way	18	17th century
9	Numbers	19	Aggregate
10	Sally Field	20	*Glasnost*

1 Ataturk airport serves which city?

2 Baccili microbes have what shape?

3 Cagliari is the main town on which island?

4 "Alluvial" describes what type of soil?

5 Baedecker guides cover which subject?

6 Chichen Itza is an archaeological site in which country?

7 Abigail was the wife of which Old Testament king, according to the book of Samuel?

8 *Ballet Shoes* was a 1936 novel by which author?

9 Cardamom belongs to which family of spices?

10 Amharic is an official language of which country?

11 Benedict Cumberbatch starred in a 2018 TV adaptation of which series of novels by Edward St Aubyn?

12 Caligula succeeded which Roman emperor?

13 Actaeon was turned into what type of creature, in Greek mythology?

14 Benghazi is the second-largest city in which country?

15 Chamonix hosted the Winter Olympics in which year?

16 Alchemists tried to turn what substances into gold?

17 Bergamot is what type of fruit?

18 Chattanooga is in which US state?

19 *Almira* (1705) was the first opera by which composer?

20 Byron Bay is a coastal town in which country?

Easy · *Medium* · *Hard*

Answers to QUIZ 198 – Rock Music

1	Rhiannon	11	Jimmy Page
2	Iron Maiden (Bruce Dickinson)	12	*Spirit of Radio*
3	Chris Cornell	13	Goo Goo Dolls
4	Radiohead	14	Dire Straits
5	Marvin Lee Aday	15	Ritchie Blackmore
6	Eddie and Alex	16	The Killers
7	Teignmouth	17	Red Hot Chili Peppers
8	*Inside*	18	Foreigner
9	Larry Mullin Jr	19	*Wind of Change*
10	Thirty Seconds to Mars	20	Stereophonics

QUIZ 201 – Pot Luck

ANSWERS ON PAGE 203

1 What was the title of the spin-off from the TV series *Bewitched*, the name of Darrin and Samantha's daughter?

2 On an Ordnance Survey map (Explorer and Landranger series), what is the interval between contour lines?

3 Which bird became extinct in 1681?

4 In which decade of the 20th century was Jack Nicklaus born?

5 What type of fabric is corduroy?

6 What is the name of the pink Nintendo® game character who has the ability to inhale enemies and gain their abilities?

7 Who wrote the screenplay for *2001: A Space Odyssey*?

8 In 1962, which sports car model was introduced by Lotus?

9 Who was the best-selling author of *Patriot Games* and *The Hunt for Red October*?

10 Who is the Roman deity of beginnings and endings?

11 Bonnie Tyler's *Holding Out for a Hero* featured on the soundtrack to which 1984 film?

12 Carillon is a popular branch of what pursuit?

13 What is a cheongsam?

14 Who directed the 1980 film *Raging Bull*?

15 Of what is hypnophobia a fear?

16 In which alphabet is the Bulgarian language written?

17 What kind of nut is used to make noisette?

18 Panama has a land border with which South American country?

19 Concorde and Louise Bonne are types of which fruit?

20 Which 2013-15 sci-fi series starring Dean Norris was based on a book by Stephen King?

Easy

Medium

Hard

Answers to QUIZ 199 – Pot Luck

1	Dress with a tartan sash	11	Ebor
2	Zeta	12	30
3	Bridgewater Canal	13	Was Not Was
4	Sicily	14	M62
5	Joss Stone	15	Elgin
6	*Absolute Power*	16	Spencer Perceval, UK Prime Minister
7	Hockenheimring	17	Granada
8	Pomegranate	18	Plastering
9	Bridge of Sighs	19	Sapphire
10	A sphere	20	Dubbin

Easy

1   Who began his first term as Ireland's Taoiseach in 1979?

2   In which year did the National Theatre open on the South Bank?

3   Introduced in 1972, what was the Sinclair Executive?

4   Which actor (b.1889) died on Christmas Day in 1977?

5   In the US, who served as both Vice President and President in the 1970s without being elected to either office?

6   On which date in 1971 did decimalisation happen in the UK?

7   In 1971, which car manufacturer was put into liquidation?

8   Who was appointed "Minister for Drought" in 1976?

9   Which board game first sold in 1970 also went by the name *Which Witch?*, with a later version being called *Ghost Castle*?

10 Which British golfer won the US Open in 1970?

Medium

11 Who was made Poet Laureate in 1972?

12 The Soviet Union invaded which country in 1979?

13 In 1971, workers in which sector went on strike in the UK for the first time?

14 Which chain opened its first UK restaurant in Woolwich in November 1974?

15 Which team won the FA cup in 1976?

16 Who became Archbishop of Canterbury in 1974?

17 In which year was the first of the *Star Wars* films released?

18 What was heard on Radio 4 for the first time in the UK in June 1975?

19 Which former monarch died on May 28, 1972?

20 Why did the Cambridge crew lose the Boat Race in 1978?

Hard

Answers to QUIZ 200 – ABC

1	Istanbul	11	*Patrick Melrose*
2	Rods	12	Tiberius
3	Sardinia	13	A stag
4	River sediment	14	Libya
5	Travel	15	1924
6	Mexico	16	Base metals
7	David	17	Citrus
8	Noel Streatfeild	18	Tennessee
9	Ginger	19	George Frederick Handel
10	Ethiopia	20	Australia

1 What is added to icing sugar to make royal icing?

2 Who is the patron saint of tax officials?

3 Destiny Hope are the real first names of which singer (b.1992)?

4 What is the English translation of the name of the city of Buenos Aires?

5 Whose law states that the pressure and volume of a gas are inversely proportional at constant temperature?

6 Which famous sporting venue has the postcode M16 0RA?

7 Which North Kent coastal resort is located approximately eight miles north of Canterbury?

8 Glen Cova and Malling Joy are types of which fruit?

9 In which century was Mozart born?

10 Which Christian statement of belief is based on the results of a Council in AD325?

11 Who starred as Professor Jarrod in *The House of Wax* in 1953?

12 In greyhound racing, what does the letter "R" stand for on the side of a dog's jacket?

13 Who wrote the 1926 novel *The Murder of Roger Ackroyd*?

14 Which American humorist (b.1902) was noted for his unconventionally rhyming poetry published in the *New Yorker* magazine?

15 In which year was *Pirates of the Caribbean: The Curse of the Black Pearl* originally released in cinemas?

16 Which US state has Santa Fe as its capital?

17 Which Jimi Hendrix hit was written and originally recorded by Bob Dylan?

18 The Cévennes are a mountain range in which country?

19 Which is the largest member of the dolphin family?

20 Which king was nicknamed "The Wisest Fool in Christendom"?

Easy

Medium

Hard

Answers to QUIZ 201 – Pot Luck

1	*Tabitha*	11	*Footloose*
2	5 or 10m	12	Bell-ringing
3	Dodo	13	An Oriental dress
4	1940s	14	Martin Scorsese
5	Cotton	15	Sleep
6	Kirby	16	Cyrillic
7	Arthur C Clarke and Stanley Kubrick	17	Hazelnut
8	Elan	18	Colombia
9	Tom Clancy	19	Pears
10	Janus	20	*Under the Dome*

Easy

1   What is the surname of the heroine in the novel *What Katy Did* (1872)?

2   Who released the 1980 album *Never Forever*?

3   Who wrote the 2005 novel *Labyrinth*?

4   What was the name of Kate O'Mara's character in the original TV series of *Dynasty*?

5   Who is Kate's sister in Shakespeare's *The Taming of the Shrew*?

6   Who wrote the 2002 autobiography *The Kindness of Strangers*?

7   Who played Kate Austen in the TV series *Lost*?

8   What is the name of Kate Beckinsale's character in the *Underworld* series of films?

9   In which 2006 film did Kate Bosworth play Lois Lane?

10 In which film adaptation of a Jane Austen book did Kate Winslet play Marianne Dashwood?

Medium

11 Which Government post did Kate Hoey hold from 1999 to 2001?

12 What was the title of Kate Atkinson's first novel?

13 Whose first album was entitled *Eye to the Telescope*?

14 Katy Fox, played by Hannah Tointon, appeared in which long-running series?

15 In which country was singer Katie Melua born?

16 Which singer's 2007 debut album was entitled *Made of Bricks*?

17 Which TV presenter served as President of the RSPB from 2009 to 2013?

18 Who wrote the 2015 children's novel *Katy*?

19 The Kate Greenaway Medal is awarded for what aspect of children's books?

20 What was the name of Kate Capshaw's character in *Indiana Jones and the Temple of Doom*?

Hard

Answers to QUIZ 202 – The 1970s

1	Charles Haughey	11	Sir John Betjeman
2	1976	12	Afghanistan
3	Pocket calculator	13	Postal workers
4	Sir Charlie Chaplin	14	McDonald's
5	Gerald Ford	15	Southampton FC
6	15th February	16	Dr Donald Coggan
7	Rolls-Royce Ltd	17	1977
8	Denis Howell (Baron Howell)	18	Proceedings from the House of Commons
9	*Haunted House*	19	Duke of Windsor (Edward VIII)
10	Tony Jacklin	20	Their boat sank

1   What is the county town of Kerry?

2   *Yes Sir, I Can Boogie* was a hit for which duo in 1977?

3   What is stucco?

4   Which statesman owned London's Apsley House?

5   Which metal is made from bauxite?

6   What are Madonna's two middle names?

7   In which year did the Berlin blockade begin, with Soviet troops blocking road and rail links between Berlin and the Allied Western Zone?

8   The Paul Ricard racing circuit is in which country?

9   Of which country is Brazzaville the capital?

10   Who plays the regional manager in the US version of *The Office*?

11   Which 17th-century philosopher wrote *An Essay Concerning Human Understanding*?

12   Which dry volume measurement equates to eight gallons?

13   Amroth is a village in which county?

14   Which actress starred in the 1995 film *Clueless*?

15   Which US church is the equivalent to Anglican?

16   What is the name given to the radiation belts 600 miles above the surface of the Earth?

17   The 1980 album *Guilty* was recorded by which singer?

18   Which pizza company was the first to offer online ordering?

19   Which port in Israel lies at the northern extremity of Haifa Bay?

20   During which battle did the Charge of the Light Brigade take place?

Answers to QUIZ 203 – Pot Luck

1	Egg white	11	Vincent Price
2	Matthew	12	Reserve
3	Miley Cyrus	13	Dame Agatha Christie
4	Fair winds, or good airs	14	Ogden Nash
5	Boyle's Law	15	2003
6	Old Trafford	16	New Mexico
7	Herne Bay	17	*All Along the Watchtower*
8	Raspberry	18	France
9	18th century	19	Orca
10	Nicene Creed	20	James I of England (VI of Scotland)

1   Which plant gets its name from the long spur on its fruit that resembles a wader's beak?

2   A tree which has a Latin name including the word *Quercus* has what common name?

3   Which tall vegetable has a head of purple hairs as its flower?

4   Filberts are produced by which nut tree?

5   What term is given to a tree that has had the top cut back to encourage the formation of a crown of branches?

6   How is the plant hypericum also known?

7   What is a segment of a flower's corolla called?

8   To which family of birds does the robin belong?

9   The fast-growing *Leylandii* is a variety of which type of tree?

10 To which botanical genus does the holly tree belong?

11 Alkanet, a member of the borage family, has flowers of what colour?

12 Which bird is referred to as a "speug" in Scotland?

13 What is the common name of *Nigella damascena*?

14 What is the name of the UK's largest dragonfly?

15 What do the letters N, P and K stand for in relation to fertiliser?

16 The fruit of which tree is known as "sloe"?

17 Calluna is a variety of which type of plant?

18 A gall grows on a plant as a result of which type of insect?

19 For what purpose would a gardener use vermiculite?

20 Which beetle which has metallic green and purple stripes feeds on herbs and similar plants?

Answers to QUIZ 204 – Kate

1	Carr	11	Minister for Sport
2	Kate Bush	12	*Behind the Scenes at the Museum*
3	Kate Mosse	13	KT Tunstall
4	Caress Morell	14	*Hollyoaks*
5	Bianca	15	Georgia
6	Kate Adie	16	Kate Nash
7	Evangeline Lilly	17	Kate Humble
8	Selene	18	Dame Jacqueline Wilson
9	*Superman Returns*	19	Illustrations
10	*Sense and Sensibility*	20	Willie Scott

1 In the context of aviation, what does the "L" stand for in STOL?

2 What is notable about a Bailey bridge?

3 The Tudor building of Nonsuch Palace was in which English county?

4 What is the name of the hotel in *Benidorm*?

5 In Morse code, which letter is represented by four dots?

6 Which creature is between the Rooster and the Pig in the Chinese calendar?

7 Of what is kinetophobia a fear?

8 What is the name of the Merchant of Venice in the play of the same name?

9 How many cards are usually used to play a game of canasta?

10 What is the method of obtaining a location based on identifying three nearby points?

11 Which 2013 film was about the life of Liberace?

12 The charity Sustrans is associated with which outdoor pursuits?

13 Rubies and sapphires are varieties of which very hard mineral?

14 Which actor starred in the 1991 film *The Last Boy Scout*?

15 Apart from whisky, what is in a Whisky Mac?

16 Who played Superman to Teri Hatcher's Lois Lane in *Lois & Clark: The New Adventures of Superman*?

17 Which football club enjoyed mild chart success with *Here We Go* and *All Together Now* in 1985 and 1995?

18 How is a soubriquet more usually referred to?

19 *A Trivial Comedy for Serious People* is the subtitle of which famous play?

20 The island of Bermuda is part of which continent?

Easy

Medium

Hard

Answers to QUIZ 205 – Pot Luck

1	Tralee	11	John Locke
2	Baccara	12	Bushel
3	Plasterwork	13	Pembrokeshire
4	Duke of Wellington	14	Alicia Silverstone
5	Aluminium	15	Episcopal
6	Louise Veronica	16	Van Allen Belts
7	1948	17	Barbra Streisand
8	France	18	Pizza Hut
9	Republic of Congo	19	Akko
10	Steve Carrell	20	Balaclava

QUIZ 208 – Spies on Television

ANSWERS ON PAGE 210

Easy

1. What was the name of Nicola Walker's character in *Spooks*?
2. In the 1960s series *The Avengers*, who played Cathy Gale?
3. Which secret agent was played by Richard Dean Anderson?
4. In the series *Agent Carter*, what was the first name of the title character?
5. Keri Russell and Matthew Rhys played Russian spies in which series?
6. Broadcast in 1982, what was the sequel to *Tinker, Tailor, Soldier, Spy*?
7. Jim Phelps was a character in which series that started in the 1960s?
8. Which 2011-16 series featured the artificial intelligence surveillance computer known as "The Machine"?
9. Which series follows the British military intelligence unit Section 20?
10. The organisation THRUSH appeared in which TV series?

Medium

11. Which animated series features three teenage girls in Beverly Hills who work as spies?
12. Who played Richard Roper in the 2016 series *The Night Manager*?
13. What was the name of Rupert Friend's *Homeland* character?
14. Which series featured the character of Sydney Bristow?
15. Which Australian actress starred in the 2012 series *Hunted*?
16. *The Saint* and *Return of the Saint* were based on books by which author?
17. Who played the title role in the 2007 remake of *The Bionic Woman*?
18. What was the name of Bodie and Doyle's boss in the series *The Professionals*?
19. Who played the title role in the 1983 series *Reilly: Ace of Spies*?
20. Corey Hawkins starred as Eric Carter in a 2017 series of which franchise?

Hard

Answers to QUIZ 206 – In the Garden

1. Cranesbill
2. Oak
3. Globe artichoke
4. Hazel
5. Pollard
6. St John's Wort
7. Petal
8. Thrush
9. Cypress
10. *Ilex*
11. Blue
12. Sparrow
13. Love-in-a-mist
14. Emperor dragonfly
15. Nitrogen, phosphorus and potassium
16. Blackthorn
17. Heather
18. Wasp
19. Germinating seeds
20. Rosemary beetle

208

ANSWERS ON PAGE **211**

1   What do the initials ISBN stand for?

2   Who played Oddjob in the Bond film *Goldfinger*?

3   Which novelist wrote *The Plumed Serpent*?

4   In 2016, which musical received a record 16 Tony award nominations, winning 11?

5   What was the name of the professor in *The Adventures of Tintin*?

6   Who starred in the 2014 film *American Sniper*?

7   Which constellation is also called Crux?

8   Of which African republic is Luanda the capital?

9   What was the first UK top ten hit for George Benson?

10   In what sport might one perform the movements quarte and quinte?

11   Which Latin case marks the indirect object of a verb?

12   The names of British racehorses are limited to how many characters?

13   In which two places is the National Waterways Museum located?

14   What colour flower is it considered unlucky to receive in Russia?

15   The name of which nut is derived from the Persian word "pesteh"?

16   In which town was William Wordsworth born?

17   Irkutsk and Omsk are located in which region of Russia?

18   In 1704, what territory was seized from the Spanish by English forces led by Admiral Rooke?

19   What is the state capital of California?

20   Who was emperor of Rome between AD54 and 68?

Easy

Medium

Hard

Answers to QUIZ 207 – Pot Luck

1	Landing	11	*Behind the Candelabra*
2	It is a temporary structure	12	Cycling and walking
3	Surrey	13	Corundum
4	Solana	14	Bruce Willis
5	H	15	Ginger wine
6	Dog	16	Dean Cain
7	Movement or motion	17	Everton
8	Antonio	18	Nickname
9	108 (two full packs and four jokers)	19	*The Importance of Being Earnest*
10	Triangulation	20	North America

1   Which country is home to the Komodo dragon?

2   The monkey puzzle tree is a conifer native to which countries?

3   What does CCS stand for in an environmental context?

4   To the nearest minute, how long does the light of the Sun take to reach the Earth?

5   On what does coral feed?

6   Which is the only deciduous conifer native to Central Europe?

7   What weather system is associated with calm fine conditions?

8   Which is the largest bay in the world by shoreline?

9   In an environmental context, what does the "C" stand for in the initials IUCN?

10 What word describes the height of a location above sea level?

11 What is a haboob?

12 Which continent of the world has no snakes?

13 In which sea is the Great Barrier Reef?

14 What term is given to a wind of force six on the Beaufort Scale?

15 The island of Mykonos is surrounded by which body of water?

16 What, in weather terms, is a chinook?

17 Which is the largest island in the world?

18 The Okavango river is on which continent?

19 What type of rock is solidified from a molten state?

20 The trees known as "ghost gums" are native to which country?

Answers to QUIZ 208 – Spies on Television

1	Ruth Evershed	11	*Totally Spies!*
2	Honor Blackman	12	Hugh Laurie
3	MacGyver	13	Peter Quinn
4	Peggy	14	*Alias*
5	*The Americans*	15	Melissa George
6	*Smiley's People*	16	Leslie Charteris
7	*Mission: Impossible*	17	Michelle Ryan
8	*Person of Interest*	18	Major George Cowley
9	*Strike Back*	19	Sam Neill
10	*The Man From U. N. C. L. E.*	20	24

1 Which car manufacturer produced the Punto?

2 Mel Gibson and Jodie Foster co-starred in which 1994 western?

3 Which part of the foot is also called the hallux?

4 Who designed the London Coliseum?

5 To which group of islands does Rhodes belong?

6 Which car manufacturer produced the Aveo?

7 In which country was Olivia Newton-John born?

8 HS is the postcode area code for which group of islands?

9 What term is given to a letter from the Pope?

10 What part of a cola tree is used to flavour drinks?

11 Which group had hits in the 1990s with *All That She Wants* and *Don't Turn Around*?

12 Who was manager of Liverpool when they won their first UEFA Cup in 1973?

13 Which star of the 1960 film *The Magnificent Seven* played Joseph Wladislaw in the 1967 film *The Dirty Dozen*?

14 What is the capital of Australia's Northern Territory?

15 In which country is the Orange River?

16 With what is food described as "fricassee" served?

17 What is the Latin phrase meaning "I think, therefore I am"?

18 Journalist and broadcaster Alastair Campbell is a supporter of which football team?

19 What is measured on the Snellen scale?

20 Which houseplant has the Latin name *Saintpaulia*?

Easy

Medium

Hard

Answers to QUIZ 209 – Pot Luck

1	International Standard Book Number	11	Dative
2	Harold Sakata	12	18 letters and spaces
3	DH Lawrence	13	Gloucester and Ellesmere Port
4	*Hamilton*	14	Yellow
5	Calculus	15	Pistachio
6	Bradley Cooper	16	Cockermouth
7	Southern Cross	17	Siberia
8	Angola	18	Gibraltar
9	*Give Me the Night*	19	Sacramento
10	Fencing	20	Nero

Easy

1 Which novel was the basis for the 1979 film *Apocalypse Now?*

2 In the 1999 film *Saving Private Ryan*, what was Private Ryan's first name?

3 Who directed the 1987 film *Full Metal Jacket?*

4 The 1953 film *The Cruel Sea* portrays which battle?

5 In the 1987 film *Good Morning, Vietnam*, what do the initials AFRS stand for in the name of the organisation for which Robin Williams' character works?

6 Which 2008 film set in Iraq won the Best Picture Oscar?

7 The 2005 film *Jarhead* was based on the memoirs of which US marine, played by Jake Gyllenhaal?

8 Who directed the 1963 film *The Great Escape?*

9 In which city was the 2010 film *Green Zone* set?

10 The 2001 film *Black Hawk Down* was set in which country?

Medium

11 Which 1977 film was based around 1944's Operation Market Garden?

12 The Battle of Rorke's Drift featured in which 1964 film?

13 Who played Colonel Nicholson in the 1957 film *The Bridge on the River Kwai?*

14 Which was the first of Oliver Stone's three Vietnam War films, released in 1986?

15 Units of the 35th Infantry Divison featured in which 1970 war film starring Clint Eastwood?

16 What was the title of the 1981 German film written and directed by Wolfgang Petersen, which was nominated for the Best Director Oscar?

17 Which battle between the USA and Japan was featured in a 2006 film starring Ken Watanabe?

18 In the 1962 film, what was the date of *The Longest Day?*

19 Wladyslaw Szpilman is the central character of which 2002 film set in Warsaw?

20 Who starred as Marcus Luttrell in the 2013 film *Lone Survivor?*

Hard

Answers to QUIZ 210 – Planet Earth

1	Indonesia	11	A sandstorm or duststorm
2	Chile and Argentina	12	Antarctica
3	Carbon capture and storage	13	Coral Sea
4	Eight minutes (and 20 seconds)	14	Strong breeze
5	Plankton	15	The Aegean Sea
6	Larch	16	Warm moist wind from the Pacific
7	Anticyclone or high pressure	17	Greenland
8	Hudson Bay	18	Africa
9	Conservation	19	Igneous
10	Elevation	20	Australia

1. What is the ninth month of the Islamic calendar?

2. Who wrote the story of *The Emperor's New Clothes*?

3. In literature, what term is given to the repetition of vowel sounds?

4. Which band released the 1972 album *Obscured by Clouds*?

5. The declaration of Scottish independence in 1320 is known by the name of which town?

6. What is majolica?

7. *Castle on the Hill* was a 2017 single by which singer?

8. Which angles are more than 180 but less than 360 degrees?

9. Of which principality is Vaduz the capital?

10. In which century was Johann Sebastian Bach born?

11. The Tour de France cycle race was first held in which year?

12. Who starred as Queen Guinevere in the 2004 film *King Arthur*?

13. What term is given to the principles concerned with taste and beauty?

14. Which famous novel features the character of Major Major?

15. Jakarta is the capital of which Indonesian island?

16. Which family of plants does garlic belong to?

17. Allopathy is another name for the practice of what?

18. Which poem begins "When the Present has latched its postern behind my tremulous stay"?

19. The Napier University is located in which city?

20. What name is given to a Spanish horseman?

Easy

Medium

Hard

Answers to QUIZ 211 – Pot Luck

1	Fiat	11	Ace of Base
2	*Maverick*	12	Bill Shankly
3	Big toe	13	Charles Bronson
4	Frank Matcham and Sir Oswald Stoll	14	Darwin
5	Dodecanese	15	South Africa
6	Chevrolet	16	White sauce
7	UK	17	*Cogito ergo sum*
8	Outer Hebrides	18	Burnley FC
9	Encyclical	19	Eyesight (visual acuity)
10	Nut	20	African violet

Easy

1   In the 1930s, which company introduced a new polymer, which they named nylon?

2   In computing, for what do the letters WORM stand, in reference to a type of disc?

3   Which company registered the first patents for the railway sleeping car?

4   The term "pixel" is formed from which two words?

5   What is metadata?

6   Which 1999 insect-based game by Pangea Software was originally created for the Mac operating system?

7   In which year was Bitcoin launched?

8   Which company launched the VHS format in 1976?

9   What do the initials CRT stand for in relation to television and computer screens?

10 What is the meaning of the name of the product WD-40®?

Medium

11 In which country was the stethoscope invented (1816)?

12 Which water-raising device was invented by the Greek who shouted "Eureka!"?

13 Which two words are the basis for the word "modem"?

14 In which year did Nintendo® release the Wii™?

15 What did Charles Goodyear invent in 1844?

16 In 1831, who invented a dynamo for generating electricity?

17 What type of skate was invented in 1760 by Joseph Merlin?

18 What was the surname of King Camp, who invented the safety razor?

19 The Scholes & Glidden was the first commercially successful version of what aid to communication?

20 For what do the letters GIF stand?

Hard

Answers to QUIZ 212 – War Films

1	*Heart of Darkness* (Joseph Conrad)	11	*A Bridge Too Far*
2	James	12	*Zulu*
3	Stanley Kubrick	13	Sir Alec Guinness
4	The Battle of the Atlantic	14	*Platoon*
5	Armed Forces Radio Service	15	*Kelly's Heroes*
6	*The Hurt Locker*	16	*Das Boot*
7	Anthony Swofford	17	Iwo Jima
8	John Sturges	18	June 6, 1944
9	Baghdad	19	*The Pianist*
10	Somalia	20	Mark Wahlberg

1 Ashley Walters and Noel Clarke co-starred in which 2018 crime series?

2 What is the English translation of the French term *esprit d'escalier?*

3 How is ale with a strength of 4.2-4.7% abv described?

4 Which strait links the Black Sea with the Sea of Marmara?

5 In which county is the National Agricultural Centre?

6 What was *Starsky and Hutch* actor David Soul's original surname?

7 The nene goose is native to which group of islands?

8 In which mountain range is Chamonix situated?

9 What is the title of a lawyer who is able to take affidavits?

10 Whom did Sir Winston Churchill once describe as "A modest man with much to be modest about"?

11 Which two fruit juices are mixed with vodka for a Sea Breeze cocktail?

12 How many points win a game of badminton?

13 In computing terms, for what do the letters ASCII stand?

14 How is the US medal, the Purple Heart, inscribed?

15 In which decade was the InterCity 125 train introduced?

16 Which London club based at 107 Pall Mall was founded in 1824?

17 Allison Janney played which character in the TV series *The West Wing?*

18 Which Dutch city stands on the River Dommel?

19 Who composed the music for *Show Boat?*

20 How old was Henry III when he inherited the throne of England?

Easy

Medium

Hard

Answers to QUIZ 213 – Pot Luck

1	Ramadan	11	1903
2	Hans Christian Andersen	12	Keira Knightley
3	Assonance	13	Aesthetics
4	Pink Floyd	14	*Catch-22*
5	Arbroath	15	Java
6	Enamelled pottery	16	Amaryllis
7	Ed Sheeran	17	Conventional medicine
8	Reflex	18	*Afterwards* (Thomas Hardy)
9	Liechtenstein	19	Edinburgh
10	17th century	20	Caballero

1 The character of Jackson Brodie first featured in which Kate Atkinson novel?

2 Which award was won in 2017 by Ruta Sepetys' *Salt to the Sea*?

3 Which forensic examiner was created by Patricia Cornwell?

4 Now known as the Costa Book Awards, what was its former name from 1971 to 2005?

5 What is the title of Jojo Moyes' 2015 sequel to *Me Before You*?

6 What nationality is author Stephenie Meyer?

7 Which 2012 novel by John Green was adapted for the cinema in 2014?

8 Harlen Coben's character Myron Bolitar played which sport before becoming an agent?

9 Who wrote the 2003 novel *Vernon God Little*?

10 Which novel by Julian Barnes won the 2011 Man Booker Prize?

11 Who won the 2015 Pulitzer Prize for fiction with *All the Light We Cannot See*?

12 The 2002 novel *Life of Pi* is set in which ocean?

13 *Needful Things* (1991) was written by which horror author?

14 Who wrote the 2014 novel *Us*?

15 Timothy Cavendish and Adam Ewing are characters from which 2004 novel?

16 Who is the central character of *The Girl on the Train* by Paula Hawkins?

17 *Knots and Crosses* is the first novel featuring which detective?

18 Who wrote the 2012 novel *Stonemouth*?

19 Whose novels include *The Associate* (2009) and *The Litigators* (2011)?

20 What was the title of the 2009 Robert Langdon novel by Dan Brown?

Easy

Medium

Hard

Answers to QUIZ 214 – Technology and Inventions

1	DuPont	11	France
2	Write Once Read Many (times)	12	Archimedean screw
3	Pullman	13	Modulator/demodulator
4	Picture element	14	2006
5	Data about data	15	Vulcanised rubber
6	*Bugdom*	16	Michael Faraday
7	2009	17	Inline skate
8	JVC	18	Gillette
9	Cathode-ray tube	19	Typewriter
10	Water Displacement, 40th formula	20	Graphic interchange format

1   Who won the first series of UK *Big Brother* in 2000?

2   Which central Asian inland sea lies between Kazakhstan and Uzbekistan?

3   Near which city on the Forth river is the Wallace Monument?

4   Which actor starred in the 1992 film *Patriot Games*?

5   Which year saw the death of Queen Elizabeth I of England?

6   The public school of Charterhouse is located in which county?

7   Which Indian city is the centre of the Sikh religion?

8   Touchstone the jester appears in which Shakespeare play?

9   What was the title of Dave Edmunds' 1970 chart-topping single?

10 Diamante and Elsanta are varieties of which fruit?

11 In which country is the ski resort of Courmayeur?

12 From which fibre is grosgrain usually made?

13 Who wrote the 1959 novel *Billy Liar*?

14 Which US president immediately succeeded George Washington?

15 Which actress starred in the 2003 film *Agent Cody Banks*?

16 What term is given to the belief that God exists?

17 In which decade of the 18th century did the first convict ships arrive at Botany Bay in Australia?

18 What was the nationality of the person who assassinated Archduke Ferdinand in 1914?

19 Which memorial to the dead of WWI can be found at Ypres in Belgium?

20 Which sisters famously sang *Boogie Woogie Bugle Boy*?

Answers to QUIZ 215 – Pot Luck

1	Bulletproof	11	Cranberry and grapefruit
2	The wit of the staircase	12	21
3	Best bitter	13	American Standard Code for Information Interchange
4	Bosphorus	14	For Military Merit
5	Warwickshire	15	1970s (1976)
6	Solberg	16	Athenaeum
7	Hawaii	17	CJ Cregg
8	The Alps	18	Eindhoven
9	Commissioner for oaths/Notary Public	19	Jerome Kern
10	Clement Attlee (First Earl Attlee of Walthamstow)	20	Nine

QUIZ 218 – Words

1 Which Italian word can mean a Mafia boss or a device attached to a guitar?

2 What animal's name is it considered good luck to say at the start of the month in the UK?

3 Of what is brontophobia the fear?

4 What is the meaning of "distaff"?

5 What term is given to the physical and chemical study of the stars?

6 The lyrics to the classic song *My Way* were written by which singer/songwriter?

7 What part of a building may be described as "hammerbeam"?

8 Which trade name is derived from the Latin words for "strength of man"?

9 What three-word phrase refers to the medieval practice of illustrating potentially hazardous areas of maps with mythical monsters?

10 What are the two countries referenced in the name of stations on the London Underground Jubilee Line, one by name and one by nationality?

11 What is a coif?

12 A chiromancy practitioner has what more common name?

13 What does the Latin expression *Habeas corpus* translate as?

14 What is a goosefoot?

15 Which fabric derives its name from the city of Mosul, where it was supposedly first manufactured?

16 "Brevity is the soul of wit" is a quote from which Shakespeare play?

17 What is the translation of "Volkswagen"?

18 Which line from the poem *Lady of Shalott* did Agatha Christie use for the title of a 1962 detective novel?

19 The Plantaganet name is reputed to have been inspired by which plant?

20 Which planet's satellites are named after Shakespearean characters Miranda, Ariel, Titania and Oberon?

Easy / Medium / Hard

Answers to QUIZ 216 – Modern Fiction

1	*Case Histories*	11	Anthony Doerr
2	Carnegie Medal	12	Pacific
3	Dr Kay Scarpetta	13	Stephen King
4	Whitbread Prize	14	David Nicholls
5	*After You*	15	*Cloud Atlas* (David Mitchell)
6	American	16	Rachel Watson
7	*The Fault in Our Stars*	17	Inspector Rebus
8	Basketball	18	Iain Banks
9	DBC Pierre	19	John Grisham
10	*The Sense of an Ending*	20	*The Lost Symbol*

1   Mary of Guise was married to which Scottish king?

2   In which country is the Order of the Elephant the highest and oldest honour?

3   Who was the Greek goddess equivalent to the Roman Aurora?

4   On which inlet is Aberystwyth situated?

5   Who was the lyricist for *Starlight Express*?

6   Which London building has the postcode SW1A 1AA?

7   Which three South American countries does the Equator cross?

8   Which poem was never completed because the author was interrupted by "a person from Porlock"?

9   What is the name of the blood spatter specialist featured in a series of books by Jeff Lindsay?

10   In which country do cricket teams compete for the Sheffield Shield?

11   Who was the sorceress who aided Jason to steal the Golden Fleece?

12   The character of Sheldon in *The Big Bang Theory* is originally from which state?

13   A traditional Chinese meat substitute made from wheat gluten is known by what name?

14   Which singer teamed up with the Cardigans in 1999 on *Burning Down the House*?

15   What is the French term for the large double-lobed nut of the Seychelles palm?

16   In Roald Dahl's *Matilda*, what is the first name of Miss Trunchbull?

17   When did the Super League begin in Rugby League?

18   What type of creature is a whirligig?

19   Assisi is in which region of Italy?

20   Margarine was named after the Greek word for what?

Easy
Medium
Hard

Answers to QUIZ 217 – Pot Luck

1	Craig Phillips	11	Italy
2	Aral	12	Silk
3	Stirling	13	Keith Waterhouse
4	Harrison Ford	14	John Adams
5	1603	15	Hilary Duff
6	Surrey	16	Theism
7	Amritsar	17	1780s (1788)
8	*As You Like It*	18	Serbian
9	*I Hear You Knocking*	19	Menin Gate
10	Strawberry	20	The Andrews Sisters

Easy

1   How many sovereign countries comprise South America?

2   What is the term for a positive integer that is equal to the sum of all its factors, excluding itself?

3   How many counters does backgammon have of each colour?

4   Counting the annuli rings on which part of a fish's body will give its age?

5   In 1066 how many monarchs ruled England in the year?

6   In which year did the Wimbledon tennis match between John Isner and Nicolas Mahut finish on 70-68?

7   In billiards how many points are scored for a cannon?

8   How many bones are in the adult human body?

9   Which element has the atomic number 3?

10 What is the dialling code for Oxford?

Medium

11 By what unit are angles measured other than degrees?

12 In feet, how wide is a field hockey goal?

13 "PC" is the traditional bingo call for which number?

14 Which Hollywood actress (d.1973) had her legs insured for a million dollars?

15 Who had a 1978 hit with *Because the Night*?

16 What is the square root of 289?

17 In darts, what is the minimum number of throws to score 301?

18 How many cards are dealt to each player in a game of rummy with more than two players?

19 In 2018, which football team became the first to score 100 points in the Premier League?

20 What is 0.375 expressed as a fraction?

Hard

Answers to QUIZ 218 – Words

1	Capo	11	Cap
2	Rabbit	12	Palmist
3	Thunder	13	You may have the body
4	Of or concerning women	14	A plant
5	Astrophysics	15	Muslin
6	Paul Anka	16	*Hamlet*
7	Roof	17	People's car
8	Hovis, from *hominis vis*	18	The mirror crack'd from side to side
9	Here be dragons	19	Broom (*Planta genista*)
10	Canada (Canada Water) and Switzerland (Swiss Cottage)	20	Uranus

1 Which sea lies between western Greece and southern Italy?

2 Where is Sir Isaac Newton buried?

3 What was the occupation of Cardinal Thomas Wolsey's father thought to be?

4 In the classic film noir *Chinatown*, which part of Jack Nicholson's body is injured?

5 For what purpose is an autoclave used?

6 Which singer hosted the game show *Family Fortunes* from 1983 to 1985?

7 *Das Rheingold* and *Götterdämmerung* are part of which opera cycle?

8 What was the title of The Police's fourth studio album?

9 Which PlayStation® driving game first released in 1997 has a title that translates as "Grand Touring"?

10 Which woodland creature of Greek myth has a man's body and goat's legs?

11 What relation was Napoleon III to Napoleon Bonaparte?

12 A brigantine has how many masts?

13 Which creature precedes the Monkey in the Chinese calendar?

14 Which famous figure was killed by Ramon Mercader in Mexico in 1940?

15 Which classic comedy won BAFTA best British film in 1952?

16 In which county did the the water sport of gig racing originate?

17 Which author's last written words include the line "No coward soul is mine"?

18 Who was the UK Prime Minister from 1905 to 1908?

19 In which decade was the first Test Match played between England and Australia?

20 What term describes the slope of a road from the centre to the edge?

Easy

Medium

Hard

Answers to QUIZ 219 – Pot Luck

1	James V	11	Medea
2	Denmark	12	Texas
3	Eos	13	Seitan
4	Cardigan Bay	14	Sir Tom Jones
5	Sir Richard Stilgoe	15	Coco de mer
6	Buckingham Palace	16	Agatha
7	Brazil, Colombia and Ecuador	17	1996
8	*Kubla Khan* (Samuel Taylor Coleridge)	18	A beetle
9	Dexter	19	Umbria
10	Australia	20	Pearl

Easy

1 Which Shakespeare play is subtitled *Prince of Tyre*?

2 The princes known as "the Princes in the Tower" were the sons of which 15th-century king?

3 Who played Edward VIII in the 2010 film *The King's Speech*?

4 Which English king founded the Most Noble Order of the Garter?

5 In which royal residence is the Waterloo Chamber?

6 Which English king was known as "Curtmantle"?

7 Which king summoned the "Model Parliament" in 1295?

8 In which decade did Prince Albert buy Balmoral Castle?

9 Who sailed to safety in France aboard *L'Heureux* in 1746?

10 Which American author wrote the novel *The Prince and the Pauper*?

Medium

11 In which castle was Edward II murdered?

12 Which king did William the Conqueror succeed in 1066?

13 Which legendary courtier of King Dionysius was forced to sit beneath a dangling sword?

14 In 1984, which single by the band King reached no.2 in the UK charts?

15 Which King of England established the Forest Laws in 1014 in which only noblemen could own greyhounds?

16 Anne of Bohemia was married to which English king?

17 In 1065, which king founded a church on the site where Westminster Abbey now stands?

18 Which German duchy was associated with Queen Mary, consort of George V?

19 Which archbishop annulled the marriage of Henry VIII and Catherine of Aragon?

20 Who was the father of Henry IV?

Hard

1   Which Jane Austen novel features the Woodhouse family?

2   In a three-pin plug, what is the colour of the live wire?

3   Who left the Go-Go's in 1985 and had her first UK no.1 in 1987?

4   Cambridge Favourite and Cambridge Vigour are types of which fruit?

5   Which tributary of the Thames flows through Godalming and Guildford?

6   Which US state is abbreviated to IA?

7   Which upmarket car make has been part of Volkswagen since 1998?

8   In which fictional county is Ambridge, setting for *The Archers* radio series?

9   Clint Eastwood was born in which city?

10 Grid reference numbers are usually given as the northings number followed by what?

11 Which is Egypt's second-largest city and largest port?

12 In the books by Colin Dexter, where does Robbie Lewis come from?

13 Which film company produced the 1975 film *One of Our Dinosaurs Is Missing*?

14 "Cottonopolis" was the 19th-century nickname of which British city?

15 In which county is the Isle of Oxney?

16 What type of creature is a tarantula hawk?

17 Which US state is renowned for its Black Hills?

18 Dr John Pemberton invented which drink in 1886?

19 Which band's first UK hit single was *I'm Stone in Love with You*?

20 Who was the Venetian explorer who discovered Newfoundland?

Answers to QUIZ 221 – Pot Luck

1	Ionian	11	Nephew
2	Westminster Abbey	12	Two
3	Butcher	13	Goat
4	His nose	14	Leon Trotsky
5	Sterilising apparatus	15	*The Lavender Hill Mob*
6	Max Bygraves	16	Cornwall
7	*Ring*	17	Emily Brontë
8	*Ghost in the Machine*	18	Sir Henry Campbell-Bannerman
9	*Gran Turismo*	19	1870s (1877)
10	Satyr	20	Camber

223

Easy

Medium

Hard

Easy

1   Bi is the symbol for which chemical element?

2   In 1896, what was Dmitri Mendeleev the first person to publish?

3   Which silvery-white metal element has the atomic number 13?

4   All acids contain which element?

5   Which gas is made from molecules of one nitrogen atom and three hydrogen atoms?

6   The process of galvanising uses which bluish-white metallic element?

7   Sodium hydroxide has what other name?

8   What term describes the chemical ability to form bonds?

9   Which English scientist is credited with the discovery of oxygen?

10 Which element is found on the head of matches?

Medium

11 Which metallic element was used in old light bulb filaments?

12 Combining an acid with an alcohol results in which type of molecule?

13 What is the lightest metallic element?

14 What is the technique of chromatography used for?

15 In relation to analysing elements, for what do the initials MS stand?

16 In what sort of bonding do two atoms share electrons in their outer shell?

17 What gas is given off by pouring dilute sulphuric acid onto granulated zinc?

18 What does an anoxic environment lack?

19 Which metal with the atomic number 76 is used to make record-player needles and pen tips?

20 As of 2018, how many elements were named after the Swedish village of Ytterby?

Hard

Answers to QUIZ 222 – Royalty

1	Pericles	11	Berkeley Castle
2	Edward IV	12	Harold II
3	Guy Pearce	13	Damocles
4	Edward III	14	*Love & Pride*
5	Windsor Castle	15	King Canute
6	Henry II	16	Richard II
7	Edward I	17	Edward the Confessor
8	1850s (1852)	18	Teck
9	Bonnie Prince Charlie	19	Thomas Cranmer
10	Mark Twain	20	John of Gaunt

1   What do the Aboriginal people of Australia refer to as "the beginning of knowledge"?

2   The Irish port of Drogheda lies near the mouth of which river?

3   Which actress was Sacha Baron Cohen's co-star in the 2012 film *The Dictator*?

4   Which is the largest city in the US state of New Mexico?

5   What was the nickname of Frederick I of Germany?

6   On an Ordnance Survey map, what is indicated by a blue triangle containing a blue dot?

7   Who starred as Roy McAvoy in the 1996 film *Tin Cup*?

8   Which singer released the albums *Trespassing* (2012) and *The Original High* (2015)?

9   In the 2004 film *Garfield: The Movie*, who provided the voice of Garfield?

10 Which historic Scottish county borders Stirling, Fife and Perth and Kinross?

11 The Eisenhower Trophy is awarded to amateur teams in which sport?

12 Which model wrote the 1994 novel *Swan*?

13 What is the lowest UK hereditary title?

14 ELO's *All Over the World* was written for which 1980 film?

15 What were added to London postcodes in 1917?

16 What is the name of the short to medium distance Indian train service operated by Indian Railways?

17 How many strings does a Spanish guitar have?

18 The loofah scrubbing brush is from which fruit family?

19 The word *hygge*, meaning "cosy", is from which language?

20 How many gold medals did Scotland win at the Commonwealth Games in 2018?

Easy

Medium

Hard

Answers to QUIZ 223 – Pot Luck

1	Emma	11	Alexandria
2	Brown	12	Wales
3	Belinda Carlisle	13	Disney
4	Strawberry	14	Manchester
5	Wey	15	Kent
6	Iowa	16	A wasp
7	Bentley	17	South Dakota
8	Borsetshire	18	Coca-Cola®
9	San Francisco	19	The Stylistics
10	Eastings	20	John Cabot

Easy

1 What was the real first name of jazz musician Bix Beiderbecke?

2 Which type of instrument was made by the Amati family?

3 *Tom's Diner* was a 1989 single by which singer?

4 Which composer was the subject of a 1975 Ken Russell film?

5 Who had a hit in 1964 with *My Guy*?

6 *Draw the Line* was a 2009 album by which singer/songwriter?

7 What is indicated by the musical direction "pesante"?

8 In which year was Wolfgang Amadeus Mozart born?

9 Who had a hit in 2017 with *What about Us*?

10 *One Song Glory* and *Seasons of Love* are songs from which musical?

Medium

11 Who formed the duo Soft Cell along with Marc Almond?

12 Which group had a 1969 hit with *Build Me Up Buttercup*?

13 The ballet *Appalachian Spring* was written by which American composer?

14 Who recorded the 1997 album *Come On Over*?

15 The first Eurovision Song Contest was hosted by which country?

16 Which 1960s group had hits with *Summer in the City* and *Do You Believe in Magic*?

17 Which Gilbert and Sullivan operetta features the soprano role of Phyllis?

18 *Graffiti on the Train* was a 2013 album for which band?

19 Which note has the time value of 1/32 of a semibreve?

20 Which Verdi opera features the character of Alfredo?

Hard

Answers to QUIZ 224 – Chemistry

1	Bismuth	11	Tungsten
2	A recognisable periodic table	12	Ester
3	Aluminium	13	Lithium
4	Hydrogen	14	Separating mixtures of coloured compounds
5	Ammonia	15	Mass spectrometry
6	Zinc	16	Covalent
7	Caustic soda	17	Hydrogen
8	Valency	18	Oxygen
9	Joseph Priestley	19	Osmium
10	Phosphorus	20	Four (ytterbium yttrium, terbium, and erbium)

ANSWERS ON PAGE 229

1   What is the name of the small knob on the side of an analogue watch, which is used to adjust the time?

2   The area of the Pacific that lies off the north-east coast of Australia is known by what name?

3   Who was the 1998 US women's singles tennis champion?

4   In 1938, who opened Regent's Park Children's Zoo?

5   When were Premium Bonds introduced in Britain?

6   Who landed a light aircraft in Red Square in 1987?

7   In which Georgia city was US president Jimmy Carter born?

8   Which jockey had his first Derby win on Shergar in 1981?

9   What was discovered by Allan Quartermain?

10 Contrary to tradition, whose presence was not required at the birth of Prince Charles?

11 Which old Spanish coin was so named because it was worth twice a pistole?

12 Which people suffer from the injury known as "Gamekeeper's Thumb"?

13 Who was the wife of Alfred the Great?

14 In which year was the first book printed in England by William Caxton?

15 How did Gavrilo Princip affect the course of history?

16 Which year saw the founding of the Territorial Army?

17 What is a mordant?

18 Which Old Testament book comes between Jonah and Nahum?

19 Which actor published his autobiography in parts, the second of which was entitled *Snakes and Ladders*?

20 What is armure?

Easy

Medium

Hard

Answers to QUIZ 225 – Pot Luck

1	The Dreamtime	11	Golf
2	Boyne	12	Naomi Campbell
3	Anna Faris	13	Baronet
4	Albuquerque	14	*Xanadu*
5	Barbarossa	15	Numbers
6	Triangulation pillar	16	Shatabdi Express
7	Kevin Costner	17	Six
8	Adam Lambert	18	Curcubits
9	Bill Murray	19	Danish
10	Clackmannanshire	20	Nine

1   What is the world's third-largest island?

2   What is the third-largest constellation in the northern sky?

3   In the Old Testament, who was the third son of David?

4   Who played Dr Dick Solomon in *3rd Rock from the Sun*?

5   What is the third largest city of Afghanistan, after Kabul and Kandahar?

6   Who was the third man to walk on the moon?

7   Who won the London Marathon women's elite race for the third time in 2017?

8   What is the title of the third novel in Bernard Cornwell's *Saxon Tales* series?

9   Which comedian provided the voice of Merlin in the 2007 film *Shrek the Third*?

10 Beethoven's third symphony is known by what name?

11 Who was the third Prime Minister of the United Kingdom, from 1743 to 1754?

12 Who directed the 1949 film *The Third Man*?

13 Who was the UK's third Poet Laureate (1692-1715)?

14 Which is the third most common gas in the Earth's atmosphere?

15 In *As You Like It*, what does Shakespeare describe as the "third age of man"?

16 Who wrote the novel *The Third Policeman*, published in 1967...?

17 ...and which enigmatic TV series briefly featured it in a 2005 episode, leading to a sudden rise in sales?

18 Who was King of England from 1216 to 1272?

19 Which celebrity won the third series of *Strictly Come Dancing*?

20 What was the title of Westlife's third no.1 UK single?

Answers to QUIZ 226 – Music

1	Leon	11	David Ball
2	Violin	12	The Foundations
3	Suzanne Vega	13	Aaron Copland
4	Franz Liszt	14	Shania Twain
5	Mary Wells	15	Switzerland
6	David Gray	16	The Lovin' Spoonful
7	In a forceful or weighty manner	17	*Iolanthe*
8	1756	18	Stereophonics
9	Pink	19	Demisemiquaver
10	*Rent*	20	*La Traviata*

1   What nationality was Henry the Navigator?

2   In which country are 100 öre worth one krona?

3   What word denotes the central governing body of the Roman Catholic Church?

4   What is the full name of the person whom James Bond knows as "M"?

5   Under what name is Gregor Efimovich better known?

6   At the start of *Day Of The Triffids*, what causes most of the Earth's population to go blind?

7   Of what is kenophobia a fear?

8   How many winners did Sir Gordon Richards ride in the 1947 season?

9   What is the official name of the currency of the People's Republic of China?

10 *Papa's Got a Brand New Bag* and *It's a Man's Man's Man's World* were hits for who?

11 What trade did a webster follow?

12 Who was the Secretary General of the United Nations from 1953 to 1961?

13 Which Dutch scholar edited the Greek New Testament in the 16th century?

14 Of which city was Neville Chamberlain once Lord Mayor?

15 Who is Portia's maid in Shakespeare's *The Merchant of Venice*?

16 Which profession has St Apollonia as its patron saint?

17 Pierre Omidyar was the founder of which multinational corporation?

18 What is a paronomasia?

19 In which year was William Golding awarded the Nobel Prize in Literature?

20 What was the fictional setting for the TV series *Juliet Bravo*?

Easy

Medium

Hard

Answers to QUIZ 227 – Pot Luck

1	The crown	11	Doubloon
2	Coral Sea	12	Skiers
3	Lindsay Davenport	13	Ealhwith
4	Robert and Edward Kennedy	14	1477
5	1956	15	He assassinated Archduke Franz Ferdinand
6	Mathias Rust	16	1908
7	Plains	17	A substance used to fix colours in dyeing
8	Walter Swinburn	18	Micah
9	King Solomon's Mines	19	Dirk Bogarde
10	Home Secretary	20	Fabric

Easy

1   The port of Archangel lies on the coast of which sea?

2   Which is Nigeria's largest city after Lagos?

3   What is the capital of Samoa?

4   The name of which Caribbean island means "the bearded ones"?

5   Which river of modern Pakistan was the site of the ancient Harappan civilisation?

6   Mount Elbert is the highest peak in which US state?

7   In which country is the highest waterfall in Europe?

8   Adelie Land is a French territory on which continent?

9   Delhi is on which river?

10 In which city can China's famous terracotta warriors be seen?

11 Which Australian city has the largest public tram system in the world?

12 Vientiane is the capital city of which country?

13 Which is the largest active volcano on Earth?

14 What is the capital of Malawi?

Medium

15 In which country is the oasis city of Kashgar?

16 Which is the largest island of the Philippines?

17 Which is the only country crossed by the equator and a tropic?

18 Mount Toubkal is the highest peak of which mountain range?

19 Which river flows through the Irish city of Kilkenny?

20 What is the capital of Yemen?

Hard

Answers to QUIZ 228 – Third Place

1	Borneo	11	Henry Pelham
2	Ursa Major	12	Carol Reed
3	Absalom	13	Nahum Tate
4	John Lithgow	14	Argon
5	Herat	15	The Lover
6	Charles "Pete" Conrad	16	Flann O'Brien
7	Mary Keitany	17	Lost
8	The Lords of the North	18	Henry III
9	Eric Idle	19	Darren Gough
10	Eroica	20	Flying without Wings

QUIZ 231 – Pot Luck

1 Which Old Testament book follows Daniel?

2 Which island was conquered by Velazquez de Cuéllar, who became its self-appointed governor in the early part of the 16th century?

3 In 1997, who was the first winner on Wimbledon's new No.1 court?

4 Which country has Bandar Seri Begawan as its capital?

5 Which football club's home ground is Adams Park?

6 The Morava, the Drava, and the Sava are all principal tributaries of which river?

7 Who wrote the 1991 novel *Gridlock*?

8 Which US state's flag incorporates the union flag?

9 Whose exploits behind Iraqi lines during the Gulf War were detailed in *The One That Got Away*?

10 Which Saharan country has the capital Niamey?

11 By what name is Port Jackson better known?

12 Which writer produced the novel versions of the *Star Wars*, *Aliens* and *Alien³* films?

13 In which country is the lek the unit of currency?

14 Albert Einstein was born in which German city?

15 What were based on the Victorian game called Magic Square?

16 Which style of painting is associated with Viktor Vasarely?

17 In *The Night of the Hunter* (1955), what was Robert Mitchum's profession?

18 Which of Shakespeare's plays is the longest?

19 How is singer Gaynor Hopkins better known?

20 In which European country is Lake Inari?

Easy

Medium

Hard

Answers to QUIZ 229 – Pot Luck

1 Portuguese
2 Sweden
3 Curia
4 Admiral Sir Miles Messervy
5 Rasputin
6 Watching a meteor shower
7 Empty spaces
8 269
9 Renminbi
10 James Brown
11 Weaving
12 Dag Hammarskjöld
13 Desiderius Erasmus
14 Birmingham
15 Nerissa
16 Dentists
17 eBay
18 A play upon words
19 1983
20 Hartley

1   Who won the 2017 Turner Prize?

2   What was the name by which Frida Kahlo's artist husband was known?

3   Which Swiss abstract painter (b.1879) taught at the Bauhaus with Kandinsky?

4   *Metamorphosis of Narcissus* (1937) was painted by which artist?

5   What is the subtitle of John Constable's painting *Flatford Mill*?

6   Which 16th-century German artist is renowned for *The Ambassadors*?

7   The surrender of which Dutch city was immortalised in paint by Velazquez?

8   Which Renaissance painter taught Michelangelo?

9   Which French landscape painter, 1796-1875, was a leading member of the Barbizon school?

10 Marcel Duchamp was associated with which early 20th-century art movement?

11 Who painted a portrait of Sir Winston Churchill, which was destroyed by Lady Churchill?

12 Primarily a portrait painter, whose work *The Storm on the Sea of Galilee* was stolen in 1990?

13 What was the name of the movement led in Britain by Percy Wyndham Lewis, using angular, abstract shapes?

14 In which country was Alfred Sisley born?

15 Which famous painting is actually entitled *Arrangement in Grey and Black*?

16 Who painted *Family of Saltimbanques* (1905)?

17 In the 1960s, who painted *Noli Me Tangere* and *Christ in Glory*?

18 *Painter in His Studio*, also known as *The Allegory of Painting*, was a work by which Dutch artist?

19 In 1967, whose painting *Children Coming Out of School* featured on the highest value stamp of a special commemorative issue?

20 Who features with his wife-to-be Bella in a 1915 painting entitled *The Birthday*?

Answers to QUIZ 230 – Geography

1	White Sea	11	Melbourne
2	Kano	12	Laos
3	Apia	13	Mauna Loa, Hawaii
4	Barbados	14	Lilongwe
5	Indus	15	China
6	Colorado	16	Luzon
7	Norway	17	Brazil
8	Antarctica	18	Atlas Mountains
9	Yamuna	19	Nore
10	Xi'an	20	Sana'a

1 Which African country has the capital Bujumbura?

2 Who wrote *Love in a Cold Climate* (1949)?

3 In which part of Australia is the Kakadu National Park?

4 What is the official currency unit of the Czech Republic?

5 What traditional form of entertainment is the Japanese bunraku?

6 The 1880 novel *Ben-Hur* was written by which author?

7 What was the first UK top ten hit for The Trammps?

8 What type of creature is a gharial?

9 *Micro* is a thriller completed by Richard Preston after the death of which author?

10 Who played Mel Gibson's wife in *Braveheart*?

11 Of which royal family is Het Loo the summer residence?

12 In what discipline did Richard Meade win a gold medal at the Munich Olympics in 1972?

13 Which Portuguese archipelago has Ponta Delgada as its capital?

14 The Tsar Kolokol is the biggest what in the world?

15 The Melbourne Cup is run at which racecourse?

16 In *Robinson Crusoe*, how long was Crusoe alone on the island before Friday arrived?

17 Salisbury Crags loom over which British city?

18 What was the title of James Joyce's only play?

19 Which river splits into the Lek and Waal in the Netherlands?

20 Before the invention of the clock what was "clockwise" known as?

Easy

Medium

Hard

Answers to QUIZ 231 – Pot Luck

1	Hosea	11	Sydney Harbour
2	Cuba	12	Alan Dean Foster
3	Tim Henman	13	Albania
4	Brunei	14	Ulm
5	Wycombe Wanderers	15	Crossword puzzles
6	Danube	16	Op art
7	Ben Elton	17	Preacher
8	Hawaii	18	*Hamlet*
9	Chris Ryan	19	Bonnie Tyler
10	Niger	20	Finland

Easy

1   In which year was the £1,000 note last issued by the Bank of England?

2   To which stricken ship did Grace Darling row a lifeboat in 1838?

3   When was slavery abolished in the British Empire by the Abolition Act?

4   During the 1988 US presidential elections, who was George Bush's Democrat opponent?

5   Which Sunday newspaper was founded in 1791 by WS Bourne?

6   In which cathedral was Henry III first crowned?

7   In which decade were traveller's cheques introduced?

8   Who was George II's mother?

9   In which year was the first London police force established at Scotland Yard?

10 From 1556 to 1605, who was the Mogul emperor of India?

11 Who sailed in the *Half Moon* in an attempt to discover a north-west passage to the orient?

12 Who was the last prisoner of the Tower of London?

13 In the 1950s and 1960s, who was the leading statesman of East Germany?

14 In which year did the Portuguese discover the Spice Islands?

Medium

15 What was a stater in Ancient Greece?

16 At the beginning of the Falklands War, who was the leader of Argentina?

17 Which country did Britain fight in the War of Jenkins' Ear?

18 Who was president of Malawi from 1966 to 1994?

19 What was the name of the ship used by both Fridtjof Nansen and (later) Roald Amundsen?

20 What name was given to the 8-24 page pamphlets that were widely circulated in Western Europe in the early 16th century?

Hard

Answers to QUIZ 232 – Art

1	Lubaina Himid	11	Graham Sutherland
2	Diego Rivera	12	Rembrandt
3	Paul Klee	13	Vorticism
4	Salvador Dali	14	France
5	*Scene on a Navigable River*	15	*Whistler's Mother*
6	Hans Holbein	16	Pablo Picasso
7	Breda	17	Graham Sutherland
8	Ghirlandaio	18	Johannes Vermeer
9	Corot	19	LS Lowry
10	Dada	20	Marc Chagall

1   Which well-known writer was born in Elstow near Bedford in 1628?

2   On a ship or boat what is a painter?

3   In John Le Carré's book, what was the name of the spy who came in from the cold?

4   Who was the last person to hold the UK office of Postmaster General before it was abolished in 1969?

5   The part of a sundial which casts a shadow is given what name?

6   Which 1964 play opens with the line "This is my lounge"?

7   Whose first novel was entitled *Pamela*?

8   Where was Tess of the d'Urbervilles arrested and charged with murder?

9   In 2012 in which Scottish town were lyrics from Marillion's *Kayleigh* inscribed in the market square?

10 Which Italian-born architect designed The Shard in London?

11 Thimphu is the capital of which small Asian country?

12 What name is given to a boy from a public school founded in 1572?

13 Who was the first female jockey to complete the Grand National?

14 In which Asian country is the city of Luang Prabang?

15 Which duo had a hit with *In the Year 2525* in 1969?

16 What is the Latin phrase usually abbreviated to QED?

17 The resort of Queenstown is in which New Zealand province?

18 Which band's seventh album was entitled *Think Tank*?

19 In which county was Southfork Ranch in *Dallas*?

20 What is the name of the castle estate that is home to the titular character of *Citizen Kane*?

Answers to QUIZ 233 – Pot Luck

1	Burundi	11	Dutch
2	Nancy Mitford	12	Three-Day Eventing
3	Northern Territory	13	Azores
4	Czech koruna	14	Bell
5	Puppet theatre	15	Flemington
6	Lew Wallace	16	24 years
7	*Hold Back the Night*	17	Edinburgh
8	Crocodile	18	*Exiles*
9	Michael Crichton	19	Rhine
10	Catherine McCormack	20	Sunwise

Easy

Medium

Hard

Easy

1 Which Danish architect designed the Sydney Opera House?

2 Where was Edward VIII born?

3 Which iconic Frank Lloyd Wright house overhangs a river in Pennsylvania?

4 The Bank for International Settlements has its headquarters in which city?

5 Where is the Shwedagon Pagoda?

6 Where in Paris would you go to see Napoleon's tomb?

7 Which UK university college is informally known as Castle?

8 In which building is the famous clock tower in Philadelphia, Pennsylvania?

9 Which is the largest Gothic church in northern Europe?

10 Why is the White House white?

11 Eton College was founded by which monarch?

12 Which French city contains a famous 13th-century Gothic cathedral, the largest in France?

13 The Radcot Bridge is the oldest bridge still standing across which river?

Medium

14 Whose seat is Eaton Hall in Cheshire?

15 What is the name of the aqueduct in America which is the world's longest tunnel?

16 To which country would you travel to see Kandy's Temple of the Tooth?

17 George I was born in which castle?

18 What is the name of the official church of the Lord Mayor of London?

19 Where in Britain is the Robert Gordon University?

20 What was the name of the tower occupied by Saruman in *Lord of the Rings*?

Hard

Answers to QUIZ 234 – History

1	1943	11	Henry Hudson
2	*Forfarshire*	12	Rudolph Hess
3	1833	13	Walter Ulbricht
4	Michael Dukakis	14	1511
5	*Observer*	15	A coin
6	Gloucester	16	Leopoldo Galtieri
7	1770s	17	Spain
8	Sophia Dorothea of Celle	18	Hastings Banda
9	1829	19	*Fram*
10	Akbar	20	Chapbooks

1   Who released the 2006 album *Back to Basics*?

2   Who had a hit with *The Riverboat Song* in 1996?

3   Under what name was Manchester United FC originally formed?

4   The sackbut was an early English name for which instrument?

5   The 1974 novel *Centennial* was written by which author?

6   Who created the fictional collie Lassie?

7   The ruins of Leptis Magna are in which country?

8   What is the main colour on the Tunisian flag?

9   Who wrote the poem *September 1, 1939*?

10   Which Israelite leader succeeded Moses?

11   In *Middlemarch* by George Eliot, what is the name of Celia's sister?

12   Which river on Tasmania's central plateau flows into the Derwent?

13   Who duetted with Britney Spears on *Pretty Girls*, released in May 2015?

14   Which Earl of Derby gave his name to the race?

15   The village of Fritham is in which county?

16   Who said: "You know you're getting old when the candles cost more than the cake"?

17   Which Greek goddess was the personification of the rainbow?

18   *When I Was Your Man* was a top ten single in 2013 for which singer?

19   In which year were MPs first paid in the UK?

20   Which singer and entertainer had a 1968 top 10 hit with *1-2-3 O'Leary*?

Easy

Medium

Hard

Answers to QUIZ 235 – Pot Luck

1	John Bunyan	11	Bhutan
2	A rope	12	Harrovian
3	Alec Leamas	13	Geraldine Rees
4	John Stonehouse	14	Laos
5	A gnomon	15	Zager and Evans
6	*Entertaining Mr Sloane*	16	*Quod erat demonstrandum*
7	Samuel Richardson	17	Otago
8	Stonehenge	18	Blur
9	Galashiels	19	Braddock County
10	Renzo Piano	20	Xanadu

Easy

1 Who starred as Mortimer Brewster in the 1944 film *Arsenic and Old Lace*?

2 Who played James Rhodes/War Machine in the 2018 film *Avengers: Infinity War*?

3 In the film *2001: A Space Odyssey*, what was the name of the spaceship sent to explore Jupiter?

4 Which Donald won an Oscar in 1942 for his performance in *How Green Was My Valley*?

5 In *Earth vs. the Flying Saucers* (1956) which famous animator created the effects?

6 Which actor played James Bond's contact, Henderson, in one film and went on to portray Blofeld two films later?

7 Who directed *Great Expectations* in 1946?

8 Which Peter won a posthumous Oscar for the 1976 film *Network*?

9 In the 1960 film *Village of the Damned*, what was the name of the town?

10 Who played Joel Cairo in *The Maltese Falcon* (1941)?

11 Who starred as the one-armed war veteran in *Bad Day at Black Rock* (1955)?

Medium

12 On whose life was the 1985 film *Heart of a Champion* based?

13 In *Sahara* (2005), which actress starred as a United Nations scientist?

14 Who played Snoke in the 2017 film *Star Wars: The Last Jedi*?

15 Which George directed *My Fair Lady* (1964)?

16 Which 1956 film starred Kevin McCarthy, who also played a cameo role in the 1978 re-make?

17 Who starred in the 1941 film *Dr. Jekyll and Mr. Hyde*?

18 How is the film director Sándor Kellner better known?

19 What was the surname of Lotte, who played Rosa Klebb in *From Russia with Love* (1963)?

20 Which 1968 musical film, about the life of Gertrude Lawrence, starred Dame Julie Andrews?

Hard

Answers to QUIZ 236 – Buildings

1 Utzon
2 White Lodge, Richmond
3 Fallingwater
4 Basel
5 Yangon, Myanmar (Burma)
6 Les Invalides
7 University College, Durham
8 Philadelphia City Hall
9 Cologne cathedral
10 To cover smoke stains (It was set on fire by the British in 1814)
11 Henry VI
12 Amiens
13 The Thames
14 The Duke of Westminster
15 The Delaware Aqueduct
16 Sri Lanka
17 Osnabrück (Hanover)
18 St Lawrence Jewry
19 Aberdeen
20 Orthanc

QUIZ 239 – Pot Luck

1 In which country were cultured pearls first obtained?

2 Which was the first UK racecourse equipped with a photo-finish camera?

3 In whose reign was the British sovereign monetary unit introduced?

4 What is the name of the domed hills near Uluru?

5 4:44 was a 2017 album by which artist?

6 Which couple lived at 12 Coleridge Close, Climthorpe?

7 Which Essex town was established as the site of a market in 1247?

8 Other than in Scotland, where is there a capital called Edinburgh?

9 Which first-class county club did Phil Tufnell play for from 1986 to 2002?

10 Which river flows through Munich?

11 Which country has borders with both Suriname and Brazil?

12 In which year was the US university Yale founded?

13 Which is the second largest of the Hawaiian islands?

14 Which politician owned a dog called "Dizzy", named in honour of Benjamin Disraeli (First Earl of Beaconsfield)?

15 The Great Smoky Mountains National Park straddles the border between North Carolina and which other US state?

16 Who followed Sir Robert Walpole as Prime Minister of the UK?

17 If it is eight o'clock on a July morning in the UK, what time is it in Los Angeles, California?

18 Which football team plays at Cappielow Park?

19 Who had hits in 1969 and 1970 with *Wonderful World, Beautiful People* and *Wild World*?

20 What is the capital of Madagascar?

Easy / **Medium** / **Hard**

Answers to QUIZ 237 – Pot Luck

1	Christina Aguilera	11	Dorothea
2	Ocean Colour Scene	12	Ouse
3	Newton Heath Lancashire & Yorkshire Railway Football Club	13	Iggy Azalea
4	Trombone	14	12th
5	James Michener	15	Hampshire
6	Eric Knight	16	Bob Hope
7	Libya	17	Iris
8	Red	18	Bruno Mars
9	WH Auden	19	1911
10	Joshua	20	Des O'Connor

1 Which bird has the longest migration route?

2 What is the process of nidulation more commonly known as?

3 *Alcea* are garden flowering plants more commonly known by what name?

4 What is another name for the plantain lily?

5 Which tree is associated with the Latin name *Juglans*?

6 Which is the world's longest insect?

7 A tree of the genus *Fraxinus* has what common name?

8 What sort of bird is a Cinnamon Norwich?

9 What word describes an insect that lives for only one day?

10 Which part of its body does a snake use to detect noise?

11 What would you not find in an aphotic zone?

12 The sweetbriar has what alternative name?

13 What sort of creature is a cisticola?

14 If an animal is described as an endotherm, what type of creature is it?

15 What is a group of tortoises called?

16 To which botanic family do Swiss cheese plants belong?

17 The kangaroo paw plant is an emblem of which Australian state?

18 What is another name for the extinct Tasmanian Tiger?

19 What is Sweden's national flower?

20 What is another name for the bird sometimes known as a laverock?

Answers to QUIZ 238 – Film

1	Cary Grant	11	Spencer Tracy
2	Don Cheadle	12	Ray Mancini
3	*Discovery*	13	Penélope Cruz
4	Crisp	14	Andy Serkis
5	Ray Harryhausen	15	Cukor
6	Charles Gray	16	*Invasion of the Body Snatchers*
7	Sir David Lean	17	Spencer Tracy
8	Finch	18	Alexander Korda
9	Midwich	19	Lenya
10	Peter Lorre	20	*Star!*

QUIZ 241 – Pot Luck

ANSWERS ON PAGE 243

1   In which country is Friulian a regional language?

2   Who appeared on the first two US adhesive stamps?

3   Which New Zealand river flows south-west from the Tararua Range?

4   In which year was the first credit card issued in the UK?

5   Who wrote *The Prisoner of Zenda* (1894)?

6   Which South African town was subjected to a four-month siege during the Second Boer War?

7   Which trench lies between Jamaica and Cuba?

8   Who was the first female jockey to ride in the Derby?

9   In John Osborne's play *Look Back in Anger*, what sort of stall does Jimmy Porter have in the market?

10 On which Caribbean island would you find the resort of Varadero?

11 Which girl's name is derived from the Hebrew word for "lily"?

12 In which European country is Lake Mamry?

13 On which river does Dumfries stand?

14 Which member of Queen wrote *Radio Ga Ga*?

15 When did Cleopatra become queen of Egypt?

16 In which country was the first modern motorway created?

17 Which monarch is buried in Canterbury Cathedral?

18 What was the last symphony written by Mozart?

19 Which is the most southerly race course on mainland Britain?

20 *All Quiet on the Western Front* (1929) was written by which author?

Easy
Medium
Hard

Answers to QUIZ 239 – Pot Luck

1	Japan	11	Guyana
2	Epsom	12	1701
3	Henry VII	13	Maui
4	Olgas	14	Michael Foot
5	Jay-Z	15	Tennessee
6	Reggie and Elizabeth Perrin	16	Spencer Compton, first Earl of Wilmington
7	Romford	17	Midnight
8	Tristan da Cunha	18	Greenock Morton
9	Middlesex	19	Jimmy Cliff
10	Isar	20	Antananarivo

1   Which two astronomers discovered the cosmic microwave background radiation in the 1960s?

2   What is studied by an orthopterologist?

3   How is the medical condition of Daltonism more commonly referred to?

4   In which constellation are the Pleiades?

5   What is the measurement of ocean depths called?

6   Who was the sister of a famous astronomer who between 1786 and 1797 discovered several new comets herself?

7   What title was first held by John Flamsteed in 1675?

8   Of what is somatology the science?

9   What is a lotion containing malathion used to treat?

10 The disease Leptospirosis has which common name?

11 Betz cells are found in which part of the body?

12 Pyorrhoea is an inflammation of what part of the body?

13 Which constellation contains the bright star Procyon?

14 Which is the hottest planet in our solar system?

15 What name is given to the bending of the winds caused by the Earth spinning on its axis?

16 What does the Mercalli scale measure?

17 What is an eidograph?

18 Ac is the chemical symbol for which element?

19 Which English biologist first coined the term "dinosaur" in the early 1840s?

20 Which viral disease is also called grippe?

Answers to QUIZ 240 – Natural World

1	Arctic tern	11	Light
2	Nest-building	12	Eglantine
3	Hollyhocks	13	Bird
4	Hosta	14	Warm-blooded
5	Walnut	15	A creep
6	Chinese stick insect	16	Arum
7	Ash	17	Western Australia
8	Canary	18	Thylacine
9	Ephemeral	19	Twinflower
10	Jaw	20	Lark

ANSWERS ON PAGE 245

1   In which country are Arequipa and Ayacucho?

2   Who with royal connections had the maiden name Warfield?

3   Whose diary, *The Actor's Life*, was published in 1978?

4   Which band headlined the first ever Glastonbury Festival in 1970?

5   Which institution was founded in 1694 and nationalised in 1946?

6   Who was the Russian author of *Dead Souls* (1842)?

7   Whose Symphony No.69 in C is known as the "Laudon" symphony?

8   Which football team plays at Bayview Stadium?

9   To what did the British Protectorate of Bechuanaland change its name, after becoming independent on 30 September 1966?

10 Who released the 2015 single *Lush Life?*

11 What was the name of the largest carnivorous dinosaur ever to be discovered?

12 *Wings of the Wild* was the fifth studio album by which Australian singer?

13 In the King James Bible, what is the 26th book of the Old Testament?

14 Which is England's deepest lake?

15 What does "psso" mean in knitting?

16 In which country are there a river and lake called Athabasca?

17 The Efteling theme park is in which country?

18 What nationality was composer Giacomo Meyerbeer?

19 In Greek mythology, which weaver was turned into a spider by Athena?

20 In 2000, which boy band had a hit with their cover of Queen's *We Will Rock You?*

Easy

Medium

Hard

Answers to QUIZ 241 – Pot Luck

1	Italy	11	Susan
2	Benjamin Franklin and George Washington	12	Poland
3	Hutt	13	Nith
4	1966	14	Roger Taylor
5	Anthony Hope	15	51BC
6	Ladysmith	16	Italy
7	Cayman	17	Henry IV
8	Alex Greaves	18	*Jupiter* (No.41)
9	Sweets	19	Newton Abbot
10	Cuba	20	Erich Maria Remarque

1   Which novel, subsequently made into a film, features the stricken ship the *SS Cabinet Minister*?

2   Which family features in John Steinbeck's *The Grapes of Wrath*?

3   Which famous author penned the catchphrase "naughty but nice" when referring to fresh cream cakes?

4   *Dead Famous* and *Past Mortem* are books by which comedian turned novelist?

5   The TV series *Bones* is based on the books from which author?

6   In *Lady Chatterley's Lover* by DH Lawrence, what is Lady Chatterley's first name?

7   Who wrote the war poem *Naming of Parts*?

8   Who wrote the series of novels *The Power of Five*?

9   In *Little Women* which of the March girls went to bed with a clothes peg on her nose to try to improve its shape?

10 In which Dickens novel does Bradley Headstone appear?

11 Which poet wrote *The Love Song of J Alfred Prufrock*?

12 In which novel by Jane Austen does Captain Wentworth feature?

13 Of whom did Shakespeare write: "Age cannot wither her, nor custom stale her infinite variety"?

14 The group Mungo Jerry got their name from which book?

15 John Masefield wrote "I must go down to the seas again" in which poem?

16 Whose address is 56B Whitehaven Mansions, Sandhurst Square, London W1?

17 Who wrote the 1980 novel *The Clan of the Cave Bear*?

18 In which country is Edgar Allen Poe's *The Pit and the Pendulum* set?

19 Which 19th-century French novelist wrote *Germinal*?

20 Who wrote the 1956 novel *Time for a Tiger*?

Answers to QUIZ 242 – Science

1	Arno Penzias and Robert Wilson	11	The brain
2	Cockroaches and grasshoppers etc	12	Gums
3	Colour blindness	13	Canis Minor
4	Taurus	14	Venus
5	Bathymetry	15	Coriolis effect
6	Caroline Herschel	16	Earthquake intensity
7	Astronomer Royal	17	An instrument for enlarging or reducing drawings
8	The human body	18	Actinium
9	Infestations such as head lice or scabies	19	Sir Richard Owen
10	Weil's disease	20	Influenza

QUIZ 245 – Pot Luck

ANSWERS ON PAGE 247

1. Where is the Lambert-Fisher glacier, the longest in the world?
2. In Finland, Santa is associated with which type of animal?
3. What was the family name of Kaiser Wilhelm II of Germany?
4. Which Russian river flows into the Volga at Nizhni Novgorod?
5. Which suborder of dinosaurs are the evolutionary ancestors of modern birds?
6. In which country is Lake Manyara?
7. Which great metropolis grew from a fishing village called Edo?
8. Which group were the first to be signed to Tamla Motown?
9. In what year was the word "selfie" included in the online *Oxford English Dictionary*?
10. The Triassic period occurred during which geological era?
11. What nationality is fashion designer Dries Van Noten?
12. Who remains at the end of Joseph Haydn's *Farewell* symphony?
13. Which band had a hit with *King of the Road* in 1990?
14. Which Sir Noël Coward musical features the song *I'll See You Again*?
15. Why was the 1955 Royal Ascot meeting postponed for a month?
16. What is Stanley's surname in the play *A Streetcar Named Desire*?
17. In which Kent town is Pocahontas buried?
18. Which author wrote the *Barsoom* series featuring the character of John Carter?
19. Of what is logophobia a fear?
20. Which of the Leeward Islands lies north-east of Montserrat?

Easy

Medium

Hard

Answers to QUIZ 243 – Pot Luck

1	Peru	11	Spinosaurus
2	Mrs Wallis Simpson	12	Delta Goodrem
3	Charlton Heston	13	Ezekiel
4	T Rex	14	Wastwater
5	The Bank of England	15	Pass slipped stitch over
6	Nikolai Gogol	16	Canada
7	Haydn	17	Holland
8	East Fife	18	German
9	Botswana	19	Arachne
10	Zara Larsson	20	Five

Easy

1 How many goals did Sir Bobby Charlton score for Manchester United?

2 In 1973, who was the male player who competed in a mixed singles match billed as the "Battle of the Sexes"?

3 When did synchronised swimming become an Olympic event?

4 In which city were the first Commonwealth Games held?

5 James Naismith invented which sport?

6 How many riders compete in a standard speedway race?

7 Who were the first American Football Super Bowl winners, in 1967?

8 Which football team plays at Kirklees Stadium?

9 For which Spanish football club did Mark Hughes play?

10 Tennis legend Andre Agassi's father was a former Olympic contestant in which sport?

11 Who won the PDC World Darts Championship in 2018 in his first year as a professional?

12 In which sport is the Corbillon Cup awarded?

13 Who played the putt that clinched the 2004 Ryder Cup for Europe?

14 Who achieved the first televised nine dart finish in 1984?

Medium

15 In which sport did Irina Rodnina win 24 world, Olympic and European gold medals?

16 Whom did Frank Bruno beat to become World Heavyweight Champion in 1995?

17 In the 200m freestyle at Palma in 1993, who became the first British woman to win a world swimming title?

18 Who was the first woman to win gold at winter and summer Games?

19 How many times did the great Sir Gordon Richards win the Epsom Derby?

20 How many dimples are there on a standard golf ball?

Hard

Answers to QUIZ 244 – Literature

1	*Whisky Galore!*	11	TS Eliot
2	The Joad Family	12	*Persuasion*
3	Salman Rushdie	13	Cleopatra
4	Ben Elton	14	*Old Possum's Book of Practical Cats*
5	Kathy Reichs	15	*Sea Fever*
6	Constance	16	Hercule Poirot
7	Henry Reed	17	Jean Auel
8	Anthony Horowitz	18	Spain
9	Amy	19	Zola
10	*Our Mutual Friend*	20	Anthony Burgess

1. In which year was the Glyndebourne Opera theatre opened?

2. For what is the Kremer prize awarded?

3. Which West African country was formerly called Dahomey?

4. Which rugby league team was known as the Blue Sox?

5. Which US state is nicknamed "The Centennial State"?

6. In which European city was the Kellogg-Briand Pact, otherwise known as the Treaty for the Renunciation of War, signed in 1928?

7. Who wrote incidental music for the Bjørnson play *Sigurd the Crusader*?

8. What was Shakespeare's first comedy?

9. A score of 111 by a team or batsman is known by what name?

10. Which river forms part of the boundary between Germany and the Netherlands?

11. What textile is sometimes known as a "poor man's velvet"?

12. Other than cricket, what sport is played at Lord's?

13. Which *The X Factor* runner-up released the single *Sax* in 2015?

14. What was the nationality of the composer Svend Schultz?

15. Whom did Henry I marry in 1100?

16. Who wrote the 1920s books *To the Lighthouse* and *Orlando*?

17. To which country does the Sea of Marmara belong?

18. What was the address of Lord Peter Wimsey's bachelor flat in London?

19. Which Joseph Conrad novel features the ill-fated ship, the *Patna*?

20. In which south-east Cornish village is the Heritage Museum of Smuggling and Fishing located?

Answers to QUIZ 245 – Pot Luck

1	Antarctica	11	Belgian
2	Goat	12	The conductor and two violinists
3	Hohenzollern	13	The Proclaimers
4	Oka	14	*Bitter Sweet*
5	Theropods	15	Because of a railway strike
6	Tanzania	16	Kowalski
7	Tokyo	17	Gravesend
8	The Miracles	18	Edgar Rice Burroughs
9	2013	19	Words
10	Mesozoic	20	Antigua

1   What word, derived from Greek, means "thunder lizard"?

2   Of what is nyctophobia a fear?

3   What is a toxopholite?

4   From which language does the word "kiosk" originate?

5   What is the name of the three collections of books that make up the Buddhist scriptures?

6   At the start of the traditional Hippocratic oath, the words "I swear by" led to the naming of which Greek god as "healer"?

7   What does "photography" mean in Greek?

8   What name is given to a salmon returning upstream?

9   Nephophobia is a fear of what?

10 What is a feijoda?

11 What is considered to be the first work of literature printed in America?

12 What was ogham?

13 If you suffered with anosmia, what would you be unable to do?

14 What name is given to the service at the start of Passover?

15 Who signs with the name "Sarum"?

16 Which philosopher wrote "Where there is no common power, there is no law. Where no law, no justice" (1651)?

17 What is the opposite of aestivation?

18 In culinary terms, what does "farci" mean?

19 Which speech includes the words "that government of the people, by the people, and for the people, shall not perish from the earth"?

20 Of what is demophobia a fear?

Answers to QUIZ 246 – Sport

1	249	11	Rob Cross
2	Bobby Riggs (against Billie Jean King)	12	Women's table tennis
3	1984	13	Colin Montgomerie
4	Hamilton, Canada	14	John Lowe
5	Basketball	15	Figure skating
6	Four	16	Oliver McCall
7	Green Bay Packers	17	Karen Pickering
8	Huddersfield Town	18	Christa Luding-Rothenburger
9	Barcelona	19	Once
10	Boxing	20	336

ANSWERS ON PAGE 1

1   From which language does the word "ranch" originate?

2   In which island is Chaguanas the largest settlement?

3   Which Jane Austen novel features Eleanor Tilney?

4   The ghost town of Pripyat is in which country?

5   Which London thoroughfare, originally called Catherine Street, was renamed after a game played there during the reign of Charles II?

6   In which Dickens novel does Jerry Cruncher appear?

7   Into which sea does the Tiber flow?

8   From which city did the Spanish Armada set sail?

9   Which Swiss artist, playwright and novelist wrote *Homo Faber* (1957)?

10 Which rock singer has a bench dedicated to his memory at Pembroke Lodge in Richmond Park?

11 Who wrote the words to Petula Clark's no.1 hit *This Is My Song*?

12 What is a lacuna?

13 In which decade was the Prix de L'Arc de Triomphe first run?

14 When was Napoleon Bonaparte first proclaimed Emperor of France?

15 Who released a 1972 album entitled *Never a Dull Moment*?

16 Which jockey won the Grand National in 2010 at his 15th attempt?

17 Which river in South Australia is named after a battle in France?

18 What sort of book was compiled by Moody and Sankey?

19 Of which country is *La Brabançonne* the national anthem?

20 As what did couturier Pierre Balmain originally train?

Easy

Medium

Hard

Answers to QUIZ 247 – Pot Luck

1	1934	11	Corduroy
2	Human-powered flight	12	Real Tennis
3	Benin	13	Fleur East
4	Halifax	14	Danish
5	Colorado	15	Matilda of Scotland
6	Paris	16	Virginia Woolf
7	Grieg	17	Turkey
8	*Two Gentlemen of Verona*	18	110a Piccadilly
9	Nelson	19	*Lord Jim*
10	Ems	20	Polperro

Easy

1 Who was the first lawgiver of ancient Athens, who gave his name to any harsh system?

2 What was the title of the French royal house from 1328 to 1589?

3 Who was the Spartan admiral who defeated the Athenians in the Peloponnesian War?

4 In which town or city is Italy's oldest opera house, the Teatro di San Carlo?

5 In 1979, which country won the Eurovision Song Contest but declined to host the event in 1980?

6 Which French photographer (b.1908) was among the first to adopt 35 mm film?

7 What is the name of the Flemish cartographer who is recognised as the creator of the first modern atlas?

8 Which European capital city was destroyed by an earthquake in 1755?

9 What was the nationality of the composer Matyas Gyorgy Seiber?

10 In which year did France present the USA with the Statue of Liberty?

11 Which Norwegian port was the country's capital during the Viking period?

12 The Oise and the Marne are tributaries of which river?

13 In which area of water are the Kekennah Islands?

Medium

14 Who was the 18th-century German composer of the opera *Orfeo ed Euridice*?

15 In which year did Napoleon Bonaparte die in exile?

16 In which city in Italy was the violin-maker Antonio Stradivarius born?

17 On which Greek island is the great temple and shrine to Apollo?

18 Which saint founded the monastic site of Glendalough in the Republic of Ireland?

19 If you were holidaying in Fuengirola, on which of the Spanish Costas would you be?

20 Which German author wrote *Steppenwolf* in 1927?

Hard

Answers to QUIZ 248 – Words

1	Brontosaurus	11	*Bay Psalm Book*
2	Night or darkness	12	An ancient alphabetical system
3	Archer	13	Smell
4	Turkish	14	Seder
5	*Tripitaka*	15	The Bishop of Salisbury
6	Apollo	16	Thomas Hobbes
7	Drawing with light	17	Hibernation
8	Grilse	18	Stuffed
9	Clouds	19	The Gettysburg Address
10	A Brazilian stew	20	Crowds

250

1 In the rhyme often quoted when magpies are seen, what is associated with one magpie?

2 What was the composer Stravinsky's first name?

3 *Neither Here Nor There: Travels in Europe* is a 1991 book by which US author?

4 Which category is represented by the colour pink in a game of Trivial Pursuit™?

5 What is an aperitif of white wine and cassis called?

6 *I Should Be So Lucky* was a hit for which Australian singer?

7 Who managed the England football team at the 1996 European Championships?

8 What is the radio operators' code word between Mike and Oscar?

9 "Let me drown in your laughter, Let me die in your arms" is a lyric from which song?

10 On a standard computer keyboard, which letter is between S and F?

11 If two straight lines are always the same distance apart what are they said to be?

12 Which material is associated with the Irish county of Donegal?

13 What are ensigns or standards of a particular regiment generally called?

14 Who came to visit for the sake of my little nut tree?

15 What was the name of Gavin's mum in the TV series *Gavin & Stacey*?

16 How many points are there in a perfect turn in a driving test?

17 In which country is the city of Stuttgart?

18 Which studio produced the 2018 film *Early Man*?

19 During which month do Muslims fast from before sunrise until just after sunset?

20 Which company manufactures the MX5?

Answers to QUIZ 499 – Pot Luck

1	Josiah	11	The Broadway League and American Theatre Wing
2	Aldous Huxley	12	1911
3	Rossini	13	Sydney, Australia
4	Christmas Island	14	Shawn Mendes
5	A strong broth	15	Captain Marryat
6	Pork	16	Quagga
7	Madagascar	17	*How to Succeed in Business without Really Trying*
8	Jupiter (or Jove)	18	Kümmel
9	Two	19	Crocodile
10	Nick Skelton	20	Canada

ANSWERS ON PAGE 254

1   Electric power that flows one way only is given what name?

2   What term is given to two spirals coiled round an axis, as in the DNA molecule?

3   What is measured to assess the concentration of glucose in the body?

4   The mandible has what more common name?

5   What is the radioactive form of an element called?

6   How is the central part of an atom referred to?

7   Which membrane covers the front of the eye?

8   How is acetic acid more commonly known?

9   What travels at 186,281 miles per second?

10   Which scientist is associated with the theory of gravity?

11   The letter F represents which chemical element?

12   Which element has atomic number 1?

13   What, in the context of blood coagulation, is the common word for a thrombus?

14   In which part of the body is the duodenum?

15   Which part of the brain lies immediately behind the forehead?

16   Cl is the symbol for which chemical element?

17   Which is the fourth planet from the Sun?

18   Which US communications satellite launched in 1962?

19   Of what is cardiology the science?

20   Which planet in the solar system is the home of the Great Red Spot, a giant spinning storm in the planet's atmosphere?

Answers to QUIZ 500 – Photography

1	Brian Duffy	11	Times Square, New York
2	Steven Sasson	12	1900
3	1810s	13	Annie Leibovitz
4	Diane Arbus	14	Norman Anderson
5	Nicephore Niepce	15	Brian May
6	1820s	16	Lausanne
7	Exchangeable image file	17	Deutsches Institut für Normung
8	Mexico	18	David Heneker
9	Patrick Lichfield (Fifth Earl of Lichfield)	19	Kevin Systrom and Mike Krieger
10	Lunch atop a Skyscraper	20	Robert Goddard

1 What word can refer both to a horse colour and a loading area?

2 What did Old Mother Hubbard find in her cupboard?

3 Which British playwright wrote the trilogy *The Norman Conquests*?

4 Which star constellation represents a hunter with his club and shield raised?

5 On an Ordnance Survey map, what is indicated by the abbreviation Sta?

6 Who wrote the classic novel *Jane Eyre*?

7 What does the time abbreviation pm stand for?

8 Russets and Braeburns are varieties of which type of fruit?

9 Which mythical creature is between the Rabbit and the Snake in the Chinese calendar?

10 What did the USA buy from Russia for $7.2 million dollars in 1867?

11 Which surname is shared by the fourth and sixth stars of the TV series *Doctor Who*?

12 What is the traditional bingo call for the number 65?

13 Who had a 2003 hit with *Rock Your Body*?

14 Which boxer took part in the 2018 series of *I'm a Celebrity...Get Me Out of Here*?

15 Gareth Southgate appeared in a 1990s advert for which fast food chain?

16 In which county is Biggin Hill airport?

17 In Scrabble® what is the value of the blank tile?

18 On UK roads, what colour of cats eyes are used to mark the left edge of the carriageway?

19 Mo Salah plays football for which national team?

20 How many Ugly Sisters feature in *Cinderella*?

Easy

Medium

Hard

Answers to QUIZ 251 – Pot Luck

1	Sorrow	11	Parallel
2	Igor	12	Tweed
3	Bill Bryson	13	Colours
4	Entertainment	14	The King of Spain's daughter
5	Kir	15	Pam
6	Kylie Minogue	16	Three
7	Terry Venables	17	Germany
8	November	18	Aardman Animations
9	*Annie's Song* (John Denver)	19	Ramadan
10	D	20	Mazda

Easy

1 What colour is the tractor symbol that denotes food quality in the UK?

2 Which cookery term means to fry quickly in a little hot fat?

3 What is coley?

4 A Caesar salad usually contains which cheese?

5 What is the German word for a veal cutlet?

6 The milk of which legume is used to make tofu?

7 Rioja is a wine from which country?

8 Raita traditionally consists of buttermilk, cucumber, mint and what other ingredient?

9 Which musician was involved in the creation of "Little Wallop" cheese?

10 What confection is generally a combination of sugar or honey, roasted nuts and whipped egg white?

Medium

11 What spice is made from dried red capsicum fruit?

12 Acorn and kabocha are varieties of which fruit commonly used as a vegetable?

13 What is the name of the dish with toasted muffins, ham and hollandaise sauce?

14 In which country did clootie dumplings originate?

15 What is the main ingredient of tabbouleh?

16 *Roti* is another name for which popular Indian flatbread?

17 From which country does paella originate?

18 What is the main alcholic ingredient in a Cosmopolitan?

19 What, traditionally, forms the outside of a dolma?

20 A pomelo belongs to which family of fruit?

Hard

Answers to QUIZ 252 – Science

1	Direct current	11	Fluorine
2	Double helix	12	Hydrogen
3	Blood sugar	13	Clot
4	Jawbone	14	Small intestine
5	Radioisotope	15	Frontal lobe
6	Nucleus	16	Chlorine
7	Cornea	17	Mars
8	Vinegar	18	*Telstar*
9	Light	19	The heart
10	Sir Isaac Newton	20	Jupiter

QUIZ 255 – Pot Luck

QUIZ 255 – Pot Luck

1 Who was the mother of Edward VI?

2 *The Dark Side of the Moon* is a 1973 album by which band?

3 In song, which two words go before, "...how sweet the sound, That saved a wretch like me"?

4 In which county is the stately home of Wimpole Hall?

5 Which Shakespearean character has been played on screen by both Mel Gibson and Sir Laurence Olivier?

6 In which Scottish region is Inverary Castle?

7 Which chemical element has the atomic number 12?

8 Which 1990s TV series about the Larkins starred Sir David Jason?

9 What is the radio operators' code word for the letter between Juliet and Lima?

10 Who played Idi Amin in the film *The Last King of Scotland*?

11 Which animal represents the zodiac sign Capricorn?

12 Which castle overlooks the Llŷn peninsula?

13 Each chess player starts a game with how many pieces?

14 The twin doctors who present series including *Operation Ouch!* have what first names?

15 What word can mean both "seaside" and "freewheel"?

16 What geometrical name is given to an area in the north Atlantic Ocean?

17 What astronomical event took place on August 11, 1999?

18 Which chain of convenience stores was founded in the Netherlands in 1932?

19 On which racecourse is the Steward's Cup run?

20 Which British tennis player played his first match as a seed at the 2018 French Open?

Easy
Medium
Hard

Answers to QUIZ 253 – Pot Luck

1	Bay	11	Baker
2	Nothing	12	Old age pension
3	Sir Alan Ayckbourn	13	Justin Timberlake
4	Orion	14	Amir Khan
5	Station	15	Pizza Hut™
6	Charlotte Brontë	16	Kent
7	Post meridiem	17	Nil
8	Apple	18	Red
9	Dragon	19	Egypt
10	Alaska	20	Two

ANSWERS ON PAGE **258**

1 Which Russian author wrote the novel *Crime and Punishment*?

2 What term is given to the use in literature of several words close together which begin with similar sounds?

3 What was the first name of *The Other Boleyn Girl* in the novel by Philippa Gregory?

4 Who wrote the classic novel *Gone with the Wind*?

5 In a literary context, for what does the abbreviation "ms" stand?

6 Which Transylvanian count was created by Bram Stoker?

7 What was the title of the first of Sir Terry Pratchett's *Discworld* novels?

8 Who are the main characters in Milton's *Paradise Lost*?

9 *Of Mice and Men* (1937) was written by which author?

10 Who wrote the novels which have been adapted for TV as the series *Shetland*?

11 In Jane Austen's *Pride and Prejudice*, who is Mr Darcy's friend and Netherfield tenant?

12 In which century was Charlotte Brontë born?

13 Which novel features the character of Long John Silver?

14 Creatures from which planet invaded Earth in HG Wells' *The War of the Worlds*?

15 Who wrote the novel *Hard Times*?

16 After which London terminus was Michael Bond's fictional bear named?

17 "Earth has not anything to show more fair" is the opening line of which poem by William Wordsworth?

18 Where was *Our Man* in the title of a novel by Graham Greene?

19 The 1977 TV series *Roots* and a 2016 remake were based on a novel by which author?

20 In which county is Hardy's Cottage, now in the care of the National Trust?

Answers to QUIZ 254 – Food and Drink

1	Red	11	Paprika
2	Sauté	12	Squash
3	A fish	13	Eggs Benedict
4	Parmesan	14	Scotland
5	Schnitzel	15	Cracked wheat
6	Soya bean	16	Chapati
7	Spain	17	Spain
8	Yoghurt	18	Vodka
9	Alex James	19	Vine leaf
10	Nougat	20	Citrus

ANSWERS ON PAGE **259**

1   What is the surname of Lynda in the radio series *The Archers*?

2   In which county is Fishguard?

3   What term is given to the transposition of word sounds, such as "you have hissed the mystery lecture"?

4   Which airport has the international code FRA?

5   The Polo is manufactured by which car company?

6   Who designed Queen Elizabeth II's wedding gown?

7   Which anniversary did the USA celebrate in 1976?

8   What word can mean both to go fishing and a viewpoint?

9   Fusing sand, soda and lime at a high temperature creates which substance?

10 Which Irish rock band appeared on the front cover of *Time* magazine in 1987?

11 On mobile phones with a keypad on the handset, which letters appear on the number 7 key?

12 The UK was involved in which conflict between April and June 1982?

13 What is the administrative centre for the county of West Midlands?

14 What was the name of the train service created in 1883 on which a famous Dame Agatha Christie novel was set?

15 Who played Billy Costigan in the 2006 film *The Departed*?

16 Of which Native American people was Sitting Bull the chief?

17 For which football club did Harry Kane play before joining Tottenham Hotspur?

18 *I Am the Very Model of a Modern Major-General* is from which work by Gilbert and Sullivan?

19 What is a panatella?

20 In the Old Testament, the queen of which land famously visited King Solomon?

Easy

Medium

Hard

Answers to QUIZ 255 – Pot Luck

1	Jane Seymour	11	Goat
2	Pink Floyd	12	Harlech Castle
3	Amazing Grace	13	16
4	Cambridgeshire	14	Chris and Xand
5	Hamlet	15	Coast
6	Argyll and Bute	16	Bermuda Triangle
7	Magnesium	17	Solar eclipse
8	*The Darling Buds of May*	18	Spar
9	Kilo	19	Goodwood
10	Forest Whitaker	20	Kyle Edmund

1 From which part of its body does a firefly emit light?

2 Which bird has song and mistle species?

3 What kind of creature is a gecko?

4 Is the Australian barramundi a freshwater or sea fish?

5 What is the main food of the aardvark?

6 What term is given to a whale's nostril?

7 Which yellow-and-black striped insect is named after a US state?

8 Yellow-necked, wood and house are species of which small rodent?

9 Which species of dog is most commonly used in sled racing?

10 What does an apiarist keep or study?

11 Which breed of cat originated in the country that can also be referred to as Myanmar?

12 Which water-bird got its name because it was once thought to grow from shellfish?

13 The wildebeest is native to which continent?

14 Which creature has fallow and roe species?

15 Are reptiles cold-blooded or warm-blooded?

16 The fetlock is found on which part of a horse?

17 What name is given to a litter of piglets?

18 What type of creature is a pearl-bordered fritillary?

19 The giant otter is native to which continent?

20 Where do female marsupials carry their young?

Answers to QUIZ 256 – Literature

1	Dostoevsky	11	Mr Bingley
2	Alliteration	12	19th century
3	Mary	13	*Treasure Island*
4	Margaret Mitchell	14	Mars
5	Manuscript	15	Charles Dickens
6	Dracula	16	Paddington
7	*The Colour of Magic*	17	*Upon Westminster Bridge*
8	Adam and Eve	18	Havana
9	John Steinbeck	19	Alex Haley
10	Ann Cleeves	20	Dorset

1   Whose 1989 debut album was entitled *Raw Like Sushi*?

2   Which musical note is equivalent in length to two crotchets?

3   In 1992, who won the Wimbledon women's singles title?

4   In literature, who was master of the submarine *Nautilus*?

5   The character of Dorothy Boyd says "You had me at hello" in which film?

6   In relation to communications, what do the letters TPS stand for?

7   On which day of the week are people encouraged to go meat-free?

8   For what did YUP stand for in the 1980s-coined term "yuppies"?

9   In which country is the port of Livorno?

10 Which Scottish town lies on Loch Linnhe?

11 Which word means both a jump and an underground storeroom?

12 A Sealyham is what type of dog?

13 Who is the host of the TV series *Love Island*?

14 Which band released the single *Livin' on a Prayer* in 1986?

15 What microscopic fungus is used in brewing and baking?

16 How is the constellation Ursa Major more commonly known?

17 What is India's national fruit?

18 Frances Gumm was the birth name of which actress?

19 In which fast food chain would you find the Whopper® and Royale?

20 Belgrade is the capital of which country?

Answers to QUIZ 257 – Pot Luck

1	Snell	11	PQRS
2	Pembrokeshire	12	The Falklands War
3	Spoonerism	13	Birmingham
4	Frankfurt	14	The Orient Express
5	Volkswagen	15	Leonardo DiCaprio
6	Sir Norman Hartnell	16	Sioux
7	Bicentennial	17	Leicester City FC
8	Angle	18	*Pirates of Penzance*
9	Glass	19	Cigar
10	U2	20	Sheba

Easy

1   Fluck and Law designed the puppets for which satirical show?

2   Which comedian presents *The Mash Report*?

3   Who played reporter Damian Day in *Drop the Dead Donkey…*?

4   …and what was the name of his long-suffering cameraman, voiced by Andy Hamilton?

5   In 2016, which MP was replaced by a handbag on *Have I Got News for You* when she cancelled her planned appearance?

6   Who presented *The Daily Show* in the US from 1999 to 2015?

7   What was the full title of the TV show known as *TW3*?

8   In which decade did *Saturday Night Live* begin broadcasting in the US?

9   Which topical show's theme tune is *News of the World* by The Jam…?

10 …and which comedian presents it?

11 What was the name of Peter Capaldi's character in *The Thick of It*?

Medium

12 Who created and presented the series *Brass Eye*?

13 In *Yes Minister* and its sequel, what was the name of Nigel Hawthorne's character?

14 Which fictional TV presenter created by Steve Coogan made his first TV appearance on *The Day Today*?

15 Who created *The Simpsons*?

16 Which impressionist was joined on a Channel 4 series by John Bird and John Fortune?

17 *The Liberty Bell* was the theme tune to which series that ran from 1969 to 1974?

18 Who played Jack Donaghy in the TV series *30 Rock*?

19 Which radio show starring Jon Culshaw and Jan Ravens also had a TV version from 2002 to 2007?

20 Amy Poehler played which character in *Parks and Recreation*?

Hard

Answers to QUIZ 258 – Animal World

1	Its abdomen	11	Burmese
2	Thrush	12	Barnacle goose
3	Lizard	13	Africa
4	Freshwater	14	Deer
5	Ants and termites	15	Cold-blooded
6	Blowhole	16	Its leg
7	Colorado beetle	17	Farrow
8	Mouse	18	Butterfly
9	Husky	19	South America
10	Bees	20	In a pouch

1 Which river flows through Totnes?

2 What word describes a letter, figure or symbol printed below the line?

3 How many words are there in the shortest verse of the Bible (John, Chapter 11, verse 35)?

4 Which company makes the 787 Dreamliner?

5 What was the name of the racehorse that was stolen from the Ballymany Stud in 1983?

6 James I became King of England following the death of which monarch?

7 Required in selling a house, what is an EPC?

8 Which 1980 film starring Leslie Nielsen is a parody of disaster movies?

9 Who played Gunner "Lofty" Sugden in *It Ain't Half Hot Mum*?

10 Who was appointed Archbishop of Canterbury in 1980?

11 In which country was the group Franz Ferdinand formed?

12 What is the name of the formal gardens in Paris which are all that remain of Catherine de Medici's 16th-century palace?

13 Uttar Pradesh is a state in which country?

14 On which island is the city of Catania?

15 What is a substance with a pH greater than seven?

16 Which word meaning "declare" is also used to refer to an area within a federal republic?

17 In which sport has Claudia Fragapane won Commonwealth gold medals for England?

18 In which year did breakfast TV start broadcasting in the UK?

19 Which city of New Zealand shares its name with an Oxford college?

20 Who featured in the TV series *An Idiot Abroad*?

Easy

Medium

Hard

Answers to QUIZ 259 – Pot Luck

1	Neneh Cherry	11	Vault
2	Minim	12	Terrier
3	Steffi Graf	13	Caroline Flack
4	Captain Nemo	14	Bon Jovi
5	*Jerry Maguire*	15	Yeast
6	Telephone Preference Service	16	Great Bear
7	Monday	17	Mango
8	Young Urban Professional	18	Judy Garland
9	Italy	19	Burger King®
10	Fort William	20	Serbia

Easy

1 Wing attack, goal defence and goal shooter are positions in which sport?

2 Which Berkshire racecourse east of Bracknell was founded by Queen Anne?

3 Which London football club plays at Craven Cottage?

4 In snooker what is the white ball called?

5 What sport is played by the Chicago Bulls?

6 In 1896, in which city were the Olympic Games held?

7 Which prestigious golf tournament is held in Augusta, Georgia?

8 What is the name of the venue for the Australian Grand Slam?

9 How high is the tallest diving platform in the Olympics?

10 Who was England's goalkeeper for the 1966 World Cup?

11 Headingley cricket ground is located in which English city?

Medium

12 Which New York Yankees baseball player was briefly married to Marilyn Monroe?

13 In 1976 who became the first gymnast to be awarded ten points?

14 Which French town is famous for its 24-hour motor race?

15 Which US swimmer won seven Olympic gold medals in 1972?

16 What was the nickname of the 1980s US basketball player Earvin Johnson?

17 The first Invictus Games were held in which city?

18 What term is applied to an over in cricket in which no runs are scored?

19 Which sporting event involves pistol shooting, fencing, swimming, show jumping and cross-country running?

20 Which figure-skating jump begins on the back outer edge of one foot, and ends on the other?

Hard

Answers to QUIZ 260 – Television Satire

1	*Spitting Image*	11	Malcolm Tucker
2	Nish Kumar	12	Chris Morris
3	Stephen Tompkinson	13	Sir Humphrey Appleby
4	Gerry	14	Alan Partridge
5	Nicky Morgan	15	Matt Groening
6	Jon Stewart	16	Rory Bremner
7	*That Was the Week That Was*	17	*Monty Python's Flying Circus*
8	1970s	18	Alec Baldwin
9	*Mock the Week*	19	*Dead Ringers*
10	Dara Ó Briain	20	Leslie Knope

ANSWERS ON PAGE **265**

1   What number is represented by the Roman numerals XCI?

2   John Knox was the founder of which branch of the Protestant religion?

3   Monophobia is the fear of what?

4   Which *Star Trek* captain was played by William Shatner?

5   What is the symbol of the star sign Libra?

6   Which type of fat has a high proportion of fatty acid molecules?

7   "Why do birds suddenly appear, Every time you are near?" is a lyric from which 1970 song?

8   In which National Park is Ambleside?

9   On which island is the city of Kyrenia?

10 Which UK motorway crosses the River Severn, alongside the M4?

11 What is a person who believes that there is no God called?

12 Who played the title role in the TV series *Father Ted*?

13 Where is the famous Moorish Palace of The Alhambra situated?

14 Cass Elliot was a member of which 1960s group?

15 Who managed the England football team from 1990 to 1993?

16 The shipping areas of Lundy and Plymouth are to the north and south of which two counties?

17 Which edible bulb is said to ward off vampires?

18 Is a Bramley apple a cooking apple or an eating apple?

19 How were the group including Virginia Woolf, Leonard Woolf, and John Maynard Keynes collectively known?

20 What note is written in the space below the middle line of the treble clef?

Easy

Medium

Hard

Answers to QUIZ 261 – Pot Luck

1	Dart	11	Scotland
2	Subscript	12	Tuileries
3	Two (Jesus wept)	13	India
4	Boeing	14	Sicily
5	Shergar	15	Alkali
6	Elizabeth I	16	State
7	Energy Performance Certificate	17	Gymnastics
8	*Airplane!*	18	1983
9	Don Estelle	19	Christchurch
10	Robert Runcie (Baron Runcie)	20	Karl Pilkington

1   In which century did the Black Death occur?

2   Which garden flower suffers from black spot?

3   What is a blackcap?

4   What type of creature was the famous Black Bess?

5   If a car is shown a black flag in Formula 1, what must the driver do?

6   In which county is Blackburn?

7   *Blackstar* (2016) was the final studio album by which singer?

8   The Blackwall tunnel goes under which river?

9   What was Cilla Black's real surname?

10 *Black Velvet*, released in 1989, was a hit for which singer?

11 Who created the TV series *Black Mirror*?

12 What was the first UK no.1 for The Black Eyed Peas?

13 Which actor starred in the 2012 film *The Woman in Black*?

14 The Black Mountains are in which part of the UK?

15 What was the name of Bernard Hill's character in the TV series *Boys From the Blackstuff*?

16 Which 1997 film features agents Kay and Jay?

17 In which year was the Penny Black stamp introduced?

18 What did Sir Winston Churchill describe as a "black dog"?

19 In which month does the retail event Black Friday occur?

20 The Black Isle peninsula is in which region of Scotland?

Answers to QUIZ 262 – Sport

1	Netball	11	Leeds
2	Ascot	12	Joe di Maggio
3	Fulham	13	Nadia Comaneci
4	Cue ball	14	Le Mans
5	Basketball	15	Mark Spitz
6	Athens	16	Magic
7	Masters	17	London
8	Melbourne Park	18	Maiden
9	Ten metres	19	Modern Pentathlon
10	Gordon Banks	20	Lutz

1 Which year did Queen Elizabeth II describe as her "annus horribilis"?

2 Of which archipelago of more than seven thousand islands is Manila the capital?

3 In which *Carry On* film did Roy Castle play Captain Keene?

4 Athlete Laura Muir was born in which country in 1993?

5 What other name for a Dublin Bay prawn has a Scandinavian connection?

6 Which letter is between E and T on a standard computer keyboard?

7 "Hello, Possums!" is a greeting favoured by which comedy creation?

8 Who played Dr Tony Hill in the TV series *Wire in the Blood*?

9 On an Ordnance Survey map, what is indicated by the abbreviation FM?

10 Which group had a 1981 hit with *Prince Charming*?

11 What title is given to a graduate who has studied tort and jurisprudence?

12 In the song, "if that diamond ring turns brass", what is Mama going to buy you?

13 Inventor Sir Joseph Swan was involved in the development of which everyday object?

14 What colour dye is obtained from the plant woad?

15 Who was known as the "Merry Monarch"?

16 What is the nationality of a native of Johannesburg or Bloemfontein?

17 A circle with a cross through it on a clothing label indicates that the item cannot be cleaned by what method?

18 What term is used to describe the distance between where food is consumed and where it was grown?

19 In the children's song, what was packed by Nellie the Elephant?

20 0116 is the dialling code for which English city?

Answers to QUIZ 263 – Pot Luck

1	91	11	Atheist
2	Church of Scotland	12	Dermot Morgan
3	Being alone	13	Granada, Spain
4	Captain James T Kirk	14	The Mamas and the Papas
5	Scales	15	Graham Taylor
6	Saturated	16	Devon and Cornwall
7	*Close to You*	17	Garlic
8	Lake District	18	Cooking apple
9	Cyprus	19	The Bloomsbury Group
10	M48	20	A

Easy

1 How were Roy Jenkins, Shirley Williams, David Owen and William Rodgers, all subsequently members of the House of Lords, known in the early 1980s?

2 *Diaries Volume Three: Power and Responsibility 1999–2001* was written by which former political aide?

3 Which political group joined forces with the Liberals in 1981?

4 What is the title of the chief legal adviser to the government?

5 Who was Neil Kinnock's (Baron Kinnock's) predecessor as Labour leader?

6 Who was appointed Foreign Secretary in July 2016?

7 In which decade did Helmut Kohl serve as Chancellor of Germany?

8 What term is given to a government in which the governing party has most seats but still less than half the total?

9 Which 1990s UK Prime Minister was noted for his "Back to Basics" campaign?

10 How old was William Pitt the Younger when he became Prime Minister in 1783?

11 In which London building is the Cabinet Room?

12 What is the title given to the senior politician who makes others toe the party line?

Medium

13 Who was Chancellor of the Exchequer from 2007-10?

14 Which former Hollywood actor became US President in 1981?

15 What term is given to the spot at which speeches are made by ministers in the House of Commons?

16 What is the term for the group of people represented by an MP?

17 In which city is Stormont?

18 The leaders of which two countries met for the first time on their border in April 2018?

19 Which US president set the goal of "landing a man on the Moon and returning him safely to the Earth"?

20 Whom did Nicola Sturgeon succeed as First Minister of Scotland?

Hard

1 Which publisher of children's books has a type of beetle for its logo?

2 Ra is the chemical symbol for which element?

3 What type of food is paneer?

4 In music, if a piece is in three flats which notes will be flat?

5 Who starred in the film *Close Encounters of the Third Kind*?

6 "But then again, too few to mention" is a line from which song?

7 How is the sport of clay-pigeon shooting otherwise known?

8 Who co-wrote the *Dad's Army* scripts with David Croft?

9 In which month do the Heritage Open Days take place in the UK?

10 Which plant has a swollen nutritious root used to make sugar?

11 What is the term for blue in heraldry?

12 In which country did the famous Battle of the Bulge (the Ardennes Offensive) take place?

13 In 1986, who won the FIFA World Cup?

14 In which area of outer London was the TV series *The Good Life* set?

15 Helmsley is a town in which county?

16 What French term is used to describe a romantic letter?

17 The 1897 novel *The Invisible Man* was written by which author?

18 Oxford and which other city in the UK have a "Bridge of Sighs", named after the Venetian bridge?

19 What is the name of the Egyptian hieroglyph of life?

20 What is the name of the fictional steam train in the 2004 Christmas film of the same name?

Easy

Medium

Hard

Answers to QUIZ 265 – Pot Luck

1	1992	11	Bachelor of Law
2	Philippines	12	A looking glass
3	*Carry On up the Khyber*	13	Light bulb
4	Scotland	14	Blue
5	Norway lobster	15	Charles II
6	R	16	South African
7	Dame Edna Everage	17	Dry cleaning
8	Robson Green	18	Food mile
9	Farm	19	Her trunk
10	Adam and the Ants	20	Leicester

Easy

1 Moving clockwise on a dartboard, which number is next to 17?

2 How many sides has a dodecahedron?

3 What is the square root of four?

4 What is three eighths of 96?

5 How many minutes are there in five hours?

6 What is the next highest prime number above 23?

7 How many kilograms are there in seven tonnes?

8 How many legs are shown on the Isle of Man flag?

9 What is 15% of 300?

10 How is 77 represented in Roman numerals?

11 What do the numbers add up to on the opposite sides of a die?

12 How many degrees are there in a circle?

13 How many do you get if you add a baker's dozen to a score?

14 What prefix indicates 10^{-3}?

15 How many sides are there in 15 triangles?

16 How does 7.20 pm appear on a 24-hour clock?

17 How many milligrams are there in a gram?

18 What shape would you get if you deduct the number of sides of a pentagon from the number of sides of an octagon to form another shape?

19 How many minutes are there in half a day?

20 What is the Roman numeral for 500?

Medium

Hard

Answers to QUIZ 266 – Politics

1	The Gang of Four	11	10 Downing Street
2	Alastair Campbell	12	Chief whip
3	(SDP) Social Democratic Party	13	Alistair Darling (Baron Darling of Roulanish)
4	Attorney General	14	Ronald Reagan
5	Michael Foot	15	Dispatch box
6	Boris Johnson	16	Constituency
7	1980s	17	Belfast
8	Minority government	18	North and South Korea
9	Sir John Major	19	John F Kennedy
10	24	20	Alex Salmond

1 Which satirical magazine ceased publication in 1992 after 150 years?

2 What is the term given to the stalks of reaped corn left after a harvest?

3 What term was coined in the USA for a popular, long-running TV serial?

4 Released in 2016, what was the title of the second film in the *Cloverfield* franchise?

5 Who was President of the National Union of Mineworkers from 1981 to 2002?

6 Who played Steve Biko in the film *Cry Freedom*?

7 The TV series *Asian Provocateur* featured which comedian?

8 What is the title given to the head of the BBC?

9 Carnophobia is a fear of what?

10 What type of bird is a teal?

11 What may be bugs in the body, or in a computer?

12 At which airport was the Brink's-Mat robbery carried out in 1983?

13 Which army rank is immediately below Major?

14 What is a clove hitch?

15 What does *son et lumière* mean?

16 Which port in Georgia lies just south of the border with South Carolina?

17 According to Frederic Austin's 1909 version of the carol, what did my true-love give to me on the eighth day of Christmas?

18 In which county is the village of Market Deeping?

19 With which sport is the song *Swing Low, Sweet Chariot* associated?

20 The Stone of Scone was captured and placed in Westminster Abbey by which English king?

Easy

Medium

Hard

Easy

1 After which German city was a British royal house named?

2 German director Werner Herzog directed which 2006 fim starring Christian Bale?

3 What are *Kartoffeln*, in English?

4 Before the euro, what was the unit of currency in Germany?

5 What bird appears on the German coat of arms?

6 What is the surname of brothers Jacob and Wilhelm who published collections of folk tales including Hansel and Gretel?

7 In which year did Nico Rosberg win the Formula 1 World Championship?

8 What is the official name of Germany?

9 Which German-born theoretical physicist is responsible for developing the theory of relativity?

10 What is the name for a German beer mug?

Medium

11 German composer Hans Zimmer wrote the music for which 2010 sci-fi film directed by Christopher Nolan?

12 What was the name of the structure which divided Germany's current capital city from 1961 to 1989?

13 Which German composer wrote *Lohengrin*?

14 Germany had their first 21st-century win in the FIFA World Cup in which year?

15 Which city was the capital of West Germany until 1990?

16 How many times did Boris Becker win the Wimbledon men's singles championship?

17 Which German composer wrote the popular *Moonlight Sonata*?

18 The Moselle is a tributary of which major river?

19 In which year did Angela Merkel become Chancellor of Germany?

20 Which country shares a border with the north of Germany?

Hard

Answers to QUIZ 268 – Numbers

1	3	11	Seven
2	12	12	360
3	Two	13	33
4	36	14	Milli
5	300	15	45
6	29	16	19:20
7	7000	17	1000
8	Three	18	Triangle
9	45	19	720
10	LXXVII	20	D

1 How often are the show-jumping World Championships held?

2 Why did Merseyside couple Graham and Janet Walton hit the headlines in 1983?

3 What is the prime cut of beef taken from the upper middle of the body?

4 In which city is Charles de Gaulle airport?

5 In which county is Newquay?

6 The kea, native to New Zealand's South Island, is a large species of which bird?

7 Who played Norman Scott in the 2018 mini-series *A Very English Scandal*?

8 Who had a hit with *Rocket Man* (1972)?

9 What is the code word for the seventh letter of the alphabet in radio communications?

10 Which word referring to an actor's assistant also refers to an item of furniture?

11 In relation to families, what do the initials NCT stand for?

12 What was the subtitle of the second film in the *Hunger Games* series?

13 Which plant is the national emblem of Ireland?

14 What is the fifth book of the Old Testament?

15 The US state of Nebraska has which city as its capital?

16 The bingo call for which number can be subject to change after a general election?

17 Which blues guitarist formed Cream with Ginger Baker and Jack Bruce?

18 What crystallised mineral acts as an oscillator in an electronic watch?

19 Who created the fictional character The Jabberwock?

20 The Suez Canal and the Sinai Peninsula are in which African country?

Easy

Medium

Hard

Answers to QUIZ 269 – Pot Luck

1	*Punch*	11	Viruses
2	Stubble	12	Heathrow
3	Soap	13	Captain
4	*10 Cloverfield Lane*	14	A knot
5	Arthur Scargill	15	Sound and light
6	Denzel Washington	16	Savannah
7	Romesh Ranganathan	17	Eight maids a-milking
8	Director General	18	Lincolnshire
9	Meat	19	Rugby Union
10	Duck	20	Edward I

1   What is the top of a polar mountain called?

2   What term is given to the tremors that follow a major earthquake?

3   What name is given to the flat area of a river that becomes inundated when the river rises?

4   In which month of 1987 did the Great Storm occur in the UK?

5   Of what is conchology the study?

6   What type of animal is an iguana?

7   Which spiky tree has the scientific name *Ilex aquifolium*?

8   In an environmental context, what do the letters MCS stand for?

9   Which river flows through Lake Geneva?

10 The Kruger national park is in which country?

11 The Seven Sisters cliffs are in which English county?

12 In the north of England, what name is given to mountains and hills?

13 In which US state is Bryce Canyon National Park?

14 What word is given to an extended period where no rain falls?

15 The tea tree is native to which country?

16 What does the process of irrigation supply to an area of land?

17 The general name for what type of ancient remains comes from the Latin for "to dig"?

18 In which continent is the Gobi Desert?

19 Called magma when it is underground, by what name is it known when it erupts from a volcano?

20 Which island in the Indian Ocean is famed for its biodiversity and large percentage of species that grow nowhere else in the world?

Answers to QUIZ 270 – Germany

1	Hanover	11	*Inception*
2	*Rescue Dawn*	12	The Berlin Wall
3	Potatoes	13	Wagner
4	The Mark	14	2014
5	An eagle	15	Bonn
6	Grimm	16	Three (1985, 86, and 89)
7	2016	17	Ludwig van Beethoven
8	Federal Republic of Germany	18	Rhine
9	Albert Einstein	19	2005
10	Stein	20	Denmark

ANSWERS ON PAGE 275

1   If it is 12 noon GMT, what time is it in Helsinki?

2   Glacier Point is a viewpoint in which US National Park?

3   Who wrote the travelogues *The Lost Continent* and *Made in America*?

4   Which sitcom's theme tune was performed by The Rembrandts?

5   Who created the character of Sergeant Bilko?

6   Who replaced Lacey Turner as the star of the TV series *Our Girl*?

7   The RHS garden of Harlow Carr is in which city?

8   Which Queen was called "The Flanders Mare"?

9   In the periodic table, which element has the atomic number 6?

10 Rathlin Island is off the coast of which Northern Irish county?

11 "Parting is such sweet sorrow" is a line from which Shakespeare play?

12 Which Welsh singing legend is a judge on *The Voice UK*?

13 Which actress starred as Elizabeth in the 2011 film *Bad Teacher*?

14 In which year did the "Big Bang" stock market deregulation take place?

15 In which county is Clitheroe?

16 What nationality was Jules Léotard, who popularised the one-piece outfit that bears his name?

17 British Summer Time ends on the last Sunday of which month?

18 In which city did the fictional detective Maigret operate?

19 What is the next-highest prime number above 43?

20 What was the name of the horse that won the 2018 Epsom Derby?

Easy

Medium

Hard

Answers to QUIZ 271 – Pot Luck

1	Every four years	11	National Childbirth Trust
2	They had sextuplets, all girls	12	*Catching Fire*
3	Sirloin	13	Shamrock
4	Paris	14	Deuteronomy
5	Cornwall	15	Lincoln
6	Parrot	16	Ten
7	Ben Whishaw	17	Eric Clapton
8	Sir Elton John	18	Quartz
9	Golf	19	Lewis Carroll
10	Dresser	20	Egypt

Easy

1   Which group had a hit in 1979 with *Sultans of Swing*?

2   Under what name did Gary Numan have his first hit, *Are Friends Electric*?

3   Which song, used as the theme to a TV documentary series, was a no.1 hit for Sir Rod Stewart in 1975?

4   Which *Dad's Army* star topped the charts with *Grandad*?

5   Which group had a top 10 hit in 1979 with *Breakfast in America*?

6   *Rivers of Babylon* and *Daddy Cool* were hits for which group?

7   Which duo had a no.1 hit with *Up Town Top Ranking*?

8   What completes the title of the 1975 Judy Collins hit, *Send in the _*?

9   *I Want Your Love* was a hit for which group in 1979?

10   The Sex Pistols were the leaders of which movement?

11   Who had a hit with *Hold Me Close* in 1975?

12   What were the initials of the group that had a 1976 hit with *Livin' Thing*?

13   YMCA was a 1978 hit for which group?

14   What was the first British top ten hit for the Cars?

Medium

15   Who had a no.1 single in 1972 with his tribute to Vincent Van Gogh?

16   Who won the Eurovision Song Contest for the UK in 1976?

17   *Don't Give Up On Us* was a hit for which actor?

18   Which band had a 1973 hit with *Wishing Well*?

19   *Superstition* was a 1972 hit for which singer?

20   Who sang *The Eton Rifles* in 1979?

Hard

Answers to QUIZ 272 – Planet Earth

1	Snowcap	11	East Sussex
2	Aftershock	12	Fells
3	Flood plain	13	Utah
4	October	14	Drought
5	Shells	15	Australia
6	Lizard	16	Water
7	Holly	17	Fossils
8	Marine Conservation Society	18	Asia
9	Rhône	19	Lava
10	South Africa	20	Madagascar

1   Arborio or Carnaroli rice forms the chief ingredient of which Italian dish?

2   How many spots are there in total on a standard six-sided die?

3   Azaleas are a variety of which shrub?

4   Which classic 1979 sci-fi thriller starred Sigourney Weaver?

5   What age was Ruth Lawrence when she gained a 1st class honours degree in mathematics in 1985?

6   What prefix indicates 10^3?

7   What name is given to a person born under the sign of the Archer?

8   Tribeca is a district of which New York borough?

9   Which planet was discovered in 1846?

10   In *Hey Diddle Diddle*, who or what ran away with the spoon?

11   Kenny Ball had a 1961 hit mentioning *Midnight* in which city?

12   How many kings and queens are there in a standard pack of cards?

13   What name is given to a cabbage that has been grown for its appearance rather than flavour?

14   What term is given to the shortened version of a larger work?

15   What word describes a musical note that is lowered by half a tone?

16   A hospital room and a local electoral district share what name?

17   Which city was threatened by a volcano in the 1997 film starring Tommy Lee Jones?

18   In which century was Richard the Lionheart born?

19   Who hosts the celebrity TV quiz *House of Games*?

20   In which county is Barrow-in-Furness?

Easy

Medium

Hard

Answers to QUIZ 273 – Pot Luck

1	14:00	11	*Romeo and Juliet*
2	Yosemite	12	Sir Tom Jones
3	Bill Bryson	13	Cameron Diaz
4	*Friends*	14	1986
5	Phil Silvers	15	Lancashire
6	Michelle Keegan	16	French
7	Harrogate	17	October
8	Anne of Cleves	18	Paris
9	Carbon	19	47
10	Country Antrim	20	Masar

Easy

1 Which Mexican hat takes its name from the Spanish for "shade"?

2 Who provided the voice of the Cat in the Hat in the 2003 film?

3 What informal name for a hat comes from Cockney rhyming slang?

4 Comedian Tommy Cooper was associated with which type of hat?

5 Who wrote the music and lyrics for the 1935 film *Top Hat*?

6 What is the French word for "hat"?

7 Which English footballer scored a hat-trick against Poland in the 1986 FIFA World Cup?

8 In which 1964 film is George Banks' bowler hat ritually destroyed when he is fired?

9 Ten-gallon and cowboy hats are chiefly associated with which US brand?

10 Which Bedfordshire hat-making town is home to a football team known as the Hatters?

11 What headgear is associated with the accident-prone 1970s sitcom character Frank Spencer?

Medium

12 What style of hat links Prime Ministers Eden and Churchill with The Godfather and Tony Hancock?

13 What boat-shaped cap, worn by the Royal Regiment of Scotland, is in the title of a David Mamet play and film?

14 *Wherever I Lay My Hat (That's My Home)* was a 1983 single by which singer?

15 Which woolly hat that covers the head and part of the face was originally worn by soldiers in the Crimea?

16 In *Alice's Adventures in Wonderland*, how much did the Mad Hatter's hat cost?

17 Which tall silk hat takes its name from a flue to a cooker?

18 Which edible item lends its name to a hat with a flat crown and a turned-up brim?

19 What is on the top of a bobble hat?

20 How many points are there on a tricorn hat?

Hard

Answers to QUIZ 274 – 1970s Music

1	Dire Straits	11	David Essex
2	Tubeway Army	12	ELO
3	*Sailing*	13	Village People
4	Clive Dunn	14	*My Best Friend's Girl*
5	Supertramp	15	Don McLean
6	Boney M	16	Brotherhood of Man
7	Althia and Donna	17	David Soul
8	*Clowns*	18	Free
9	Chic	19	Stevie Wonder
10	Punk	20	Jam

1   Of which form of precautionary treatment was Edward Jenner the pioneer?

2   What is a third of 1,200?

3   Who was the English author of *The Canterbury Tales*?

4   In the context of education, what do the initials OU stand for?

5   *The Guns of Navarone* (1961) was based on a novel by which author?

6   Edinburgh and Perth are connected by which motorway?

7   On a standard computer keyboard, the buttons which control different applications and operating systems all start with which letter?

8   Which luxury car company based in Northern Ireland went into receivership in 1982?

9   In which poem did TS Eliot assert that "April is the cruellest month"?

10 Which famous sitcom couple first appeared as the landlord and landlady in *Man About the House*?

11 In which year was Nelson Mandela released from prison?

12 Advocaat is a traditional alcoholic drink from which country?

13 Which administrative body in the English capital was abolished in 1986?

14 What title did Meghan Markle receive on her wedding day?

15 What is the two-word term for a forceful shot in basketball?

16 In June 2018, which tennis player dropped his first set at the French Open since 2015?

17 On the scale of A to G, which letter indicates the most energy efficient appliance?

18 Who was the first Hanoverian ruler of England?

19 What surname was shared by French writer Françoise and US astronomer Carl?

20 Which word can mean both "bid" and "sore"?

Easy

Medium

Hard

Answers to QUIZ 275 – Pot Luck

1	Risotto	11	Moscow
2	21	12	Eight (four of each)
3	Rhododendron	13	Ornamental cabbage
4	*Alien*	14	Abridgement
5	13	15	Flat
6	Kilo	16	Ward
7	Sagittarian	17	Los Angeles
8	Manhattan	18	12th century
9	Neptune	19	Richard Osman
10	The dish	20	Cumbria

1 What flower, often purple, is named after an animal native to the UK and an item of clothing worn in cold weather?

2 An animal popularised as a soft toy and an embrace give the name of which wrestling hold?

3 Which four-legged pet and a bed for a baby combine to give the name of a child's game involving string?

4 What type of four-legged animal present should you not look in the mouth?

5 Which season and bird combine to give a term for a young person?

6 Which four-legged animal should be worried near a chatterbox?

7 When linked with a religious building, what small rodent is proverbially poor?

8 What profitable venture links money with a farm animal?

9 A messy situation links which animal with a morning meal?

10 Which sea creature is used to describe a money-lender?

11 Which farm animal's ear would not make a silk purse?

12 The largest share of something would go to which big cat?

13 In which area of Cardiff might you see a big cat?

14 In which country did the phrase "Don't come the raw prawn with me" originate to indicate scepticism?

15 What animal is referred to in a false cry for help?

16 The traditional pre-wedding parties for a bride and groom are named after which two animals?

17 A small compartment or a category combine the name of which bird with a small space?

18 Which bovine animal's organ of sight is the name of a member of the daisy family?

19 Which rodent can also be a deserter?

20 A deceitful person may be likened to which reptile in vegetation?

Answers to QUIZ 276 – Hats

1	Sombrero	11	Beret
2	Mike Myers	12	Homburg
3	Titfer (tit for tat)	13	Glengarry (*Glengarry Glen Ross*)
4	Fez	14	Paul Young
5	Irving Berlin	15	Balaclava
6	*Chapeau*	16	Ten shillings and sixpence
7	Gary Lineker	17	Stovepipe
8	*Mary Poppins*	18	Pork-pie hat
9	Stetson	19	Pompom
10	Luton	20	Three

Easy

Medium

Hard

ANSWERS ON PAGE 281

1. In which language does the TV channel S4C broadcast?

2. In greyhound racing, what colour jacket is worn by the dog in trap two?

3. Lambrettas and Vespas are examples of which two-wheeled motor vehicles?

4. Wombats are native to which country?

5. The film *Maleficent* was inspired by which fairytale?

6. In which battle was Harold Godwinson killed?

7. Who was the original presenter of *The Apprentice: You're Fired!*?

8. Who wrote the 1908 handbook *Scouting for Boys*?

9. From 1976 to 1979, who was the Prime Minister of Cambodia?

10. In which English county is the town of Harlow?

11. Which US public official acts as prosecutor for the state or federal government?

12. Which state did band Lynyrd Skynyrd call *Sweet Home*?

13. What word links "Fisherman's" in San Francisco with "Canary" in London?

14. A "sky rocket" means what in Cockney rhyming slang?

15. After which queen is a plain sponge cake named?

16. What does GMT stand for?

17. What is the square root of 64?

18. In what type of building is the US TV series *Code Black* set?

19. Which musician and singer won a Grammy with John Lee Hooker for *I'm in the Mood*?

20. In which country was actress Penélope Cruz born?

Easy

Medium

Hard

Answers to QUIZ 277 – Pot Luck

1	Vaccination	11	1990
2	400	12	The Netherlands
3	Chaucer	13	Greater London Council
4	Open University	14	Duchess of Sussex
5	Alistair MacLean	15	Slam dunk
6	M90	16	Rafael Nadal
7	F	17	A
8	De Lorean Motor Company	18	George I
9	*The Waste Land*	19	Sagan
10	George and Mildred	20	Tender

Easy

1   In which county is the RHS garden of Rosemoor?

2   Which A road would you use to drive from Newcastle to Carlisle?

3   Who was Governor of the Bank of England from 2003 to 2013?

4   In which resort was the first pleasure pier opened in England in 1823?

5   Which Oxfordshire palace is the seat of the Duke of Marlborough?

6   In which county is Dewsbury?

7   Which city is at the western end of Hadrian's Wall?

8   Hardknott Pass is in which county?

9   In which city is the Barbican arts centre?

10 What is the name of the famous passenger train operating between Edinburgh and London?

11 Who or what returned to Piccadilly Circus in 1947, after being kept in hiding during the Second World War?

12 0118 is the dialling code for which town?

13 Which East Sussex abbey town's name means "fight"?

14 Which RAF rank is the higher, Air Commodore or Group Captain?

15 Which river flows through Glasgow?

16 British Summer Time begins on the last Sunday of which month?

17 Which town is home to the University of Essex?

18 On UK roads, what is the background colour of the road sign denoting the national speed limit?

19 What is the name of the famous tea rooms based in Harrogate?

20 Which area of London is associated with Jack the Ripper?

Answers to QUIZ 278 – Animal Inspiration

1	Foxglove	11	Sow
2	Bear hug	12	Lion
3	Cat's cradle	13	Tiger Bay
4	Gift horse	14	Australia
5	Spring chicken	15	Wolf
6	Donkey (talk the hind leg off)	16	Hen and stag
7	Church mouse	17	Pigeon hole
8	Cash cow	18	Ox-eye
9	Dog (Dog's breakfast or dinner)	19	Rat
10	Shark (loan shark)	20	Snake in the grass

1 What term is given to sea undulation caused by a distant gale or earthquake?

2 Which band released the album *Forty Licks*?

3 Who played Mark Zuckerberg in the film *The Social Network*?

4 What was the name of ITV's first breakfast show?

5 Kincardine is situated on which estuary?

6 What term is given to the illegal use of confidential information on the stock exchange?

7 How is a competitor at the rear of a race referred to?

8 What first name was shared by the two famous potters Wedgwood and Spode?

9 In which century did James I & II and Charles I & II reign?

10 What is the name of Vicki McClure's *Line of Duty* character?

11 "Put a tiger in your tank" was the slogan of which fuel company?

12 What term is given to someone who does not eat meat but does eat dairy produce?

13 What is the name of the first regiment of the royal household infantry?

14 An Affenpinscher is what type of creature?

15 In which county is Wilmslow?

16 Which protein is the chief constituent of hooves and horns?

17 What is the Scottish equivalent of A-Levels?

18 What is considered to be the second deadly sin?

19 In football, what term describes the gap between goals scored and conceded?

20 Who co-starred with Dame Judi Dench in the film *Philomena*?

Easy

Medium

Hard

Answers to QUIZ 279 – Pot Luck

1	Welsh	11	District attorney
2	Blue	12	Alabama
3	Scooters	13	Wharf
4	Australia	14	Pocket
5	*Sleeping Beauty*	15	Victoria
6	Battle of Hastings	16	Greenwich Mean Time
7	Adrian Chiles	17	Eight
8	Robert Baden-Powell (First Baron Baden-Powell)	18	A hospital
9	Pol Pot	19	Bonnie Raitt
10	Essex	20	Spain

1   The character of Big Ears was created by which author?

2   Maurice Sendak wrote which 1963 picture book, which was adapted into a feature-film in 2009?

3   What 1970 novel by Roald Dahl tells the story of a creature who must outwit three farmers?

4   Which 1999 Julia Donaldson book tells the story of a mouse travelling through a forest?

5   AA Milne created which bear?

6   Which 1950 fantasy novel features siblings Peter, Susan, Edmund and Lucy Pevensie?

7   *The Wind in the Willows* was written by which author?

8   What is the title of EB White's novel about a pig called Wilbur and his arachnid friend?

9   Which story, first published in book form in 1906, features siblings Roberta (Bobbie), Phyllis and Peter and their move to Yorkshire?

10   In which book do a Gryphon and a Mock Turtle dance to the Lobster Quadrille?

11   *A Child's Garden of Verses* (1885) was written by which Scottish author better known for his adventure novels?

12   Which author wrote *The Tale of Peter Rabbit*?

13   Which 1952 fantasy novel focuses on a family of fictional miniscule people and their interactions with "human beans"?

14   In Philip Pullman's trilogy of books *His Dark Materials*, what is the title of the first novel?

15   Who wrote *The Secret Garden* (1911)?

16   What is Charlie's surname in the story of *Charlie And The Chocolate Factory*?

17   *The World's Worst Children* series is written by which comedian and author?

18   Who wrote *The Tiger Who Came to Tea*?

19   *The Curious Incident of the Dog in the Night-Time* by Mark Haddon takes its title from a quote by which fictional detective?

20   John Boyne's *The Boy in the Striped Pyjamas* is set during which conflict?

Answers to QUIZ 280 – The UK

1	Devon	11	The statue of Eros
2	A69	12	Reading
3	Sir Mervyn King	13	Battle
4	Brighton	14	Air Commodore
5	Blenheim	15	Clyde
6	West Yorkshire	16	March
7	Carlisle	17	Colchester
8	Cumbria	18	White
9	London	19	Betty's
10	*Flying Scotsman*	20	Whitechapel

1   Who succeeded Ed Miliband as Labour Party leader?

2   Which two colours feature on the shirts of the Barbarians rugby team?

3   Worcestershire Beacon is the highest point in which range of hills?

4   What is the US right to silence to avoid self-incrimination called?

5   Ross and Larsen are examples of what natural occurrence?

6   What was the real name of the character nicknamed "Baby" in the film Dirty Dancing?

7   Who directed the film *Captain Phillips*?

8   In the TV series *The Musketeers*, which character did Santiago Cabrera play?

9   Which group released the 1991 single *I Can't Dance*?

10 In which county is Falmouth?

11 Germany's financial centre is based in which city?

12 What was the Welsh setting for the TV series *Gavin & Stacey*?

13 On a dartboard, which number is bottom centre?

14 Which Scottish town has an "Academicals" football club?

15 In Greek celebrations, which crockery items are traditionally smashed?

16 What Latin phrase means "acting as mother or father"?

17 In June 2016, which association did Britain vote to leave?

18 Who is the main presenter of the TV series *Love Your Garden*?

19 What was the name of George Michael and Andrew Ridgeley's 1980s pop group?

20 In which year of the 1990s was the Grand National declared void?

Answers to QUIZ 281 – Pot Luck

1	Groundswell	11	Esso
2	The Rolling Stones	12	Lacto-vegetarian
3	Jesse Eisenberg	13	Grenadiers
4	TV-am	14	Dog
5	Firth of Forth	15	Cheshire
6	Insider dealing	16	Keratin
7	Back-marker	17	Highers
8	Josiah	18	Gluttony
9	17th century	19	Goal difference
10	Kate Fleming	20	Steve Coogan

1 Who directed the 2004 film *The Passion of the Christ*?

2 What is the name of Viggo Mortensen's character in the *Lord of the Rings* films?

3 In the 1951 fim *The Man in the White Suit*, who played the title role?

4 What was the title of Scott Joplin's theme music to the film *The Sting*?

5 In the *X-Men* films, who played Charles Xavier?

6 Who starred in the 1927 film *The Jazz Singer*, the first "talkie"?

7 Who directed the 1968 film *Once Upon a Time in the West*?

8 How many *Degrees of Separation* were there in the title of a 1993 Will Smith film?

9 Who acted opposite Tom Cruise in *Eyes Wide Shut*?

10 Who played the female lead in the sci-fi spoof *Galaxy Quest*?

11 Boris Karloff was noted for appearing in which genre of film?

12 Which Michael directed *Heat, Ali* and *Collateral*?

13 In the 1984 film *Beverly Hills Cop*, who starred as Axel Foley?

14 Who directed the 1984 film *A Passage to India*?

15 Who sang *Blaze of Glory* in the movie *Young Guns II*?

16 "The point is, ladies and gentlemen, that greed, for lack of a better word, is good" is a line from which 1987 film?

17 Which 1987 comedy film was about bachelors looking after a child?

18 What was the surname of Grace Kelly's character Tracy in *High Society*?

19 What was the subtitle of the third film in the *Hobbit* series?

20 Whom did Meryl Streep play in the 2015 film *Suffragette*?

Answers to QUIZ 282 – Children's Literature

1	Enid Blyton	11	Robert Louis Stevenson
2	*Where the Wild Things Are*	12	Beatrix Potter
3	*Fantastic Mr Fox*	13	*The Borrowers*
4	*The Gruffalo*	14	*Northern Lights*
5	Winnie-the-Pooh	15	Frances Hodgson Burnett
6	*The Lion, the Witch and the Wardrobe*	16	Bucket
7	Kenneth Grahame	17	David Walliams
8	*Charlotte's Web*	18	Judith Kerr
9	*The Railway Children*	19	Sherlock Holmes
10	*Alice's Adventures in Wonderland*	20	WWII

ANSWERS ON PAGE **287**

1   How many cards does each player start with in a game of gin rummy?

2   What name is given to the emergency method of dislodging an obstruction from the windpipe?

3   Who was the British monarch at the start of WWI?

4   Port of Spain is the capital of which Caribbean country?

5   Honeydew and charentois are varieties of which fruit?

6   What is the name of Tamara Wall's character in *Hollyoaks*?

7   What was the title of Sister Sledge's 1986 no.1 record?

8   In which city are Partick Thistle FC based?

9   Which white-flowered wild plant has a name that combines that of a ruminant and a herb?

10 What is the setting for the 2005 Wes Craven thriller *Red Eye*?

11 What term is given to continuous electricity flow that periodically reverses direction?

12 What is Dwayne Johnson's nickname from his wrestling days?

13 The zodiac sign Gemini covers which two calendar months?

14 Entertainer Mike Yarwood (b.1941) appeared regularly on TV in the 1960s-80s in what capacity?

15 What do the letters stand for in the Latin term NB?

16 What word is given to products that are made from man-made artificial substances rather than natural ones?

17 Entertainers Sinatra, Davis Jr, Martin, Lawford and Bishop were collectively known as what?

18 What term is given food that has been soaked before cooking to absorb flavour?

19 More than half the human race lives on which continent?

20 The Kent town of Hythe is on the edge of which wetland area?

Easy

Medium

Hard

Answers to QUIZ 283 – Pot Luck

1	Jeremy Corbyn	11	Frankfurt
2	Black and white	12	Barry Island
3	Malverns	13	3
4	The Fifth Amendment	14	Hamilton
5	Ice shelf	15	Plates
6	Frances	16	*In loco parentis*
7	Paul Greengrass	17	European Union
8	Aramis	18	Alan Titchmarsh
9	Genesis	19	Wham!
10	Cornwall	20	1993

Easy

1   Who wrote the Father Brown novels...?

2   ...and who plays him in the TV adaptation that started in 2013?

3   Who created the private detectives *Tommy and Tuppence*?

4   The novel *The Sign of Four* (1890) featured which fictional sleuth?

5   What was the title of the late 1970s TV series featuring Nicholas Ball as a private investigator?

6   Which private investigator did James Garner play on TV in the 1970s?

7   Precious Ramotse is the main character in which novel and TV series?

8   Which author created the character of Dirk Gently?

9   Who played the title role in the 1980s series *Magnum P.I.?*

10   What is the first name of Holliday Grainger's character in the TV series *Strike*?

11   The character of Philip Marlowe was created by which author?

12   Cameron Diaz, Lucy Liu and which other actress starred in the 2011 film *Charlie's Angels...*?

13   ...and who replaced Farrah Fawcett in the 1970s TV series?

Medium

14   Which band had a no.2 hit in 1982 with *Private Investigations*?

15   Who created the TV series *Jonathan Creek*?

16   What is the name of private investigator Ralph Dibny's superhero in the TV series *The Flash*?

17   In which village do Sidney Chambers and Geordie Keating solve crimes?

18   How was Harry Orwell known in the title of a 1970s TV series?

19   Who created the character of VI Warshawski?

20   What was the name of the detective agency in the TV series *Moonlighting*?

Hard

1	Mel Gibson	11	Horror
2	Aragorn	12	Mann
3	Sir Alec Guinness	13	Eddie Murphy
4	*The Entertainer*	14	Sir David Lean
5	Sir Patrick Stewart	15	Jon Bon Jovi
6	Al Jolson	16	*Wall Street*
7	Sergio Leone	17	*Three Men and a Baby*
8	Six	18	Lord
9	Nicole Kidman	19	*The Battle of the Five Armies*
10	Sigourney Weaver	20	Emmeline Pankhurst

QUIZ 287 – Pot Luck

ANSWERS ON PAGE 289

1 In which season does the Hunter's Moon appear?

2 Axel is a term used in which sport?

3 What term is given to the seven-day period of fund-raising by students in the UK?

4 As well as Real, what is the other major football team that is based in Madrid?

5 What type of creature is the Tasmanian devil?

6 Is Sauternes a sweet or dry wine?

7 The subject of a 1993 film, what name is given to February 2 in the US?

8 The town of Ipswich is on the estuary of which river?

9 Which brothers starred in the 2017 film *The Disaster Artist*?

10 Which singer had a 1993 hit with *Dreams*?

11 In which US state is Chattanooga?

12 Which group had a hit in 1975 with *You Sexy Thing*?

13 Who played Albert Stroller in the TV series *Hustle*?

14 The Komodo dragon is a species of what type of reptile?

15 What term for a very low lease fee takes its name from a condiment?

16 What name is given to the outer covering of sweetcorn?

17 In *Pygmalion* and *My Fair Lady*, what was the name of Eliza's father?

18 What term is given to someone who is abnormally anxious about their health?

19 In *Coronation Street*, what is the name of Audrey's daughter?

20 The Jet Propulsion Laboratory is part of which US organisation?

Easy

Medium

Hard

Answers to QUIZ 285 – Pot Luck

1	Ten	11	Alternating current
2	Heimlich manoeuvre	12	The Rock
3	George V	13	May and June
4	Trinidad and Tobago	14	Impressionist
5	Melon	15	Nota bene
6	Grace Black	16	Synthetics
7	*Frankie*	17	The Rat Pack
8	Glasgow	18	Marinated
9	Cow parsley	19	Asia
10	A plane	20	Romney Marsh

Easy

1   Saturn's rings are almost entirely made of what?

2   How many planets have there been in our system since Pluto was demoted?

3   How are Jupiter, Saturn, Uranus and Neptune collectively known on account of their composition and size?

4   What term is given to the eruptions from the Sun that can disrupt radio communication?

5   Which planet takes longer to rotate on its axis that it does to orbit around the Sun?

6   What compound gives Mars its unique red colouring?

7   In 1989, *Voyager 2* became the first spacecraft to observe which planet?

8   Which planet in the solar system has only one moon?

9   What name is given to a dark cool patch that appears on the surface of the Sun?

10 Which two planets lie between Earth and the Sun?

11 "The Jewel of the Solar System" is used to describe which planet?

12 What is Pluto now classified as given that it is no longer recognised as a planet?

13 Which is the smallest planet in our solar system?

Medium

14 Which is the only planet in our solar system not to be named after a Greek or Roman god?

15 What is the name of the NASA rover that landed on Mars in 2012?

16 The Sun is composed of which two gases?

17 The *Juno* space probe was launched to explore which planet?

18 Does the planet Mercury have any moons?

19 Approximately how many times wider than the Earth is Uranus?

20 Which planet's moons are named after sea gods and nymphs?

Hard

Answers to QUIZ 286 – Private Investigations

1	GK Chesterton	11	Raymond Chandler
2	Mark Williams	12	Drew Barrymore
3	Dame Agatha Christie	13	Cheryl Ladd
4	Sherlock Holmes	14	Dire Straits
5	*Hazell*	15	David Renwick
6	Jim Rockford	16	The Elongated Man
7	*The No.1 Ladies Detective Agency*	17	Grantchester
8	Douglas Adams	18	*Harry O*
9	Tom Selleck	19	Sara Paretsky
10	Robin	20	The Blue Moon Detective Agency

ANSWERS ON PAGE **291**

1 What nationality was the philosoher Søren Kierkegaard?

2 Obstetrics is the branch of medicine concerned with what process?

3 Peas and beans belong to which family of vegetables?

4 The series *The Secret Life of the Zoo* goes behind the scenes of which zoo?

5 Sam Rockwell starred as Sam Bell in which 2009 sci-fi film?

6 What is the sixth book of the New Testament?

7 Which player at the time was the youngest man ever to win a Wimbledon title, and also the first German and the first unseeded player to do so?

8 Who was Chancellor of the Exchequer from 1974 to 1979?

9 What colour is the Geography category represented by in Trivial Pursuit™?

10 For what is the London store Foyles famous?

11 In which county is the gothic mansion of Knebworth House?

12 What nationality was inventor John Logie Baird?

13 *Swords of a Thousand Men* was a 1981 hit for which group?

14 What term is given to someone who eats eggs and cheese but not meat?

15 Who is the Muppet's drummer?

16 What is the surname of the *Psycho* character Norman?

17 Which motorway connects Hull and Liverpool?

18 Jonagold and Spartan are varieties of which fruit?

19 How many sides are there in four oblongs?

20 Which English city was a European Capital of Culture in 2008?

Answers to QUIZ 287 – Pot Luck

1	Autum	11	Tennessee
2	Figure skating	12	Hot Chocolate
3	Rag Week	13	Robert Vaughn
4	Atlético	14	Monitor lizard
5	Marsupial	15	Peppercorn rent
6	Sweet	16	Husk
7	Groundhog Day	17	Alfred Doolittle
8	Orwell	18	Hypochondriac
9	James and Dave Franco	19	Gail
10	Gabrielle	20	NASA

ANSWERS ON PAGE **292**

Easy

1 How many different colours feature on the Romanian flag?

2 Which city is served by Schiphol airport?

3 Palma is the capital of which island in the Balearics?

4 Which country is nicknamed "the Lucky Country"?

5 In which county is Ashby-de-la-Zouch?

6 What has East Pakistan been called since 1971?

7 On which island is the city of Palermo?

8 In which US state is Amarillo?

9 Which sea lies between the St George's Channel and North Channel?

10 The state of Kerala is in which country?

11 HKG is the code for which airport?

12 Which mountains of North Africa extend from Morocco to Tunisia in a series of chains?

13 Which Minnesotan port lies at the western end of Lake Superior?

14 What name is given to a South African of Dutch descent?

Medium

15 Which country has the capital Baghdad?

16 In which country is Mayrhofen?

17 In which country was the language Sanskrit used?

18 Which country owned Louisiana before it was bought by the USA in 1803?

19 Which river flows through Perth, in Australia?

20 In which Irish province is the town of Cork?

Hard

Answers to QUIZ 288 – Solar System

1	Ice	11	Saturn
2	Eight	12	A dwarf planet
3	Gas giants	13	Mercury
4	Solar flares	14	Earth
5	Venus	15	Curiosity
6	Iron oxide	16	Hydrogen and helium
7	Neptune	17	Jupiter
8	Earth	18	No
9	Sunspot	19	Four
10	Mercury and Venus	20	Neptune

1   What is the county town of Pembrokeshire?

2   How is Pentecost also known?

3   What is a quisling?

4   In which sport do competitors follow the Queensberry Rules?

5   Who recorded the 1986 album *Graceland*?

6   Who played Bridget's father in the 2001 film *Bridget Jones's Diary*?

7   An aubergine is what colour?

8   Which New York street runs from Harlem to Washington Square?

9   Who wrote the famous poem *If*?

10 Which famous ancient Greek conqueror became king of Macedonia at the age of 20?

11 The process of obtaining early and tender stems on rhubarb is referred to by what term?

12 "The Restoration" applied to the reign of which monarch?

13 Which branch of philosophy maintains that existence is without objective meaning or purpose?

14 Who played Charlotte in *Sex and the City*?

15 Which sport is referred to as "the beautiful game"?

16 On which Italian lake is the town of Stresa situated?

17 In a majority verdict, at least how many of the jurors must agree?

18 Which manmade waterway passes through Milton Keynes?

19 The letter K is on which row of a typewriter or computer keyboard?

20 Pachyderms are mammals with what characteristic?

Answers to QUIZ 289 – Pot Luck

1	Danish	11	Hertfordshire
2	Pregnancy and childbirth	12	Scottish
3	Legumes	13	Tenpole Tudor
4	Chester Zoo	14	Lacto-ovo vegetarian
5	*Moon*	15	Animal
6	Romans	16	Bates
7	Boris Becker	17	M62
8	Denis Healey (Baron Healey)	18	Apple
9	Blue	19	16
10	Books	20	Liverpool

Easy

1. What name is given to a person who covers furniture?
2. The type of song known as a shanty is traditionally sung by people in which occupation?
3. Who deals with sports injuries requiring exercise and massage?
4. Which expert treats communication and language disorders?
5. A trichologist is concerned with what part of the body?
6. What does a graphologist study?
7. Wainwrights traditionally make which type of vehicle?
8. Who studies diseases of the blood?
9. What is the job title of someone who creates words for advertisements?
10. Collectively, what name is given to barristers?

Medium

11. What name is given to a shop selling writing materials?
12. What did a scribe do?
13. In which profession is Roy Lancaster a well-known name?
14. The main characters featured in the TV series *All Creatures Great and Small* were in which profession?
15. Where does a stoker stand in a steam train?
16. In what subject does a herpetologist have expertise?
17. Which consultant is reponsible for identifying the likely costs of a building project?
18. For what was Mabel Lucie Attwell famous?
19. Before he achieved stardom in *Star Wars*, what was the occupation of Harrison Ford?
20. What do the letters GP stand for in a medical context?

Hard

Answers to QUIZ 290 – Geography

1. Three
2. Amsterdam
3. Majorca
4. Australia
5. Leicestershire
6. Bangladesh
7. Sicily
8. Texas
9. The Irish Sea
10. India
11. Hong Kong
12. Atlas
13. Duluth
14. Boer
15. Iraq
16. Austria
17. India
18. France
19. The Swan
20. Munster

1   What is Bruce Oldfield (b.1950) famous for?

2   Raclette cheese is made from the milk of which animal?

3   Whitby is close to which National Park?

4   What is the most prestigious trophy presented at the Cannes film festival?

5   In 2000, which group had a hit with *Don't Call Me Baby*?

6   Who played the title role in the 1998 film *There's Something About Mary*?

7   Who hosts the quiz show *Curious Creatures*?

8   In which place did England finish in the 1990 FIFA World Cup?

9   Which ancient Greek philosopher (d.399BC) do many credit with being the founder of Western philosophy?

10 What is the name of Taylor Schilling's character in the series *Orange is the New Black*?

11 What is the allergy test called that is carried out before using chemicals such as hair dye?

12 In the Shakespeare play, who is the youngest daughter of King Lear?

13 What general title is given to a bishop?

14 With which instrument was Paganini (b.1782) associated?

15 *The Honorary Consul* (1973) was written by which author?

16 "Halfway there" is the traditional bingo call for which number?

17 In skiing, what term is given to the controlled descent down a slope?

18 The Chevette was made by which car company?

19 *Forever Love* was a 1996 solo hit for which member of Take That?

20 Which line on a map identifies the east-west position of a point?

Answers to QUIZ 291 – Pot Luck

1	Haverfordwest	11	Forcing
2	Whit Sunday	12	Charles II
3	A traitor	13	Nihilism
4	Boxing	14	Kristin Davis
5	Paul Simon	15	Association football
6	Jim Broadbent	16	Maggiore
7	Purple	17	Ten
8	Fifth Avenue	18	Grand Union Canal
9	Rudyard Kipling	19	Middle letters row
10	Alexander the Great	20	Thick skin

Easy

1 What is the first name of the title character in the TV series *Luther*?

2 What was the nickname of the vehicle which had a number plate WHO 1?

3 In *The Magic Roundabout* what sort of animal was Dylan?

4 Who played Private Pike in the original TV series of *Dad's Army*?

5 Which of his wives did *Coronation Street*'s Ken Barlow marry twice?

6 What is the name of Mandy Patinkin's *Homeland* character?

7 Which crime series features Detective Jimmy Perez?

8 Ellie Harrison began co-presenting which programme in 2009?

9 What is the name of the fictional island on which *Death in Paradise* is set?

10 The US TV version of a modern Sherlock Holmes has what title?

Medium

11 What was the name of Jane Horrocks' character in *Absolutely Fabulous*?

12 In the TV series *Peaky Blinders*, who plays Tommy Shelby?

13 What is the name of William Beck's character in *Casualty*?

14 Who was the cartoon friend of Muskie?

15 In *The Two Ronnies*, what were the names of the bungling private investigators played by Messrs Corbett and Barker?

16 Who are the co-writers and co-stars of the TV series *Catastrophe*?

17 How many Teletubbies were there?

18 Who played the title role in the TV series *Frasier*?

19 *Laverne and Shirley* was a spin-off from which show?

20 In *Thunderbirds*, which of the Tracy brothers generally manned the space station, Thunderbird 5?

Hard

Answers to QUIZ 292 – Occupations

1	Upholsterer	11	Stationer
2	Sailors	12	Write or copy letters
3	Physiotherapist	13	Gardening
4	Speech therapist	14	Veterinary medicine
5	Hair	15	On the footplate
6	Handwriting	16	Reptiles
7	Wagons	17	Quantity Surveyor
8	Haematologist	18	Illustrating books
9	Copywriter	19	Carpenter
10	The Bar	20	General practitioner

1   In which century was Thomas Becket born?

2   Which radio code word alphabetically follows Oscar?

3   Which group formed from a talent show had a 2002 hit with *Just a Little*?

4   Which 2007 thriller starred Reese Witherspoon, Meryl Streep and Jake Gyllenhaal?

5   For which gland is iodine necessary for the production of hormones?

6   What is the name of the theatre in Liverpool that was reopened in 2014?

7   Who was Henry VIII's first child, and by whom?

8   What is the dialling code for Manchester?

9   What term is given to the four-sided inner court of a building?

10 The Skylon structure was a feature of which 1951 event?

11 Which is the world's oldest football tournament?

12 What is the name of Linda Bassett's *Call the Midwife* character?

13 Linzer torte is a pastry dish originating in which country?

14 What is the Latin phrase used to mean "while not present"?

15 Which university is located in Egham?

16 In which Beatles song is "a barber showing photographs"?

17 Who is also known as the Pontiff?

18 In which decade was the Official Secrets Act introduced in the UK?

19 Who presented the game show *The Cube*?

20 In food preparation, which is used to crush items: the pestle or the mortar?

Easy

Medium

Hard

Answers to QUIZ 293 – Pot Luck

1	Fashion design	11	Patch test
2	Cow	12	Cordelia
3	North York Moors	13	Right Reverend
4	Palme d'Or	14	Violin
5	Madison Avenue	15	Graham Greene
6	Cameron Diaz	16	45
7	Kate Humble	17	Glissade
8	Fourth	18	Vauxhall
9	Socrates	19	Gary Barlow
10	Piper Chapman	20	Longitude

Easy

1. The *Victory* was the flagship of which naval hero?

2. The 1746 Battle of Culloden took place near which Scottish city?

3. Strathclyde was an early kingdom of which country?

4. What was the name of Zimbabwe until 1979?

5. The Battle of Bosworth Field took place in which county?

6. In the UK, the strike-bound months of 1978-79 became known as the Winter of what?

7. What adjective is applied to the period of British history from 1901 to 1910?

8. Stalin was leader of which country from 1922 to 1952?

9. What name was given to the wheeled hut that swimmers used in Victorian times?

10. The dissolution of what type of establishment was ordered by Henry VIII in 1536?

Medium

11. Gebhard Leberecht von Blücher commanded which country's troops at the Battle of Waterloo?

12. Who succeeded Richard I as King of England?

13. In which city was Archduke Franz Ferdinand assassinated?

14. Which pope visited Britain in 1982?

15. In 1994, what did Queen Elizabeth II and President Mitterand jointly open?

16. Michael Savage was the first Labour Prime Minister of which country?

17. What name was given to the attempt to overthrow James II in 1685?

18. In 1964, which art historian confessed to being a Russian spy?

19. Which Tudor queen was said to possess an extra finger on her body?

20. What was the name of the main welfare provision for those on low incomes in the UK from 1948 to 1966?

Hard

Answers to QUIZ 294 – Television

1	John	11	Bubble
2	Bessie	12	Cillian Murphy
3	Rabbit	13	Dylan Keogh
4	Ian Lavender	14	Deputy Dawg
5	Deirdre	15	Charley Farley and Piggy Malone
6	Saul Berenson	16	Sharon Horgan and Rob Delaney
7	*Shetland*	17	Four
8	*Countryfile*	18	Kelsey Grammer
9	Saint Marie	19	*Happy Days*
10	*Elementary*	20	John Tracy

1   The 1990 single *Vision of Love* was the first UK top ten hit for which singer?

2   From which country does fondue originate?

3   What term is given to the centre of a pitch in football?

4   In which county is Fowey?

5   The redshank is a member of which family of birds?

6   At which notorious fictional hotel were Miss Tibbs and Miss Gatsby residents?

7   What type of fruit is an ugli fruit?

8   Which Communion is an affiliation of Churches headed by the Archbishop of Canterbury?

9   The Civic is manufactured by which car company?

10 What term is given to the curved upper surface of liquid in a tube?

11 What is the French word for the direction "left"?

12 On which estuary is Rosyth situated?

13 What is the thin flap that prevents food entering the windpipe?

14 In what type of building does a maltster work?

15 Which US agency has an academy at Quantico, Virginia?

16 Which direction-finding system was pioneered by Sir Robert Watson-Watt?

17 What is the state capital of Arizona?

18 What is the US term for a baby's dummy or teething-ring?

19 Sir Joshua Reynolds and Hans Holbein were particularly noted for what genre of painting?

20 What colour bottle top does skimmed milk usually have?

Answers to QUIZ 295 – Pot Luck

1	12th century	11	FA Cup
2	Papa	12	Phyllis Crane
3	Liberty X	13	Austria
4	*Rendition*	14	*In absentia*
5	The thyroid	15	Royal Holloway
6	Everyman	16	*Penny Lane*
7	Mary I, borne by Catherine of Aragon	17	The Pope
8	0161	18	1910s (1911)
9	Quadrangle	19	Phillip Schofield
10	Festival of Britain	20	Pestle

Easy

1 Satchmo was the nickname of which jazz musician...?

2 ...and which instrument did he play?

3 Jazz icon Eleanora Fagan, nicknamed Lady Day, was better known by what name?

4 What type of animal is jazz-loving King Louie in Disney's animation of *The Jungle Book*?

5 *Swing When You're Winning* was a hit album for which former boyband star?

6 *Unforgettable* and *Mona Lisa* were 1950s hits for which jazz singer?

7 Which instrument did the "King of Swing" Benny Goodman play?

8 BB King was best known for playing what genre of music?

9 Which 1974 vigilante film starring Charles Bronson was scored by Herbie Hancock?

10 Stephane Grappelli is renowned for playing which instrument?

Medium

11 What phone number, for the Hotel Pennsylvania in New York, formed the title of a big-band standard?

12 Which Hoboken-born star played Nathan Detroit in the 1955 film *Guys and Dolls*?

13 What is the name of Ryan Gosling's jazz pianist in *La La Land*?

14 *It Don't Mean a Thing (If It Ain't Got that Swing)* was composed by which bandleader?

15 What type of creature plays trumpet in Disney's *The Princess and the Frog*?

16 *It's Time, Crazy Love* and *Nobody But Me* are albums by which Canadian singer?

17 Which British musician co-founded a Soho jazz club with fellow tenor sax player Pete King?

18 What were the forenames of John Belushi and Dan Aykroyd's *Blues Brothers* characters?

19 The song *All That Jazz* is from which musical?

20 *Moonlight Serenade* was the signature tune of which wartime bandleader?

Hard

Answers to QUIZ 296 – History

1	Horatio Nelson (Viscount Nelson)	11	Prussian
2	Inverness	12	King John
3	Scotland	13	Sarajevo
4	Rhodesia	14	John Paul II
5	Leicestershire	15	The Channel Tunnel
6	Discontent	16	New Zealand
7	Edwardian	17	Monmouth rebellion
8	USSR	18	Sir Anthony Blunt
9	Bathing machine	19	Anne Boleyn
10	Monastery	20	National Assistance

1 Which actor starred as Dennis in the 2007 film *Run, Fatboy, Run*?

2 The wine-growing region of Mainz-Bingen is in which country?

3 Which 1960s TV pop show was hosted by Cathy McGowan?

4 Which actress appeared in the TV series *Glee* as teacher Holly Holliday?

5 What name is given to the public-spending watchdog in the UK?

6 The macadamia nut is native to which country?

7 How many times did Nick Faldo win the Open?

8 Wild rice is not a grain: what is it?

9 What was the first name of Laurie Brett's character in *EastEnders*?

10 Which fictional detective is associated with the phrase "The game is afoot"?

11 Bolognese sauce is named after which city?

12 What device is used to control current in an electric circuit?

13 What was the name of the robotic dog in *Dr Who*?

14 Which famous Scottish public school is located near Elgin?

15 The zodiac sign Aquarius covers which two calendar months?

16 Which US resort is the easternmost town in Florida?

17 Which is the only mammal that produces eggs?

18 In the front row of a scrum, which rugby forward plays on the hooker's left?

19 The electronics manufacturer Panasonic was founded in which country?

20 What relation was Elizabeth I to Mary I?

Easy

Medium

Hard

Answers to QUIZ 297 – Pot Luck

1	Mariah Carey	11	*Gauche*
2	Switzerland	12	Firth of Forth
3	Midfield	13	Epiglottis
4	Cornwall	14	Brewery
5	Snipe	15	FBI
6	*Fawlty Towers*	16	Radar
7	Citrus	17	Phoenix
8	Anglican	18	Pacifier
9	Honda	19	Portraits
10	Meniscus	20	Red

Easy

1 What is the name of the hero in the Matrix movie series?

2 Which famous TV producer is associated with *Thunderbirds*, *UFO* and *Joe 90*?

3 George Lucas is famous for which series of sci-fi films?

4 Which South American city is flattened in an attack by the bugs in *Starship Troopers*?

5 Joanna Lumley and David McCallum played which TV sci-fi investigators?

6 *2001: A Space Odyssey* was written by which author?

7 What colour is the TARDIS in *Doctor Who*?

8 Which country originally produced the Godzilla movies?

9 What are Peter, Drax, Gamora, Rocket and Groot better known as?

10 *The Lone Gunmen* was a spin-off from which series?

Medium

11 Which *Naked Gun* actor starred in the 1950s sci-fi classic *Forbidden Planet*?

12 What is the name of the giant robot in the 1951 film *The Day The Earth Stood Still*?

13 Who starred in *Doctor Who* immediately after Patrick Troughton?

14 In *Star Trek*, what is the name of Mr Spock's home planet?

15 What was the name of the moonbase in the TV series *Space: 1999*?

16 Which 2001 film directed by Steven Spielberg starred Haley Joel Osment?

17 Who wrote the book on which *Blade Runner* was based?

18 In the original *Alien* film, what is the name of the ship?

19 What is the nickname for Dr McCoy in *Star Trek*?

20 Which sci-fi TV series, first broadcast in the late 1970s, had a ship's computer called Zen?

Hard

Answers to QUIZ 298 – Jazz and Blues

1 Louis Armstrong
2 Trumpet
3 Billie Holiday
4 Orang-utan
5 Robbie Williams
6 Nat King Cole
7 Clarinet
8 Blues
9 *Death Wish*
10 Violin

11 (Pennsylvania) 6-5000
12 Frank Sinatra
13 Sebastian Wilder
14 Duke Ellington
15 Alligator
16 Michael Bublé
17 Ronnie Scott
18 Jake and Elwood
19 *Chicago*
20 Glenn Miller

ANSWERS ON PAGE **303**

1 Where would an Alice band be worn?

2 In which year did Baroness Margaret Thatcher become leader of the Conservative party?

3 Phil Coulson is a central character in which TV sci-fi series?

4 Which coarse plant is used to help stabilise sand dunes?

5 Of the alkaline earth metals, which is the heaviest?

6 Which *Springwatch* presenter wrote the award-winning memoir *Fingers in the Sparkle Jar*?

7 Providence is the largest city of which US state?

8 What type of vegetable is a Pentland Squire?

9 In which county is Morpeth?

10 Which game show was hosted by Jim Bowen and had a theme song by Chas'n'Dave?

11 Which band had two top ten hits in the 1980s, one with The Dubliners, and the other featuring Kirsty MacColl?

12 What is the capital of Rajasthan?

13 Which organisation produces the shipping forecast?

14 Proverbially, what should you "Ne'er cast" "till May be out"?

15 Which West Country city with Roman remains is associated with Beau Nash?

16 In which county is Rickmansworth?

17 In which century was Jane Austen born?

18 Which novelist (d.2018) wrote *An Absolute Scandal* and *The Best of Times*?

19 Which is the longest word that can be made using only one row of letters on a standard keyboard, "typewriter", "salad" or "harvest"?

20 In which month was Horatio Nelson (Viscount Nelson) mortally wounded at the Battle of Trafalgar?

Easy **Medium** **Hard**

Answers to QUIZ 299 – Pot Luck

1	Simon Pegg	11	Bologna
2	Germany	12	Resistor
3	*Ready Steady Go!*	13	K-9
4	Gwyneth Paltrow	14	Gordonstoun
5	National Audit Office	15	January and February
6	Australia	16	Palm Beach
7	Three (1987, 1990 and 1992)	17	Platypus
8	A grass	18	Loose head prop
9	Jane	19	Japan
10	Sherlock Holmes	20	Half-sister

Easy

1. In which city is Red Square?
2. On an Ordnance Survey map, what is indicated by a black square with a "t" shape on top of it?
3. In geometry, what is drawn using a T-square?
4. In which city is Times Square?
5. Which polar point is contained within the Arctic Circle?
6. Square leg is a fielding position in which sport?
7. In chess, how many squares can the king move at a time?
8. In Scrabble®, what colour are the double-word-score squares?
9. Proverbially, into what can you not fit a square peg?
10. What colour is the Circle Line on a London Underground map?
11. The song *Circle of Life* is from which Disney film…?
12. …and who wrote it?

Medium

13. Who released the 1980 single *Bermuda Triangle*?
14. Which Berkshire town has a theatre called The Hexagon?
15. What is the name of the V-shaped stripe on an NCO's badge?
16. The Pentagon is the headquarters of which US department?
17. Is Sloane Square in east or west London?
18. What term is given to a sports tournament in which the competitors play all the other competitors?
19. In which Scottish town is there a large land transformation project known as the Helix?
20. Which legendary king had a round table?

Hard

Answers to QUIZ 300 – Science Fiction

1	Neo	11	Leslie Nielsen
2	Gerry Anderson	12	Gort
3	*Star Wars*	13	Jon Pertwee
4	Buenos Aires	14	Vulcan
5	Sapphire and Steel	15	Alpha
6	Arthur C Clarke	16	*AI: Artificial Intelligence*
7	Blue	17	Philip K Dick
8	Japan	18	Nostromo
9	The Guardians of the Galaxy	19	Bones
10	*The X-Files*	20	*Blake's 7*

1 Which actress starred in the 1985 film *Prizzi's Honor*?

2 What name is given to the layer of soil that remains below 0°?

3 Moving clockwise on a dartboard what number is next to 11?

4 Which piece of the wicket is furthest from the batsman?

5 What was Sir Roger Moore's first James Bond film?

6 0115 is the dialling code for which city?

7 A brock is what type of animal?

8 Which song title links Go West and Blondie?

9 What type of food is the Greek spanikopita?

10 In which county is Clumber Park?

11 Which TV chef is associated with Padstow in Cornwall?

12 O' Connell Street is a famous thoroughfare in which European city?

13 Who wrote the late 1980s series of TV monologues entitled *Talking Heads*?

14 What is the name of Duncan Preston's *Emmerdale* character?

15 What is the main religion of Portugal?

16 In which Canadian province was the novel *Anne of Green Gables* set?

17 How are the Irish police force referred to?

18 How is a Commonwealth or US student with an award to study at Oxford University described?

19 What is the meaning of the French phrase *chacun à son goût*?

20 Which jazz pianist wrote the tune *Honeysuckle Rose*?

Easy

Medium

Hard

Answers to QUIZ 301 – Pot Luck

1	On the head	11	The Pogues
2	1975	12	Jaipur
3	*Agents of SHIELD*	13	The Met Office
4	Marram grass	14	A clout
5	Radium	15	Bath
6	Chris Packham	16	Hertfordshire
7	Rhode Island	17	18th century
8	Potato	18	Penny Vincenzi
9	Northumberland	19	Typewriter
10	*Bullseye*	20	October

Easy

1. "Friends, Romans, countrymen" is said by which character in Shakespeare's *Julius Caesar*?

2. Which two languages provide most of the influence for modern English?

3. What do Americans call a flyover?

4. According to the saying, what is made by "many a mickle"?

5. What is the French term for a pseudonym used during a conflict?

6. The German sign "*Rauchen verboten*" prohibits what activity?

7. "China" refers to what in Cockney rhyming slang?

8. What do Americans call a drawing pin?

9. According to the proverb, beauty is only what?

10. What is a non-sequitur?

Medium

11. What term is given to data relating to the structure of a population?

12. Which word of German origin means excessive sentimentality?

13. What term describes the measurement of height?

14. A long-legged bird and a hoisting device share what name?

15. Which Latin phrase means "by that very fact"?

16. What word can mean "a container" and "to throw punches"?

17. A determiner, such as "a" or "an" in English, is described by what two-word term?

18. What is the literal meaning of "hypodermic"?

19. What is the grammatical term for a unit of pronunciation containing one vowel sound?

20. What word describes a person between 60 and 69?

Hard

Answers to QUIZ 302 – Shapes

1	Moscow	11	*The Lion King*
2	A place of worship with a tower	12	Sir Elton John
3	Right angle	13	Barry Manilow
4	New York	14	Reading
5	North Pole	15	Chevron
6	Cricket	16	Department of Defense
7	One	17	West
8	Pink	18	Round robin
9	Round hole	19	Falkirk
10	Yellow	20	King Arthur

QUIZ 305 – Pot Luck

ANSWERS ON PAGE **307**

1   What was the first name of Pam St Clement's *EastEnders* character

2   In *The Canterbury Tales*, who tells the last tale?

3   Which member of the Beatles died in 2001?

4   What was the surname of brothers Joseph-Michel and Jacques-Étienne, who pioneered the hot air balloon?

5   What is a tamarillo?

6   What completes the slogan used in the American War of Indepence: "No taxation without _"?

7   In cookery, which unit of measurement is approximately 15ml?

8   By what name is the groundhog also known?

9   What shape is a parabola?

10   For how many years did Frank Lampard play for Chelsea?

11   In which Greek city were the 2000 Summer Olympic Games held?

12   Which boat lends its name to a suspended cabin on a cable car?

13   Which army rank is immediately above Lance Corporal?

14   In which part of London is the famous King's Road?

15   What is the first name of famous astrologer Mr Grant?

16   Which US state gives its name to cookies and a chicken dish?

17   What is the name of the active volcano south-east of Mexico City?

18   Proceedings in the House of Commons were suspended for 20 minutes in 1976 when which Conservative MP picked up the ceremonial mace?

19   Beyoncé and Shakira collaborated on what 2007 hit?

20   Who became questionmaster on the TV series *Child Genius* in 2016?

Answers to QUIZ 303 – Pot Luck

1	Kathleen Turner	11	Rick Stein
2	Permafrost	12	Dublin
3	14	13	Alan Bennett
4	Off stump	14	Douglas Potts
5	*Live and Let Die*	15	Roman Catholic
6	Nottingham	16	Prince Edward Island
7	Badger	17	The Garda
8	*Call Me*	18	A Rhodes Scholar
9	A savoury pastry	19	Each to his or her own taste
10	Nottinghamshire	20	Fats Waller

1 "You have got to swing it, shake it, move it, make it" is a line from which song?

2 Who sang *Cover Me* and *The River* in the 1980s?

3 Who had a 1991 no. 1 with *The One and Only*?

4 Singer Céline Dion was born in which country?

5 What was the first no 1. single for The Boomtown Rats?

6 Glen Campbell sang about what type of *Cowboy*?

7 *Big For Your Boots* was a no.1 hit for which rapper in 2017?

8 In what state was Alvin Stardust's *Mind* in 1974?

9 Which singer had a 1993 hit with *I'd Do Anything For Love (But I Won't Do That)*?

10 Which singer recorded the 2017 single *Shape of You*?

11 What was the only single by The Clash to make the top ten, reaching no.1 in 1991?

12 *I'm Outta Love* was a hit for which singer in 2000?

13 Which Welsh group recorded *Mulder & Scully* in 1998?

14 Which boy-band had UK no.1 hits with *You Got It (The Right Stuff)* and *Hangin' Tough*?

15 *The Great Escape* was a 1995 album by which band?

16 "Give me time to realise my crime, Let me love and steal" is a lyric from which song?

17 In 1966, who sang about a *Dedicated Follower of Fashion*?

18 Who had a hit in 1956 with *Hound Dog*?

19 Which US rock band had a 2003 hit with *Bring Me to Life*?

20 Which goddess provided a hit for Bananarama in 1986?

Answers to QUIZ 304 – Words

1	Mark Antony	11	Demographics
2	Latin and French	12	Schmaltz
3	Overpass	13	Altimetry
4	A muckle	14	Crane
5	*Nom de guerre*	15	*Ipso facto*
6	Smoking	16	Box
7	China plate (Mate)	17	Indefinite article
8	Thumbtack	18	Under the skin
9	Skin deep	19	Syllable
10	A remark that does not logically follow	20	Sexagenarian

1   Which 1990s band featured the Appleton sisters?

2   In which county is the stately home of Saltram?

3   Is a Portobello mushroom a large or small mushroom?

4   Richmond Castle in North Yorkshire overlooks which river?

5   In Scrabble®, how many points is the letter A worth?

6   What was the first name of the cartoon character Captain Pugwash?

7   Which playwright died on 23rd April 1616?

8   What colour bottle top does semi-skimmed milk usually have?

9   What were the more liberal members of the Conservative party described as in the 1980s?

10 Which Eleanor H Porter heroine lends her name to an optimistic person?

11 Which is the only US state's name that can be typed using just the middle row of a standard computer keyboard?

12 Which 1970s prog-rock band had Rick Wakeman among its members?

13 What is the fee paid to an author as a result of the book being borrowed?

14 Which French town is famous for its nougat?

15 The state of South Australia has what nickname?

16 What is the cockney term for a dreadful smell?

17 Which car company manufactures the TT?

18 James II converted to which religion?

19 What is the American term for a purse or wallet?

20 Which knighted actor played Obi-Wan Kenobi in the original *Star Wars* film?

Answers to QUIZ 305 – Pot Luck

1	Pat	11	Athens
2	The parson	12	Gondola
3	George Harrison	13	Corporal
4	Montgolfier	14	Chelsea
5	A fruit	15	Russell
6	Representation	16	Maryland
7	Tablespoon	17	Popocatépetl
8	Woodchuck	18	Michael Heseltine (Baron Heseltine)
9	Curve	19	*Beautiful Liar*
10	13 years	20	Richard Osman

QUIZ 308 – Technology

ANSWERS ON PAGE 310

Easy

1. In which city does Sony have its headquarters?
2. For what is "blog" an abbreviation?
3. Instagram™ was bought by which company in 2012?
4. What verb describes the copying of files from the internet onto a computer or phone?
5. Which conflict featured in the 2017 release of *Call of Duty*?
6. Nokia was founded in which country?
7. What is the name of Apple's virtual assistant?
8. What do the letters DVD stand for?
9. What word can apply to a piece of glass fitted in front of a camera's lens to give a special effect, or a special effect applied by computer?
10. For what do the initials PDA stand for in relation to a small computer?

Medium

11. What term describes the process of taking a copy of data in case of damage to the original?
12. Which image and video hosting service, popular with photographers, was launched by Ludicorp in 2004?
13. Blogger is owned by which company?
14. What term is given to data transmission capacity?
15. In 2018, which British consulting firm closed after revelations about its data collection activities?
16. Which two letters are immediately above the letter M on a standard computer keyboard?
17. What is the term given to malicious software that demands payment to restore access to files and systems?
18. What term is given to the degree of detail visible in a photo or TV image?
19. In the communications method abbreviated to VOIP, for what does the "V" stand?
20. What name is given to someone who illegally accesses computer data?

Hard

Answers to QUIZ 306 – Pop Music

1. *Who Do You Think You Are* (Spice Girls)
2. Bruce Springsteen
3. Chesney Hawkes
4. Canada
5. *Rat Trap*
6. *Rhinestone*
7. Stormzy
8. *Jealous*
9. Meat Loaf
10. Ed Sheeran
11. *Should I Stay or Should I Go?*
12. Anastacia
13. Catatonia
14. New Kids On The Block
15. Blur
16. *Do You Really Want to Hurt Me?*
17. The Kinks
18. Elvis Presley
19. Evanescence
20. Venus

1 In which county is Weymouth?

2 Which singer is most associated with the song *Fly Me to the Moon*?

3 Which toy's name is derived from the Danish for "play well"?

4 In which country would you find the airport with the code BVA?

5 In the musical *West Side Story*, who were the gang rivals of the Jets?

6 What is the name of the kiosk in which electors cast votes?

7 Jean Boht played the matriarch in which Carla Lane sitcom?

8 A native of Russia's capital is referred to by what name?

9 What general term is given to a Holy day with no fixed date?

10 What name is given to the building from which astronomers view the night sky?

11 How would 14 be written in Roman numerals?

12 In which county is Workington?

13 What is another name for the monkey nut?

14 What is the literal meaning of the word "antediluvian"?

15 What is a French shoe made from a single block of wood?

16 The Pentland Hills lie south-west of which UK city?

17 How many grand slam tennis titles did Pete Sampras win?

18 Which family member's name is used to describe a pawnbroker?

19 What vegetable is used to make hash browns?

20 In which city can you visit the SS *Great Britain*?

Easy

Medium

Hard

Answers to QUIZ 307 – Pot Luck

1	All Saints	11	Alaska
2	Devon	12	Yes
3	Large	13	Public Lending Right
4	The Swale	14	Montelimar
5	One	15	Festival state
6	Horatio	16	Pen and ink
7	William Shakespeare	17	Audi
8	Green	18	Catholicism
9	"Wets"	19	Pocket book
10	Pollyanna	20	Sir Alec Guinness

Easy

1   What is the name of the highest mountain in the Alps?

2   In the late 1800s, which monument was gifted to the USA from the people of France?

3   In WWII, the D-Day landings were an invasion of which part of France?

4   Prior to the euro, what was the currency unit in France?

5   Which French phrase used in English means "already seen"?

6   Which of these countries does not share a border with France: The Netherlands, Italy or Switzerland?

7   The French flag features which three colours?

8   Which country has a border with France to the south west…?

9   …and what is the name of the mountain range which runs along this border?

10 What is the name of the art museum in Paris which has a glass pyramid in the courtyard?

11 Who was nicknamed the "Maid of Orleans"?

Medium

12 What is the English translation of the national motto of France?

13 In 1804, which political leader declared himself Emperor of France?

14 What are edible snails known as?

15 In *The Adventures of Asterix*, what is the name of Asterix's friend?

16 Which 1996 Disney film was set in Paris?

17 The period of upheaval that occurred in France between 1789 and 1799 is referred to by what name?

18 Which French-nationalised physicist was the first woman to win a Nobel Prize?

19 What does the French phrase *au revoir* mean?

20 For what is the Médoc region well-known?

Hard

Answers to QUIZ 308 – Technology

1	Tokyo	11	Backing up
2	Web log	12	Flickr®
3	Facebook™	13	Google
4	Downloading	14	Bandwidth
5	WWII	15	Cambridge Analytica
6	Finland	16	J and K
7	Siri	17	Ransomware
8	Digital versatile disk	18	Resolution
9	Filter	19	Voice
10	Personal Digital Assistant	20	Hacker

QUIZ 311 – Pot Luck

1   An Egremont Russet is what type of fruit?

2   Which song was a hit for Robbie Williams and Kylie Minogue in 2000?

3   Which drink involving an egg is reputed to be a hangover cure?

4   What is the Scottish variant of the English name James?

5   Which language is spoken in the Azores?

6   In which decade was the Royal Festival Hall built in London?

7   What is the title given to the head of a county's magistrates?

8   In relation to the body, what is a capillary?

9   "Uh, Houston, we've had a problem here" is a line from which 1995 film?

10 In which county is Bude?

11 What term is given to the court verdict if a defendant fails to appear?

12 Which comedian used the catchphrase, "Rock on, Tommy"?

13 In some traditional pendulum clocks, what automated bird moves or calls out every hour?

14 Desiccated coconut is coconut that has undergone what process?

15 What is the name of the pump used in land-based oil wells?

16 Pashka is a Russian dish traditionally eaten at what time of year?

17 What general term is given to substance in physics, as opposed to energy?

18 On an Ordnance Survey map, what is indicated by a blue square containing oak leaves?

19 In which county is the stately home of Chatsworth?

20 What nationality was George Ferris, inventor of the wheel that bears his name?

Easy

Medium

Hard

Answers to QUIZ 309 – Pot Luck

1	Dorset	11	XIV
2	Frank Sinatra	12	Cumbria
3	Lego®	13	Peanut
4	France	14	Before the flood
5	Sharks	15	Sabot
6	Booth	16	Edinburgh
7	*Bread* (Nellie Boswell)	17	14
8	Muscovite	18	Uncle
9	Movable feast	19	Potato
10	Observatory	20	Bristol

Easy

1   Who wrote the play *Lady Windemere's Fan*?

2   What term is given to a sold-out performance in a theatre?

3   Mungojerrie and Bombalurina are characters in which musical?

4   Which small British mammal is featured in the title of a Shakespeare play?

5   What name is given to the stage curtain and its framework?

6   In which German town is a famous Passion Play performed every ten years?

7   In which century was playwright JB Priestley born?

8   What name is given to a performance where the audience are arranged on all sides of the action?

9   Who wrote the one-act plays *The Bear* (1888) and *The Wedding* (1900)?

10 At the end of a performance, what two-word term is given to the actors' final appearance?

11 What term is given to the ability to make the voice heard at a distance?

12 Who wrote the farce *Hotel Paradiso*?

Medium

13 Whose hits are featured in Tim Firth's musical *The Band*?

14 *Accidental Death of an Anarchist* (1970) was written by which playwright?

15 The character of Willy Loman features in which Arthur Miller play?

16 The play *Dancing at Lughnasa* by Brian Friel is set in which country...?

17 ...and who played oldest sister Kate in the 1998 film adaptation?

18 Which sport features in *Up 'n' Under* by John Godber?

19 *The House of Bernarda Alba* and *Blood Wedding* are set in which country?

20 The 1987 film *Prick Up Your Ears* featured the life of which British playwright?

Hard

Answers to QUIZ 310 – France

1	Mont Blanc	11	Joan of Arc
2	The Statue of Liberty	12	Liberty, equality and fraternity
3	Normandy	13	Napoleon Bonaparte
4	Franc	14	Escargot
5	Déjà vu	15	Obelix
6	The Netherlands	16	*The Hunchback of Notre Dame*
7	Blue, white and red	17	The French Revolution
8	Spain	18	Marie Curie
9	The Pyrenees	19	Until we meet again
10	Louvre	20	Wine production

1 Who wrote the 1960 play *The Dumb Waiter*?

2 Salerno is on which Italian coast?

3 What term is given to a holy place of refuge?

4 Which Isle of Wight resort shares its name with a Surrey racecourse?

5 In 1989 and 1990, which tennis player won the Australian Open men's singles championship?

6 What astrological term describes a person born under the second sign of the zodiac?

7 The 1987 novel *Moon Tiger* was written by which author?

8 Which actress received an Oscar nomination for her role in the 2017 film *The Shape of Water*?

9 In which county is Bury St Edmunds?

10 Which football team has had "Royal" and "Woolwich" as part of its name in the past?

11 What type of vegetable can be described as waxy or floury?

12 In which county is Redditch?

13 Peritonitis is inflammation of which part of the body?

14 What term is given to the areas of the economy under state control?

15 What was the first British top ten hit for the Korgis?

16 In which sport did Beth Tweddle compete?

17 Which UK scat-singing star, with a range of well over three octaves, was made a Dame in 1997?

18 Who played Captain Mainwaring in the original TV series of *Dad's Army*?

19 Which London Underground route was named in 1977?

20 What is Rambo's first name?

Easy

Medium

Hard

Answers to QUIZ 311 – Pot Luck

1	Apple	11	Judgement by default
2	*Kids*	12	Bobby Ball
3	Prairie oyster	13	Cuckoo
4	Hamish	14	It has been dried
5	Portuguese	15	Nodding donkey
6	1950s (1951)	16	Easter
7	Lord Lieutenant	17	Matter
8	Blood vessel	18	National Trust
9	*Apollo 13*	19	Derbyshire
10	Cornwall	20	American

Easy

1   Which 1998 film starred Morgan Freeman and Christian Slater?

2   Which character sings *The Impossible Dream* in the musical *Man of La Mancha*?

3   For which 2015 film did Tom Hardy receive an Oscar nomination?

4   The 1970 single *It's Impossible* was a hit for which singer?

5   Who released the 2000 single *Trouble*?

6   What was the subtitle of the 2015 film in the *Mission: Impossible* series?

7   In which country was the Labour Party founder Keir Hardie born?

8   In which year was the film *Hard Day's Night* released?

9   Who played the EastEnders character Richard Cole, nicknamed "Tricky Dicky"?

10 Who recorded the 2008 album *Hard Candy*?

11 Who played villain Hans Gruber in the 1988 film *Die Hard*?

12 In the 1854 novel *Hard Times*, in what type of establishment did Mr Gradgrind work?

13 What term is given to a printed copy of something viewed on screen?

14 Eric Monkman and Bobby Seagull were contestants on which series in 2017?

15 In the well-known phrase, what is the other end of a hard place when faced with a dilemma?

16 In which county is Hardwick Hall?

17 Proverbially, what is a trouble shared?

18 Who was reported to have said "Kiss me, Hardy" on his deathbed?

19 How is singer Adrian Thaws better known?

20 Which *Doctor Who* character was described as the "impossible girl"?

Medium

Hard

Answers to QUIZ 312 – On Stage

1	Oscar Wilde	11	Projection
2	Full house	12	George Feydeau
3	*Cats*	13	Take That's
4	Shrew	14	Dario Fo
5	Proscenium	15	*Death of a Salesman*
6	Oberammergau	16	Ireland
7	19th century	17	Meryl Streep
8	Theatre in the round	18	Rugby League
9	Anton Chekhov	19	Spain
10	Curtain call	20	Joe Orton

1 What is the RAF rank between wing commander and air commodore?

2 The mantilla is a head-dress originating from which country?

3 Who released the 2016 single *Perfect Illusion*?

4 How is the BBC time signal usually referred to?

5 What is the name of David Nielson's character in *Coronation Street*?

6 On mobile phones with a keypad on the handset, which letters appear on the number 4 key?

7 *A Whiter Shade Of Pale* was a transatlantic hit for which group?

8 London and Folkestone are connected by which motorway?

9 Which comedienne wrote the 2016 book *A Mindfulness Guide for the Frazzled*?

10 Which French phrase describes something that is already done?

11 Who played Paul Spector in the crime drama series *The Fall*?

12 In 1988, who became the first leader of the Social and Liberal Democrats?

13 What was the name of the 6' 9" servant in *The Addams Family*?

14 A pithivier is what type of food item?

15 Which fracture in the Earth caused the 1906 San Francisco earthquake?

16 What is a Sam Browne?

17 Who recorded *I Shot the Sheriff* in 1974?

18 The island of Lampedusa belongs to which country?

19 What is the term used for a prepared series of movements in football?

20 In the Chinese calendar, which year comes before the year of the Horse?

Easy

Medium

Hard

Answers to QUIZ 313 – Pot Luck

1	Harold Pinter	11	Potato
2	Amalfi coast	12	Worcestershire
3	Sanctuary	13	Abdomen
4	Sandown	14	Public sector
5	Ivan Lendl	15	*Everybody's Got To Learn Sometime*
6	Taurean	16	Gymnastics
7	Penelope Lively	17	Dame Cleo Laine
8	Sally Hawkins	18	Arthur Lowe
9	Suffolk	19	Jubilee Line
10	Arsenal FC	20	John

Easy

1   Which West Sussex stately home is the country seat of the Dukes of Richmond?

2   Burghley House represented the setting of Castel Gandolfo in the film adaptation of which Dan Brown novel...?

3   ...and which famous landscape architect designed the gardens?

4   In which county is Blickling Hall?

5   In which stately home was *Downton Abbey* mostly filmed?

6   Downhill House in Northern Ireland is perched on clifftops near Castlerock on which ocean?

7   Which stately home in Somerset was used to represent Greenwich Palace in the television adaptation of *Wolf Hall*?

8   Which former monastery in Dorset has a postal address in Somerset?

9   In which country in the UK is Bodrhyddan Hall?

10 Which TV adaptation of an Evelyn Waugh novel featured Castle Howard in Yorkshire as the setting for the fictional home of Sebastian Flyte?

11 Ham House is situated on which river?

Medium

12 Which stately home in Wiltshire is home to the TV series *Animal Park*?

13 Speke Hall is near which city?

14 At which Cheshire stately home, owned by the National Trust, does an annual RHS flower show take place?

15 With which 1960s scandal was Cliveden associated?

16 The parents of which TV chef (b.1972) were farmers on the Castle Howard estate in North Yorkshire?

17 Which stately home in Northumberland was the first house in the world to be lit by hydroelectric power?

18 Kenwood House lies on the edge of which London park?

19 Lyme Park in Cheshire was the location of which fictional house in the 1995 TV adaptation of *Pride and Prejudice*?

20 In which county is Woburn Abbey?

Hard

Answers to QUIZ 314 – Hard Times

1	*Hard Rain*	11	Alan Rickman
2	Don Quixote	12	A school
3	*The Revenant*	13	Hard copy
4	Perry Como	14	*University Challenge*
5	Coldplay	15	A rock
6	*Rogue Nation*	16	Derbyshire
7	Scotland	17	A trouble halved
8	1964	18	Horatio Nelson (Viscount Nelson)
9	Ian Reddington	19	Tricky
10	Madonna	20	Clara Oswald

1 On which river do Bewdley and Bridgnorth stand?

2 Paddington Bear came from which country?

3 In Scotland, what term is given to the first visitor in the New Year?

4 What colour is Vouvray wine?

5 What nationality was the composer Sergei Rachmaninov?

6 The Penrith Panthers compete in which sport?

7 Who played Sir Winston Churchill's wife in the 2017 film *Darkest Hour*?

8 What is another name for a one-armed bandit?

9 Is the seaside of Salcombe in North Devon or South Devon?

10 On which UK island is Blackgang Chine?

11 What is a schottische?

12 What is a Winnebago?

13 The 1959 short story *The Loneliness of the Long-Distance Runner* was written by which author?

14 What term is given to someone who specalises in X-rays?

15 In the film *The Sting*, who was Robert Redford's co-star?

16 Which is California's second largest city?

17 Morecambe and Wise mocked which conductor by calling him Andrew Preview?

18 Which edible seaweed is also known as carrageen?

19 What word describes the sole growth of one crop?

20 Who won *Celebrity MasterChef* in 2017?

Easy

Medium

Hard

Answers to QUIZ 315 – Pot Luck

1	Group captain	11	Jamie Dornan
2	Spain	12	Paddy Ashdown (Baron Ashdown of Norton-sub-Hamdon)
3	Lady Gaga		
4	The pips	13	Lurch
5	Roy Cropper	14	A pie
6	GHI	15	San Andreas Fault
7	Procul Harum	16	A belt
8	M20	17	Eric Clapton
9	Ruby Wax	18	Italy
10	*Fait accompli*	19	Set piece
		20	The year of the snake

Easy

1 In Olympic boxing, what two colours are used for gloves, headgear and uniform?

2 What number is at the "9 o'clock position" on a dartboard?

3 Which surfboard takes its name from a Californian beach?

4 What type of golf club is usually used to tee off?

5 What piece of equipment did Fatima Whitbread throw?

6 In Olympic archery, where would you find the fletching?

7 In which sport are a ball, mallet and a horse essential equipment?

8 In weightlifting, what is the name of the long bar which holds the weights at both ends...?

9 ...and what is the name of the short bar with weights at either end that is used in fitness training?

10 Basketballs are usually what colour?

11 What is attached to the end of a lacrosse stick?

12 What substance do snooker players put on the end of the cue to ensure the ball does not slip?

Medium

13 In which sport are the balls identified by coloured dots?

14 What piece of equipment does a sweeper use in curling?

15 What is the diameter, in inches, of a basketball hoop?

16 The device that connects a ski to a ski boot is referred to by what name?

17 What type of sportsperson would need their footwear "regrinding", or sharpening?

18 In an Olympic throwing field event, which item weighs 4lb 6oz?

19 What is the name of the items against which sprinters place their feet to start a race?

20 Which golfing iron is used to hit the ball out of a bunker?

Hard

Answers to QUIZ 316 – Stately Homes

1	Goodwood	11	River Thames
2	*The Da Vinci Code*	12	Longleat
3	Lancelot "Capability" Brown	13	Liverpool
4	Norfolk	14	Tatton Park
5	Highclere Castle	15	The Profumo affair
6	Atlantic Ocean	16	James Martin
7	Montacute House	17	Cragside
8	Forde Abbey	18	Hampstead Heath
9	Wales	19	Pemberley
10	*Brideshead Revisited*	20	Bedfordshire

1 In greyhound racing, what colour jacket is worn by the dog in trap four?

2 The Puy lentil originates from which country?

3 Which "judge" took part in the 2016 series of *Strictly Come Dancing*?

4 In which country is the city of Poznań?

5 In which Sussex village was a supposed "missing link" found in 1912?

6 Who released the 1989 single *Opposites Attract*?

7 On a dartboard what number is opposite 20?

8 Hughtown is the capital of which of the Isles of Scilly?

9 In relation to education, for what do the letters HND stand?

10 Which gas mark is equivalent to 190 degrees Celsius?

11 What term describes someone in his or her 90s?

12 In the *Pitch Perfect* films, which actress plays Fat Amy?

13 Is tagliatelle a short or long form of pasta?

14 Which queen was known as "Bloody"?

15 Which French phrase describes something to jog your recollection?

16 "If you build it, he will come" is a line from which film?

17 Which Surrey film studio became part of the Pinewood group in 2001?

18 In which county is Folkestone?

19 What general term is given to an artificial limb?

20 The Proton car company was founded in which country?

Easy

Medium

Hard

Answers to QUIZ 317 – Pot Luck

1	River Severn	11	A dance
2	(Darkest) Peru	12	A motor home
3	First foot	13	Alan Sillitoe
4	White	14	Radiologist
5	Russian	15	Paul Newman
6	Rugby League	16	San Diego
7	Dame Kristin Scott Thomas	17	André Previn
8	Fruit machine	18	Irish moss
9	South Devon	19	Monoculture
10	Isle of Wight	20	Angellica Bell

1 By what surname is actor Sir David White better known?

2 Which English town is famous for its white cliffs?

3 Which of Snow White's dwarfs has the shortest name?

4 Who wrote the 1860 novel *The Woman in White*?

5 Who had a UK top five hit in 1977 with *White Christmas*?

6 What was Barry White's only UK no.1 single?

7 A large and unwanted gift is referred to as what type of animal?

8 A white feather is traditionally a derogatory symbol indicating what about the recipient?

9 What is a White Admiral?

10 Who said "There can be no whitewash at the White House"?

11 Rupert Penry-Jones and Phil Davis starred in which London-based crime series?

12 Which creature does Alice follow when she falls down the rabbit hole in *Alice's Adventures in Wonderland*?

13 In the 18th century, what was George Hepplewhite famous for making?

14 In general terms, what are put forward in a government White Paper?

15 The term "white goods" is used to describe items that are used in which room of the house?

16 What is the name of Jack Whitehall's father, who has appeared with him on TV?

17 For what event was London's former White City stadium originally built?

18 What is snooker player Jimmy White's nickname?

19 Who was head chef on two series of the UK version of *Hell's Kitchen*?

20 Betty White played Rose Nyland in which US sitcom?

Answers to QUIZ 318 – Sporting Equipment

1	Red and blue	11	A net
2	11	12	Chalk
3	Malibu	13	Squash
4	Driver	14	Broom
5	Javelin	15	18 inches
6	On the back of an arrow	16	Binding
7	Polo	17	Ice skater
8	Barbell	18	A discus
9	Dumbbell	19	Blocks
10	Orange	20	Sand wedge

QUIZ 321 – Pot Luck

ANSWERS ON PAGE **323**

1 Which actor's last film was *The Shootist* (1976)?

2 The British Saddleback is a breed of what type of animal?

3 Which vegetable develops "eyes" if left exposed to light?

4 On what type of instrument would you find a fretboard?

5 In business terms, how is a potential client referred to?

6 Who wrote the 1993 novel *The Night Manager*?

7 The song *We'll Gather Lilacs* was written by which composer?

8 Which rank is the immediate junior of a sea captain?

9 Which sea area is south of Sole?

10 In the TV series *Holby City*, what is the name of Bob Barrett's character?

11 Who topped the charts in 1973 with *Can the Can*?

12 What is the term for formal admission to a university, particularly Oxford?

13 Santander is a port in which country?

14 What salad item has cherry and beefsteak varieties?

15 Who was Neil Kinnock's (Baron Kinnock's) deputy when he became leader of the Labour Party?

16 How was French tightrope walker Philippe Petit described in the title of a 2008 documentary film...?

17 ...and what was the title of the dramatised version of events released in 2015?

18 A slapshot is a strike in which sport?

19 What is a corsage?

20 Moving clockwise on a dartboard what number is next to 6?

Answers to QUIZ 319 – Pot Luck

1 Black
2 France
3 Judge Rinder
4 Poland
5 Piltdown
6 Paula Abdul
7 3
8 St Mary's
9 Higher National Diploma
10 Gas mark 5
11 Nonagenarian
12 Rebel Wilson
13 Long
14 Mary I
15 *Aide-memoire*
16 *Field of Dreams*
17 Shepperton
18 Kent
19 Prosthetic
20 Malaysia

321

1   What term is given to a broadcast consisting of all the week's episodes of a series such as *EastEnders* or *Coronation Street*?

2   In *Casualty*, what is the name of George Rainsford's character?

3   What is the name of the surgery in BBC's *Doctors*?

4   In which TV competition did original presenter Loyd Grossman announce the results by saying "We've deliberated, cogitated and digested"?

5   Which building has the fictional address of 46 Albert Square, Walford, E20?

6   Ashley Taylor Dawson is best known for playing which *Hollyoaks* character?

7   Who won *Strictly Come Dancing* in 2016?

8   What was the name of the Watts family's dog in *EastEnders*?

9   In which decade was *Emmerdale Farm* screened for the first time?

10 Who plays *Emmerdale*'s Rodney Blackstock?

11 On which programme did Petra, Shep and Goldie find fame?

12 Michelle Connor in *Coronation Street* is played by which actress and singer?

13 What are the names of Homer and Marge Simpson's daughters?

14 Who was cast as Joel Dexter in *Hollyoaks* when the character returned to the series in 2016?

15 In *Coronation Street*, who plays Leanne?

16 What was the name of Jill Halfpenny's character in *Waterloo Road*?

17 What is the name of Bart Simpson's pet greyhound?

18 In *Doctor Who*, what is the name of the home planet of the Daleks?

19 What is the name of the wedding planning business in *Emmerdale*?

20 On April 1, 1957, which current affairs programme broadcast a hoax film about a spaghetti tree?

Answers to QUIZ 320 – White

1	Jason	11	*Whitechapel*
2	Dover	12	White rabbit
3	Doc	13	Furniture
4	Wilkie Collins	14	Proposals
5	Bing Crosby	15	Kitchen or utility room
6	*You're the First, the Last, My Everything*	16	Michael
7	White elephant	17	Olympic Games (1908)
8	They are a coward	18	*The Whirlwind*
9	Butterfly	19	Marco Pierre White
10	Richard Nixon	20	*The Golden Girls*

ANSWERS ON PAGE **325**

1   In which Tanzanian national park does the "Great Migration" take place?

2   What is the translation of the RAF's motto, *"Per ardua ad astra"*?

3   In the 1959 film *Some Like it Hot*, what were the female names adopted by Joe and Jerry?

4   In cricket, what is the term for the large white board used to help the players see the ball?

5   What term is given to the process of shaping the bodywork of a motor vehicle?

6   Which English poet (b.1922) was also a university librarian?

7   In which year did the cross-channel hovercraft begin operating…?

8   …and in which year did it cease operations?

9   If a person is described as a quinquagenarian, they are between what two ages?

10   Who composed the 1881 opera *The Tales of Hoffmann*?

11   London's Monument commemorates which event?

12   *Atomic* was a hit for which group in 1980?

13   How many celebrities compete in each edition of *House of Games*?

14   Saffron Walden is in which English county?

15   Which county of England is famous for its hotpot?

16   What is the first name of Jennifer Metcalfe's *Hollyoaks* character?

17   In which year did Elvis Presley have a hit with *Heartbreak Hotel*?

18   What is measured in millibars?

19   A high hat is what type of musical instrument?

20   What term describes a country run by a presidential government?

Answers to QUIZ 321 – Pot Luck

1	John Wayne	11	Suzi Quatro
2	Pig	12	Matriculation
3	Potato	13	Spain
4	Stringed instrument	14	Tomato
5	Prospect	15	Roy Hattersley (Baron Hattersley)
6	John le Carré	16	*Man on Wire*
7	Ivor Novello	17	*The Walk*
8	First mate	18	Ice hockey
9	Fitzroy	19	A small bouquet of flowers
10	Sacha Levy	20	Ten

Easy

1. What was the profession of Robin Williams' character in the film *Dead Poets Society*?
2. Along with Phillip Schofield, who was the main presenter of *Going Live!* when it began in 1983?
3. What was the venue for the English Live Aid concert in 1985?
4. Who directed the 2004 film *Shaun of the Dead*?
5. The 1983 film *Staying Alive* starred which actor?
6. How many deadly sins are there?
7. Which comedian starred in the 1991 film *Drop Dead Fred*?
8. Which Sir Noël Coward play features a divorced couple who are honeymooning in the same hotel?
9. Which dairy product can be described as "live"?
10. Who directed the 1991 film *Dead Again*?

Medium

11. The 1992 song *I'll Sleep When I'm Dead* was by which band?
12. Who would leave or collect a message from a dead letter box?
13. Which group released the 2010 single *The Club is Alive*?
14. If someone has a lot of energy, what "live" item are they compared to?
15. Proverbially, what animal is flogged in a hopeless situation?
16. *I'm Alive* was a 1965 no.1 hit for which band?
17. What is the setting for the 1989 film *Dead Calm*?
18. The "Live Lounge" features on which national radio station?
19. What is the title of the BBC comedy series based at a West London venue?
20. Which band recorded the 1996 song *Drop Dead Gorgeous*?

Hard

Answers to QUIZ 322 – Long-Running Television Series

1	Omnibus edition	11	Blue Peter
2	Ethan Hardy	12	Kym Marsh
3	The Mill Health Centre	13	Lisa and Maggie
4	*MasterChef*	14	Rory Douglas-Speed
5	The Queen Vic (*EastEnders*)	15	Jane Danson
6	Darren Osborne	16	Izzie Redpath
7	Ore Oduba	17	Santa's Little Helper
8	Roly	18	Skaro
9	1970s	19	*Take a Vow*
10	Patrick Mower	20	*Panorama*

QUIZ 325 – Pot Luck

1 What nationality is actor Michael Sheen?

2 Porter is a dark form of which drink?

3 Algy Pug and Ferdy Fox are friends of which cartoon bear?

4 Is Piedmont in in the north or south of Italy?

5 In which county is Thirsk?

6 Which field of medicine deals with bones and muscles?

7 In which country did the Rottweiler originate?

8 Who wrote the 1948 play *The Browning Version*?

9 What is the Jewish festival of Yom Kippur also known as?

10 What type of fruit is a mineola?

11 Which vegetable can be red, white or Savoy?

12 Friars Crag is a promontory jutting into which body of water?

13 In which political TV series does Kerry Washington play Olivia Pope?

14 In which county is Spalding?

15 What name is given to a Parliamentary board that investigates complex issues?

16 The video for which Robbie Williams song featured ice skating?

17 What is the state flower of Hawaii?

18 How many different colours are used on the squares on a chessboard?

19 Which Indian actor played Mowgli in 1942's *Jungle Book*?

20 In which decade was the Polaroid instant camera introduced?

Easy

Medium

Hard

Answers to QUIZ 323 – Pot Luck

1 Serengeti
2 Through struggles to the stars
3 Josephine and Daphne
4 Sight screen
5 Panel beating
6 Philip Larkin
7 1968
8 2000
9 50-59
10 Offenbach
11 Great Fire of London
12 Blondie
13 Four
14 Essex
15 Lancashire
16 Mercedes
17 1956
18 Air pressure
19 Cymbals
20 Republic

Easy

1 What term was given to the process that occurred in Germany after the fall of the Berlin Wall?

2 Which famous Paris landmark can you visit on the Île de la Cité?

3 The island of Naxos is surrounded by which body of water?

4 What is the name of the Tuscan city where the Palio horse race is held?

5 What colour is the cross on the Greek flag?

6 In 1985, which city became the first to be awarded the title "European City of Culture"...?

7 ...and which Scottish city held that title in 1990?

8 Grossglockner is the highest peak in which country?

9 Which European Basilica was started in 1886 and is still unfinished?

10 Which Portuguese island is famous for its wine?

11 *Le Figaro* is a newspaper published in which country?

12 Wroclaw lies on the banks of which river?

13 What was the currency unit of Greece before the adoption of the euro in 2002?

14 What is the main religion of Lithuania?

Medium

15 Proverbially, taking an irrevocable step is compared to crossing which Italian river?

16 Which central European city is served by John Paul II International Airport?

17 Which Paris art gallery opened in 1986 on the site of a former railway station?

18 Popular in Belgium, moules-frites is a dish of what type of seafood?

19 The Red Cross was founded in which European country?

20 In which decade did the European Economic Community drop the "Economic" from its name?

Hard

Answers to QUIZ 324 – Dead or Alive

1 Teacher
2 Sarah Greene
3 Wembley Stadium
4 Edgar Wright
5 John Travolta
6 Seven
7 Rik Mayall
8 *Private Lives*
9 Yoghurt
10 Sir Kenneth Branagh
11 Bon Jovi
12 A spy
13 JLS
14 Live wire
15 Dead horse
16 The Hollies
17 A boat
18 Radio 1
19 *Live at the Apollo*
20 Republica

1   The film *Titanic* received 14 Oscar nominations, but how many did it actually win?

2   What links the Oscars won by Peter Finch and Heath Ledger?

3   Which former *Play Away* presenter was made a Life Peer in 2010?

4   The cartoonist Matt is associated with which daily newspaper?

5   What name is given to a the basis for a sauce where flour and butter are cooked together before adding liquid?

6   Pink eye is another name for what condition?

7   Which soul duo comprised CeeLo Green and Danger Mouse?

8   What nationality is author John Grisham?

9   The Murray River is the longest river in which country?

10   In which state is Disney World?

11   Which delivery company shares its name with an explosive?

12   In which year did the first London Marathon take place?

13   What type of animal is a skink?

14   Who founded The Body Shop in 1976?

15   How many players are allowed on the ice in an ice hockey team?

16   *Gigi* was written by which duo?

17   With whom did Trinny Woodall present *What Not To Wear*?

18   The single *Over My Shoulder* was released in 1995 by which band?

19   Chihuahuas originate from which country?

20   Which car manufacturer produces the Xsara?

Answers to QUIZ 325 – Pot Luck

1	Welsh	11	Cabbage
2	Beer	12	Derwentwater, Cumbria
3	Rupert	13	*Scandal*
4	North	14	Lincolnshire
5	North Yorkshire	15	Select committee
6	Orthopaedics	16	*She's the One*
7	Germany	17	Hibiscus
8	Sir Terence Rattigan	18	Two
9	The Day of Atonement	19	Sabu
10	Citrus	20	1940s

ANSWERS ON PAGE **330**

Easy

1 *The Son of Man* and *Man in a Bowler Hat* are works by which Belgian surrealist artist?

2 In which London building is the Courtauld Gallery?

3 The horn of plenty is given what name when depicted in art?

4 What was the 19th-century movement exemplified by Morris, Voysey and Ruskin?

5 What Latin expression means "a great work" when referring to art?

6 Which open-air exhibition is situated at West Bretton, south-west of Wakefield?

7 A statue by Rodin and paintings by Klimt and Max Ernst share what name?

8 Which artist exhibited an unmade bed at the Tate Gallery in 1999?

9 In which country was Frida Kahlo born?

10 The Scottish National Gallery is in which city?

11 What was the first name of Impressionist painter Cézanne?

12 Who painted *Poppies* (1873) and *Waterloo Bridge* (1903)?

13 What term is given to an artist's painting of his or her own face?

14 Which French expression is used to refer to artistically experimental work?

Medium

15 In which London park are the Serpentine Galleries?

16 Pointillism is a method of painting that uses what instead of brush strokes?

17 With what flat implement might an artist apply paint?

18 What nationality was the artist Camille Pissaro (b.1830)?

19 In which county is Flatford Mill, subject of several paintings by Constable...?

20 ...and which cathedral did he paint a view of from the Meadows in 1831?

Hard

Answers to QUIZ 326 – Europe

1	Reunification	11	France
2	Notre-Dame	12	Oder
3	Aegean Sea	13	The drachma
4	Siena	14	Roman Catholicism
5	White	15	Rubicon
6	Athens	16	Krakow
7	Glasgow	17	Musée d'Orsay
8	Austria	18	Mussels
9	Sagrada Familia	19	Switzerland
10	Madeira	20	1990s (1993)

ANSWERS ON PAGE 331

1 Which BBC period drama follows the trials and tribulations of the French Court of Louis XIV?

2 In cookery, what does "to chiffonade" mean?

3 "Dirty knee" is the traditional bingo call for which number?

4 What is the largest island in Europe?

5 Journalist Sarah Vine is married to which politician?

6 Zazu and Pumbaa are characters from which musical?

7 Which gormless character did Bernard Bresslaw play in the TV series *The Army Game*?

8 How many years are there in a decade?

9 Who starred as Marge in the 1996 film *Fargo*?

10 Who would wear a wimple?

11 The Stoop is the home ground of which Rugby Union team?

12 Which European republic has the kuna as its unit of currency?

13 In which state is Palm Springs?

14 *Bufo bufo* is the scientific classification for which common animal?

15 Which band, formed in the 1970s, took their name from an aeroplane and a hairstyle?

16 Baz Luhrmann directed which 2001 musical film?

17 Which sport's name derives from the Norwegian for "sloping path"?

18 What type of animal is Hobbes, from *Calvin and Hobbes*?

19 Which country won Olympic Gold in the 2018 men's 5,000 metre short-track speed skating relay?

20 As well as being a mythical creature, what type of animal is a kelpie?

Easy

Medium

Hard

Answers to QUIZ 327 – Pot Luck

1	11	11	TNT
2	They were awarded posthumously	12	1981
3	Floella Benjamin	13	A lizard
4	*The Daily Telegraph*	14	Dame Anita Roddick
5	A roux	15	Six
6	Conjunctivitis	16	Lerner and Loewe
7	Gnarls Barkley	17	Susannah Constantine
8	American	18	Mike & the Mechanics
9	Australia	19	Mexico
10	Florida	20	Citroën

Easy

1 The pink stem of which vegetable is eaten as a fruit?

2 What type of vegetable is an Estima?

3 What name is given to the central part of a globe artichoke?

4 Radicchio is an Italian variety of which salad plant?

5 Known as *cebolla* in Spanish and *cipolla* in Italian, what is it in English?

6 A Hallow'een lantern is traditionally carved from which orange vegetable?

7 What flavour is fennel?

8 What name is given to an individual piece of asparagus?

9 What type of vegetable is January king?

10 Which orchard fruit is mentioned in a phrase indicating that things are going wrong?

11 Calabrese is a variety of which vegetable?

12 How is the carambola fruit better known?

13 Which vegetable is traditionally used as a snowman's nose?

14 A Lexia is what type of dried fruit?

Medium

15 Which red fruit has wild and alpine varieties?

16 What type of salad item is an oak leaf?

17 An embarrassed person is said to be as red as which vegetable?

18 Which part of a boxer's body may be likened to a cauliflower?

19 What type of fruit is a plantain?

20 Framboise liqueur is flavoured with which fruit?

Hard

Answers to QUIZ 328 – Art

1	René Magritte	11	Paul
2	Somerset House	12	Claude Monet
3	Cornucopia	13	Self-portrait
4	Arts and crafts	14	*Avant-garde*
5	*Magnum opus*	15	Kensington Gardens
6	Yorkshire Sculpture Park	16	Dots
7	*The Kiss*	17	Palette knife
8	Tracey Emin	18	French
9	Mexico	19	Suffolk
10	Edinburgh	20	Salisbury

1 How many points do players aim to reach in the game of pontoon?

2 0113 is the dialling code for which city?

3 What is the name of Apple's digital media player application?

4 Which magazine was founded in 1991 by John Bird (Baron Bird) and Gordon Roddick?

5 *Too Darn Hot* is a song from which musical?

6 The Romanovs were a ruling dynasty in which country?

7 What is a "Gibson Flying V"?

8 What is a dunlin?

9 Who had a hit song with *Drive* in 1984?

10 The rubber plant belongs to which family?

11 The Golden Raspberry Awards are also known by what short form?

12 How many times did John McEnroe win Wimbledon?

13 Cordoba is a city in which European country?

14 São Tomé and Príncipe is an island nation off the west coast of which continent?

15 Which numerical quantity can be described as "vulgar"?

16 In which county is Melton Mowbray?

17 Which actor starred in the 1990s sitcom *The Piglet Files*?

18 At which stately home on the River Thames is there an annual flower show run by the RHS?

19 What was the name of the first King of England and Scotland?

20 In which form of wrestling do competitors only use their arms and upper bodies to attack their opponent?

Easy

Medium

Hard

Answers to QUIZ 329 – Pot Luck

1	*Versailles*	11	Harlequins
2	To shred finely	12	Croatia
3	33	13	California
4	Great Britain	14	Toad
5	Michael Gove	15	The B-52s
6	*The Lion King*	16	*Moulin Rouge!*
7	Private "Popeye" Popplewell	17	Slalom
8	Ten	18	A tiger
9	Frances McDormand	19	Hungary
10	A nun	20	A dog

QUIZ 332 – Human Biology

1 Folic acid is added to food to help prevent which birth defect?

2 Which blood vessel leads from the heart's right ventricle?

3 Where in the body are the pectoral muscles?

4 Which hormone is secreted in response to stress?

5 Encephalitis affects which organ of the body?

6 Umami is detected by which part of the body?

7 What type of joint is the human hip or shoulder?

8 A benign cystic lesion in a tendon sheath is given what name?

9 What is the study of the blood's physiology?

10 What type of gene needs to be inherited from both parents to have an impact on the offspring?

11 A low body temperature is referred to by what medical term?

12 What is the US term for hypermetropia?

13 Otitis affects which part of the body?

14 A wart growing on the foot is given what name?

15 Which gas is produced on breathing out?

16 What type of injury may be hairline or greenstick?

17 What is lost from the bones in the condition osteoporosis?

18 Psoriasis affects which part of the body?

19 How is a myocardial infarction more commonly referred to?

20 What do the initials SAD stand for in the winter-related condition?

Easy / **Medium** / **Hard**

Answers to QUIZ 330 – Fruit and Vegetables

1	Rhubarb	11	Broccoli
2	Potato	12	Star fruit
3	Heart	13	Carrot
4	Chicory	14	Raisin
5	Onion	15	Strawberry
6	Pumpkin	16	Lettuce
7	Aniseed	17	Beetroot
8	Spear	18	Ear
9	Cabbage	19	Banana
10	Pear	20	Raspberry

1   Who composed *Maple Leaf Rag* (1899)?

2   In what discipline did Amy Williams win gold in the 2010 Winter Olympics?

3   Springfield is the capital of which US state?

4   Who played the housekeeper in the TV series *Downton Abbey*?

5   Which team won the FA Cup in 1966, Liverpool or Everton?

6   In which county is Haywards Heath?

7   The former region of Picardy, now part of Hauts-de France, has a coastline on which body of water?

8   "At first I was afraid, I was petrified" are the opening words to which song?

9   Which geometric shape is found in the percussion section of the orchestra?

10 If someone is described as a "klutz", what behaviour are they displaying?

11 What name is given to a female red deer, especially one over the age of three?

12 What type of food item is a morel?

13 Under what astrological sign is a "moonchild" born?

14 Who directed the 1936 thriller *Sabotage*?

15 The Hoosiers are a band from which US state?

16 What is the name of James Norton's *Happy Valley* character?

17 Phlebitis is a disorder relating to which part of the body?

18 Which type of financial fund shares its name with a garden barrier?

19 What is the name of the panel of people who make decisions about releasing prisoners?

20 What type of creature is a Gila monster?

Answers to QUIZ 331 – Pot Luck

1	21	11	Razzies
2	Leeds	12	Three (1981,1983 and 1984)
3	iTunes	13	Spain
4	*The Big Issue*	14	Africa
5	*Kiss Me Kate*	15	Fraction
6	Russia	16	Leicestershire
7	An electric guitar	17	Nicholas Lyndhurst
8	Bird	18	Hampton Court Palace
9	The Cars	19	James I of England and VI of Scotland
10	Fig	20	Greco-Roman wrestling

QUIZ 334 – Fighting Talk

Easy

Medium

Hard

ANSWERS ON PAGE 336

1 "In the deserts of Sudan and the gardens of Japan" are the opening lyrics to which song?

2 JMW Turner's *The Fighting Temeraire* is on display in which art gallery?

3 In sporting terms, what do the initials MMA stand for?

4 The line "Run the straight race through God's good grace" is from which hymn?

5 Proverbially, which two animals fight constantly...?

6 ...and which two body parts are involved in a bitter struggle?

7 What is the opposite response to "fight" in a threatening situation?

8 Who returned as host of the BBC Radio 5 Live show *Fighting Talk* in 2016?

9 Who played the title role in the 2012 film *The Fighter*?

10 Which music programme voted new records a hit or a miss?

11 The *Cormoran Strike* novels are written by JK Rowling under what name?

12 According to the 1999 film, what is the first rule of Fight Club?

13 *Fight For This Love* was a 2009 UK no.1 for which singer?

14 What is the alcoholic ingredient in a Planter's Punch?

15 In which year was *The Empire Strikes Back* released in cinemas?

16 Who is Punch's wife in the traditional seaside puppet show?

17 In 1979, which band recorded *I Fought the Law*?

18 Which pop magazine was published from 1978 to 2006?

19 Which of the members of Busted formed the group Fightstar?

20 In which sport is there a strike zone?

Answers to QUIZ 332 – Human Biology

1	Spina bifida	11	Hypothermia
2	Pulmonary artery	12	Far-sightedness
3	In the chest	13	The ear
4	Adrenaline	14	Verruca
5	The brain	15	Carbon dioxide
6	The tongue (it is one of the five tastes)	16	Fracture
7	Ball and socket	17	Calcium
8	Ganglion	18	Skin
9	Haematology	19	Heart attack
10	Recessive	20	Seasonal Affective Disorder

334

1 What word for a study can also describe an animal's lair?

2 The country of St Kitts and Nevis is located in which island group?

3 Which fictional character, created in the early 20th century, was raised in the African jungle by the Mangani great apes?

4 What does the Italian word *penne* translate to?

5 In 2008, a monologue episode of *EastEnders* featured which character?

6 What is the yellow part of an egg called?

7 What word refers to the part of a ticket you keep and to hurt one's toe?

8 Where in the body are the alveoli?

9 *Cuzznz* is a collaborative album by Daz Dillinger and which other hip-hop artist?

10 The description "Salopian" refers to a resident of which county?

11 In cricket, what name is given to a medium-pace bowler who can make the ball bounce so that it will change direction?

12 Which actress co-starred with Leonardo DiCaprio in *The Wolf of Wall Street* (2013)?

13 In which month does the autumnal equinox occur in the UK?

14 The Grizedale Forest is in which National Park?

15 Which game features Miss Scarlet and the Reverend Green?

16 Which poet (d.1963) was married to Ted Hughes?

17 By what French name is the snow pea also known?

18 The Burning Man event takes place in which US state?

19 In 1965, who became the first British-born driver to win the Indy 500?

20 Which is the largest container shipping company in the world?

Easy

Medium

Hard

Answers to QUIZ 333 – Pot Luck

1	Scott Joplin	11	Hind
2	Skeleton	12	Mushroom
3	Illinois	13	Cancer
4	Phyllis Logan	14	Sir Alfred Hitchcock
5	Everton	15	Indiana
6	West Sussex	16	Tommy Lee Royce
7	English Channel	17	The veins
8	*I Will Survive* (Gloria Gaynor)	18	Hedge
9	Triangle	19	Parole board
10	Clumsiness	20	Lizard

Easy

1   In ice hockey, what is the sin bin?

2   In which country were the the first Winter Olympics held?

3   Who came last representing Great Britain in ski-jumping at the 1988 Winter Olympics...?

4   ...and in which year was a film featuring Hugh Jackman released based on his story?

5   What material is a curling stone made from?

6   In which year were the first Winter Olympics?

7   Which former British Olympic gold medallist was a judge on the original series of *Dancing on Ice*?

8   In which country were the 1972 Winter Olympics held, the first time they had been held outside of Europe or North America?

9   Do competitors in the luge travel face-up or face-down?

10   What was Christopher Dean's occupation before he became a professional ice dancer?

Medium

11   What name is given to the mounds of hard snow on a ski slope in some competitions?

12   Which American city has hosted the Winter Olympics twice?

13   What name is given to the semi-circular ditch dug into a mountain for freestyle snowboarding and skiing competitions?

14   The National Hockey League consists of ice hockey teams from which two countries?

15   In which year did Torvill and Dean perform their famous gold-medal winning Bolero routine?

16   What two sizes of team are there in bobsleigh racing?

17   Who won Britain's first Olympic gold medal in figure skating?

18   Which town is the centre of the Scottish winter sports industry?

19   In which decade did ice dancing become a Winter Olympic sport?

20   In which country were the 2018 Winter Olympics held?

Hard

Answers to QUIZ 334 – Fighting Talk

1   *Hit Me With Your Rhythm Stick* (Ian Dury and the Blockheads)
2   The National Gallery
3   Mixed martial arts
4   *Fight the Good Fight*
5   Cat and dog
6   Tooth and nail
7   Flight
8   Colin Murray
9   Mark Wahlberg
10   *Juke Box Jury*
11   Robert Galbraith
12   You do not talk about Fight Club
13   Cheryl
14   Rum
15   1980
16   Judy
17   The Clash
18   *Smash Hits*
19   Charlie Simpson
20   Baseball

QUIZ 337 – Pot Luck

ANSWERS ON PAGE 339

1   The Sir Alan Ayckbourn play *Season's Greetings* takes place at what time of year?

2   In which TV series did the lawyer Saul Goodman first appear?

3   Which promissory note is purchased at the Post Office?

4   How is the lima bean better known in the UK?

5   What term is given to the programs and instructions that run a computer?

6   What term is given to an MP's constituency with only a small majority?

7   In which century was Charles Dickens born?

8   Which type of bridge carries water?

9   What term is given to someone who records the news in images?

10 Which 2015 film about a children's character starred Hugh Jackman and Rooney Mara?

11 Which actress starred in the 1954 film *Dial M for Murder*?

12 In which city does UNICEF have its headquarters?

13 "I don't wanna talk about the things we've gone through, Though it's hurting me, now it's history" are the opening lines of which ABBA song?

14 In the 1951 novel *Tom Brown's Schooldays*, which school did Tom attend?

15 The first names of which "Duke" (b.1899) were Edward Kennedy?

16 *All Eyez on Me* was a 1996 album by which rap artist?

17 Actor Samuel West is the son of which famous actress?

18 In which county is Knutsford?

19 What is the meaning of the Latin phrase *Semper fidelis*?

20 What colour wine is Valpolicella?

Easy

Medium

Answers to QUIZ 335 – Pot Luck

1	Den	11	Seam bowler
2	West Indies	12	Margot Robbie
3	Tarzan	13	September
4	Quills	14	Lake District National Park
5	Dot	15	Cluedo®
6	The yolk	16	Sylvia Plath
7	Stub	17	Mangetout
8	In the lungs	18	Nevada
9	Snoop Dogg	19	Jim Clark
10	Shropshire	20	Maersk

Hard

ANSWERS ON PAGE 340

Easy

1   Sir Adrian Boult was associated with a number of orchestras in what capacity?

2   Who composed the opera *La Traviata*?

3   In which area of London is the Royal Albert Hall?

4   What name is given to a broken chord, where notes are played in a rising or descending order?

5   Who composed the *Water Music* (1717)?

6   What does the musical term "pizzicato" mean?

7   Which musical steel tool provides a true pitch?

8   *The Carnival of the Animals* was an 1886 work by which composer?

9   Whose second symphony, first performed in 1895, is known as the "Resurrection" symphony?

10   What is the musical term indicating a reduction in volume?

11   Robert Schumann (b.1810) was what nationality?

12   Who composed the *St Matthew Passion* (1729)?

Medium

13   What was the name of the TV classical music quiz, originally presented by Joseph Cooper?

14   What is the name of the pace-setting musical pendulum?

15   *The Flight of the Bumblebee* was the work of which composer?

16   Which classical guitarist (d.1987) had the title Marquis of Salobreña?

17   In the opera *Carmen*, what is the profession of Escamillo?

18   Who composed *Don Giovanni* (1787)?

19   Which musical term indicates that notes should be played in a short and sharp manner?

20   The opening notes of which Beethoven symphony are the same as the Morse Code for the letter V?

Hard

Answers to QUIZ 336 – Winter Sports

1	The penalty box where players infringing the rules sit out	11	Moguls
2	France	12	Lake Placid (1932 and 1980)
3	Eddie "The Eagle" Edwards	13	Half-pipe
4	2016	14	USA and Canada
5	Granite	15	1984
6	1924	16	Two or four people
7	Robin Cousins	17	John Curry
8	Sapporo, Japan	18	Aviemore
9	Face-up	19	1970s (1976)
10	Policeman	20	South Korea

ANSWERS ON PAGE 341

1 Petty officer is a rank in which of the services?

2 What breathing tubes are used by those swimming just beneath the water's surface?

3 In which country was playwright Samuel Beckett born?

4 What dish is made using green leaves, tomato, bacon, chicken, egg, chives, Roquefort and vinaigrette?

5 Who wrote the 1930 novel *Memoirs of an Infantry Officer*?

6 Which Elvis song includes the words "You ain't never caught a rabbit"?

7 What is a mangrove?

8 What two-word term describes the status of a property for sale that is empty?

9 In rugby, what three-word term is also used to describe the garryowen?

10 What is Dungeness B?

11 What is the name of the latitude line at about $23\frac{1}{2}$ degrees north of the equator?

12 Times Roman and Courier are examples of what?

13 What was the title of the TV series that ran from 2006 to 2009 and starred Dexter Fletcher as Tony Casemore?

14 In which year did Gordon Brown become Prime Minister?

15 The seaside town of Skegness is in which county?

16 In which decade was slavery abolished in the British Empire?

17 Which film's last line is "Tomorrow is another day"?

18 What flavour is the Italian liqueur Limoncello?

19 In which US state is Waikiki beach?

20 Which character did Sean Astin play in the *Lord of the Rings* trilogy of films?

Easy

Medium

Hard

Answers to QUIZ 337 – Pot Luck

1	Christmas	11	Grace Kelly
2	*Breaking Bad*	12	New York City
3	Postal order	13	*The Winner Takes It All*
4	Butter bean	14	Rugby
5	Software	15	Duke Ellington
6	Marginal seat	16	Tupac Shakur
7	19th century	17	Prunella Scales
8	Aqueduct	18	Cheshire
9	Photojournalist	19	Always faithful
10	*Pan*	20	Red

1 Southampton is bypassed by which motorway?

2 Which means of transport is missing from the title of the 1987 film *Planes, Trains and _*?

3 Which French phrase means "have a good journey"?

4 Which song has been used in the Jet2holidays adverts since the end of 2015?

5 What name is given to an overnight train carriage?

6 What term describes a journey by air over few miles?

7 In Britain, what standard measurement is four feet and eight and a half inches?

8 What term is given to the permission to cross land?

9 In which year was the driving test introduced in the UK...?

10 ...and in which year was a compulsory theory test introduced?

11 The Royal Docks and the Greenwich Peninsula in East London are linked by which type of transport?

12 "The Knowledge" is a test that must be passed in order to drive which vehicle?

13 In which year did the Icelandic volcano Eyjafjallajökull erupt, causing disruption to air traffic?

14 Maglev, or magnetic levitation, is a system of movement for what type of vehicle?

15 Which English airport has the code EMA?

16 How many wheels were there on a Robin Reliant?

17 What is the name of the railway line that runs from Glasgow to the ports of Oban and Mallaig?

18 In which year were BOAC and BEA merged to create British Airways?

19 What did the initials BOAC stand for...?

20 ...and what did the initials BEA stand for?

Answers to QUIZ 338 – Classical Music

1	Conductor	11	German
2	Verdi	12	JS Bach
3	Kensington	13	*Face the Music*
4	Arpeggio	14	Metronome
5	George Frederick Handel	15	Rimsky-Korsakov
6	Plucked	16	Andrés Segovia
7	Tuning fork	17	Toreador
8	Saint-Saëns	18	Wolfgang Amadeus Mozart
9	Mahler	19	Staccato
10	Diminuendo	20	Fifth symphony

1   Neil, Rik, Vyvyan and Mike were the main characters in which 1980s sitcom?

2   Which actor starred in the title role of the 2001 film *I Am Sam*?

3   What term was given to an ancient Roman ruling group of three?

4   Are maracas shaken or struck?

5   What is the capital of Cambodia?

6   The cured meat pancetta originated in which country?

7   Who co-wrote *Do They Know It's Christmas* with Bob Geldof?

8   Which number is on the left of the line of keys immediately above the above the top row of letters on a standard computer keyboard?

9   A "Gallup poll" is a survey of opinion that is used during which national event?

10   Which Greater Manchester borough includes Altrincham and Sale?

11   As at the end of the 2017-18 season, who was Arsenal FC's all-time top goal scorer?

12   Who was the star of the 1990s series *Dr Quinn, Medicine Woman*?

13   In the phrase "SWOT analysis", what does the letter "W" stand for?

14   Who is the chief law officer of the Crown in Scotland?

15   *We are Family* was a hit for which group?

16   What was unusual about the elite men's race in the first London Marathon?

17   The vegetable scorzonera is also known by what name?

18   Which material is sometimes also called sackcloth?

19   Which 1974 film sequel won the Best Picture Oscar?

20   In which European art gallery can you see Botticelli's *Venus*?

Easy

Medium

Hard

Answers to QUIZ 339 – Pot Luck

1	Royal Navy	11	Tropic of Cancer
2	Snorkels	12	Typeface or font
3	Ireland	13	*Hotel Babylon*
4	Cobb salad	14	2007
5	Siegfried Sassoon	15	Lincolnshire
6	*Hound Dog*	16	1830s (1833)
7	A tree	17	*Gone with the Wind*
8	Vacant possession	18	Lemon
9	Up and under	19	Hawaii
10	A nuclear power station	20	Sam

1   Which legendary figure did Anthony Head play in the TV series *Merlin*?

2   In which decade did Butlin's holiday camp open in Minehead...?

3   ...and in which county is Minehead?

4   Holyhead is the largest town in which county?

5   What is the name of Del Trotter's local?

6   Is Flamborough Head on the east coast or west coast of England?

7   Issued in 1981, what was the first Talking Heads single to make the UK top twenty?

8   A headbanger listens to what sort of music?

9   Birkenhead is on which river?

10 Charlie Fairhead is a character from which TV series?

11 Proverbially, which animal with a sore head is someone likened to if they are in a bad mood?

12 What name is given to the large cask that holds 54 pints of beer?

13 *Creep*, originally released in 1992, was the debut single by which band?

14 Malin Head is the most northerly point of which country?

15 Mr Potato Head is a character in which 1990s series of films?

16 *A Head Full of Dreams* is a 2015 album by which band?

17 What are you have said to hit on the head if you make an accurate statement?

18 Judith Keppel and Dave Rainford appear on which TV quiz?

19 What is the name of Sebastian's teddy bear in the 1945 novel *Brideshead Revisited*?

20 At which English cricket ground was the fourth Test in the 2009 Ashes held?

Answers to QUIZ 340 – Travelling Around

1	M27	11	Cable car
2	Automobiles	12	London black cab
3	Bon voyage	13	2010
4	Hold My Hand (Jess Glynne)	14	Train
5	Sleeper	15	East Midlands Airport
6	Short-haul	16	Three
7	Railway gauge (distance between rails)	17	West Highland Line
8	Right of way	18	1974
9	1935	19	British Overseas Airways Corporation
10	1996	20	British European Airways

ANSWERS ON PAGE 345

1   What is polenta made from?

2   In the rhyme often quoted when magpies are seen, what is associated with two magpies?

3   Which is the first sign of the zodiac?

4   *Desert Island Discs* is broadcast on which channel?

5   The city of Olbia is on which Mediterranean island?

6   The TV series *A History of Britain* was presented by which historian?

7   What term is given to the monarch's mark of approval of a product?

8   In 1875, who became the first man to swim the English Channel?

9   What is a recently hatched fish called?

10   What is "tucker" slang for in Australia?

11   Fatigues are designed for being worn by which type of personnel?

12   Which is the southernmost of India's states?

13   What is the name of the sponge that is baked over a layer of fruit and inverted for serving?

14   In the TV series *Line of Duty*, who played Lindsay Denton?

15   What name is given to the governmental principle of combining states?

16   *Son of a Preacher Man* was a 1968 hit for which singer?

17   In cookery, which unit of measurement is approximately 5ml?

18   Who was the first British athlete to win back-to-back gold medals at the Winter Olympics?

19   Who played the title role in *Doctor Who* when it was revived in 2005?

20   In which US state is the resort of Santa Barbara?

Easy

Medium

Hard

Answers to QUIZ 341 – Pot Luck

1	*The Young Ones*	11	Thierry Henry
2	Sean Penn	12	Jane Seymour
3	Triumvirate	13	Weaknesses
4	Shaken	14	Lord Advocate
5	Phnom Penh	15	Sister Sledge
6	Italy	16	Two runners tied for first place: Dick Beardsley (US) & Inge Simonsen (Norway)
7	Midge Ure	17	Black salsify
8	1	18	Hessian
9	General election	19	*The Godfather: Part II*
10	Trafford	20	The Uffizi, Florence

ANSWERS ON PAGE 346

Easy

1 How is souvlaki served?

2 Saag aloo is a dish comprised mainly of which two vegetables?

3 What is the two-word term for the percentage that may be added to a bill for the work of the waiting staff?

4 What word describes thinly sliced raw beef?

5 The chief waiter in a restaurant is referred to by which French term?

6 What is the name of the thin, crisp disc-shaped accompaniment to Indian food?

7 Dulce de leche, often served with churros, has what flavour?

8 What is a lift for food in a restaurant known as?

9 What does a sommelier advise on?

10 Kalamata olives are usually what colour?

Medium

11 Pomodoro is the Italian name for which salad fruit?

12 A gratin Dauphinois is a side dish of which vegetable?

13 What is antipasti?

14 Which type of noodles are traditionally used in a pad thai?

15 Guacamole originates from which country?

16 A dish described as *Provençal* originates from which country?

17 What is the word for a Swedish buffet?

18 What Chinese dish is cooked in a similar way to an omelette?

19 Which is typically spicier, a balti or a jalfrezi?

20 Buffalo wings are made from which meat?

Hard

Answers to QUIZ 342 – Heads Up

1	Uther Pendragon	11	Bear
2	1960s	12	Hogshead
3	Somerset	13	Radiohead
4	Anglesey	14	Ireland
5	The Nag's Head	15	*Toy Story*
6	East coast	16	Coldplay
7	*Once in a Lifetime*	17	The nail
8	Heavy metal	18	*Eggheads*
9	Mersey	19	Aloysius
10	*Casualty*	20	Headingley

1   In the nursery rhyme *Oranges and Lemons*, which bells say "When will that be?"

2   What are Garibaldi and Bath Oliver types of?

3   What is contained in a reliquary?

4   Beef Stroganoff originates from which country?

5   What was the first name of Mr Lord, after whom the cricket ground is named?

6   *Queen of My Heart* featured on which Westlife album?

7   In which *Carry On* film did Harry H Corbett make his only appearance?

8   Which Olympic water sport includes twists, tucks and pikes?

9   Benicassim is a festival in which country?

10   In 1994, who was elected leader of the Labour Party?

11   Who replaced Kate Thornton as presenter of *The X Factor*?

12   Which Jane Austen novel features Charles and Mary Musgrove?

13   What is a "via", in Rome?

14   Of what sort of night in Georgia did Brook Benton sing in 1970?

15   In which county is Huddersfield?

16   Which Mediterranean cheese is traditionally made from a mix of goat's and sheep's milk?

17   What religion was Mary I?

18   Who was appointed the political editor of BBC News in 2015?

19   Is a gudgeon a freshwater or sea fish?

20   Which two actors co-starred in the 2007 film *The Bucket List*?

Answers to QUIZ 343 – Pot Luck

1	Cornmeal	11	Military personnel
2	Joy	12	Tamil Nadu
3	Aries	13	Upside-down cake
4	BBC Radio 4	14	Keeley Hawes
5	Sardinia	15	Federalism
6	Simon Schama	16	Dusty Springfield
7	Royal Warrant	17	Teaspoon
8	Captain Matthew Webb	18	Lizzy Yarnold
9	A fry	19	Christopher Eccleston
10	Food	20	California

1 Autumn weather that is unseasonably warm is often referred to as a summer from which country?

2 Which 1938 novel takes its name from the first Mrs De Winter?

3 Who left the main presenting team of *Springwatch* and its spin-offs at the end of 2017?

4 Who wrote the words "Hope springs eternal in the human breast"?

5 In which month does the summer solstice occur in the UK?

6 The song *Summertime* features in which musical by George Gershwin?

7 *Summertime Blues* was a 1958 hit for which singer?

8 Which group released the 1978 single *Summer Night City*?

9 What type of plant is winter savory?

10 Summer Bay is the setting for which long-running Australian series?

11 Spring greens belong to which family of vegetables?

12 Who wrote *Ode to Autumn*?

13 Which season do Americans call "fall"?

14 "Sleigh bells ring, are you listening? In the lane, snow is glistening" are lyrics from which song?

15 What is another name for a gazebo?

16 *A Winter's Tale* was a 1982 hit for which singer?

17 Justin Hayward's *Forever Autumn* featured on which 1978 best-selling album?

18 The town of Alice Springs is in which country?

19 Winterfell is a location in which TV series?

20 Which arboretum in Gloucestershire is famous for its autumn colour?

Answers to QUIZ 344 – Eating Out

1	On a skewer	11	Tomato
2	Spinach and potatoes	12	Potato
3	Service charge	13	Italian hors d'oeuvre
4	Carpaccio	14	Rice noodles
5	Maître d'hôtel	15	Mexico
6	Poppadom	16	France
7	Caramel	17	Smorgasbord
8	A dumb waiter	18	Foo yong
9	Wine	19	Jalfrezi
10	Black (sometimes brown)	20	Chicken

1 Pleurisy affects which part of the body?

2 What is the postcode area code for Bolton?

3 Which band recorded the 1988 song *Never Tear Us Apart*?

4 Who wrote the 1978 play *Betrayal*?

5 Who abdicated in Fontainebleau in April 1814?

6 Who starred as Philo Beddoe in *Every Which Way But Loose*?

7 Which singer was with Streetband and Q-Tips before becoming a solo artist?

8 "Jump and jive" is the traditional bingo call for which number?

9 On mobile phones with a keypad on the handset, which letters appear on the number 9 key?

10 Is Sidmouth in north Devon or south Devon?

11 What is the first name of Tina O'Brien's character in *Coronation Street*?

12 Who plays Mr Brown in the *Paddington* films?

13 Anne Boleyn was beheaded in the grounds of which building?

14 What was the name of Phoebe's twin in the TV series *Friends*?

15 Worsted is what type of fabric?

16 What is a trilobite?

17 Prince William Sound is on the south coast of which US state?

18 What is the term for the process in which liquid changes to a vapour?

19 In which country would you find the shanty towns known as favelas?

20 What is the term for a small earthquake?

Answers to QUIZ 345 – Pot Luck

1	Stepney	11	Dermot O'Leary
2	Biscuit	12	*Persuasion*
3	Relics	13	A road
4	Russia	14	Rainy
5	Thomas	15	West Yorkshire
6	*World of Our Own*	16	Halloumi
7	*Carry On Screaming*	17	Roman Catholic
8	Diving	18	Laura Kuenssberg
9	Spain	19	Freshwater
10	Tony Blair	20	Jack Nicholson and Morgan Freeman

ANSWERS ON PAGE 350

1 What is the name of Superman's home city?

2 Who is Bruce Wayne's butler...?

3 ...and who plays him in the TV series *Gotham*?

4 What is the nickname of Virginia Potts in the Marvel films?

5 Which superhero is nicknamed the "Caped Crusader"?

6 Who made his first outing as Captain America in the 2011 film in the Marvel franchise?

7 Which comic-book hero is from the planet Krypton?

8 Which superhero starred in a 2017 film in the *Lego Movie* series?

9 In *The Flash*, who is Barry Allen's adoptive father...?

10 ...and what is the name of his daughter, who becomes Barry's wife?

11 Who starred as Lex Luthor in *Superman* (1978)?

12 What is the name of Scarlett Johansson's Marvel character?

13 In the name of the comic range, the initials "DC" were taken from which original publication?

14 What is the name of the psychiatric hospital that serves Gotham City?

15 Which former *Doctor Who* actor plays Rip Hunter in *Legends of Tomorrow*?

16 In which year did Deadpool appear on the big screen for the first time?

17 Adam West and Burt Ward played which superheroes in a 1960s TV series?

18 Who plays Ray Palmer in *Arrow* and *Legends of Tomorrow*?

19 Which Marvel superhero's name appeared in the title of the 2007 *Fantastic Four* film?

20 Describing a collection of superheroes, for what do the initials JLA stand?

Answers to QUIZ 346 – Seasons

1	India	11	Cabbage
2	*Rebecca*	12	John Keats
3	Martin Hughes-Games	13	Autumn
4	Alexander Pope	14	*Winter Wonderland*
5	June	15	Summerhouse
6	*Porgy and Bess*	16	David Essex
7	Eddie Cochran	17	*Jeff Wayne's Musical Version of The War of the Worlds*
8	ABBA	18	Australia
9	A herb	19	*Game of Thrones*
10	*Home and Away*	20	Westonbirt

1 In which county is the town of Horsham?

2 What word, from the French for a large case, describes a combination of two words?

3 0141 is the dialling code for which Scottish city?

4 From which country does biscotti originate?

5 For which 1986 film did Marlee Matlin win the Best Actress Oscar?

6 Called Río Bravo del Norte in Mexico, how is it referred to in the US?

7 The town of Launceston is in which county?

8 On a dartboard, what number is opposite 5?

9 What is Staffordshire's largest city?

10 Sumatra is an island belonging to which country?

11 Which religion uses a fish as a symbol?

12 Full-fat milk is sold in bottles with what colour top?

13 What name is given to a boundary on a football or rugby pitch?

14 What type of food item is a chanterelle?

15 What sport does Bernhard Langer play?

16 The zodiac sign Pisces covers which two calendar months?

17 What nationality was playwright Sean O'Casey (d.1964)?

18 The giant-impact hypothesis relates to the formation of which celestial body?

19 A book by Jennifer Worth was the basis for which TV series, first shown in 2012?

20 Which newspaper is nicknamed "The Thunderer"?

Easy

Medium

Hard

Answers to QUIZ 347 – Pot Luck

1	The lungs	11	Sarah
2	BL	12	Hugh Bonneville
3	INXS	13	Tower of London
4	Harold Pinter	14	Ursula
5	Napoleon I	15	Woollen
6	Clint Eastwood	16	A fossil
7	Paul Young	17	Alaska
8	35	18	Evaporation
9	WXYZ	19	Brazil
10	South Devon	20	Tremor

Easy

1   What word describes a heavy snowstorm accompanied by strong winds?

2   "Smog" is a combination of which two words?

3   On a weather map, what colour is a line indicating a warm front?

4   The Enhanced Fujita scale is used to measure the damage caused by which weather event?

5   What general term is given to rain, snow and hail?

6   Is a cirrus cloud thick or wispy?

7   During the spring and summer, the Met Office provides a forecast for grass, weed and what other type of pollen?

8   How is a UV index reading of between 3 and 5.9 classed in terms of risk of sun exposure?

9   What is the third colour of the rainbow...?

10   ...and by what other name is a "white rainbow" known, sometimes seen in cloudy conditions?

Medium

11   What weather-related event can also be described as an inundation?

12   What does an anemometer measure?

13   A reading of 0 on the Beaufort Scale indicates what type of weather?

14   In a Met Office weather warning, what name is given to the table indicating the likelihood of the event occurring against the likely outcome?

15   Which map line joins points of equal atmospheric pressure?

16   What is the profession of someone who studies the weather?

17   What is the heavy rain of summer called in Asia?

18   On hot days, what term is applied to the misty phenomenon that can develop?

19   The mistral wind occurs on which continent?

20   What symbol on a weather map indicates overcast weather?

Hard

Answers to QUIZ 348 – Superheroes

1	Metropolis	11	Gene Hackman
2	Alfred	12	Black Widow
3	Sean Pertwee	13	Detective Comics
4	Pepper Potts	14	Arkham Asylum
5	Batman	15	Arthur Darvill
6	Chris Evans	16	2016
7	Superman	17	Batman and Robin
8	Batman	18	Brandon Routh
9	Joe West	19	Silver Surfer
10	Iris	20	Justice League of America

ANSWERS ON PAGE 353

1 In the Netherlands, what name is given to land reclaimed from the sea?

2 What was the number allocated to Patrick McGoohan's character in the cult series *The Prisoner*?

3 What name is given to the practice of insulting an opposing player so as to affect his or her concentration?

4 Sichuan is a province in which country?

5 In which literary work does the Wife of Bath appear?

6 Who directed the 2012 film *Zero Dark Thirty*?

7 Tuvalu is in which ocean?

8 Which gas mark is equivalent to 165 degrees Celsius?

9 Selsey Bill is a headland in which county...?

10 ...and which band mentioned it in 1982's *Driving in My Car*?

11 Who won her first tennis Grand Slam title at the French Open in 2018?

12 Who is Kim's mother in the Australian sitcom starring Gina Riley and Jane Turner?

13 The 2003 film *I Capture the Castle* was based on a book by which author?

14 In which county is the Fossdyke canal?

15 What was known as "Little Willie" in WWI?

16 In the initials of the campaigning organisation, for what do the letters PETA stand?

17 Who recorded *Bad Case Of Loving You (Doctor Doctor)* in 1979?

18 Which French phrase describes camaraderie, particularly amongst soldiers?

19 In which sport would a Western roll be used?

20 What word can refer to both a card game and part of the nose?

Answers to QUIZ 349 – Pot Luck

1	West Sussex	11	Christianity
2	Portmanteau	12	Blue
3	Glasgow	13	Touchline
4	Italy	14	Mushroom
5	*Children of a Lesser God*	15	Golf
6	Rio Grande	16	February and March
7	Cornwall	17	Irish
8	17	18	The Moon
9	Stoke-on-Trent	19	*Call the Midwife*
10	Indonesia	20	*The Times*

Easy

Medium

Hard

1 Who was the first British driver to win the World Rally Championship?

2 Which late Formula 1 driver was the subject of a 2010 documentary?

3 In which country is Lamborghini based?

4 What term is given to an area where your view is obstructed, particularly when driving?

5 What was cyclist Laura Kenny's maiden name?

6 How many wheels are there on a rickshaw?

7 The team pursuit race in cycling has a maximum of how many riders in each team?

8 Which general type of petrol is obtained from a pump marked in green?

9 In which two years did Barry Sheene win the 500cc motorcycle World Championships?

10 Which luxury car manufacturer produces the Veyron?

11 Which motor-racing circuit is located near Towcester?

12 Former presenters of which motoring programme include Angela Rippon, Noel Edmonds and Tiff Needell?

13 What name is given to the form of transport with one wheel, often seen in a circus?

14 What early type of transport was a velocipede?

15 As at the end of the 2017 season, who is the only Polish driver to have won a Formula 1 Grand Prix?

16 Ansel Elgort played the lead role in which 2017 film?

17 Who is the only man to have won world motor racing championships on both two and four wheels?

18 How many lights are used to start a Formula 1 race?

19 Which 1969 car caper ends with a bus teetering on the edge of a cliff?

20 What term was given to the outdoor site at the 2012 Olympics where the BMX and mountain bike competitions took place?

Answers to QUIZ 350 – Weather

1	Blizzard	11	Flood
2	Smoke and fog	12	Wind speed
3	Red	13	Calm weather
4	Tornado	14	Impact matrix
5	Precipitation	15	Isobar
6	Wispy	16	Meteorologist
7	Tree	17	Monsoon
8	Moderate	18	Haze
9	Yellow	19	Europe
10	Fogbow	20	A grey cloud

1 Who won the "Golden Boot" award for being the top scorer in the 2014 FIFA World Cup Finals?

2 What is a cultivator used for in the garden?

3 In which county is the town of Sheerness?

4 Stonehenge is situated on which area of land?

5 Which US state is nicknamed "the First State"?

6 What term is generally used as an index of water height?

7 In cookery, which unit of measurement is approximately 10ml?

8 A trattoria is the name of a small restaurant in which country?

9 What nationality was the novelist Gabriel García Márquez?

10 Hyssop is a member of which family?

11 With what part of the body is a treadle operated?

12 Provolone is what type of food?

13 Which weight category is below feather and bantam in professional boxing?

14 Who starred in the 2011 film *The Rum Diary*?

15 Which actress co-starred with Mel Gibson in the 1990 film *Bird on a Wire*?

16 The artificial island of Palm Jumeirah is on the coast of which city?

17 Who recorded *Back in the USSR* in 1968?

18 Which motorway runs from London to Leeds?

19 In what type of building would you find a backcloth or backdrop?

20 Moving anticlockwise on a dartboard what number is next to 17?

Easy

Medium

Hard

Answers to QUIZ 351 – Pot Luck

1	Polder	11	Simone Halep
2	Six	12	Kath
3	Sledging	13	Dodie Smith
4	China	14	Lincolnshire
5	*The Canterbury Tales*	15	The first prototype tank
6	Kathryn Bigelow	16	People for the Ethical Treatment of Animals
7	Pacific Ocean	17	Robert Palmer
8	Gas mark 3	18	*Esprit de corps*
9	West Sussex	19	High jump
10	Madness	20	Bridge

Easy

1   Jaundice causes the skin and eyes to become what colour?

2   What is the colour of mourning in China and Japan?

3   A Norfolk Grey is what type of creature?

4   Which European country first produced orange carrots?

5   What does Shakespeare refer to as "the green-eyed monster"?

6   What colour blood is used to describe those of a high social rank?

7   On a Monopoly™ board, what colour is Trafalgar Square?

8   Which group released the 1981 song *Golden Brown*?

9   What colours are the five rings on the Olympic flag?

10 What colour represents the art and literature category in a standard edition of Trivial Pursuit™?

11 An optimist is said to wear what colour glasses?

12 What colour is Cabernet Sauvignon wine?

13 What name is given to someone who sells fruit and vegetables?

14 Who co-starred with Michelle Williams in the 2010 film *Blue Valentine*?

Medium

15 Robert Llewellyn is best known for playing which character in the TV series *Red Dwarf*?

16 Which country is referred to as the Rainbow Nation?

17 If you are very pleased about something, what colour are you said to be tickled?

18 Who starred as Celie Johnson in the 1984 film *The Color Purple*?

19 How many colours are there on a tricolour flag?

20 What colour is spaghetti verde?

Hard

Answers to QUIZ 352 – On Wheels

1	Colin McRae	11	Silverstone
2	Ayrton Senna (*Senna*)	12	*Top Gear*
3	Italy	13	Unicycle
4	Blind spot	14	Bicycle
5	Trott	15	Robert Kubica
6	Two	16	*Baby Driver*
7	Four	17	John Surtees
8	Unleaded	18	Five
9	1976 and 1977	19	*The Italian Job*
10	Bugatti	20	Velopark

1 Who plays Sophie in the *Mamma Mia* films?

2 In which year did Piers Morgan join *Good Morning Britain* as a presenter?

3 What is the term for a law proposed by a back-bencher?

4 In which of the *Star Trek* films did humpback whales play a major part in the plot?

5 What is the first name of Bonnie Langford's *EastEnders* character?

6 The character of Jimmy Porter features in which 1956 play?

7 By what three letters is the radio frequency 300-3000 megahertz referred to?

8 What type of fish has species that include silver and chinook?

9 In which country is the village of Grindelwald?

10 Which actor starred as Henry Willows the 1980s sitcom *Home to Roost*?

11 What was the first UK top ten hit for James Brown?

12 Which curved type of cavalry sword has a single cutting edge?

13 What flavour is stracciatella ice cream?

14 A continual annoyance may be described as what in the side?

15 How is gluhwein known in English?

16 When were NHS prescription charges first introduced?

17 Who wrote the 1940 novel *Farewell, My Lovely*?

18 In which New Mexico town did a crash occur in 1947, prompting speculation about flying saucers?

19 What is the highest point in the range of hills east of Jerusalem?

20 Approximately how long is a squash court in English singles?

Easy

Medium

Hard

Answers to QUIZ 353 – Pot Luck

1	James Rodriguez (Colombia)	11	The foot
2	Turning over soil	12	Cheese
3	Kent	13	Flyweight
4	Salisbury Plain	14	Johnny Depp
5	Delaware	15	Goldie Hawn
6	Sea level	16	Dubai
7	Dessert spoon	17	The Beatles
8	Italy	18	M1
9	Colombian	19	A theatre
10	Mint	20	2

Easy

1 Which film ends with Sam Baldwin and Annie Reed meeting at the top of the Empire State Building?

2 Who played The Grandfather in the 1987 film *The Princess Bride*?

3 The 2011 film *I Don't Know How She Does It* was based on a book by which author?

4 Who won the Best Actress Oscar for her role in the film *Moonstruck*?

5 In the 2004 film *Along Came Polly*, who co-starred with Jennifer Aniston?

6 Which actress starred in the 1953 film *Roman Holiday*?

7 Who played Harry in the 1989 film *When Harry Met Sally*?

8 Who wrote and directed the 2013 film *About Time*?

9 In which year was the first *Sex and the City* film released?

10 In the 1993 film *Much Ado About Nothing*, who played Beatrice and Benedick?

Medium

11 Who got married in the title of a 1986 film directed by Francis Coppola?

12 How many things did *I Hate About You* in the title of the 1999 film?

13 The 1984 film *Romancing the Stone* was set in which South American country?

14 In which country was the 1992 film *Strictly Ballroom* set?

15 In the 1967 film *The Graduate*, what was the name of Mrs Robinson's daughter?

16 The 2009 film *Ghosts of Girlfriends Past* was inspired by which Charles Dickens novel?

17 Who played the title role in the 2008 film *Forgetting Sarah Marshall*?

18 Which singer and actress starred in the 2010 film *The Back-up Plan*?

19 The characters of Robert Kincaid and Francesca Johnson featured in which 1995 film?

20 Which 1986 romantic comedy was named after a song by the Psychedelic Furs?

Hard

Answers to QUIZ 354 – Colours

1	Yellow	11	Rose-tinted
2	White	12	Red
3	Chicken	13	Greengrocer
4	The Netherlands	14	Ryan Gosling
5	Jealousy	15	Kryten
6	Blue	16	South Africa
7	Red	17	Pink
8	The Stranglers	18	Whoopi Goldberg
9	Blue, black, red, yellow and green	19	Three
10	Brown	20	Green

1   What was the name of Neil Morrissey's character in the TV series *Men Behaving Badly*?

2   In which county is Huntingdon?

3   With which group is singer Pauline Black associated?

4   The Trebbiano grape makes what colour wine?

5   What was the name of Rebecca Front's character in the TV series *Lewis*?

6   A linebacker plays which sport?

7   Who directed the 1996 film *Romeo + Juliet*?

8   In which decade was the RSPCA established?

9   Which animal is used as a quality mark on British eggs?

10 The novel *All Quiet on the Western Front* was set during which conflict?

11 What term is used to describe a boxing match ended by the referee?

12 In Scrabble®, how many points is the letter S worth?

13 What term is used to describe the condition when a human's body temperature drops below 35°C?

14 For which 2009 film did Sandra Bullock win the Best Actress Oscar?

15 In which country is the city of Tijuana?

16 Who was the first actor to be posthumously nominated for a Best Actor Oscar?

17 Which literary figure tilted at windmills?

18 St Crispin is the patron saint of which profession?

19 Which singer released the song, *I'm Lovin' it*, used in the jingle for the McDonald's adverts?

20 What does a lacewing feed on?

Answers to QUIZ 355 – Pot Luck

1	Amanda Seyfried	11	*Living In America*
2	2015	12	Sabre
3	Private Member's Bill	13	Chocolate-chip
4	*Star Trek IV: The Voyage Home*	14	A thorn
5	Carmel	15	Mulled wine
6	*Look Back in Anger*	16	1952
7	UHF (Ultra-high frequency)	17	Raymond Chandler
8	Salmon	18	Roswell
9	Switzerland	19	Mount of Olives
10	John Thaw	20	10m

1 What product is Singer® best known for manufacturing?

2 What would you be doing if you practised a strathspey and a pas de basque?

3 The Acol bidding system is used in which card game?

4 In what game do you peg, and score for pairs and fifteens?

5 How many playing cards are there in each suit?

6 What is Margarete Steiff famous for making?

7 What kind of entertainment did Barnum call "the Greatest Show on Earth"?

8 On a dartboard what number is opposite 19?

9 What is the hobby of someone who is described as a "twitcher"?

10 Which building toy was designed by a Dane, Ole Kirk Christiansen?

11 How many different digits are used in a standard Sudoku grid?

12 In which card game can you stick and twist?

13 What was developed to experience the excitement of surfing on land?

14 In which county is Thorpe Park?

15 What term describes transmitting a film or programme direct to a computer, rather than downloading it?

16 Where would someone practise parkour?

17 What is the name of the hanging rollercoaster ride at Alton Towers that was opened in 1994?

18 In a game of whist, what term is given to the winning of all the tricks?

19 What term is given to forwarding a message on Twitter™?

20 On an Ordnance Survey map, what is indicated by a blue duck symbol?

Answers to QUIZ 356 – Romantic Comedies

1	*Sleepless in Seattle*	11	*Peggy Sue*
2	Peter Falk	12	Ten
3	Allison Pearson	13	Colombia
4	Cher	14	Australia
5	Ben Stiller	15	Elaine
6	Audrey Hepburn	16	*A Christmas Carol*
7	Billy Crystal	17	Kristen Bell
8	Richard Curtis	18	Jennifer Lopez
9	2008	19	*The Bridges of Madison County*
10	Dame Emma Thompson and Sir Kenneth Branagh	20	*Pretty in Pink*

1   What is a slingback?

2   What was the title of the TV series that starred Donald Sinden and Elaine Stritch?

3   What is the old name for the UK Army Reserve?

4   The dish Tournedos Rossini is made from which meat?

5   Quingha is a province in which country?

6   Which animal is also known as the carcajou and the skunk bear?

7   What is the term given to ice at the northern or southern end of the Earth?

8   Which small county borders Northamptonshire and Lincolnshire?

9   What is fenugreek?

10 Who directed the 1982 film *Gandhi*?

11 What nationality was Rudolf Diesel, inventor of the engine that bears his name?

12 What term is given to a Japanese administrative area?

13 In which US city is the Smithsonian Institution based?

14 Alderley Edge is in which county?

15 In which year did ABBA have a hit with *The Name of the Game*?

16 In cricket, what term describes a bowler who spins the ball from the batsman's leg side to off side?

17 The city of Messina is on which Mediterranean island?

18 What term is given to government by a temporary ruler due to the monarch's absence or incapacity?

19 What is the purpose of an escape valve?

20 Which word can mean both "attending" and "gift"?

Easy
Medium
Hard

Answers to QUIZ 357 – Pot Luck

1	Tony	11	Technical knock-out
2	Cambridgeshire	12	One
3	The Selector	13	Hypothermia
4	White	14	*The Blind Side*
5	Chief Superintendent Innocent	15	Mexico
6	American Football	16	James Dean (for two different films)
7	Baz Luhrmann	17	Don Quixote
8	1820s (1824)	18	Shoemakers
9	Lion	19	Justin Timberlake
10	WWI	20	Aphids (and similar pests)

Easy

1   How many people take part in a paso doble?

2   The macarena originates from which country?

3   Which European capital is particularly associated with the waltz?

4   In which European city is the Moulin Rouge...?

5   ...and what red building is shown on its roof?

6   In ballet, what is a barre?

7   Which ballet features Odette and Odile?

8   In which year was *Strictly Come Dancing* first broadcast...?

9   ...and who was the only female judge on the panel?

10 In which country was dancer Michael Flatley born...?

11 ...and in which theatrical show did he become famous?

12 What was the title of the 2008 sequel to *Step Up?*

13 Which style of dance requires shoes that have a metal part on the toe and heel?

14 The Bollywood style of dancing originated in which country?

Medium

15 In which party dance do people form a long winding line?

16 Which band recorded the 1994 single *Discothèque?*

17 In which US state did the hula dance originate?

18 How many beats to the bar are there in waltz music?

19 Which singer popularised the moonwalk?

20 Which runner's celebratory dance is nicknamed the "Mobot"?

Hard

Answers to QUIZ 358 – Leisure

1	Sewing machines	11	Nine
2	Scottish dancing	12	Pontoon
3	Bridge	13	Skateboard
4	Cribbage	14	Surrey
5	13	15	Streaming
6	Toy bears	16	In an urban environment
7	Circus	17	*Nemesis*
8	1	18	Grand slam
9	Birdwatching	19	Retweeting
10	Lego®	20	Nature reserve

1 Scarborough is in which county?

2 Who wrote the novel *A Portrait of the Artist as a Young Man*?

3 Which tennis player won the French Open in 2018 for a record eleventh time?

4 Which 1995 film starred Nicole Kidman as an ambitious weather reporter?

5 Prospero is the central character in which of Shakespeare's plays?

6 In which decade of the 20th century was snooker champion Steve Davis born?

7 A shaslik kebab is made from which meat?

8 Who said in 1980 "You turn if you want to. The lady's not for turning"?

9 Which classic love song was a no.1 hit for Lionel Richie in 1984?

10 BS is the postcode area code for which city?

11 What was the name of Michael J Fox's character in the *Back to the Future* films?

12 What is the name of Lacey Turner's character in *EastEnders*?

13 A swallowtail is what type of creature?

14 On which row of a standard computer keyboard is the letter J found?

15 Which unit of distance took its name from the Latin for 1000?

16 Which nut is the basis of satay sauce?

17 What are farfalle, pansotti and rigati?

18 What number does the Roman numeral IV stand for?

19 Which newspaper started life as the *Daily Univeral Register*?

20 On which continent did Europeans first encounter turkeys?

Easy

Medium

Hard

Answers to QUIZ 359 – Pot Luck

1	A shoe	11	German
2	*Two's Company*	12	Prefecture
3	Territorial Army	13	Washington DC
4	Beef	14	Cheshire
5	China	15	1977
6	Wolverine	16	Leg-spinner
7	Polar cap	17	Sicily
8	Rutland	18	Regency
9	A spice	19	To let out air or steam to reduce pressure
10	Sir Richard Attenborough	20	Present

Easy

1   What name was given to the short socks worn by teenagers in the 1950s?

2   Which long-running play opened in the West End in 1952?

3   Chris Chataway and Chris Brasher were pacemakers for which world-record-breaking athlete in 1954?

4   In which year did the M1 open?

5   In which year did all rationing end in the UK?

6   Eamon de Valera became the president of which country in 1959?

7   Who won five Formula 1 World Championships between 1951 and 1957?

8   The Treaty of Rome in 1957 was fundamental in establishing which organisation?

9   Opened in 1956, what was Calder Hall?

10 Who was US President at the start of the 1950s...?

11 ...and who succeeded him in 1953?

12 Which UK Prime Minister who took office during the 1950s was nicknamed "Supermac"?

Medium

13 Which Israeli Prime Minister resigned in 1954 but took up office again in 1955?

14 In 1959, which two states became the 49th and 50th states of the USA?

15 Queen Elizabeth II's coronation took place in which year...?

16 ...and in which building?

17 In 1954, the CERN research facility was established near which European city?

18 Which country hosted the 1950 FIFA world cup...?

19 ...and which country won it?

20 What prompted the Suez crisis in 1956?

Hard

Answers to QUIZ 360 – Dance

1	Two	11	Riverdance
2	Spain	12	*Step Up 2: The Streets*
3	Vienna	13	Tap dance
4	Paris	14	India
5	A windmill	15	Conga
6	A rail	16	U2
7	*Swan Lake*	17	Hawaii
8	2004	18	Three
9	Arlene Phillips	19	Michael Jackson
10	USA	20	Sir Mo Farah

1 In which sport might someone have the position of second slip?

2 Whose face appeared on a 1914 poster encouraging men to enlist in the British Army?

3 The sternum is the medical name for which bone?

4 In *The Matrix* series of films, who played Agent Smith?

5 Who were musically *Reunited* in 1979?

6 What type of creature is a leatherback?

7 Which Irish poet and playwright died in Paris in 1900 at the age of 44?

8 How is a computerised axial tomography examination more usually referred to?

9 Herne Bay is a coastal resort in which county?

10 Which Austrian town's name translates as "Salt town"?

11 What type of foodstuff is naan?

12 "Freo" is the nickname of which Australian port?

13 Galveston is a coastal city in which US state?

14 What surname did Thomas Hicks (b.1936) adopt as a stage name?

15 What name is given to the day before Good Friday?

16 Which sign of the zodiac is represented by the Scales?

17 What was the title of Helen Reddy's first UK hit?

18 In which century was William Shakespeare born?

19 What number equates to four dozen?

20 Who resigned as Labour leader in 1980?

Answers to QUIZ 361 – Pot Luck

1	North Yorkshire	11	Marty McFly
2	James Joyce	12	Stacey
3	Rafael Nadal	13	Butterfly
4	*To Die For*	14	Middle row of letters
5	*The Tempest*	15	Mile
6	1950s	16	Peanut
7	Mutton	17	Pasta shapes
8	Margaret Thatcher (Baroness Thatcher)	18	Four
9	*Hello*	19	*The Times*
10	Bristol	20	North America

Easy

1   Tog is a rating applied to which household item?

2   *From Me to You* was released as a single by the Beatles in which year?

3   Tony Soprano was played by which actor in the TV series?

4   *Frozen* (2013) was inspired by which Hans Christian Andersen tale?

5   Tomsk is a city in which area of Russia?

6   Frodo Baggins was played by which actor in the *Lord of the Rings* films directed by Peter Jackson?

7   Toytown was created by which children's author?

8   Frome is a town in which county?

9   *Tombstone* (1993) starred which actor as Doc Holliday?

10 Frogs' eggs are collectively given what name?

11 Tobruk is a port in which country?

12 Frosty the Snowman's eyes were made from what, in the Christmas song?

13 Topiary is the art of cutting what into artistic shapes?

14 Fromage frais is what type of foodstuff?

Medium

15 Tom Barnaby was the original main character in which TV series?

16 "Front of house" is a term used in which building?

17 *Top of the Pops* was cancelled in which year?

18 *From Russia with Love* (1963) starred which actor as James Bond?

19 Tower Hamlets is a borough of which English city?

20 *From Here to Eternity* (1953) starred which actor as Sgt Milton Warden?

Hard

Answers to QUIZ 362 – 1950s

1   Bobby sox
2   *The Mousetrap* (Dame Agatha Christie)
3   Sir Roger Bannister
4   1959
5   1954
6   Ireland
7   Juan Manuel Fangio
8   European Union
9   Nuclear power station
10 Harry S Truman
11 Dwight D Eisenhower
12 Harold Macmillan
13 David Ben-Gurion
14 Alaska and Hawaii
15 1953
16 Westminster Abbey
17 Geneva
18 Brazil
19 Uruguay
20 Nationalisation of the canal

QUIZ 365 – Pot Luck

ANSWERS ON PAGE 367

1 Who played Ma Larkin in the 1990s TV series *The Darling Buds of May*?

2 Why was the 1912 University Boat Race abandoned?

3 What is the general term given to plants that have thick, fleshy leaves designed to retain water?

4 In which country is the town of Mantua, known as Mantova to the locals?

5 What is the term for an MP who does not hold a ministerial office?

6 Which French actress played Lady Macbeth in the 2015 film *Macbeth*?

7 In society terms, what is "deb" short for?

8 Who was the first artist to achieve a simultaneous no.1 chart topper in the UK & US?

9 Chocolate is made from the seeds of which tree?

10 In 1908, who became the first person to fly a heaver-than-air machine in Britain?

11 How many shakes of a lamb's tail are used in a phrase to indicate an immediate response?

12 What is the more common name for allergic rhinitis?

13 Which band released the 1979 single *Don't Stop Me Now*?

14 Who was the star of the 1954 film *On the Waterfront*?

15 Is the London borough of Lewisham in north or south London?

16 In which lagoon was a German fleet scuttled in 1919?

17 "Ask for more" is the traditional bingo call for which number?

18 What builds up in a kettle in a hard water area?

19 In the picture-book series by Lucy Cousins, what type of creature is Maisy?

20 Where in the body are the quadriceps?

Answers to QUIZ 363 – Pot Luck

1	Cricket	11	Flatbread
2	Lord Kitchener	12	Fremantle
3	Breastbone	13	Texan
4	Hugo Weaving	14	Steele
5	Peaches and Herb	15	Maundy Thursday
6	Turtle	16	Libra
7	Oscar Wilde	17	*Angie Baby*
8	CAT scan	18	16th century
9	Kent	19	48
10	Salzburg	20	James Callaghan (Baron Callaghan)

Easy

1 "Thoroughbred" is used to describe what type of animal?

2 A jittery person is described as being like a cat on what surface?

3 What was the name of Ethel Skinner's pug dog in *EastEnders*?

4 Which German Shepherd dog was a screen star of the 1920s?

5 Which horse race is the first leg of the English Triple Crown?

6 The title character of which animated television series, first aired in 1961, was the leader of a gang of alley cats?

7 From which country does the pug dog originate?

8 Which dog's name comes from the German *Pudelhund*?

9 What two colours are the hat belonging to *The Cat in the Hat*?

10 Proverbially, what killed the cat?

11 What was the name of the black and white cartoon cat created during the silent-film era?

12 Which part of a cat is compared to an excellent thing?

13 Which children's book features the character of the Cheshire Cat?

Medium

14 What name is given to a the maze of tunnels in which rabbits live in the wild?

15 A dog that has been trained to assist with locating drugs or explosives by scent is given what name?

16 Which insurance company has a bulldog as its mascot?

17 The cartoon dog Huckleberry Hound is what colour?

18 A black horse is the logo of which bank?

19 Which BBC consumer affairs programme is named after a canine guard?

20 Which animal lends its name to a short sleep?

Hard

Answers to QUIZ 364 – To And Fro

1 Duvet
2 1963
3 James Gandolfini
4 *The Snow Queen*
5 Siberia
6 Elijah Wood
7 Enid Blyton
8 Somerset
9 Val Kilmer
10 Frogspawn
11 Libya
12 Two pieces of coal
13 Hedges (trees and shrubs)
14 Soft cheese
15 *Midsomer Murders*
16 Theatre
17 2006
18 Sir Sean Connery
19 London
20 Burt Lancaster

Easy

1   The port of Archangel is in which country?

2   In which decade was the early May Bank Holiday introduced?

3   Harry Vardon (b.1870) was famous for playing which sport?

4   In relation to light bulbs, for what do the letters LED stand?

5   At which consecutive Olympic games did Sir Steve Redgrave and Sir Matthew Pinsent win gold in the coxless pairs?

6   In which country was chef Giorgio Locatelli born?

7   Which UK political party was formed in 1900?

8   Is hypothyroidism the medical name for an under-active thyroid or an over-active thyroid?

9   What is the name of the group appointed to advise the British monarch on political matters?

10   What was the title of Showaddywaddy's 1976 no.1 hit?

11   From what animal is lard obtained?

12   In which county is Lanhydrock House?

13   Which word for a shrub associated with Scotland is also the name of a fish?

14   Tommy Lee Jones and Samuel L Jackson co-starred in which 2000 war film?

15   What is the purpose of a flue on a cooker or stove?

16   Which author (d.1976) was married to archaeologist Max Mallowan?

17   Which *Heroes* actress went on to play Juliette Barnes in the TV series *Nashville*?

18   Alphabetically, what is the first sign of the zodiac?

19   Which football team plays home games at Ibrox Park?

20   Which of Queen Elizabeth II's children was first to marry?

Medium

Hard

Answers to QUIZ 365 – Pot Luck

1	Pam Ferris	11	Two
2	Both boats sank	12	Hay fever
3	Succulent	13	Queen
4	Italy	14	Marlon Brando
5	Back-bencher	15	South
6	Marion Cotillard	16	Scapa Flow
7	Debutante	17	34
8	Perry Como (*Don't Let the Stars Get in Your Eyes*)	18	Limescale
9	Cacao tree	19	A mouse
10	Samuel Cody	20	In the leg

1 Which hard-sounding British cake contains dried fruit and has a rough surface?

2 What is the name of the pudding which consists of ice cream on a sponge cake, covered with meringue?

3 Which Derbyshire town gives its name to an almond-flavoured tart?

4 Kulfi is ice cream from which country?

5 What is the name of the baked French dessert of fruit, traditionally black cherries, in a thick, flan-like batter?

6 What dessert, named after a British school, consists of strawberries, broken meringue and whipped cream?

7 Shortbread is a speciality of which country?

8 Which ice cream dessert shares part of its name with a pair of short trousers?

9 Stollen is a fruit loaf originating from which country?

10 In America, what is the traditional Thanksgiving Day dessert?

11 What is the name of the dessert of thin French pancakes flamed in alcohol?

12 Which vegetable is used to make a popular sweet cake?

13 Is short-grain or long-grain rice used to make rice pudding?

14 Which chocolate bar was once advertised with the slogan that it would help you "work, rest and play"?

15 Along with peach and Melba sauce, what is the third ingredient of a Peach Melba?

16 A classic tarte tatin is made with which fruit?

17 Water ice is another name for which sweet item?

18 What is a brûlée topped with?

19 With which famous summer sporting event are strawberries and cream traditionally associated?

20 Which Italian dessert has a name that translates to "pick me up"?

QUIZ 369 – Pot Luck

ANSWERS ON PAGE 371

1 Paul Michael Glaser played which 1970s detective?

2 Which classic 1960s sitcom took place in the workshop of Fenner Fashions?

3 Eliza Acton (b.1799) produced one of Britain's first books on what subject?

4 Which cartoon character first appeared in 1930 in *Dizzy Dishes*?

5 In 1910, who became the first person to be arrested as the result of wireless communication?

6 In which decade was Rolls-Royce originally founded?

7 As what was Laurence Sterne (b.1713) famous?

8 What type of creature is a turbot?

9 Sorghum is what type of crop?

10 Which Californian city was originally called Yerba Buena?

11 Which group sang *Losing My Religion* in 1991?

12 The yeast-extract paste Vegemite comes from which country?

13 Rosacea affects which part of the body?

14 What is the name of the profession of someone who fits glass into windows?

15 Who starred in the 2004 adventure film *National Treasure*?

16 What is the name of the latitude line at about $23^1/2$ degrees south of the equator?

17 In which county is the Wildfowl and Wetlands Trust reserve of Slimbridge?

18 What was the 1964 no.1 hit for Peter and Gordon?

19 The ancient Ring of Brodgar is located in which group of islands?

20 In the 1977 Academy Awards ceremony, which actor did Muhammad Ali come on stage to spar with?

Easy / Medium / Hard

Answers to QUIZ 367 – Pot Luck

1 Russia
2 1970s (1978)
3 Golf
4 Light-emitting diode
5 Barcelona 1992 & Atlanta 1996
6 Italy
7 Labour Party
8 Under-active
9 Privy council
10 *Under the Moon of Love*
11 Pig
12 Cornwall
13 Ling
14 *Rules of Engagement*
15 It diverts smoke
16 Dame Agatha Christie
17 Hayden Panettiere
18 Aries
19 Rangers FC
20 Princess Anne

ANSWERS ON PAGE 372

1   What is the term for a fixed amount of money given to a church or priest?

2   The Midland Bank became part of which banking group?

3   Before decimalisation, what three letters were used to refer to pounds, shillings and pence?

4   What is the technical term for increasing the amount of money in circulation to encourage spending?

5   What word is given to a fixed regular payment by an employer?

6   Whose picture features on the £10 note that was first issued in 2017?

7   What does ROI stand for in a financial context?

8   A financial supporter of a theatre venture is given what heavenly name?

9   The old £1 coin was withdrawn from circulation in which year?

10 Traditionally, what colour is the briefcase that the Chancellor of the Exchequer uses on Budget Day?

11 Which banking group took over the Post Office Girobank in 1990...?

12 ...and was subsequently bought out by which group in 2008?

13 What two-word term is given to all the currency in circulation?

14 Stamp duty is payable when buying what?

15 Which coin is worth one fifth of a pound?

16 What is a company's list of income and outgoings called?

17 Portugal had what unit of currency before adopting the euro?

18 How is interest referred to that is calculated both on the sum borrowed and on the interest repayable?

19 At the time of decimalisation, how many sides did the old threepenny bit have?

20 The £50 note first issued in 2011 depicts Matthew Boulton and which other engineer?

Answers to QUIZ 368 – Sweet Things

1	Rock cake	11	Crêpes Suzette
2	Baked Alaska	12	Carrot
3	Bakewell	13	Short-grain
4	India	14	Mars
5	Clafoutis	15	Ice cream
6	Eton Mess	16	Apples
7	Scotland	17	Sorbet
8	Knickerbocker glory	18	Caramelised sugar
9	Germany	19	Wimbledon
10	Pumpkin pie	20	Tiramisu

1 In which county are Goodwin Sands?

2 Who became Saracens' leading points scorer of all time in 2017?

3 Battersea is located in which borough of London?

4 In which country was writer Germaine Greer born?

5 What is the official language of the island of Martinique?

6 What is the term for a clause in a contract that sets out the circumstances under which the contract can be broken?

7 In Scrabble® what colour are the triple-letter score squares?

8 What are the initials TB short for in the name of the disease?

9 Which actor starred in the 2008 remake of *The Day the Earth Stood Still*?

10 Rennet is traditionally used in the production of what foodstuff?

11 What nationality is wildlife broadcaster Iolo Williams?

12 What is a medlar?

13 The TV drama series *The 100* follows the survivors of what catastrophic event?

14 What was the profession of Auguste Escoffier (d.1935)?

15 On which river in the north of England is the High Force waterfall located?

16 In which month is St David's Day celebrated?

17 The 2017 film *It* was based on a book by which author?

18 In the Bible, who famously cut off Samson's hair?

19 Which three colours appear on the flag of Bulgaria?

20 The bobcat is a species of which big cat?

Easy

Medium

Hard

Answers to QUIZ 369 – Pot Luck

1	Starsky	11	R.E.M.
2	*The Rag Trade*	12	Australia
3	Cookery	13	The face
4	Betty Boop	14	Glazier
5	Dr Crippen	15	Nicolas Cage
6	1900s (1906)	16	Tropic of Capricorn
7	An author	17	Gloucestershire
8	Fish	18	*World Without Love*
9	Cereal or grain crop	19	Orkney Islands
10	San Francisco	20	Sylvester Stallone

ANSWERS ON PAGE **374**

Easy

1. What is the stage name of magician Steven Frayne?
2. What relation is Sinéad Cusack to Niamh Cusack?
3. Ferne McCann is a former cast member of which structured reality series?
4. Which actor turned politician launched the cartoon series *The Governator*?
5. Whom did Beyoncé marry in 2008...?
6. ...and what is the name of their daughter, born in 2012?
7. What is the relationship between the actors who play Agnes and Cathy in *Mrs Brown's Boys*?
8. How many children does Katie Price have with ex-husband Peter Andre?
9. How is Michael Ebenazer Kwadjo Omari Owuo Jr better known?
10. Which musician was actress Kate Hudson engaged to from 2011 to 2014?
11. Born in 2017, the son of which two singers was named Bear?
12. Which actress married Daniel Craig in 2011?
13. Which comedian's self-titled sitcom has aired on BBC3 since 2015?

Medium

14. By what name is actor Thomas Mapother IV better known?
15. Which member of The Saturdays took part in *Strictly Come Dancing* in 2017...?
16. ...and in which place did she finish?
17. What nationality is actress Sofia Vergara?
18. On which programme did presenter and singer Stacey Solomon first find fame?
19. The TV series *In the Long Run* is based on the early life of which actor, who also stars in it?
20. What relation is actor Nicolas Cage to director Francis Ford Coppola?

Hard

Answers to QUIZ 370 – Money

1	Tithe	11	Alliance and Leicester
2	HSBC	12	Santander
3	L,S and D	13	Money supply
4	Quantitative easing	14	A property
5	Salary	15	Twenty pence
6	Jane Austen	16	Balance sheet
7	Return on investment	17	Escudo
8	Angel	18	Compound interest
9	2017	19	12
10	Red	20	James Watt

QUIZ 373 – Pot Luck

ANSWERS ON PAGE 375

1   In the saying indicating that something has been completed, who is your uncle?

2   In which country is the Gilles Villeneuve motor racing circuit?

3   The Folies Bergère is in which European city?

4   Who presents the TV series *Grand Designs*?

5   Iritis is an inflammation of which part of the body?

6   St Stephen's Green and Phoenix Park can be visited in which capital city?

7   How many Wonders of the Ancient World were there?

8   The Spanish holiday resort of Torremolinos is situated in which seaside region…?

9   …and what does the region's name translate to in English?

10 "Whispering" is the nickname of which DJ and presenter (b.1946)?

11 On a Monopoly™ board, what colour is Oxford Street?

12 What nationality is singer Bonnie Tyler?

13 Who wrote the 1981 children's book *George's Marvellous Medicine*?

14 In the rhyme often quoted when magpies are seen, what is associated with six magpies?

15 Moving anti-clockwise on a dartboard, what is the number next to 4?

16 In which century was poet Robert Burns born?

17 The castles of Pendennis and St Mawes lie close to which Cornish town?

18 What word meaning "dull" refers to a poet when read backwards?

19 Who released the 1985 single *We Don't Need Another Hero*…?

20 …and in which 1985 film did it feature?

Easy

Medium

Hard

Answers to QUIZ 371 – Pot Luck

1	Kent	11	Welsh
2	Owen Farrell	12	Fruit
3	Wandsworth	13	Nuclear apocalypse
4	Australia	14	Chef
5	French	15	Tees
6	Escape clause	16	March
7	Dark blue	17	Stephen King
8	Tuberculosis	18	Delilah
9	Keanu Reeves	19	White, green and red
10	Cheese	20	Lynx

1   The practice of removing some seedlings to allow the rest space to grow is known by what two-word term?

2   Which garden ornament can be used to tell the time?

3   What name is given to a plant which dies down at the end of the growing season?

4   Which purple plant has "dog" and "sweet" varieties?

5   What can be floribunda or a rambler?

6   What two-word term is given to the process of gradually acclimatising plants grown indoors to the outdoors?

7   For what would you use a dibber?

8   Which machine with spikes is used for breaking up the surface of a lawn?

9   Which herb has the botanical name *Allium schoenoprasum*?

10 Popular in fishponds, what type of fish are koi?

11 What term is given to the practice of removing the growing tips of plants to encourage side shoots to grow?

12 Are rhododendrons generally lime-tolerant or lime-hating plants?

13 Which TV gardener received an OBE in the Birthday Honours List in June 2018?

14 The cherry tree belongs to which family?

15 What informal style of garden takes its name from a rural building?

16 The shrub *Lavandula* has what common name?

17 What term is given to partly decomposed matter in soil?

18 Which freestanding outdoor fireplace takes its name from the Spanish for "chimney"?

19 On which garden makeover programme did Charlie Dimmock first find fame?

20 What term is given to a shrub which grows most of its branches on or just above the ground?

Answers to QUIZ 372 – Celebrity

1	Dynamo	11	Liam Payne and Cheryl
2	Sister	12	Rachel Weisz
3	*The Only Way is Essex*	13	Josh Widdicombe
4	Arnold Schwarzenegger	14	Tom Cruise
5	Jay-Z	15	Mollie King
6	Blue Ivy Carter	16	Fifth place
7	Husband and wife	17	Colombian
8	Two (Junior and Princess)	18	*The X Factor*
9	Stormzy	19	Idris Elba
10	Matthew Bellamy	20	Nephew

1   In relation to connecting electronic devices, what do the letters "HD" stand for in HDMI?

2   What is the colour of the cross on the Jamaican flag?

3   Who had a 1968 hit with *For Once in My Life*?

4   The Gewürztraminer grape is used to make which colour wine?

5   In which county are the villages of Great Walsingham and Little Walsingham?

6   Which mythical creature is St George said to have fought?

7   In which decade of the 20th century was singer Ray Charles born?

8   Which word can mean both a formal dance and an item of sports equipment?

9   Which impressionist played "Spock" in the TV series *Preston Front* (originally *All Quiet on the Preston Front*)?

10 Which BBC radio station plays predominantly classical music?

11 Which number is "top of the shop" in bingo?

12 The normal body temperature for a human is around how many degrees?

13 On which day is St Andrew's Day celebrated?

14 In which county is Belsay Hall?

15 What term is given to a constituency with a large majority?

16 Who starred in the 1983 film *Scarface*?

17 What is the name of Hugh Quarshie's *Holby City* character?

18 Racing driver Graham Hill was what relation to Damon Hill?

19 In which month did WWI commence?

20 Who played the title role in the 2006 film *Miss Potter*?

Answers to QUIZ 373 – Pot Luck

1	Bob	11	Green
2	Canada	12	Welsh
3	Paris	13	Roald Dahl
4	Kevin McCloud	14	Gold
5	The iris	15	18
6	Dublin	16	18th century
7	Seven	17	Falmouth
8	Costa del Sol	18	Drab
9	Coast of the Sun	19	Tina Turner
10	Bob Harris	20	*Mad Max Beyond Thunderdome*

Easy

1. In metres, how long is an Olympic-sized swimming pool?

2. In which sport did Geoff Hunt become the inaugural World Champion in 1976?

3. Which wrestler's real name was Shirley Crabtree?

4. Is bantamweight or featherweight the heavier in the weight classes of boxing?

5. What is the name of the flexible plank used in diving competitions?

6. Which American boxer was known as "The Greatest"?

7. With which swimming stroke do races begin in the water?

8. In gymnastics, what name is given to the "horse"?

9. Which gymnast (b.1955) won three Olympic gold medals for the Soviet Union at the 1972 Summer Olympics?

10. How many gold medals did Rebecca Adlington win at the 2008 Olympic Games?

11. In darts, what is the lowest score for three trebles?

12. What sport do the Washington Wizards play?

13. Which indoor sport was featured in the 2004 Ben Stiller film, subtitled *A True Underdog Story*?

Medium

14. In which sport does Elise Christie (b.1990) compete?

15. A carom is a shot in which sport?

16. In centimetres, how wide is the balance beam in gymnastics?

17. What colour is the surface of a snooker table?

18. Which stately home in the borough of Richmond-on-Thames has the oldest surviving real tennis court in England?

19. The Toronto Maple Leafs compete in which sport?

20. In which discipline of men's gymnastics might competitors perform the "Iron Cross"?

Hard

Answers to QUIZ 374 – In the Garden

1	Thinning out	11	Pinching out
2	Sundial	12	Lime-hating
3	Herbaceous	13	Monty Don
4	Violet	14	*Prunus*
5	A rose	15	Cottage garden
6	Hardening off	16	Lavender
7	Making a hole in soil to plant seeds	17	Humus
8	Scarifier	18	Chimenea
9	Chives	19	*Ground Force*
10	Carp	20	Prostrate

ANSWERS ON PAGE 379

1   How many days of Christmas are there, according to the festive song?

2   Who created the series *The Thick of It* and the spin-off film *In the Loop*?

3   What is the name of the *First Dates* barman?

4   What nationality was philosopher Jean-Paul Sartre?

5   How many minutes are there in six hours?

6   Who had hits with *Dancing in the Dark* and *Born to Run*?

7   What would be fired in a kiln?

8   Which American singer is remembered for the song *When I Fall in Love*?

9   What does the "G" stand for in the film company name MGM?

10 In the organisation FTSE, what do the letters "SE" stand for?

11 In which county is Keswick?

12 Which part of the body is affected by macular degeneration?

13 Which country lends its name to a cocktail made from gin and cherry brandy?

14 What was the first name of Sigourney Weaver's character in the *Alien* series of films?

15 The square and compasses are the symbol of which secret society?

16 What tourist attraction was opened at Woburn in 1970?

17 Artist Salvador Dali was what nationality?

18 What is the county town of Lancashire?

19 Which empire-building video game first released in 1991 bears the name of its creator, Sid Meier?

20 Holden Caulfield is the main character in which 1951 novel?

Easy

Medium

Hard

Answers to QUIZ 375 – Pot Luck

1	High Definition	11	90
2	Yellow	12	37 degrees C (99 degrees F)
3	Stevie Wonder	13	30th November
4	White	14	Northumberland
5	Norfolk	15	Safe seat
6	Dragon	16	Al Pacino
7	1930s	17	Ric Griffin
8	Ball	18	Father
9	Alistair McGowan	19	July 1914
10	Radio 3	20	Renée Zellweger

1 Which member of the Monty Python team co-wrote the musical Spamalot?

2 *I Could Have Danced All Night* is a song from which musical?

3 *Cabaret* is set in which city?

4 Who had a hit in 1980 with *Take That Look off Your Face*?

5 Kurt, Brigitta and Gretl featured in which 1964 film musical?

6 Which actor was the star of the 2014 film version of *Annie*?

7 The Pink Ladies feature in which musical?

8 Which *Glee* actress won an Olivier award for her performance in the West End version of *Dreamgirls*?

9 In the 2017 musical *Everybody's Talking About Jamie*, as what does Jamie perform?

10 Christine Daaé is a lead character in which musical?

11 *Wicked* tells the backstory of characters from which other musical?

12 *I Dreamed A Dream* is a song from which musical?

13 ...and which character sings it?

14 Velma Kelly is a character in which musical?

15 Which Welsh actress (b.1969) played a leading role in the West End production of *42nd Street* in the late 1980s?

16 In which decade was *The Boy Friend* set?

17 In which musical is Arthur Kipps the main character?

18 Which musical features the song *Luck Be a Lady*?

19 Who starred in the 1951 film *An American in Paris*?

20 Which 1983 musical features the twins Mickey and Eddie?

Answers to QUIZ 376 – Indoor Sports

1	50 metres	11	Nine
2	Squash	12	Basketball
3	Big Daddy	13	Dodgeball
4	Featherweight	14	Speed skating (short track)
5	Springboard	15	Billiards
6	Muhammad Ali	16	10cm
7	Backstroke	17	Green
8	Pommel	18	Hampton Court Palace
9	Olga Korbut	19	Ice hockey
10	Two	20	Rings

ANSWERS ON PAGE 381

1   What is the English meaning of the Spanish word *tostada?*

2   Edgar Linton is a character in which 1847 novel?

3   What do the initials SIM stand for in relation to a mobile phone?

4   What was Carrie's surname in *Sex and the City?*

5   How are Inky, Blinky, Pinky and Clyde better known in a computer game?

6   In which year was *Jaws 2* released in cinemas?

7   In which county is the town of Thame?

8   In the nursery rhyme, what was purchased along with half a pound of tuppenny rice?

9   How often is the census taken in the UK?

10 How many old pennies were there in a "bob"?

11 Glossitis affects which part of the body?

12 The theme tune to the series *W1A* was originally used for which children's series?

13 What was Emma Bunton's Spice Girls' nickname?

14 Which river of south-west England is noted for its tidal bore?

15 The Tower of London is the setting for which Gilbert and Sullivan opera?

16 Which actress starred with James Stewart in the 1954 film *Rear Window?*

17 In 1955, who was the last woman to be hanged in Britain?

18 Which animal's footwear is considered lucky?

19 The Oval cricket ground is in which London borough?

20 What foodstuff is made using the Chorleywood process?

Easy

Medium

Hard

Answers to QUIZ 377 – Pot Luck

1	12	11	Cumbria
2	Armando Iannucci	12	The eyes
3	Merlin	13	Singapore (Sling)
4	French	14	Ellen
5	360	15	Freemasons
6	Bruce Springsteen	16	Safari park
7	Pottery	17	Spanish
8	Nat King Cole	18	Lancaster
9	Goldwyn	19	*Civilization*
10	Stock Exchange	20	*Catcher in the Rye*, JD Salinger

1 Which kitchen item was entrepreneur Ken Wood involved in developing?

2 The confectioner Tom Smith is credited with inventing which seasonal item?

3 What type of pens were invented by the Tokyo Stationery Company, later renamed Pentel?

4 The inventor known as Brains, first seen on TV in the 1960s, appears in which series?

5 Sir Frank Whittle was an officer in which branch of the forces?

6 In which English county was inventor and engineer Richard Trevithick born?

7 The Glasgow School of Art is most associated with which architect (b.1868)?

8 Who was known as "The Wizard of Menlo Park"?

9 Who played inventor Dr Emmett Brown in the *Back to the Future* series of films?

10 Opened in 1830, between which two English cities did the first railway run that used only steam power?

11 What is measured by the SI unit, previously known as cycle per second, that was named after physicist Heinrich Hertz?

12 Inventor and mathematician Blaise Pascal was born in which country?

13 Which evil genius was portrayed by Alfred Molina in the 2004 film *Spider-Man 2*?

14 Which English inventor (b.1947) is famous for his bagless vacuum cleaner?

15 In the TV series *Person of Interest*, what was the usual name used by the reclusive billionaire inventor?

16 Which Hollywood actress (d.2000) was also an inventor in the field of telecommunications?

17 In which decade was Microsoft® founded?

18 Who invented the 1985 electric vehicle the C5?

19 In the 1968 film *Chitty Chitty Bang Bang*, what is the name of the inventor who creates the car?

20 What is Charles Macintosh (b.1766) famous for inventing?

Answers to QUIZ 378 – Musicals

1	Eric Idle	11	*The Wizard of Oz*
2	*My Fair Lady*	12	Les Misérables
3	Berlin	13	Fantine
4	Marti Webb	14	*Chicago*
5	*The Sound of Music*	15	Catherine Zeta-Jones
6	Jamie Foxx	16	1920s
7	*Grease*	17	*Half a Sixpence*
8	Amber Riley	18	*Guys and Dolls*
9	A drag queen	19	Gene Kelly
10	*The Phantom of the Opera*	20	*Blood Brothers*

1   Which 2014 TV series took its title from a Wham! single?

2   Who wrote the children's poem about a dormouse who liked to sleep amongst blue delphiniums and red geraniums?

3   In which county of Northern Ireland is the Giant's Causeway?

4   In the nursery rhyme *Mary, Mary Quite Contrary*, what type of shells does she have in her garden?

5   Which actor starred in the 1995 film *Waterworld*?

6   Which German sports car company makes the 911?

7   Justine Roberts founded which website in 2000?

8   Pevensey castle is in which county?

9   What is the background colour on the Danish flag?

10 Difficulty in sleeping has what medical term?

11 What was the subtitle of the 2017 *King Kong* film?

12 What is the second colour of the rainbow?

13 Who had a hit in 1990 with *Nothing Compares 2 U*?

14 Robin Hood's Bay is located in which National Park?

15 Which comedian hosts *Eight out of Ten Cats*?

16 What colour dress does Cinderella wear to the ball?

17 Which 1946 film featured an angel called Clarence?

18 Which English city has a suburb called Jericho?

19 The tight head prop is on which side of the hooker in the front row of a rugby scrum?

20 As is the chemical symbol for which element?

Answers to QUIZ 379 – Pot Luck

1	Toasted	11	Tongue
2	*Wuthering Heights*	12	*Animal Magic*
3	Subscriber Identity Module	13	Baby
4	Bradshaw	14	River Severn
5	Pac Man™ ghosts	15	*The Yeomen of the Guard*
6	1978	16	Grace Kelly
7	Oxfordshire	17	Ruth Ellis
8	Half a pound of treacle	18	Horse (horseshoe)
9	Every ten years	19	Lambeth
10	12	20	Bread

Easy

1   Who was the Greek goddess of beauty?

2   Which planet is named after the Roman god of war?

3   Which war in Greek mythology was waged when Helen fell in love with Prince Paris and left her husband, the king of Sparta...?

4   ...and what was the title of the 2018 BBC series that told the story of the conflict?

5   The Roman god Janus is depicted as having how many faces?

6   What legendary Greek hero is the protagonist of the *Odyssey*?

7   In Norse mythology, who took the dead heroes to Valhalla?

8   Which bird was associated with Jupiter in Roman mythology?

9   Which chemical element is named after the Roman god of messages?

10 What natural phenomenon is Zeus often depicted as holding?

11 Which 1972 disaster film starring Gene Hackman features the name of a Greek god in the title?

12 In Greek mythology, when the 100-eyed guardian Argus died, his eyes were transferred to the tail of which bird?

Medium

13 The statue known as Eros can be seen at which London road junction?

14 Who were the daughters of Zeus, who personified and bestowed charm and beauty?

15 In Greek mythology, what did the Gorgons have instead of hair?

16 In the *Thor* films, who plays Loki, the Norse god of mischief?

17 Which sportswear company takes its name from that of a Greek goddess?

18 Which planet is named after the Roman god of agriculture?

19 What type of creature was Cerberus?

20 How many prongs are there on Neptune's trident?

Hard

1	Food mixer	11	Frequency
2	Christmas cracker	12	France
3	Felt tips	13	Doctor Octopus
4	*Thunderbirds*	14	Sir James Dyson
5	RAF	15	Harold Finch
6	Cornwall	16	Hedy Lamarr
7	Charles Rennie Mackintosh	17	1970s
8	Thomas Edison	18	Sir Clive Sinclair
9	Christopher Lloyd	19	Caractacus Potts
10	Liverpool and Manchester	20	Waterproof material

ANSWERS ON PAGE 385

1   What nationality was the composer Ralph Vaughan Williams?

2   Who was the runner-up on the first series of *Pop Idol*?

3   What number is represented by the Roman numerals LXIII?

4   How were Windsor's wives described in the title of a Shakespeare play?

5   The 2008 Olympic Games were held in which city?

6   Waldorf salad takes its name from what type of establishment?

7   Who portrayed Inspector Rebus on TV before Ken Stott took over the role?

8   What was the title of the second studio album released by Oasis?

9   The town of Lyndhurst is in which National Park?

10 In which decade did hot pants become fashionable?

11 Who co-starred with Nicole Kidman in the 2005 film *Bewitched*?

12 How many musicians are there in a septet?

13 Who had a UK no.1 hit in 1992 with *Ain't No Doubt*?

14 What, in law, is spoken defamation of character?

15 In which county is Stroud?

16 Silverskin is a variety of which vegetable?

17 Who created the 1982 graphic novel *When the Wind Blows*?

18 Who composed the theme music for the *Indiana Jones* series of films?

19 What term is given to a Cabinet minister who does not have responsibility for a particular area?

20 How many pounds are there in a half a stone?

Easy

Medium

Hard

Answers to QUIZ 381 – Pot Luck

1	*Edge of Heaven*	11	*Skull Island*
2	AA Milne	12	Orange
3	Antrim	13	Sinead O'Connor
4	Cockle	14	North York Moors
5	Kevin Costner	15	Jimmy Carr
6	Porsche	16	Blue
7	Mumsnet	17	*It's a Wonderful Life*
8	East Sussex	18	Oxford
9	Red	19	On the right
10	Insomnia	20	Arsenic

Easy

1 What was the name of the former guarded border between the Soviet bloc and the rest of Europe?

2 What term is given to seclusion or remoteness from the realities of everyday life?

3 A nation or institution that appears powerful but is in fact weak is known by what name?

4 A serialised drama on TV or radio, usually depicting domestic themes, is called what?

5 What warm two-word term describes a precarious, dangerous or difficult situation?

6 An equal mixture of stout and champagne creates which drink?

7 Which former band of Liam Gallagher's shares its name with a term meaning "keen watchfulness"?

8 What is the name of the US president's retreat in Maryland?

9 What is meant by the term "dog days"?

10 Which rhyming term describes an old-fashioned person?

11 What is a revolving table-top tray?

12 If someone is well-heeled, what are they?

13 What is the British association of conjurers called?

Medium

14 The Nazi dictatorship from 1933 to 1945 was denoted by what two-word term?

15 What device contains an air bubble to accurately give horizontal surfaces?

16 A set of members of an organisation who split from the main body can be described by what two-word term?

17 Which old TV show takes its name from a term meaning a sudden, significant advance or breakthrough?

18 What two-word term describes the bulb-shaped roofs characteristic in Russian architecture?

19 What is a *femme fatale*?

20 From Greek legend, what term means a complicated and intricate problem?

Hard

Answers to QUIZ 382 – Mythology

1	Aphrodite	11	*The Poseidon Adventure*
2	Mars	12	Peacock
3	The Trojan War	13	Piccadilly Circus
4	*Troy: Fall of a City*	14	Three Graces
5	Two	15	Serpents or snakes
6	Odysseus	16	Tom Hiddelston
7	The Valkyries	17	Nike (goddess of victory)
8	Eagle	18	Saturn
9	Mercury	19	A dog
10	Thunderbolt or lightning bolt	20	Three

1 What colour is the background on the Chinese flag?

2 Where would you find a flying buttress?

3 Who played President Bartlet's wife in the TV series *The West Wing*?

4 Who won the Wimbledon women's singles title in 1975?

5 Laurence Llewelyn-Bowen and Graham Wynne were designers on which 1990s makeover show?

6 In which country is the city of Kobe?

7 Who became leader of the Labour party in 1983?

8 To the nearest 10,000, how many casualties did the British Army suffer on the first day of the Somme?

9 Who plays "Sunny" Khan in the TV series *Unforgotten*?

10 In which country is the winter sports resort of Innsbruck?

11 What is the family name of Romeo in Shakespeare's play?

12 Which 1986 film starred Christopher Lambert as an immortal sword fighter?

13 Who partnered Oliver Hardy in a comedy double-act?

14 *Brown Eyed Girl* was a 1967 single by which musician?

15 The country house of Rokeby Park is in which English county?

16 Rotherham is in which county?

17 Who was elected the first Mayor of London in 2000?

18 Morten Harket was the lead singer of which band?

19 In which century was author Joseph Conrad born?

20 What is the first prime number that has two digits?

Easy

Medium

Hard

Answers to QUIZ 383 – Pot Luck

1	English	11	Will Ferrell
2	Gareth Gates	12	Seven
3	63	13	Jimmy Nail
4	*Merry*	14	Slander
5	Beijing	15	Gloucestershire
6	Hotel	16	Onion
7	John Hannah	17	Raymond Briggs
8	*What's the Story (Morning Glory)*	18	John Williams
9	New Forest	19	Minister without portfolio
10	1970s	20	Seven

Easy

1 *My Generation* was a 1965 single released by which band?

2 Who wrote and sang the 1960s hit *Blowin' in the Wind*?

3 Mick Hucknall is the lead singer of which band?

4 *Ruins* is a 2018 album by which Swedish group?

5 Which musician released the single *An Englishman in New York* in 1988?

6 *Someone Like You* was a 2011 single by which singer?

7 *In it For The Money* was a 1997 album by which group?

8 Who released the 1974 album *Diamond Dogs*?

9 What instrument did John Deacon play with Queen?

10 *Build a Rocket Boys!* was a 2011 album by which band...?

11 ...and who is their frontman?

12 Jon Bonham was best known as the drummer with which group?

13 *Face the Music* and *Discovery* were 1970s albums by which band?

14 In which country did the band Rush form?

Medium

15 What is the first name of the frontman of Mumford & Sons?

16 By what name is guitarist David Evans better known?

17 *Band on the Run* was a 1973 album released by which group formed by Sir Paul McCartney?

18 Alex Turner is the lead vocalist and guitarist with which band?

19 *No Jacket Required* was a 1985 album by which musician?

20 Originally a single by Fleetwood Mac, *Black Magic Woman* was a 1970 hit for which band?

Hard

Answers to QUIZ 384 – Two-word Terms

1	Iron Curtain	11	Lazy Susan
2	Ivory tower	12	Wealthy
3	Paper tiger	13	Magic Circle
4	Soap opera	14	Third Reich
5	Hot seat	15	Spirit level
6	Black Velvet	16	Splinter group
7	Beady Eye	17	*Quantum Leap*
8	Camp David	18	Onion dome
9	A hot period of summer	19	An alluring or seductive woman
10	Fuddy-duddy	20	Gordian knot

1   LL is the postcode area code for which town?

2   Which Cistercian monks are known for their austerity and vows of silence?

3   Which *Doctor Who* character was portrayed by Roger Delgado in the 1970s?

4   In which county is Bideford?

5   What is the name of Selma's twin in *The Simpsons*?

6   The letter X is on which row of a typewriter or computer keyboard?

7   Which Danish gardens share their name with the location of a famous villa near Rome?

8   Which sport is referred to as "The sport of kings"?

9   In which country of the UK is the Gleneagles golf course?

10 Edinburgh and Glasgow are connected by which motorway?

11 What word for an unpleasant habit also describes a tool used to hold an object?

12 How would 42 be written in Roman numerals?

13 Which film won the Best Picture Oscar in 1979?

14 Burdock is traditionally made into a drink with which wild flower?

15 Which type of drum is associated with the Caribbean?

16 Noel Edmonds, Keith Chegwin and Maggie Philbin released the 1981 song *I Wanna Be a Winner* under what name?

17 In relation to communications, what do the letters MPS stand for?

18 Which British Grand Prix motorcycle racer (d.1981) was known as "Mike the Bike"?

19 Native to New Zealand, what is a weta?

20 Which comedian (b.1967) is nicknamed "The Punslinger"?

Easy

Medium

Hard

Answers to QUIZ 385 – Pot Luck

1	Red	11	Montague
2	On the outer wall of a church	12	*Highlander*
3	Stockard Channing	13	Stan Laurel
4	Billie Jean King	14	Van Morrison
5	*Changing Rooms*	15	County Durham
6	Japan	16	South Yorkshire
7	Neil Kinnock (Baron Kinnock)	17	Ken Livingstone
8	57,000 (57,470) casualties	18	A-Ha
9	Sanjeev Bhaskar	19	19th century
10	Austria	20	11

Easy

1 Who wrote the poem *The Tyger*?

2 "If I should die, think only this of me" was written by which poet?

3 What nationality was the poet Ezra Pound?

4 Which poet wrote *The Waste Land* (1922)?

5 William Wordsworth, Samuel Taylor Coleridge and Robert Southey were the main figures of which group of poets, named after the area in which they lived?

6 The eponymous hero of a Robert Burns poem gave his name to which hat?

7 What is the term for lines of poetry grouped together into sections or units within a poem?

8 What was the first name of the poet Mr Browning (b.1812)?

9 From which country does the haiku originate?

10 The 2008 film *The Edge of Love* was about the life of which poet?

11 A section of which London building is known as "Poets' Corner"?

Medium

12 *Anthem for Doomed Youth* (1917) was written by which poet?

13 Who was the first woman to be appointed Poet Laureate?

14 What were the first names of the poet Longfellow?

15 How many lines are there in a couplet?

16 What term is given to a collection of poems by different authors?

17 How long is the Children's Laureate position held for...?

18 ...and who was awarded it in 2017?

19 What was "written in a country churchyard" according to the poem by Thomas Gray?

20 Which poet's 1960 autobiography, written in verse, was entitled *Summoned by Bells*?

Hard

Answers to QUIZ 386 – Musicians

1	The Who	11	Guy Garvey
2	Bob Dylan	12	Led Zeppelin
3	Simply Red	13	Electric Light Orchestra
4	First Aid Kit	14	Canada
5	Sting	15	Marcus
6	Adele	16	The Edge
7	Supergrass	17	Wings
8	David Bowie	18	The Arctic Monkeys
9	Bass guitar	19	Phil Collins
10	Elbow	20	Santana

1 Who is the owner of the Springfield power plant in *The Simpsons*?

2 What is a sinecure?

3 The character of Esmerelda appears in which 1831 novel by Victor Hugo?

4 Do stalactites grow up or down?

5 Traditionally, to which Scottish village did eloping English couples go to marry?

6 *Exodus* was a 1977 album by which group?

7 What type of creature is an agouti?

8 What is a linctus?

9 In which chapel did the Duke and Duchess of Sussex get married?

10 Which fairy-tale character spun straw into gold?

11 On which part of the body would you wear a loafer?

12 What was the first name of Shakespeare's wife?

13 How is movement towards the audience indicated in a stage direction?

14 Who was the French president from 2007 to 2012?

15 What is three score and ten?

16 Pudsey is a town in which county?

17 Who played the title role in the 2015 film *The Intern*?

18 *Turn it Up* was the debut studio album by which singer?

19 Matthew Fort and Oliver Peyton are judges on which culinary competition?

20 In which country were the Summer Olympic Games held in 1980?

Easy

Medium

Hard

Answers to QUIZ 387 – Pot Luck

1	Llandudno	11	Vice
2	Trappists	12	XLII
3	The Master	13	*The Deer Hunter*
4	Devon	14	Dandelion
5	Patty	15	Steel
6	The bottom row	16	Brown Sauce
7	Tivoli Gardens	17	Mailing Preference Service
8	Horse racing	18	Mike Hailwood
9	Scotland	19	Insect
10	M8	20	Tim Vine

Easy

1. 5-7-0-5 was a hit for which group in 1978?
2. What is the cube root of 64?
3. The Alarm had a hit in 1983 with which song?
4. Which 2016 horror film starred John Goodman and Mary Elizabeth Winstead?
5. How many episodes of *Fawlty Towers* were made?
6. Which month has 29 days in a leap year?
7. What is the eighth sign of the zodiac?
8. How long is a marathon?
9. What is the national speed limit on a UK motorway?
10. Tchaikovsky wrote which piece of music to commemorate Russia's defence of the motherland?

Medium

11. Traditionally, at what age do you get the key to the door?
12. Who had a 1985 hit with *One Vision*?
13. Which vehicle had the number plate GEN11?
14. Dodie Smith wrote which novel in 1956?
15. At what number in Festive Road did Mr Benn live?
16. A billion has how many zeros?
17. What is a petit four?
18. In which decade was the TV series *Thirtysomething* first broadcast?
19. Which numbers describe someone who is in a state of confusion?
20. How many turtle doves are there in the song *The Twelve Days of Christmas*?

Hard

Answers to QUIZ 388 – Poetry

1	William Blake	11	Westminster Abbey
2	Rupert Brooke	12	Wilfred Owen
3	American	13	Carol Ann Duffy
4	TS Eliot	14	Henry Wadsworth
5	The Lake Poets	15	Two
6	Tam O'Shanter	16	Anthology
7	Stanza	17	Two years
8	Robert	18	Lauren Child
9	Japan	19	Elegy
10	Dylan Thomas	20	Sir John Betjeman

ANSWERS ON PAGE **393**

1   In which county is Tamworth?

2   Who directed the 1955 film *To Catch A Thief*?

3   In which pursuit was Boris Spassky world champion?

4   Ajax football team are based in which country?

5   A macaw is a member of which bird family?

6   The phrase "Salad days" was first said by which character in a Shakespeare play?

7   What was the subtitle of the 2017 film in the *Pirates of the Caribbean* series?

8   Which three colours appear on the flag of Belgium?

9   What is the name of the strong adhesive fabric used in electrical repairs?

10 What does a three-line whip order an MP to do?

11 Redcar was once part of which historic county?

12 How many feet are there in five yards?

13 What is the name of Fred and Wilma's daughter in *The Flintstones*?

14 In which city would you find an avenue of sphinxes?

15 What is the title of the panel game hosted by Dara Ó Briain where teams compete by playing video games?

16 Is Prestatyn in North Wales or South Wales?

17 What does a campanologist do?

18 Who had a 1978 hit with *I'm Every Woman*?

19 In the *Avengers* series of films who is Tony Stark's alter-ego?

20 The song *Wind Beneath My Wings* featured in which 1988 film?

Easy

Medium

Hard

Answers to QUIZ 389 – Pot Luck

1	Mr Burns	11	On the foot
2	A paid job involving little work or responsibility	12	Anne
3	*The Hunchback of Notre-Dame*	13	Downstage
4	Down	14	Nicolas Sarkozy
5	Gretna Green	15	70
6	Bob Marley and the Wailers	16	West Yorkshire
7	A rodent	17	Robert De Niro
8	A cough syrup	18	Pixie Lott
9	St George's Chapel, Windsor Castle	19	*Great British Menu*
10	Rumplestiltskin	20	Soviet Union

1   In which 1972 film did Barbra Streisand co-star with Ryan O'Neal?

2   The Barossa Valley is a wine-growing region in which country?

3   What term is given to a boxing match where gloves are not worn?

4   Barbara Cartland was known for writing what type of fiction?

5   The area of medicine called bariatrics deals with what condition?

6   Barnstaple is in which county?

7   Which writer created the fictional region of Barsetshire?

8   In which year did Barack Obama become US President?

9   What type of apes are associated with Gibraltar?

10   In which 1982 film did Drew Barrymore play Gertie?

11   Which arts complex in London shares its name with the fortified entrance to a city?

12   What is the capital of Barbados?

13   Barbour is particularly associated with which type of clothing?

14   What word can mean both an ancient burial mound and a street trader's cart?

15   Which comedian wrote sketches under the pseudonym "Gerald Wiley"?

16   In the US TV series Barney & Friends, what type of creature is Barney?

17   *Coronation Street*'s Tracy Barlow has been portrayed by which actress since 2002?

18   What nationality was composer Béla Bartók?

19   What type of creature is a barbel?

20   Bari is the capital of which Italian region?

Answers to QUIZ 390 – It Figures

1	City Boy	11	21
2	Four	12	Queen
3	*68 Guns*	13	*Chitty Chitty Bang Bang*
4	*10 Cloverfield Lane*	14	*The Hundred and One Dalmatians*
5	12	15	52
6	February	16	Nine
7	Scorpio	17	A small cake
8	26 miles 385 yards	18	1980s
9	70 mph	19	Six and seven (At sixes and sevens)
10	*1812 Overture*	20	Two

1   What is Tom Hanks' middle name?

2   On which course was the 2010 Ryder Cup played?

3   What is a clean serve in tennis called where the receiver does not manage to get a racket on it?

4   What is the sequel to *The Phantom of the Opera*?

5   Which stand-up comedian wrote the book *We Will Rock You* on which the musical of the same name is based?

6   What is a goitre?

7   Snap, Crackle and Pop are associated with which cereal?

8   With what type of publication is Collins associated?

9   What does the acronym YOLO stand for?

10 What does Waterstones predominantly sell?

11 Who would most likely be a filibusterer?

12 Tagalog is a language of which country?

13 What is the practice of sorting emergency patients into categories to prioritise treatment?

14 What can be a vigil before a funeral or the tracks left by a vessel moving through water?

15 What is a decoration filled with sweets and hung up at parties, only to be broken for its contents?

16 In the film *All the President's Men*, which president is being referred to?

17 The Solent is off which coast of England?

18 What colour bear is Yogi?

19 What name is given to the young of an eagle?

20 In which county of Scotland is the road known as "Electric Brae", where cars appear to roll uphill?

Easy
Medium
Hard

Answers to QUIZ 391 – Pot Luck

1	Staffordshire	11	North Riding of Yorkshire
2	Sir Alfred Hitchcock	12	15 feet
3	Chess	13	Pebbles
4	The Netherlands	14	Luxor, Egypt
5	Parrots	15	*Dara O Briain's Go 8 Bit*
6	Cleopatra	16	North Wales
7	*Salazar's Revenge*	17	Ring bells
8	Black, yellow and red	18	Chaka Khan
9	Gaffer tape	19	Iron Man
10	Vote	20	*Beaches*

1. What nationality was the founder of Selfridges?

2. Which is the only bridge over the Thames in central London that can be raised?

3. Marble Arch was originally designed as the entrance to which building?

4. In which decade did Starbucks open its first British coffee shop?

5. A statue of which American President stands in Trafalgar Square, presented to London by the Commonwealth of Virginia?

6. Which area of London is particularly associated with cinemas?

7. In which building is the London Aquarium?

8. A true Cockney must be born within the sound of which bells?

9. As what was the Tate Modern building used before it became an art gallery?

10. Which annual sporting event starts at Blackheath?

11. Which is the oldest Royal Park in London?

12. Leadenhall Market was used to represent which location in the *Harry Potter* films?

13. What type of buildings are The Dorchester and Claridge's?

14. Who is commemorated by the fountain in Hyde Park which opened in 2004?

15. Newgate was what type of establishment?

16. Which entertainment venue is close to the Liberty department store?

17. In which museum can you attempt to lift a gold bar?

18. The Royal Courts of Justice are on which thoroughfare?

19. In which park is the ArcelorMittal Orbit tower?

20. In which area of London is the Science Museum?

Answers to QUIZ 392 – Bars

1	*What's Up, Doc?*	11	The Barbican
2	Australia	12	Bridgetown
3	Bare-knuckle	13	Outdoor jackets
4	Romance	14	Barrow
5	Obesity	15	Ronnie Barker
6	Devon	16	A dinosaur
7	Anthony Trollope	17	Kate Ford
8	2009	18	Hungarian
9	Barbary apes	19	Fish
10	*E.T. the Extra-Terrestrial*	20	Apulia

ANSWERS ON PAGE 397

1 In which county is the city of Winchester?

2 To what does the word "fiscal" relate?

3 In which year did The Jam top the charts with *Start!*?

4 Who was the 38th President of the United States?

5 Who played villain Howard Payne in the 1994 film *Speed*?

6 What nationality was playwright Henrik Ibsen?

7 From which 1980s sitcom did the phrase "Language, Timothy!" originate?

8 Which sport do the Green Bay Packers play?

9 Who played Celia in *Last Tango in Halifax*?

10 The Austrian flag features two red horizontal stripes on either side of what colour band?

11 Who played author Paul Sheldon in the 1990 film *Misery*?

12 Which superhero was played on screen by Eric Bana in 2003 and Edward Norton in 2008?

13 What is the Latin phrase used to describe solid earth?

14 How many fluid ounces are there in half a pint?

15 What is the Italian word for "yes"?

16 Robusta is a species of tree used to make which drink?

17 The Newlyn School was an art colony based in a fishing village in which county?

18 Which country won the 2018 Eurovision Song Contest?

19 What is an accentor?

20 In which year was *My Big Fat Greek Wedding* 2 released in cinemas?

Easy

Medium

Hard

Answers to QUIZ 393 – Pot Luck

1 Jeffrey
2 Celtic Manor
3 An ace
4 *Love Never Dies*
5 Ben Elton
6 A swelling of the thyroid gland
7 Rice Krispies®
8 Dictionaries
9 You Only Live Once
10 Books
11 A politician
12 Philippines
13 Triage
14 A wake
15 A piñata
16 Richard Nixon
17 South coast
18 Brown
19 Eaglet
20 Ayrshire

ANSWERS ON PAGE **398**

Easy

1   What is the surname of Crystal, singer of *Don't It Make My Brown Eyes Blue*?

2   What is the name of Tony Marshall's character in *Casualty*?

3   What were the names of the two main characters in the 1970 film *Love Story*?

4   Who co-wrote and starred in the 2011 film *Paul*?

5   Brothers Gary and Martin from Spandau Ballet have what surname?

6   In which religion is the prayer Hail Mary used?

7   Who plays Fred Thursday in the TV series *Endeavour*?

8   Which principle in business observes that people rise to the level at which they are not competent?

9   In which country of the UK is St David's, Britain's smallest city?

10 Beverly and Sean Lincoln are two of the main characters in which TV series?

Medium

11 What first name is shared by the actors who play Captain Kirk in the reboot of *Star Trek* and Thor in the Marvel films?

12 What is the name of the head waiter in the *First Dates* restaurant?

13 What is the surname of *Carrie* actress Sissy?

14 Stevenage is in which county?

15 Which Marvin *Heard It Through the Grapevine*?

16 Rick Springfield sang about whose girl in 1981?

17 Which short form of a man's name can also refer to towelling material?

18 What name is given in the UK to a typical or unknown man...?

19 ...and what is the US equivalent?

20 Who was *Thoroughly Modern* in the title of a film starring Dame Julie Andrews?

Hard

Answers to QUIZ 394 – London

1	American	11	St James's (1532)
2	Tower Bridge	12	Diagon Alley
3	Buckingham Palace	13	Hotels
4	1990s (1998)	14	Diana, Princess of Wales
5	George Washington	15	A prison
6	Leicester Square	16	The London Palladium
7	City Hall	17	Bank of England Museum
8	Bow Bells	18	The Strand
9	Power station	19	Queen Elizabeth Olympic Park, Stratford
10	London Marathon	20	Kensington

1 *Bless Your Beautiful Hide* is a song from which musical?

2 Horseshoe Cloister and The Curfew Tower are features of which historic Berkshire building?

3 Which part of the army engage in military combat on foot?

4 Out of which material were parachutes originally made?

5 Which city is situated in a bay that lies between the Po and Piave rivers?

6 In Roman times, what was a denarius?

7 Which comic's autobiographical account of his time during WWII was titled *Adolf Hitler: My Part in His Downfall?*

8 "Land of 10,000 Lakes" is a slogan applied to which US State?

9 Which gas has the chemical symbol CH_4?

10 A formicarium would contain which type of insect?

11 What is the title of Charles Aznavour's 1974 no.1 hit?

12 What is the name of Charlotte Salt's character in *Casualty*?

13 What was the name of Jason Donovan's character in the TV series *Neighbours*?

14 Is a Great Dane long or short-haired?

15 From which language does the word "chauffeur" originate?

16 What word can be a liqueur or a shade of greenish-yellow?

17 Cross Fell is the highest peak in which range of hills?

18 What is the name of the clown in *It*?

19 Which word can be either a partially dried fruit or to remove dead material from plants?

20 A snowball is a mixture of lemonade and which other drink?

Easy

Medium

Hard

Answers to QUIZ 395 – Pot Luck

1 Hampshire
2 Government or public money
3 1980
4 Gerald Ford
5 Dennis Hopper
6 Norwegian
7 *Sorry!*
8 American football
9 Anne Reid
10 White
11 James Caan
12 The Hulk
13 *Terra firma*
14 Ten
15 *Si*
16 Coffee
17 Cornwall
18 Israel
19 A type of bird
20 2016

QUIZ 398 – Lands

1 How many islands are there in the name of a popular salad dressing?

2 In the London method of transport, for what do the letters DLR stand?

3 How is the Primate of All England better known?

4 *Land of Hope and Glory* has been used as the anthem for which political party?

5 The Long Island Iced Tea cocktail is named after a part of which US state?

6 What shape is a Cumberland sausage?

7 Who is the star of the TV series *Designated Survivor*?

8 John Landis (b.1950) directed which 1983 Michael Jackson video?

9 Where do Leeds FC play their home games?

10 Who took over as the presenter of *Desert Island Discs* in 2006?

11 Eswatini (formerly Swaziland) is on which continent?

12 In printing, what is the alternative aspect to landscape format?

13 Being asleep is referred to as being in which land?

14 The Cleveland Way is on which coast of England?

15 Annapolis is the capital of which US state?

16 Zealand is an island belonging to which European country?

17 On which programme did the puppet Roland Rat first appear?

18 *Land of Our Fathers* is the national anthem of which country?

19 What is a landau?

20 In which country was actress Britt Ekland born?

Easy

Medium

Hard

---

1   Caracas is the capital of which country?

2   For which 2012 film did Jennifer Lawrence win the Best Actress Oscar?

3   Justin Rose (b.1980) is a professional in which sport?

4   NG is the postcode area code for which city?

5   Who played Raquel in the TV series *Only Fools and Horses*?

6   When is a nocturnal creature active?

7   Wendy, Scoop and Leo are friends of which fictional worker?

8   What colour is the cross on the Finnish flag...?

9   ...and what was the unit of currency in Finland before the euro?

10 Which actor starred in the film *Edge of Tomorrow* (2014)?

11 In which county is the hill of Glastonbury Tor?

12 Edwin and Angelina feature in which 1875 opera?

13 Which fruit is used to make cider?

14 Which town lies across the Mersey from Widnes?

15 What decoration can be fondant, glacé or royal?

16 Which is the second month of the year to have exactly 30 days?

17 Microsoft Excel® is an example of what type of software?

18 In the cartoon *Dastardly and Muttley in their Flying Machines*, what type of bird were the title characters trying to stop?

19 Who played Uhura in *Star Trek* (2009)?

20 How many centimeters are there in a metre?

Easy

Medium

Hard

Answers to QUIZ 397 – Pot Luck

1	*Seven Brides for Seven Brothers*	11	She
2	Windsor Castle	12	Sam Nicholls
3	Infantry	13	Scott Robinson
4	Silk	14	Short-haired
5	Venice	15	French
6	Money	16	Chartreuse
7	Spike Milligan	17	Pennines
8	Minnesota	18	Pennywise
9	Methane	19	Prune
10	Ants	20	Advocaat

Easy

1   In the poem by Robert Louis Stevenson, what is the "birdie with a yellow bill"?

2   What is the setting for the novel *Swallows and Amazons*?

3   The kiwi is the emblem of which country?

4   In the nursery rhyme, who killed Cock Robin...?

5   ...and with what?

6   Which book by Helen Macdonald won the Costa Book of the Year award in 2014?

7   The Millennium Falcon spaceship appears in which series of films?

8   What is the nickname of Newcastle United FC?

9   Which animated TV couple sailed on the *Skylark*?

10 The 1975 novel *The Eagle Has Landed* was written by which author?

11 Who was Jay McGuiness partnered with when he won *Strictly Come Dancing*?

12 Which bird is a traditional symbol of peace?

13 The TV series *Falcon Crest* was set in which US state?

14 Which Arthurian wizard shares his name with a bird?

Medium

15 Which bird lends its name to a complaint?

16 Who played Clarice Starling in the 1991 film *The Silence of the Lambs*?

17 *Reputation* was a 2017 album by which singer?

18 Which bird is said to live in a fantasy cloud land?

19 Chinstrap and rockhopper are species of which bird?

20 Which bird puppet was associated with Rod Hull?

Hard

Answers to QUIZ 398 – Lands

1	A thousand	11	Africa
2	Docklands Light Railway	12	Portrait
3	Archbishop of Canterbury	13	Land of Nod
4	Conservative Party	14	East coast
5	New York	15	Maryland
6	Spiral	16	Denmark
7	Kiefer Sutherland	17	*TV-am*
8	*Thriller*	18	Wales
9	Elland Road	19	A carriage
10	Kirsty Young	20	Sweden

1   Which famous Athenian temple on the Acropolis was built by Pericles?

2   Which element has the atomic number 2?

3   What device measures the distance travelled by a bicycle?

4   The cartilage projection at the front of the neck is usually referred to by what name?

5   What are the only three countries completely enclaved in one other country?

6   Who had a 1970 hit album with *After the Gold Rush*?

7   Which TV presenter wrote the 2008 book *Amazing Tales for Making Men out of Boys*?

8   What is the airport code for Dubai international airport?

9   The comet Shoemaker-Levy 9 broke into fragments in 1994 and struck which planet?

10   Brent Cross and Leicester Square are linked by which London Underground line?

11   *People Will Say We're in Love* is a song from which musical?

12   The baroque style of architecture first became popular in which century?

13   Berengaria of Navarre was married to which English king?

14   The Woodall, Trowell, and Tibshelf services are on which motorway?

15   What is a rambutan?

16   Which single provided the first US top ten for the Police?

17   What is the name of the children's programme, first shown in the 1970s, whose titular characters performed live at Glastonbury festival in 2011?

18   Is Bermuda ahead of or behind Greenwich Mean Time?

19   What type of bird is a wigeon?

20   In which building did the first Northern Irish Parliament open in 1921?

Easy

Medium

Hard

---

1   What does an ice hockey match begin with?

2   At which course was the Open golf championship held in 2002?

3   Which boxer was the undisputed middleweight champion from 1980 to 1987?

4   In 1990, who won her third Commonwealth Games javelin title?

5   Who was the winning jockey in the 2018 Grand National?

6   In which country is the cricket ground of Seddon Park?

7   In which year were the Winter Olympics first held in the middle of the four-year cycle of the summer games?

8   At what discipline did Denise Lewis win Olympic gold in 2000?

9   Which Olympic sport needs a planting box?

10 What is the nickname of Hull City FC?

11 In which year did Nigel Mansell last race Formula 1 cars?

12 What is the location of the Italian motor-racing circuit named after Ferrari?

13 In which sport did Isabella and Paul Duchesnay compete?

14 What name is given to a hall for practising martial arts?

15 What is the nickname of the NFL American Football team based in Miami?

16 Eusebio played for which Portuguese club?

17 Who became the youngest and oldest player to win The Masters in 1963 and 1986 respectively?

18 Which game is played to the Harvard rules?

19 How many players make up a water polo team?

20 The terms serve, dig and spike relate to which sport?

Answers to QUIZ 400 – Birds

1	A blackbird	11	Aliona Vilani
2	Lake District	12	Dove
3	New Zealand	13	California
4	The sparrow	14	Merlin
5	Bow and arrow	15	Grouse
6	*H is for Hawk*	16	Jodie Foster
7	*Star Wars*	17	Taylor Swift
8	The Magpies	18	Cuckoo
9	Noah and Nelly	19	Penguin
10	Jack Higgins	20	Emu

ANSWERS ON PAGE **405**

1 Which former International Space Station commander was the first Canadian to walk in space?

2 Jack Worthing is a central character in which play of 1895?

3 Which European flat race is run annually on the first Sunday in October?

4 Which Philippa Pearce novel won the Carnegie Medal?

5 Who played Emperor Nero in *Quo Vadis*?

6 Which African country was formerly known as Nyasaland?

7 In which decade did Yorkshire lose its historical "Ridings" as a result of government reform?

8 Which gardener is associated with Great Dixter in East Sussex?

9 In which year did the Bretton Woods economic conference take place?

10 Which three islands that lie north of Venezuela are known as the ABC islands?

11 In which fictional city is the TV series *The Flash* set?

12 What type of fruit is a Whinham's Industry?

13 In which year was the Notting Hill Carnival first held?

14 Jefferson City is the capital of which US state?

15 What is the traditional bingo call for the number 58?

16 Who captained the European Ryder cup team from 1991 to 1995?

17 On an Ordnance Survey map, what is indicated by a blue square with a white V in it?

18 Which sea lies off Phuket in Thailand?

19 What two-word term describes the rectangular proportions of a photograph, expressed as width to height?

20 In which year was *Sing* a hit for Travis?

Answers to QUIZ 401 – Pot Luck

1	Parthenon	11	*Oklahoma!*
2	Helium	12	17th century
3	Odometer	13	Richard I
4	Adam's apple	14	M1
5	San Marino, Vatican City, Lesotho	15	Fruit
6	Neil Young	16	*Don't Stand So Close to Me*
7	Neil Oliver	17	The Wombles
8	DXB	18	Behind
9	Jupiter	19	Duck
10	Northern Line	20	Belfast City Hall

Easy

Medium

Hard

1   Who wrote the novel on which *Silence of the Lambs* was based?

2   What was the title of the 1978 Ronnie Barker sitcom that was a sequel to *Porridge*?

3   What was the subtitle of the 2009 *Underworld* film, a prequel to the original?

4   In the *Stars Wars* prequel trilogy, who played Jedi Master Mace Windu?

5   Who directed the 2012 film *Prometheus*?

6   What was the title of the second book in the *Adrian Mole* series of diaries by Sue Townsend?

7   *Wide Sargasso Sea* (1966) was written by Jean Rhys as a prequel to which classic novel?

8   *Caprica* was the prequel to which sci-fi series remade in 2004?

9   Released after *Raiders of the Lost Ark*, *Indiana Jones and the Temple of Doom* is set how many years earlier?

10   What was the subtitle of the 2013 second film in *The Hobbit* series?

11   What is the name of Stephanie Cole's character in the TV series *Still Open All Hours*?

12   In the BBC TV adaptation of Michael Dobbs' novel *House of Cards*, who played Francis Urquhart?

13   What was the title of the 2013 film in the *Die Hard* series?

14   *Good Wives* (1869) was a sequel to which novel?

15   Which was the fifth novel in *The Hitchhiker's Guide to the Galaxy* "trilogy"?

16   Who directed the 2016 film *Rogue One: A Star Wars Story*?

17   What was the title of the 2015 sequel to the TV sci-fi series *Heroes*?

18   Which was the final novel in the *Chronicles of Narnia* series by CS Lewis?

19   The *Young Bond* novels published from 2005 to 2009 were written by which author and comedian?

20   Who plays the young Bruce Wayne in the TV series *Gotham*?

Answers to QUIZ 402 – Sport

1	A face-off	11	1995
2	Muirfield	12	Imola
3	Marvin Hagler	13	Ice dancing
4	Tessa Sanderson	14	Dojo
5	Davy Russell	15	The Miami Dolphins
6	New Zealand	16	Benfica
7	1994	17	Jack Nicklaus
8	Heptathlon	18	American Football
9	Pole vault	19	Seven
10	The Tigers	20	Volleyball

1   In which century was Samuel Taylor Coleridge born?

2   Inverness has what postcode area code?

3   Which city is the seat of government in Bolivia?

4   Which musical instrument did Adolph Rickenbacker create?

5   Teams in the world championships of which sport competed for the Silver Broom Trophy between 1968 and 1985?

6   What is the name of the DC superhero who is heir to the throne of Atlantis?

7   Which play by Sir Terence Rattigan is based around several people staying in a Bournemouth hotel?

8   What was manufactured by James Keiller in the 1700s?

9   In the King James version of the Bible, what is the sixth commandment?

10 Who was the Greek hero of the Trojan Wars, son of Telamon?

11 What do Australians call a budgerigar?

12 Charles I was executed in front of which London building?

13 Who directed the 1971 film *The Music Lovers*?

14 New York is known as the Empire State, but which state is known as the Empire State of the South?

15 Which Welsh county lies south-east of Gwynedd?

16 Who wrote the 1853 novel *Villette*?

17 In the BBC cult series, *The Hitchhiker's Guide to the Galaxy*, what was the name of Zaphod Beeblebrox's spaceship?

18 Which city replaced Isfahan as Persia's capital in 1788?

19 What line on a map joins points of equal height?

20 Who starred opposite Humphrey Bogart in *Dark Passage* (1947)?

Easy

Medium

Hard

Answers to QUIZ 403 – Pot Luck

1	Chris Hadfield	11	Central City
2	*The Importance of Being Earnest*	12	Gooseberry
3	The Prix de L'Arc de Triomphe	13	1966
4	*Tom's Midnight Garden*	14	Missouri
5	Sir Peter Ustinov	15	Make them wait
6	Malawi	16	Bernard Gallacher
7	1970s (1974)	17	Visitor centre
8	Christopher Lloyd	18	Andaman Sea
9	1944	19	Aspect ratio
10	Aruba, Bonaire, and Curaçao	20	2001

1   Which regiment of the British army wears maroon berets?

2   Which children's organisation was first formed in Glasgow in 1908?

3   How old was Edward VI when he inherited the throne of England?

4   What British city is associated with St Mungo?

5   How are Lady Day, Midsummer Day, Michaelmas and Christmas Day collectively known in the UK?

6   Which prestigious horse race is sometimes referred to as The Blue Riband of the Turf?

7   Which four-legged table with flaps is named after a town in South Wales?

8   DA is the postcode area code for which town?

9   Which county formerly had Abingdon as its county town?

10 What completes the title of the Welsh hymn *Cwm* ___ often played at British state occasions?

11 Which river flows through the Grampian Mountains to the Moray Firth?

12 Which British nobleman ranks between a marquis and a viscount?

13 In terms of land area, which of the following is the largest county: Gloucestershire, Warwickshire, or Wiltshire?

14 Which historic London structure has the postcode SE1 2UP?

15 Who was the first Englishman to circumnavigate the world?

16 In which decade of the 20th century was Sir Alan Ayckbourn born?

17 Which social security benefit was introduced in 1909?

18 Which West Yorkshire town shares its name with the capital of Nova Scotia?

19 Which shipping forecast area includes the Orkney and Shetland islands?

20 Earl's Court and Knightsbridge are linked by which London Underground line?

Answers to QUIZ 404 – Prequels and Sequels

1	Thomas Harris	11	Delphine Featherstone
2	*Going Straight*	12	Ian Richardson
3	*Rise of the Lycans*	13	*A Good Day to Die Hard*
4	Samuel L Jackson	14	*Little Women*
5	Sir Ridley Scott	15	*Mostly Harmless*
6	*The Growing Pains of Adrian Mole*	16	Gareth Edwards
7	*Jane Eyre*	17	*Heroes Reborn*
8	*Battlestar Galactica*	18	*The Last Battle*
9	One	19	Charlie Higson
10	*The Desolation of Smaug*	20	David Mazouz

QUIZ 407 – Pot Luck

1. In which country was Rudyard Kipling born?

2. In which year did the British South Sea Trading Company collapse?

3. Susanna Hoffs was a member of which all-girl group?

4. What is the abbreviation for the title of Baronet?

5. *Never Been Better* was a 2014 album for which singer?

6. In which city is the Sacred Temple of the Emerald Buddha?

7. In the American Civil War what colour uniform did the Union soldiers wear?

8. Which river forms part of the border between Maryland and Washington DC in the USA?

9. Which was T Rex's first UK no. 1 single?

10. In which year did William Gladstone first become Prime Minister?

11. In which decade of the 20th century was Dame Mary Quant born?

12. Who starred as Michael Bluth in the sitcom *Arrested Development*?

13. In which country is the Laurentian Plateau?

14. In which Irish county is Lurgan?

15. Who were the defending champions at the 1966 FIFA World Cup?

16. What did John Keats address in the ode beginning "Thou still unravished bride of quietness"?

17. In *Jurassic Park*, the dinosaurs were cloned from insects trapped in which material?

18. What is the naval equivalent of the army rank of General?

19. Which car manufacturer produces the Mii?

20. Who wrote the 2003 novel *Monstrous Regiment*?

Easy
Medium
Hard

Answers to QUIZ 405 – Pot Luck

1	18th century	11	Parakeet
2	IV	12	Banqueting House
3	La Paz	13	Ken Russell
4	Electric guitar	14	Georgia (also known as the Peach state)
5	Curling	15	Powys
6	Aquaman	16	Charlotte Brontë
7	*Separate Tables*	17	*Heart of Gold*
8	Marmalade	18	Tehran
9	Thou shalt not kill	19	Contour
10	Ajax	20	Lauren Bacall

1   What type of fish is used in an Omelette Arnold Bennett?

2   A sardine is the young of which fish?

3   What is the first part of the beer-brewing process known as?

4   Which poisonous fish, when prepared by highly trained chefs, is considered a delicacy in Japan?

5   Which French dessert is composed of profiteroles piled into a cone and bound with spun sugar?

6   Burger King is called Hungry Jack's in which country?

7   What does a baron of lamb consist of?

8   What is a rutabaga commonly called in England?

9   Scotch broth is traditionally made from which meat?

10   Which berries are often bounced by growers to test their ripeness?

11   What is the name of Ina Garten's Food Network show?

12   In which US state is the headquarters of Dunkin' Donuts located?

13   The aubergine belongs to which family of plants?

14   What is turrón?

15   Cinnamon is obtained from trees belonging to which family?

16   In which European city were the first coffee houses opened?

17   Alfresco, Golden Boy and Shirley are types of what?

18   In which century was tea first brought to Europe?

19   To what type of sauce is cheese added to make a mornay?

20   What is the Indian dish of tarka dal?

Answers to QUIZ 406 – UK

1	Parachute regiment	11	Spey
2	Boy Scouts	12	Earl
3	Nine	13	Wiltshire
4	Glasgow	14	Tower Bridge
5	Quarter Days	15	Sir Francis Drake
6	The Epsom Derby	16	1930s
7	Pembroke	17	Old age pension
8	Dartford	18	Halifax
9	Berkshire	19	Fair Isle
10	*Rhondda*	20	Piccadilly Line

ANSWERS ON PAGE 411

1   What date is Bastille Day?

2   Which navigable river flows through the German city of Dresden?

3   In which country was comedian Kevin Bridges born?

4   Which group had a 1964 UK hit with *Needles and Pins*?

5   Catherine of Braganza was married to which king?

6   Which planet rotates the fastest?

7   What does DSLR mean in the context of photography?

8   The Braeburn apple originated in which country?

9   Suilven is a mountain in which country?

10 Founded in 1956, which organisation consisted of states that were neutral during the Cold War?

11 Who ruled England between Henry I and Henry II?

12 What is the name of the map projection designed in 1569 as a nautical chart?

13 Tom Thumb, Tennis Ball and Winter Density are types of what?

14 On which island are the towns of Ajaccio and Bastia?

15 Which US singer issued the 2001 debut album *Songs in A Minor*?

16 What is a potager?

17 Which is the oldest British flat classic race?

18 In *Pulp Fiction*, what was the name of John Travolta's character?

19 In which country did Andreas Papandreou serve three terms as Prime Minister, which ended in 1996?

20 Which duo were stripped of a Grammy for Best New Artist in 1990 after being exposed for miming?

Answers to QUIZ 407 – Pot Luck

1	India	11	1930s
2	1720	12	Jason Bateman
3	The Bangles	13	Canada
4	Bart	14	Armagh
5	Olly Murs	15	Brazil
6	Bangkok	16	A Grecian Urn
7	Blue	17	Amber
8	Potomac	18	Admiral
9	*Hot Love*	19	Seat
10	1868	20	Sir Terry Pratchett

1   What was the first name of the wife of US President Franklin D Roosevelt?

2   Which Chinese dynasty ruled from 1368 to 1644?

3   Which country administers Easter Island?

4   Jean-Claude Juncker was Prime Minister of which country from 1995 to 2013?

5   What was the first name of "Evita" Peron's husband?

6   In which year was the US Constitution signed?

7   Which Egyptian leader was jointly awarded the Nobel Peace Prize of 1978 with Menachem Begin?

8   The Althing is the parliament of which country?

9   Who was President of Poland from 1990 to 1995?

10 Who was Ireland's first female President?

11 From 1983 to 1991, who was the Australian Prime Minister?

12 What was the name of the theatre where Abraham Lincoln was assassinated?

13 Which President created the CIA?

14 Who was the President of Kenya from 1978 to 2002?

15 Who was the first Prime Minister of independent India?

16 During WWII, who was the leader of the Free French?

17 Where in the US is the Jefferson Memorial?

18 Who was Vice President of the United States from 1993-2001?

19 Who was President of South Africa from 1999 to 2008?

20 In which building does the US Congress sit?

Answers to QUIZ 408 – Food and Drink

1	Smoked haddock	11	*Barefoot Contessa*
2	Pilchard	12	Massachusetts
3	Mashing	13	Nightshade
4	Pufferfish or fugu	14	Spanish nougat
5	Croquembouche	15	Laurel (*Lauraceae*)
6	Australia	16	Vienna
7	Two legs and saddle	17	Tomato
8	Swede	18	17th century
9	Mutton	19	Béchamel
10	Cranberries	20	Lentils with garlic

Easy

Medium

Hard

ANSWERS ON PAGE 413

1 What term is used for refining iron with heat?

2 In relation to driving, what is a V5C?

3 What is the state capital of Idaho?

4 How is movement away from the audience indicated in a stage direction?

5 Who was the friendly porter in *The Railway Children*?

6 Which group released the album *Monster* in 1994?

7 Which 1985 arcade game allowed players to be an Elf, Warrior, Wizard or Valkyrie?

8 How is magnesium sulphate more commonly referred to?

9 Which US President was known as "Old Hickory"?

10 Of which South Pacific island is Papeete the capital?

11 What was the first UK top ten hit for the Beverley Sisters?

12 Which bird of prey has a honey species?

13 What is the airport code for San Fancisco International airport?

14 Which Essex town is famous for its oyster festival?

15 Actress Pamela Anderson was born in which country?

16 Which cocktail is made from brandy, orange liqueur and lemon juice?

17 In 1953, which jockey won his first Derby at the age of 49?

18 Who wrote *The Godfather* (1969)?

19 Who wrote the lyrics for *A Funny Thing Happened on the Way to the Forum*?

20 What term is given to material that is cut diagonally across the grain of the fabric?

Easy

Medium

Hard

Answers to QUIZ 409 – Pot Luck

1	14th July	11	Stephen
2	Elbe	12	Mercator projection
3	Scotland	13	Lettuce
4	The Searchers	14	Corsica
5	Charles II	15	Alicia Keys
6	Jupiter	16	A small kitchen garden
7	Digital single-lens reflex	17	St Leger
8	New Zealand	18	Vincent Vega
9	Scotland	19	Greece
10	Non-aligned Movement	20	Milli Vanilli

1   What is the capital city of Azerbaijan?

2   The Brenner Pass links Italy with which country?

3   Which capital is known as Lefkosia or Lefkoşa by its inhabitants?

4   Sarajevo is the capital city of which country?

5   The island of Heligoland is surrounded by which body of water?

6   What status does Luxembourg have as a country?

7   What is the name of the small archipelago at the entrance to Galway Bay?

8   Which country borders Afghanistan to the south?

9   The US state of North Carolina has which city as its capital?

10   Which river flows into the Atlantic at Lisbon?

11   Which US state is nicknamed "the Pelican State"?

12   In which South American mountain range is Aconcagua located?

13   Anatolia is a peninsular landmass south of which body of water?

14   Which capital city in the Middle East houses the Great Mosque and the Gate of God?

15   Oman, Kuwait and Bahrain are located on which peninsula?

16   Which airport has the code PEK?

17   The "Land of Silver" is the nickname of which country?

18   Which country lies directly south of South Yemen, across the Gulf of Aden?

19   Which county of the Republic of Ireland is also the name of a Cambridge college?

20   Addis Ababa is the capital city of which country?

Answers to QUIZ 410 – World Politics

1	Eleanor	11	Bob Hawke
2	Ming	12	Ford's
3	Chile	13	Harry S Truman
4	Luxembourg	14	Daniel arap Moi
5	Juan	15	Nehru
6	1787	16	Charles de Gaulle
7	Anwar Sadat	17	Washington DC
8	Iceland	18	Al Gore
9	Lech Walesa	19	Thabo Mbeki
10	Mary Robinson	20	Capitol

QUIZ 413 – Pot Luck

ANSWERS ON PAGE 415

1   Which boxer retired after losing to Chris Eubank, Jr at Wembley Arena in March 2016?

2   Branches of which London Underground line end at Richmond and Ealing Broadway?

3   Which Firth lies between south-west Scotland and north-west England?

4   Which plant-eating dinosaur was the longest of the Jurassic land animals?

5   What symbol is shared by Barbados and Maserati?

6   William Pratt was the real name of which classic horror actor?

7   Where were the 2010 Winter Olympics held?

8   Which Arab state was a dependency of Abu Dhabi until 1833?

9   What term is given to the premature production of flowers and seeds on vegetables such as cabbage?

10 Who was Prussian prime minister from 1862 to 1873, and then German Chancellor until 1890?

11 On which item of clothing would a cockade be worn?

12 Which 2006 film starred Dame Judi Dench and Cate Blanchett?

13 Which was the first Genesis single to reach the top ten in the UK charts?

14 What is the most westerly part of mainland Scotland?

15 What colour is a peridot stone?

16 In Greek mythology, who was the brother of Artemis?

17 "Like a fool I went and stayed too long, Now I'm wondering if your love's still strong" is a lyric from which song?

18 Where would you look to discover the Mount of the Moon and the Girdle of Venus?

19 Which 1970s film was remade in 2000 with Samuel L Jackson in the title role?

20 Which US state is known as the "Cornhusker State"?

Answers to QUIZ 411 – Pot Luck

1	Smelting	11	*I Saw Mommy Kissing Santa Claus*
2	Vehicle log book	12	Buzzard
3	Boise	13	SFO
4	Upstage	14	Colchester
5	Perks	15	Canada
6	R. E. M.	16	Sidecar
7	*Gauntlet*	17	Sir Gordon Richards
8	Epsom salts	18	Mario Puzo
9	Andrew Jackson	19	Stephen Sondheim
10	Tahiti	20	Bias cut

1   Which group was singing about *Barbados* in 1975?

2   Which singer had hits in 2000 with *Fill Me In* and *7 Days*?

3   What is Gary Numan's real surname?

4   With whom did Calvin Harris collaborate on the 2011 single *Bounce*?

5   What was the surname of Donald Swann's singing partner in the 1950s and 60s?

6   Which pop duo released a 1992 EP called *Abba-esque*?

7   *Lilac Wine* and *Don't Cry Out Loud* were 1970s hits for which singer?

8   What was the Jimi Hendrix Experience's first chart hit, in 1966?

9   *Ladies Night* was a 2003 hit for which girl group?

10 What was the title of Fern Kinney's 1980 no.1?

11 *Lights* was whose debut album in 2010?

12 Who had a hit with *Rawhide* in 1959?

13 Who had a no.1 hit record in 1961 with *Moon River*?

14 Who had a hit with *Gambler* in 1985?

15 *A Girl Like You* was a 1995 hit for which singer?

16 Who topped the charts in 2007 with *Bleeding Love*?

17 What was the title of George McCrae's 1974 no.1 single?

18 Whose 2002 debut album was *Come Away with Me*?

19 What was the nationality of the legendary Prince Buster?

20 In which decade of the 20th century was Eric Clapton born?

Answers to QUIZ 412 – Geography

1	Baku	11	Louisiana
2	Austria	12	Andes
3	Nicosia (Cyprus)	13	Black Sea
4	Bosnia and Herzegovina	14	Damascus (Syria)
5	North Sea	15	Arabian
6	Grand Duchy	16	Beijing
7	Aran Islands	17	Argentina
8	Pakistan	18	Somalia
9	Raleigh	19	Clare
10	Tagus	20	Ethiopia

1 "Drew looks at me, I fake a smile so he won't see" is the opening line from which song?

2 What was the term given to districts around Dublin that were controlled by England for several centuries?

3 Proverbially, what is used to catch a mackerel?

4 Which team did Sunderland beat in the 1973 FA Cup Final?

5 What is the name of Rob Lowe's younger brother, who is also an actor?

6 What is the traditional bingo call for the number 81?

7 In which decade was the Bank of England founded?

8 Which women's magazine was launched in the UK in February 1972?

9 Which sport was played at Central Park in Wigan?

10 In 1702, which king died after falling from his horse?

11 To which city did the League of Nations move in November 1920?

12 In *Thunderbirds*, what was Lady Penelope's surname?

13 Who wrote the Restoration comedy *She Stoops to Conquer*?

14 In song, in which Row was Mother Kelly's doorstep?

15 What name is given to a cocktail of Scotch with lemon or lime juice?

16 TR is the postcode area code for which city?

17 Which philosopher died in February 1970 at the age of 97?

18 Who wrote the novel *The Old Man and the Sea*, published in 1952?

19 Which mountainous island of Indonesia has the chief city Denpasar?

20 Which car manufacturer produced the iQ model?

Easy

Medium

Hard

Answers to QUIZ 413 – Pot Luck

1	Nick Blackwell	11	A hat
2	District Line	12	*Notes on a Scandal*
3	The Solway Firth	13	*Follow You Follow Me*
4	Diplodocus	14	Ardnamurchan Point
5	A trident	15	Green
6	Boris Karloff	16	Apollo
7	Vancouver	17	*Signed, Sealed, Delivered, I'm Yours*
8	Dubai	18	In the palm of your hand
9	Bolting	19	*Shaft*
10	Otto von Bismarck	20	Nebraska

Easy

1. Which fraudster was portrayed by Leonardo di Caprio in the 2002 film *Catch Me if You Can...*?

2. ...and which other fraudster did he portray in the 2013 film *The Wolf of Wall Street*?

3. In which London borough is the prison Wormwood Scrubs?

4. In which English county did the "Great Train Robbery" take place?

5. What term is given to the first step in a criminal trial?

6. In which city was Martin Luther King assassinated in 1968?

7. Which US fraudster was sentenced to 150 years in prison in 2009 for operating a Ponzi scheme?

8. Which outlaw was shot by Robert Ford...?

9. ...and who played Robert Ford in the 2007 film?

10. What was Al short for in Al Capone's name?

11. Which early detective investigated the Road Hill House murder case, as documented by Kate Summerscale in a 2008 book?

12. What was the nickname of the French serial killer Henri Landru?

13. In US law, what is an offence less heinous than a felony?

Medium

14. Who assassinated Lee Harvey Oswald?

15. Who played MP Peter Bessell in the 2018 TV series *A Very English Scandal*?

16. What does the Latin phrase *mens rea* mean?

17. How many points are added to a driving licence in the UK for driving while disqualified?

18. What word is applied to the doing of a wrongful or illegal act by a public official?

19. What is the process in the USA by which the President is charged with committing a crime that makes them unfit for office?

20. Who wrote the 1991 book *Homicide: A Year on the Killing Streets*, which was adapted for television as *Homicide: Life on the Street*?

Hard

Answers to QUIZ 414 – Pop Music

1	Typically Tropical	11	Ellie Goulding
2	Craig David	12	Frankie Laine
3	Webb	13	Danny Williams
4	Kelis	14	Madonna
5	Michael Flanders	15	Edwyn Collins
6	Erasure	16	Leona Lewis
7	Elkie Brooks	17	*Rock Your Baby*
8	*Hey Joe*	18	Norah Jones
9	Atomic Kitten	19	Jamaican
10	*Together We Are Beautiful*	20	1940s

QUIZ 417 – Pot Luck

ANSWERS ON PAGE **419**

1 On which river is Astrakhan situated?

2 What Barbra Streisand film musical was based on the novel *The Matchmaker*?

3 Which pianist and conductor was married to the cellist Jacqueline Du Pré?

4 Was the Battle of Agincourt before or after the Battle of Bosworth Field?

5 To which area of London did the Billingsgate fish market move in 1982?

6 What landed at Heathrow for the first time in January 1970?

7 Which US actress wrote the 2014 book *Yes Please*?

8 Which New Zealand seaport was founded in 1848 by Scottish settlers?

9 Who was the brother of Cain and Abel in the Bible?

10 Robert Walpole, first Earl of Orford, was born in which county?

11 In 1995, which female singer went *Walking in Memphis*?

12 Who rode Nijinsky to victory in the Derby?

13 What does the "RM" stand for where a ship has the designation "RMS"?

14 Which *Game of Thrones* actor had a starring role in the 2015 film *Spooks: The Greater Good*?

15 Who led the first successful expedition to navigate the Northwest Passage?

16 A scaup is what type of bird?

17 Which word means both an allotted part of a company's capital and a plough blade?

18 Who was the original male presenter of the talent show *Fame Academy*?

19 From which English county side did Ian Botham retire from cricket?

20 In Shakespeare's *A Midsummer Night's Dream*, what is the name of the carpenter?

Easy

Medium

Hard

Answers to QUIZ 415 – Pot Luck

1	*Teardrops on my Guitar* (Taylor Swift)	11	Geneva
2	The Pale	12	Creighton-Ward
3	Sprat	13	Oliver Goldsmith
4	Leeds United	14	Paradise
5	Chad	15	Whisky sour
6	Stop and run	16	Truro
7	1690s (1694)	17	Bertrand Russell
8	*Cosmopolitan*	18	Ernest Hemingway
9	Rugby League	19	Bali
10	William III (William of Orange)	20	Toyota

417

1 Who played the local copper, "Corky", in the comedy series *Sykes*?

2 Jay Pritchett and his relatives feature in which US sitcom?

3 Which actor created the Scottish comedy character Rab C Nesbitt...?

4 ...who first appeared on which comedy sketch show?

5 Who co-starred with Robert Powell in the 1990s series *The Detectives*?

6 Jack Dee played Rick Spleen in which sitcom?

7 Which actor co-starred with Janet Dibley in the sitcom *The Two of Us*?

8 In the TV series *Extras,* which actress played Maggie?

9 Which US sitcom featured the history of Ted Mosby's relationships?

10 In which county was the series *Detectorists* set?

11 Which sitcom was set in the offices of the fictional Reynholm Industries?

12 What character did Victoria Wood play in the TV series *dinnerladies*?

13 Who starred as Fletcher's grandson in the 2017 update of *Porridge*?

14 What is the name of the supermarket in the series *Trollied*?

15 Who starred in the 1990s sitcom *Chef!*?

16 In which fictional town was the US sitcom *Parks and Recreation* set?

17 Karl Howman starred as Jacko in which 1980s sitcom?

18 The series *Brighton Belles* was based on which US sitcom?

19 The US remake of which UK series featured the paper company Dunder Mifflin?

20 Which 1979-1981 sitcom starred Maureen Lipman as Jane Lucas?

Answers to QUIZ 416 – Crime

1	Frank Abagnale Jr	11	Jack Whicher
2	Jordan Belfort	12	Bluebeard
3	Hammersmith and Fulham	13	Misdemeanour
4	Buckinghamshire	14	Jack Ruby
5	Arraignment	15	Alex Jennings
6	Memphis	16	Guilty mind
7	Bernard Madoff	17	Six
8	Jesse James	18	Malfeasance
9	Casey Affleck	19	Impeachment
10	Alphonse	20	David Simon

1   What was the ancient kingdom on the territory of what is now Sudan?

2   Which brand of hand cleaner was invented in 1947 by Audley Bowdler Williamson?

3   In which ocean is Comoros?

4   The American writers Allen Ginsberg and William S Burroughs were members of which literary group?

5   RG is the postcode area code for which town?

6   What is the administrative centre for the county of Buckinghamshire?

7   What is the name of the animal hero who starred in his first video game on PlayStation® in 1996?

8   How is rapper and singer Aubrey Graham better known?

9   What was the name of the first Duke of Buckingham (b.1592)?

10   Who, along with his assistant Nicholas Hawksmoor, was the original architect of the naval hospital at Greenwich?

11   What do the initials USAF stand for?

12   The 2001 memoir *Give Me Ten Seconds* was written by which former political correspondent?

13   Which group had a 1983 hit with *My Oh My*?

14   What is the eighth letter of the Greek alphabet?

15   Who wrote the novel *One Flew over the Cuckoo's Nest*?

16   What is burlap?

17   *Free* was a 1977 no.1 single for which singer?

18   In which county is the village of Hartley Wintney?

19   How many minutes are in a degree of an angle?

20   What name is given to a hill in the centre of any Greek city?

Easy

Medium

Hard

Answers to QUIZ 417 – Pot Luck

1	Volga	11	Cher
2	*Hello, Dolly!*	12	Lester Piggott
3	Daniel Barenboim	13	Royal Mail
4	Before	14	Kit Harington
5	Isle of Dogs	15	Roald Amundsen
6	Jumbo Jet	16	Duck
7	Amy Poehler	17	Share
8	Dunedin	18	Patrick Kielty
9	Seth	19	Durham
10	Norfolk	20	Quince

1   What is the title of the first of Roald Dahl's children's books, published in 1961?

2   Who wrote the 1904 novel *Nostromo*?

3   Shelley wrote the poem *Ozymandias* about which historical figure?

4   Wackford Squeers appears in which Charles Dickens novel?

5   *There and Back Again* is the subtitle of which children's novel?

6   Which bird did Keats describe in an ode as a "light-winged Dryad of the trees"?

7   *The Martian Chronicles* (1950) were written by which author?

8   What was Little Lord Fauntleroy's first name?

9   What word is eerily repeated by Edgar Allan Poe's raven?

10 Who was Poet Laureate from 1850 until his death in 1892?

11 *One, Two, Buckle My Shoe* and *A Pocketful of Rye* are novels by which author?

12 In 1824, which Romantic poet died at Missolonghi in Greece?

13 Who wrote the lines "On Wenlock Edge the wood's in trouble"?

14 Which ancient Greek philosopher wrote *The Republic*?

15 The novel *The Bonfire of the Vanities* was written by which author?

16 Which novel features the ship *Hispaniola*?

17 *First Among Equals* was a 1984 political novel by which author?

18 What was the pseudonym used by Emily Brontë?

19 Which US poet wrote *The Road Not Taken* (1916)?

20 Who wrote *The Trial* and *The Metamorphosis*?

---

1   Which country hosted the 2006 Winter Oympics?

2   Members of which organisation within the United Nations wear blue berets or helmets?

3   What colour is the 20 euro note introduced in 2002?

4   Which is Northern Ireland's smallest county?

5   What is the clothing worn by nurses and other hospital workers colloquially known as?

6   Lewis Carroll was born in which century?

7   Which US preacher gave a sermon at St Paul's Cathedral in December, 1964 en route to collect the Nobel Peace Prize?

8   Who wrote the poem *The Faerie Queen* (1590)?

9   Which war provided the setting for the 1979 film *Apocalypse Now*?

10   What kind of a race is a "Bumper"?

11   Former Lord Chancellor Quintin Hogg took what name when he became a Lord?

12   Mariah Carey sang *Against All Odds* with which group in 2000?

13   Who played Lori in the 1990 film *Total Recall*?

14   If you combined k and p to make cables what would your hobby be?

15   The word "aquiline" relates to which family of birds?

16   Barbara Villiers was famously a mistress of which king?

17   Which dark igneous rock is found on the Moon and Mars?

18   The single *Papa Don't Preach* was taken from which Madonna album?

19   Pinchbeck is an alloy of which two metals?

20   What is the term given to the action of a seed starting to grow?

Answers to QUIZ 419 – Pot Luck

1	Kush	11	United States Air Force
2	Swarfega	12	John Sergeant
3	Indian Ocean	13	Slade
4	The Beat Generation	14	Theta
5	Reading	15	Ken Kesey
6	Aylesbury	16	A rough fabric
7	Crash Bandicoot	17	Deniece Williams
8	Drake	18	Hampshire
9	George Villiers	19	60
10	Sir Christopher Wren	20	Acropolis

Easy

1 Which English king was the first ruler of the Angevin Empire?

2 Who was called "the Serpent of the Nile"?

3 In which century was England declared a republic?

4 What were the KGB in the Soviet Union?

5 In which year did Concorde make its final commercial flight?

6 When was British Telecom privatised?

7 In which year was the *Titanic* located by robot submarine?

8 Opened in 1955, what was the name of Dame Mary Quant's Chelsea boutique?

9 In which decade was the US state of Georgia founded?

10 A 1520 meeting was held in the "Field of the Cloth of Gold" in which country?

11 Which tsar transferred the Russian capital from Moscow to St Petersburg in 1712?

12 Which chain store proprietor commissioned the then tallest inhabitable building in the world in 1913?

13 In which century did Lambert Simnel and Perkin Warbeck lay claim to the English throne?

14 Which monarchs sponsored the explorations of Christopher Columbus?

Medium

15 Which peninsula in south-east China was established as a colony by the Portuguese in 1557?

16 In which decade was the British Legion founded?

17 In which year did the liner *Queen Elizabeth II* sail from Southampton on her maiden voyage?

18 What was the name of legendary pirate Blackbeard's famous flagship?

19 What first name did Guy Fawkes use when serving in the Spanish army?

20 In which year did Norway first give Britain a gift of the Christmas tree which stands in London's Trafalgar Square?

Hard

Answers to QUIZ 420 – Literature

1	*James and the Giant Peach*	11	Dame Agatha Christie
2	Joseph Conrad	12	Lord Byron
3	Ramesses II	13	AE Housman
4	*Nicholas Nickleby*	14	Plato
5	*The Hobbit*	15	Tom Wolfe
6	Nightingale	16	*Treasure Island*
7	Ray Bradbury	17	Jeffrey Archer
8	Cedric	18	Ellis Bell
9	Nevermore	19	Robert Frost
10	Alfred, Lord Tennyson	20	Franz Kafka

1   What children's uniform originally consisted of matching khaki shirt and shorts, a neckerchief and a campaign hat?

2   What is the English translation of the Spanish word "Nevada"?

3   In the cartoons, what colour is Scooby-Doo's collar?

4   What was the name of the battleship launched in 1906 that gave its name to the new generation of battleships?

5   What is the traditional bingo call for the number 82?

6   Which species of willow is traditionally used in basket-making?

7   Which group had a 1977 hit with *Ma Baker*?

8   Piet Oudolf (b. 1944) is a well-known name in which profession?

9   Which Cornish river flows out to the sea at Carrick Roads?

10 What was the title of the 1948 Hitchcock thriller starring James Stewart?

11 Where is the Livadia Palace, scene of a famous conference in February 1945?

12 What are sold at London's Columbia Road market?

13 Robbie Williams is a supporter of which football club?

14 The 1967 opera *Punch and Judy* was written by which composer?

15 Who wrote the 1986 autobiography *Is That It*?

16 What was the first UK solo top ten hit for Doris Day?

17 Who hosted the TV series *This Is Your Life* after Eamonn Andrews?

18 In 1987, which British golfer won the Open championship?

19 What is the twentieth letter in the Greek alphabet?

20 From what milk is Gouda cheese typically made?

Easy

Medium

Hard

Answers to QUIZ 421 – Pot Luck

1	Italy	11	Hailsham
2	UN peacekeepers	12	Westlife
3	Blue	13	Sharon Stone
4	Armagh	14	Knitting
5	Scrubs	15	Eagles
6	19th century	16	Charles II
7	Dr Martin Luther King Jr	17	Basalt
8	Edmund Spenser	18	*True Blue*
9	Vietnam	19	Copper and zinc
10	A National Hunt flat race	20	Germination

1   In which century did John Napier discover logarithms...?

2   ...and what graduated rods used for multiplication and division did he also introduce?

3   What line of a right-angled triangle is opposite the angle measuring 90°?

4   Which mathematician is known for his 1632 "Last Theorem"...?

5   ...and what is the definition of a theorem?

6   In which branch of mathematics are letters used to replace numbers?

7   If a narrow, rectangular strip of paper is twisted through 180° and the ends are joined, what name is give to the one-sided continuous surface that has been created?

8   Which fictional mathematician did Sandra Dickinson play in the TV series *The Hitchhiker's Guide to the Galaxy*?

9   The branch of mathematics concerned with calculating the side length or angles of triangles is often abbreviated to which four-letter term?

10 What nationality was the mathematician Fibonacci?

11 In which TV series did Charlie Eppes and his colleagues at the fictional California Institute of Science help the FBI in solving crimes?

12 The use of the coordinates x, y and z to represent points in space is named after which French mathematician?

13 On which Greek island was Pythagoras born?

14 What creature is often used as an illustrative example of chaos theory?

15 What name is given to the branch of mathematics that studies abstract concepts?

16 From which language is the word "mathematics" derived?

17 Who wrote the 18th-century book *Elements of Mathematics*?

18 Fractals are used in which branch of mathematics?

19 Which English mathematician (b.1945) published the *Cabinet of Mathematical Curiosities* (2008)?

20 The International Mathematical Union awards which prestigious prize, named after a Canadian mathematician, every four years?

Answers to QUIZ 422 – History

1	Henry II	11	Peter the Great
2	Cleopatra	12	FW Woolworth
3	17th century	13	15th century
4	Committee for State Security	14	Ferdinand and Isabella
5	2003	15	Macao
6	1984	16	1920s (1921)
7	1985	17	1969
8	Bazaar	18	*Queen Anne's Revenge*
9	1730s	19	Guido
10	France	20	1947

ANSWERS ON PAGE **427**

1   What is the alcoholic ingredient of a gimlet cocktail?

2   What is the capital of the US state of Wyoming?

3   Guernsey has what postcode area code?

4   In which sport does England play Scotland for the Calcutta Cup?

5   Which car company manufactures the Impreza?

6   In the Disney film, what is the name of The Little Mermaid's tropical fish friend?

7   Which Restoration comedy features Lady Teazle and Lady Sneerwell?

8   In which Kent town were Sir Malcolm Sargent and Bob Holness both born?

9   Who appeared in and co-produced *The China Syndrome* (1979)?

10 Which cartoonist created the character of Dilbert?

11 Which economic alliance comprises Iceland, Liechtenstein, Norway and Switzerland?

12 Terry Downes is associated with which sport?

13 Which musical centres on the life of the son of Captain and Mrs Walker?

14 What is the process by which sheep wool is cleaned after shearing?

15 Up until 1994, what was the eastern terminus of the Central Line on London's Underground?

16 In which ocean are the South Sandwich Islands situated?

17 Who was Billie Jean King describing when she said, "She's the greatest singles, doubles and mixed doubles player who's ever lived"?

18 The chart-topping single *Sweets for My Sweet* was the first single released by which band?

19 Which bird has red-legged and grey species?

20 How are chlorofluorocarbon gases more commonly referred to?

Answers to QUIZ 423 – Pot Luck

1	Scouts' uniform	11	Yalta
2	Snow-covered	12	Flowers
3	Blue	13	Port Vale
4	HMS *Dreadnought*	14	Harrison Birtwistle
5	Straight on through	15	Bob Geldof
6	Osier	16	*My Love and Devotion*
7	Boney M	17	Michael Aspel
8	Garden design	18	Nick Faldo
9	Fal	19	Upsilon
10	*Rope*	20	Cows' milk

Easy

Medium

Hard

ANSWERS ON PAGE 428

Easy

1 Which statesman appears on the front of the 100 dollar bill?

2 Members of which branch of the United States Armed Forces traditionally wear a blue dress uniform?

3 The Chicago Cubs play which sport?

4 Gumbo is a stew that originated in which state?

5 Which territory became a state in 1907 and was the subject of a 1943 musical?

6 Who was the only US President to serve for more than eight years?

7 Which area of New York's Central Park pays tribute to the late Beatle, John Lennon?

8 Sioux Falls and Deadwood are in which American state?

9 The Statue of Liberty is coated with what metallic substance?

10 What famous "garden" in New York is actually an arena located in Midtown Manhattan?

Medium

11 Who assassinated President Abraham Lincoln?

12 Which US political party is known as the GOP?

13 What is the longest river in the USA?

14 The state of Georgia was named after which monarch?

15 What great construction is located near near Boulder City, Nevada?

16 Where is the US National Cemetery based?

17 Launched in 1797, what is the name of the American warship which last sailed under her own power in 2012?

18 What relation was the 6th President John Quincy Adams to the 2nd US President John Adams?

19 Who composed the march *Stars and Stripes Forever*?

20 Which US state has the nickname "the Apache State"?

Hard

Answers to QUIZ 424 – Mathematics

1	17th century	11	*Numb3rs*
2	Napier's Bones	12	René Descartes (Cartesian coordinates)
3	Hypotenuse	13	Samos
4	Pierre de Fermat	14	Butterfly (butterfly effect)
5	A statement that can be proved to be true	15	Pure mathematics
6	Algebra	16	Greek
7	Möbius strip	17	Leonhard Euler
8	Trillian	18	Geometry
9	Trig (trigonometry)	19	Professor Ian Stewart
10	Italian	20	Fields Medal

1   What is the language of the RC Tridentine Mass?

2   Who wrote the story *Rip van Winkle* (1819)…?

3   …and in which mountains did the title character sleep for 20 years?

4   A cartoon character from which series inspired the name of Wimpy®?

5   In which language are the words for "four" and "nine" unlucky due to their closeness to the words for "death" and "worry"?

6   Ben Lomond and Baldwin are types of which fruit?

7   Céline Dion won the Eurovision Song Contest for Switzerland in which year?

8   What was Disney's second animated feature film?

9   Which film set in Philadelphia starred Harrison Ford as John Book?

10 What event took place in Ebbw Vale in Wales in 1992, the last of five such events?

11 Which football league club did Bradley Walsh join in 1978?

12 The Church of Scientology's "Flag Land Base" is in which American state?

13 What is the capital, jointly with Santa Cruz, of the Canary Islands?

14 What is jockey Frankie Dettori's full first name?

15 Which element has the atomic number 18 and the symbol Ar?

16 Turnhouse Airport serves which city?

17 What substance is responsible for the characteristic smell of garlic?

18 Dennis Quaid and Matthew Fox starred in whch 2008 thriller?

19 Which Australian singer (b.1975) usually performs wearing a wig to obscure her face?

20 What is the capital of Bermuda?

Easy

Medium

Hard

Answers to QUIZ 425 – Pot Luck

1	Gin	11	EFTA
2	Cheyenne	12	Boxing
3	GY	13	*Tommy*
4	Rugby Union	14	Scouring
5	Subaru	15	Ongar
6	Flounder	16	Atlantic
7	*The School for Scandal*	17	Martina Navratilova
8	Ashford	18	The Searchers
9	Michael Douglas	19	Partridge
10	Scott Adams	20	CFCs

ANSWERS ON PAGE 430

Easy

1   Which actor starred in the 1957 film *Pal Joey*?

2   What make and model of car is used as a time machine in the *Back to the Future* franchise?

3   In what film does Keanu Reeves play Jack Travern?

4   Who won the Best Actress Oscar for the 2015 film *Room*?

5   Which actor starred in *Earth Girls Are Easy* and *The Tall Guy*?

6   In the 1967 film, *Billion Dollar Brain*, who played Harry Palmer?

7   Which animated film of 2004 involves a train taking children to meet Santa?

8   Who starred as Agent Neville Flynn in the 2006 film *Snakes on a Plane*?

9   The 1985 fantasy film *Ladyhawke* starred Michelle Pfeiffer and which Dutch actor?

10   *Dream Warriors* and *The Dream Child* were two of the sequels to which film?

Medium

11   In which film was Chaplin's Little Tramp seen for the last time?

12   What did Fred Quimby produce that is still seen today?

13   In the title of the 2018 film, what *Society* was based on Guernsey?

14   Who played the title role in the 2004 film *Van Helsing*?

15   Sir Mark Rylance won a Best Supporting Actor Oscar for his role in which 2015 film?

16   In the 1986 film *Sid and Nancy*, who played Sid Vicious?

17   Who provided the voice for Lola in *Shark Tale*?

18   In which film does Tony Moran star as a character called Michael Myers?

19   Saoirse Ronan played an Irish immigrant in 1950s America in which 2015 film?

20   Which sport featured in the 1977 film *Semi-Tough* starring Burt Reynolds?

Hard

Answers to QUIZ 426 – The USA

1	Benjamin Franklin	11	John Wilkes Booth
2	Marine Corps	12	The Republican Party
3	Baseball	13	Missouri
4	Louisiana	14	George II
5	Oklahoma	15	Hoover Dam
6	Franklin D Roosevelt	16	Arlington
7	Strawberry Fields	17	USS *Constitution*
8	South Dakota	18	Son
9	Copper	19	John Philip Sousa
10	Madison Square Garden	20	Arizona

1   Who wrote the 1950 novel *Strangers on a Train*?

2   Which US President appears on the front of the five dollar bill?

3   What is Edinburgh's main shopping street?

4   The imposition of which tax led to the Peasants' Revolt of 1381?

5   The space probe *Messenger* was launched in 2004 to investigate which planet?

6   Who won an Oscar for her role in the 2003 film *Monster*?

7   In which year was the Thames Flood Barrier completed?

8   What relation was Queen Anne to Queen Mary II?

9   What is the part of a verb referring to the addressee?

10 In which mountain range does the River Po rise?

11 Who was the elf lord who ruled at Rivendell in *The Lord of the Rings*?

12 What name is given to a garden with geometrically arranged beds and small hedges?

13 In which month of 1912 did the *Titanic* sink?

14 Released in 1981, what was the title of Kim Wilde's first hit?

15 In which county is the borough of Epsom and Ewell?

16 Which two words that sound the same but are spelt differently mean "tactful" and "separate"?

17 Who was the first solo British artist to win a Grammy for Best New Artist?

18 What machine is used to polish gemstones?

19 In vertebrates, what is the main part of the brain called?

20 In which sport do the Canberra Raiders compete?

Answers to QUIZ 427 – Pot Luck

1	Latin	11	Brentford
2	Washington Irving	12	California
3	Catskill	13	Las Palmas
4	*Popeye* (J Wellington Wimpy)	14	Lanfranco
5	Japanese	15	Argon
6	Blackcurrant	16	Edinburgh
7	1988	17	Allicin
8	*Pinocchio*	18	*Vantage Point*
9	*Witness*	19	Sia
10	National Garden Festival	20	Hamilton

Easy

Medium

Hard

Easy

1 On the London Underground, which station lies between Brent Cross and Hampstead?

2 Which US state is nicknamed "the Green Mountain State"?

3 What term is used for the colour green in heraldry?

4 Singer Professor Green has what real name?

5 Which of King Arthur's knights pursued and fought the Green Knight?

6 In the 2006 version of *Casino Royale*, who played Vesper Lynd?

7 Who narrated the children's TV series *Camberwick Green*?

8 What is the capital of Greenland?

9 Who topped the charts in 1970 with *Spirit in the Sky*?

10 Of which month is emerald the birthstone?

11 The protests at Greenham Common that began in the 1980s were against siting what at the RAF base?

Medium

12 What two-word term is given to the rise in global temperature as a result of certain gases trapping heat from the sun?

13 The greengage is a variety of what type of fruit?

14 What did the Scottish team Morton FC change its name to in 1994 to mark a clear link with its home town?

15 What is the German word for "green"?

16 What difference is there between the leaves used to make green tea and the leaves used to make black tea?

17 Greenwich Village is in which borough of New York?

18 Who reached no.2 in the UK charts in 1956 with a version of *Green Door*?

19 The "Don't Make A Wave" committee, formed in 1969, evolved into which organisation?

20 From which sport is the phrase "the rub of the green" taken?

Hard

Answers to QUIZ 428 – Film

1	Frank Sinatra	11	*The Great Dictator*
2	DeLorean DMC-12	12	Tom and Jerry cartoons
3	*Speed*	13	*Literary and Potato Peel Pie*
4	Brie Larson	14	Hugh Jackman
5	Jeff Goldblum	15	*Bridge of Spies*
6	Sir Michael Caine	16	Gary Oldman
7	*The Polar Express*	17	Angelina Jolie
8	Samuel L Jackson	18	*Halloween*
9	Rutger Hauer	19	*Brooklyn*
10	*A Nightmare on Elm Street*	20	American football

ANSWERS ON PAGE **433**

1   What is the postcode area code for Silverstone Racetrack?

2   What word is given to the amount of light allowed to fall on a camera's sensor as a photograph is taken?

3   Who created the Mr Men?

4   On an Ordnance Survey map, what is indicated by the letter H in a circle?

5   Which 1960s group had a hit with *Silence Is Golden*?

6   What two-word scientific term describes momentum away from the middle?

7   In which Dickens novel does Alfred Jingle appear?

8   Which band's first double album was entitled *Physical Graffiti*?

9   In which century was John Constable born?

10 On which Greek island did the poet Sappho live?

11 In which film did Timothy Dalton make his first appearance as James Bond?

12 Who wrote the poem *The Pied Piper of Hamlyn*?

13 Which UK Eurovision Song Contest entrant recorded *Ooh Aah... Just a Little Bit*?

14 On which river is the French town of Blois?

15 What is the capital of the US state of Ohio?

16 Which creature follows the Rat in the Chinese calendar?

17 In the animal world, what type of creatures are knots, stints and snipes?

18 In the animated series *Shaun the Sheep*, what is the name of the dog?

19 What was Neville Chamberlain's real first name?

20 Fratton is an area of which English city?

Easy

Medium

Hard

Answers to QUIZ 429 – Pot Luck

1	Patricia Highsmith	11	Elrond (Halfelven)
2	Abraham Lincoln	12	Knot garden
3	Princes Street	13	April
4	Poll tax	14	*Kids in America*
5	Mercury	15	Surrey
6	Charlize Theron	16	Discreet and discrete
7	1984	17	Sir Tom Jones
8	Sister	18	Tumbler
9	Second person	19	Cerebrum
10	Alps	20	Rugby League

Easy

1   In which year was the bimetallic £2 coin first issued in general circulation?

2   In relation to economics, for what does the "B" stand in the initials PSBR?

3   The pound was withdrawn from which system on 16 September 1992...?

4   ...and who was the Chancellor of the Exchequer at the time?

5   Who was the Younger PM who introduced income tax?

6   When were PEP investment schemes introduced in the UK?

7   What is the name of the politician who is featured on the five pound note introduced in 2016?

8   In 1694, Sir John Houblon was the first person to hold which financial position?

9   In which year was the Bank of England granted operational independence on monetary policy?

Medium

10   What is the name of the summer residence that the Chancellor of the Exchequer traditionally has the right to use?

11   What is indicated by M1 or W1 at the end of a tax code?

12   In which year did the monarch's portrait first appear on Bank of England notes?

13   Where was the Royal Mint based until 1810?

14   Which of these pre-decimal currency coins is worth the least: a farthing, a guinea or a shilling?

15   What colour is the 10 euro note introduced in 2002?

16   Milton Friedman formulated what economic theory...?

17   ...and in which decade did he receive the Nobel Prize in Economic Sciences?

18   What is the name of the American president who appears on the front of the two dollar bill?

19   The International Monetary Fund has its headquarters in which city...?

20   ...and what is the name of the Managing Director who was appointed in 2011?

Hard

Answers to QUIZ 430 – Green

1	Golders Green	11	Cruise missiles
2	Vermont	12	Greenhouse Effect
3	Vert	13	Plum
4	Stephen Manderson	14	Greenock Morton FC
5	Gawain	15	Grün
6	Eva Green	16	Green tea leaves are unfermented
7	Brian Cant	17	Manhattan
8	Nuuk	18	Frankie Vaughan
9	Norman Greenbaum	19	Greenpeace
10	May	20	Golf

ANSWERS ON PAGE 435

1 Which poet wrote *Don Juan* (1819-24)?

2 What nationality was sculptor Henry Moore (b.1898)?

3 *My Everything* and *Dangerous Woman* are albums by which artist?

4 What are the first names of Bond villain Blofeld?

5 The Duchess of Marlborough, a close friend of Queen Anne's, had what first name?

6 What is a Derringer?

7 Who devised the wind scale used by mariners to this day?

8 What is the name of the multiplayer online role-playing game first released in 2004 by Blizzard?

9 After the House of Commons' debating chamber was gutted by fire in 1941, which architect redesigned it?

10 What is the capital of Sudan?

11 Which mountain range runs through Morocco?

12 The "Palace of the Peak" is a nickname of which stately home?

13 What is painted on to fabric in batik?

14 Which Wiltshire town had "Royal" added to its name in 2011?

15 In ancient myth, which woman was craftily beaten in a running race by Hippomenes?

16 What is measured by the sievert SI unit?

17 In the 1956 film *High Society*, what was the name of Frank Sinatra's character?

18 What name is shared by an inlet at County Cork in Ireland and Cape Town in South Africa?

19 The Adam and Adam Rocks car models are made by which manufacturer?

20 What is kohlrabi?

Easy

Medium

Hard

Answers to QUIZ 431 – Pot Luck

1	NN	11	*The Living Daylights*
2	Exposure	12	Browning
3	Roger Hargreaves	13	Gina G
4	Heliport	14	Loire
5	Tremeloes	15	Columbus
6	Centrifugal force	16	Ox
7	*The Pickwick Papers*	17	Wading birds
8	Led Zeppelin	18	Bitzer
9	18th century	19	Arthur
10	Lesbos	20	Portsmouth

1   The Shar Pei dog originates from which country?

2   Which breed of sheep takes its name from a range of hills in the Scottish Borders?

3   Catfish have poisonous barbs on which part of their body?

4   "Clouded" is a species of which big cat?

5   Which deep-sea creature uses a "lure" to catch its prey...?

6   ...and which fish spits streams of water at insects to knock them into the water?

7   Komodo dragons have poisons in their saliva that prevent their victims' blood from doing what?

8   When does the common lobster feed?

9   A guanaco is what type of creature?

10   What type of creature is a Birman?

11   The lemur belongs to which group of mammals?

12   Which elephants have the bigger ears, Indian or African?

13   A lorikeet is a species of which type of bird?

14   The two-toed sloth is native to which continent?

15   What type of creature is a Meadow Brown?

16   Which continent is home to the addax, a type of antelope?

17   What is the world's largest and heaviest spider?

18   Which animal is also known as the red bear-cat or red cat-bear?

19   A form is the open-air home of which creature?

20   What type of bird has little ringed, grey and golden species?

Answers to QUIZ 432 – Money

1	1998	11	It is an emergency code (month 1, week 1)
2	Borrowing	12	1960
3	ERM (Exchange Rate Mechanism)	13	The Tower of London
4	Norman Lamont (Baron Lamont)	14	Farthing
5	William Pitt	15	Pink
6	1986	16	Monetarism
7	Sir Winston Churchill	17	1970s (1976)
8	Governor of the Bank of England	18	Thomas Jefferson
9	1997	19	Washington DC
10	Dorneywood	20	Christine Lagarde

ANSWERS ON PAGE 437

1   Spaghnum is a variety of which plant?

2   Who wrote the poem *Lochinvar*?

3   Which Irish writer wrote the 1992 book *An Evil Cradling* about his time as a hostage in Beirut?

4   Which seaport on the north-east coast of Brazil was formerly called Pernambuco?

5   Who would wear a custodian helmet in England and Wales?

6   In which county is the Beamish Open Air Museum located?

7   Lapine is the fictional language spoken by rabbits in which 1972 novel?

8   What term is given to the practice of growing trees and shrubs?

9   Which actress won an Oscar for *As Good as It Gets*?

10 Who directed the 2017 film *Baby Driver*?

11 *Everlasting Love* was a 1968 UK chart-topper for which group?

12 The moon Io belongs to which planet?

13 Chile contributes about a third of the global production of which metal?

14 Of which tree are aspen and cottonwood species?

15 In which century was David Livingstone born?

16 Which English king was nicknamed "Old Rowley", after his favourite racehorse?

17 Whom did Jonathan Pryce play in the 1996 film *Evita*?

18 In which year was the Scottish Parliament opened?

19 What type of creature is a brambling?

20 In the American Civil War, what colour uniform did the Confederate soldiers wear?

Easy
Medium
Hard

Answers to QUIZ 433 – Pot Luck

1	Lord Byron	11	Atlas
2	British	12	Chatsworth
3	Ariana Grande	13	Wax
4	Ernst Stavro	14	Wootton Bassett
5	Sarah	15	Atalanta
6	A pistol	16	Effective radiation dose
7	Sir Francis Beaufort	17	Mike Connor
8	*World of Warcraft*™	18	Bantry Bay
9	Sir Giles Gilbert Scott	19	Vauxhall
10	Khartoum	20	Vegetable

1 What make of car did Peter Kay drive in *Car Share*?

2 Which 1970s singer played Eddie Moon in *EastEnders* in 2011?

3 The crime drama series *DCI Banks* starred which actor in the title role?

4 In which year did Fiona Bruce first host BBC1's *Antiques Roadshow*?

5 Which TV historian presented *Jane Austen: Behind Closed Doors*?

6 What was the nickname of *Brookside*'s window cleaner?

7 In the series *Ugly Betty*, what was the name of the magazine where Betty worked?

8 Who was the original host of the TV game show *Family Fortunes*?

9 Which family owned 165 Eaton Place, London?

10 In *EastEnders*, which character did Stacey kill with the Queen Victoria bust?

11 Whose diaries, written for the Mass Observation project, were adapted for TV as *Housewife, 49…*?

12 …and who wrote and starred in it?

13 What is the name of the underwear factory in *Coronation Street*?

14 In what year was *Blue Peter* first broadcast?

15 In the series *NCIS*, what is the name of Pauley Perette's character?

16 Which co-presenter of the CBeebies series *Down on the Farm* first found fame as a member of JLS?

17 Which actor starred in the sitcom *May to December*?

18 Who were the original two team captains on *A Question of Sport*?

19 In the series *Unforgotten*, which actor plays the father of Nicola Walker's character?

20 What is the title of the makeover series presented by Charlie Dimmock with Harry and David Rich?

Easy / **Medium** / **Hard**

---

1. Which Italian town between Venice and Vicenza is associated with St Anthony?

2. In the Mario video games, what is the name of Mario's arch nemesis, often portrayed as "King of the Koopas"?

3. What is the traditional bingo call for the number 78?

4. Annie Lennox and Dave Stewart were in which band prior to forming the Eurythmics?

5. Which English agricultural pioneer invented the horse-drawn seed drill?

6. Which cartoonist created *The Far Side*?

7. Which group had a hit with the record *Star Trekkin'*?

8. What was the subtitle of the last film in the *Maze Runner* trilogy?

9. Which noblemen hold the highest hereditary titles in the British peerage?

10. In 1993, who succeeded Norman Lamont (Baron Lamont of Lerwick) as Chancellor of the Exchequer?

11. Into which sea does the Volga flow?

12. What name is given to the set of fans behind the intake at the front of a jet engine?

13. James Edward Stuart (b.1688) was given what nickname?

14. What was Frank Sinatra's middle name?

15. What soldier's uniform can be distinguished by its red tunic with equally spaced buttons and black bearskin cap?

16. In Greek myth, who was the mother of Achilles?

17. The Prior Park landscape garden in Somerset lies just outside which city?

18. What colour vapour does iodine give off when it is heated?

19. Which peninsula of NE Egypt lies between the Mediterranean and the Red Sea?

20. Dawn Ward and Tanya Bardsley became famous from appearing in which reality TV show?

Easy

Medium

Hard

Answers to QUIZ 435 – Pot Luck

1	Moss	11	Love Affair
2	Sir Walter Scott	12	Jupiter
3	Brian Keenan	13	Copper
4	Recife	14	Poplar
5	A member of the police	15	19th century
6	County Durham	16	Charles II
7	*Watership Down*	17	Juan Perón
8	Arboriculture	18	1999
9	Helen Hunt	19	A bird
10	Edgar Wright	20	Grey

Easy

1 Anne Hyde was the first wife of which Scottish king?

2 Eritrea gained independence from which other African country in 1993?

3 Aphrodite, Athena and Hera took part in a beauty contest judged by which character in Greek mythology?

4 *Electra* was written by which ancient Greek playwright?

5 Augustus Pugin and Sir Charles Barry were responsible for building which London landmark in the mid-19th century?

6 The *Encyclopedia Britannica* was first published in which decade?

7 Akron is a city in which US state?

8 *Eurotrash* was presented by Antoine de Caunes and which fashion designer?

9 *All I Have to Give* was a 1998 no.2 hit for which group?

10 Ezra Pound, the poet and critic, was born in which century?

Medium

11 Arnold Schwarzenegger featured in which 1977 film about the Mr Olympia competition?

12 *Ex officio* has what English translation?

13 Angus Prune was a character on which 1960s-70s radio show?

14 Ergonomics is the study of what?

15 Australia and New Zealand have competed annually since 1947 for which Rugby Union trophy?

16 *Elektra* was a 2005 film starring which actress in the title role?

17 Axilla is the medical name for which part of the body?

18 Echinacea is a member of which family of plants?

19 "Avatar" originally referred to the manifestation of a deity in which religion?

20 *East Lynne* was an 1861 novel by which author?

Hard

Answers to QUIZ 436 – Television

1	Fiat	11	Nella Last
2	David Essex	12	Victoria Wood
3	Stephen Tompkinson	13	Underworld
4	2008	14	1958
5	Lucy Worsley	15	Abby Sciuto
6	Sinbad	16	JB Gill
7	*Mode*	17	Anton Rodgers
8	Bob Monkhouse	18	Cliff Morgan and Sir Henry Cooper
9	The Bellamys (*Upstairs, Downstairs*)	19	Peter Egan
10	Archie Mitchell	20	*Garden Rescue*

1 Who wrote the 1974 war novel *The Dogs of War*?

2 In darts, what is the lowest score that cannot be scored with a single dart?

3 On which river are the Victoria Falls?

4 In which city was the 2016 film *Sing Street* set?

5 Which singer released the 2016 album *A Better World*?

6 What is the code for Frankfurt airport?

7 The fig belongs to which family of plants?

8 Who wrote the novel *The African Queen*?

9 In which decade of the 20th century was George Harrison born?

10 Which film critic wrote the 2010 book *It's Only a Movie*?

11 The TV series *Angel* and *Bones* both starred which leading actor?

12 The first Battle of St Alban's (1455) marked the beginning of which conflict?

13 Which south coast city grew from an ancient settlement called Brighthelmstone?

14 In Morse code what letter is represented by one dash?

15 Clothes rationing was introduced in Britain in 1941 and abolished in which year?

16 "I stop and stare at you, walking on the shore, I try to concentrate, my mind wants to explore" is the opening line from which song?

17 The "Real Deal" was the nickname of which former heavyweight champion boxer?

18 On the introduction of the Council Tax in 1993, which London council set the lowest amount?

19 In which decade did table-tennis become an Olympic sport?

20 John Jarndyce is a character in which Charles Dickens novel?

Answers to QUIZ 437 – Pot Luck

1	Padua	11	Caspian Sea
2	Bowser	12	Compressor
3	Heaven's gate	13	The Old Pretender
4	The Tourists	14	Albert
5	Jethro Tull	15	Grenadier Guard uniform
6	Gary Larson	16	Thetis
7	The Firm	17	Bath
8	*The Death Cure*	18	Violet
9	Dukes	19	Sinai
10	Kenneth Clarke	20	*The Real Housewives of Cheshire*

Easy

1   Who became Premier of Ireland in 1982?

2   Sovereignty of which country was handed back by Britain to President Canaan Banana in 1980?

3   The proceedings from the House of Commons were first televised in which year?

4   In which year of the 1980s did Queen Elizabeth II become the first British monarch to make a state visit to China?

5   What did Sue Brown become the first woman to do in 1981?

6   How old was Michael Foot when he became Labour leader?

7   In which year was the official opening of the Humber Bridge?

8   Who won the 1980 Booker Prize with the book *Rites of Passage*?

9   Which war took place in the Middle East from 1980-88?

10 What was the name of the Russian movement that began in the 1980s, the English translation of which is "restructuring"?

Medium

11 Which popular horse won his first (of four) King George VI Chase in 1986?

12 Nicolae Ceauçescu was overthrown as leader of which country in 1989?

13 Who became US President in 1980?

14 Which two countries joined the European Union in 1986?

15 In 1985, who captained Europe to their Ryder Cup victory?

16 Who was the leader of the Soviet Union from 1984 until his death in March 1985?

17 What was the name of the space shuttle that began operations in 1988?

18 In economic terms, how was October 19, 1987 described?

19 What was the best-selling single in the UK in the 1980s?

20 Which football team won the Football League title (then called the First Division) for three consecutive years starting in 1981?

Hard

Answers to QUIZ 438 – A & E

1	James II	11	*Pumping Iron*
2	Ethiopia	12	Based on your position
3	Paris	13	*I'm Sorry, I'll Read That Again*
4	Sophocles	14	The working environment
5	Palace of Westminster	15	Bledisloe Cup
6	1770s (1771)	16	Jennifer Garner
7	Ohio	17	Armpit
8	Jean-Paul Gaultier	18	Daisy family
9	Backstreet Boys	19	Hinduism
10	19th century	20	Ellen (Mrs) Henry Wood

ANSWERS ON PAGE **443**

1 Which city is nicknamed the "Mile High City"?

2 Where was Lillie Langtry born in 1853?

3 In the late 1800s and early 1900s, firefighters wore a blue uniform made from which material?

4 What was the location of the 2002 Winter Olympics?

5 The 2008 book *Who Runs Britain?* was written by which journalist?

6 In which year was the current London Bridge formally opened…?

7 …and in which decade was its predecessor, the "New London Bridge" originally opened?

8 The branches of which evergreen tree were traditionally carried at funerals?

9 *Puttin' On the Ritz* was written by which composer?

10 In which country is Mount Pinatubo?

11 Which English king was married to Sophia Dorothea?

12 Which British general surrendered his army after the 1781 siege of Yorktown?

13 Scrapie is a viral disease in what type of animal?

14 Which marine creature has common, leafy and ruby species?

15 Who starred as Jimmy in the 1979 film *Quadrophenia*?

16 Better known as an essayist and caricaturist, who wrote the 1911 novel *Zuleika Dobson*?

17 What are Tony Blair's middle names?

18 In the 2016 film *Moana*, who voiced the character of Maui?

19 The town of Swaffham is in which county?

20 In which decade of the 20th century was astronaut Neil Armstrong born?

Easy

Medium

Hard

Answers to QUIZ 439 – Pot Luck

1	Frederick Forsyth	11	David Boreanaz
2	23	12	The Wars of the Roses
3	Zambezi	13	Brighton
4	Dublin	14	T
5	Chris de Burgh	15	1949
6	FRA	16	*Mysterious Girl* (Peter Andre)
7	*Ficus*	17	Evander Holyfield
8	CS Forester	18	Wandsworth
9	1940s	19	1980s (1988)
10	Mark Kermode	20	*Bleak House*

ANSWERS ON PAGE 444

1   What term is given to the study of plant and animal cells?

2   Botanist Sir Joseph Banks accompanied whom on their "first voyage" to Brazil, Tahiti, New Zealand and Australia?

3   Deuterium is an isotope of which element?

4   Which metal is the best conductor of electricity?

5   Fear of water is a symptom of which viral illness?

6   Which silvery-white metal is a constituent of brass?

7   Which taxonomic classification is immediately above "order"?

8   What does a syrinx help a bird to do?

9   The study of fluids moving in pipes is given what name?

10 A doctor's instrument for examining the ear has what name?

11 Which element has the atomic number 50?

12 Which radioactive isotope is used for dating old materials?

13 In our solar system, which of the planets has a diameter of approximately 72,000 miles?

14 What two-word name is given to the whole passage along which food passes?

15 What is controlled by a rheostat?

16 Between which two planets would you find the main asteroid belt in our solar system?

17 In which South American Desert is the Paranal Observatory located?

18 Who formulated the uncertainty principle in quantum mechanics?

19 What is the name of the Serbian electrical engineer best known for designing the alternating current electric system?

20 Chlorine is named after which colour?

Answers to QUIZ 440 – The 1980s

1	Garret FitzGerald	11	Desert Orchid - Dessie
2	Zimbabwe (formerly Rhodesia)	12	Romania
3	1989	13	Ronald Reagan
4	1986	14	Spain and Portugal
5	Take part in the Boat Race	15	Tony Jacklin
6	67	16	Konstantin Chernenko
7	1981	17	*Discovery*
8	William Golding	18	Black Monday (stock market crash)
9	Iran-Iraq War	19	*Do They Know it's Christmas* (Band Aid)
10	*Perestroika*	20	Liverpool FC

1 Of which US state is Trenton the capital?

2 Who played the title character in the 2016 film *Doctor Strange*?

3 If you took the shortest ferry crossing from Dublin to Wales, where would you disembark?

4 Stonecrop belongs to which family of plants?

5 What type of car was the G-Wiz?

6 The toucan is native to which continent?

7 In which country can the airport with code KUL be found?

8 What does CSR stand for in relation to a company's ethical position?

9 Rebecca Stephens became the first British woman to reach the summit of Everest in which decade?

10 Who wrote the 1850 novel *The Black Tulip*?

11 Who topped the singles charts in 1970 with *Band of Gold*?

12 Which brewing company is based at Southwold in Suffolk?

13 What is the name of the main protagonist of the *Legend of Zelda*™ series of video games?

14 In 1998, which Japanese emperor visited England?

15 Which two politicians shared the Nobel Peace Prize in 1998?

16 In which two fields of work was Johannes Kepler (b.1571) famous?

17 What is the Falkirk Wheel an example of?

18 What is the name of the Scottish economist who has featured on the £20 note since 2007?

19 In which century was Beethoven born?

20 What was Tokyo called before 1868?

Easy

Medium

Hard

Answers to QUIZ 441 – Pot Luck

1	Denver	11	George I
2	Jersey	12	Charles Cornwallis
3	Wool	13	Sheep
4	Salt Lake City	14	Sea dragon
5	Robert Peston	15	Phil Daniels
6	1973	16	Sir Max Beerbohm
7	1830s (1831)	17	Charles Lynton
8	Cypress	18	Dwayne Johnson
9	Irving Berlin	19	Norfolk
10	The Philippines	20	1930s

Easy

1. What is the name given to a Spanish chaperone?
2. Which country has the last capital alphabetically?
3. Which musical instrument featured on the original flag of the Republic of Ireland?
4. Vilnius is the capital of which small Baltic country?
5. What Ancient Roman officer traditionally wore a horse-hair crested helmet and wielded a club known as a vine staff?
6. What nationality is someone from Lublin or Lodz?
7. By what name are the Funchal Islands usually referred to?
8. To which country do the Faroe Islands belong?
9. In which country is the Court of Justice of the European Union based?
10. What is the second-longest river in Ireland?

Medium

11. Of which country is Koper a major port?
12. Which king was married to Henrietta Maria of France?
13. Which Italian coastal region extends from Tuscany to the French border?
14. Vorarlberg and Burgenland are states in which country?
15. Which three colours appear on the flag of Estonia?
16. The Riksdag is the parliament of which country?
17. The lagoon Lagoa de Obidos is in which country?
18. What is the name of the stainless steel building in Brussels, constructed in 1951?
19. What is the unit of currency in Romania?
20. The Italian region of Piedmont has which city as its capital?

Hard

Answers to QUIZ 442 – Science

1	Cytology	11	Tin
2	James Cook	12	Carbon 14
3	Hydrogen	13	Saturn
4	Silver	14	Alimentary canal
5	Rabies	15	Electric current
6	Zinc	16	Mars and Jupiter
7	Class	17	The Atacama Desert
8	Sing	18	Werner Heisenberg
9	Hydraulics/fluid dynamics	19	Nikola Tesla
10	Otoscope	20	Yellowish green

ANSWERS ON PAGE **447**

1   Which hundred-eyed giant of Greek mythology is also a common newspaper name?

2   A neuron is part of which system of the body?

3   In which county is the town of Settle?

4   Which actor is associated with a version of the Six Degrees of Separation theory?

5   Who recorded the song *Cheap Thrills* in 2016?

6   The "Sunflower State" is the nickname of which US state?

7   On an Ordnance Survey map, what is indicated by the abbreviation MP?

8   For what did the initials PG stand in PG Wodehouse's name?

9   In which century was Captain James Cook born?

10 Who rode Devon Loch in the 1956 Grand National?

11 What was the RSPCA endorsement "RSPCA Assured" formerly known as?

12 In the UK Parliament, who is the chief usher of the Lord Chamberlain's department?

13 What type of watch is specifically designed so that the wearer can view its internal parts?

14 The seguidilla is a dance from which country?

15 Which former model found fame in 1989 as co-presenter on *Wheel of Fortune*?

16 In what profession was Beth Chatto (d.2018) a famous name?

17 Which Port was founded in the 19th century by the Lever brothers?

18 Which sport is played at Odsal stadium in Bradford?

19 In 1996, who became the first person to have been awarded Oscars for both acting and screenwriting?

20 Coriander is also referred to as a parsley from which country?

Answers to QUIZ 443 – Pot Luck

1	New Jersey	11	Freda Payne
2	Benedict Cumberbatch	12	Adnams
3	Holyhead	13	Link
4	Sedum	14	Emperor Akihito
5	Electric	15	John Hume and David Trimble (Baron Trimble)
6	South America	16	Mathematics and astronomy
7	Malaysia (Kuala Lumpur)	17	Boat lift
8	Corporate Social Responsibility	18	Adam Smith
9	1990s (1993)	19	18th century
10	Alexandre Dumas	20	Edo

Easy

1   Which winter sport is governed by the WCF?

2   What is the distance between the bases in baseball?

3   How wide is a cricket pitch?

4   Who were the first country to win the World Cup four times?

5   In which sport do teams compete for the Sam Maguire Cup?

6   Where in London is the headquarters of the Football Association?

7   At which sporting venue will you find the Jack Hobbs Gates?

8   Which type of Formula 1 tyre is indicated by a red colour?

9   What were the two first names of cricket legend WG Grace?

10 Which professional sport is played by the Pittsburgh Penguins?

Medium

11 In 1996 which football team became the first club to win the double of FA Cup and League twice?

12 Which country's national cricket team is nicknamed The Tigers?

13 Who was the first man to score two triple centuries in Test Cricket?

14 Which Rugby League team won the "grand slam" of trophies in 1995?

15 In which sport do teams complete for the Swaythling Cup?

16 Murderball was the original name for which sport?

17 Which team won the FA Cup Final in 2009?

18 In which sport do teams compete for the Cowdray Park Gold Cup?

19 At the European athletics championships in 1986, who famously ran a leg of the gold-medal winning men's 4x400 metre relay race wearing only one shoe?

20 In which year did the Five Nations Rugby tournament become the Six Nations?

Hard

Answers to QUIZ 444 – Europe

1	Duenna	11	Slovenia
2	Croatia (Zagreb)	12	Charles I
3	The harp	13	Liguria
4	Lithuania	14	Austria
5	Centurion	15	Blue, black and white
6	Polish	16	Sweden
7	Madeira	17	Portugal
8	Denmark	18	The Atomium
9	Luxembourg	19	Leu
10	Barrow	20	Turin

ANSWERS ON PAGE **449**

1 Which 2017 short film about a deaf girl won an Oscar for Best Short Film (Live Action)?

2 *Cold Lazarus* and *Karaoke* were the last works of which playwright?

3 Which chef is best known for being the *haute cuisine* teacher on the reality show *Ladette to Lady*?

4 Jacinda Ardern became the Prime Minister of which country in 2017?

5 In 1993 Barbara Harmer became the first woman to fly which plane?

6 What type of bird is a shoveler?

7 What is the state capital of Montana?

8 In 1963, who knocked Muhammad Ali to the canvas in the fourth round of their contest at Wembley Stadium?

9 Which type of tyre is indicated by a yellow colour in F1?

10 The island of Guam is in which ocean?

11 In which Surrey town was Paul Weller born?

12 The James Norris trophy is awarded annually to the defence player who demonstrates throughout the season the greatest all-around ability in the position: in which sport?

13 On an Ordnance Survey map, what is indicated by a light orange area speckled with black?

14 In which year was the National Minimum Wage introduced?

15 How many children were there in Enid Blyton's *Famous Five*?

16 What is the term for a wide railway track measurement?

17 What do the initials LPG stand for in relation to driving?

18 George III's "madness" was caused by which disease?

19 What was Harold Macmillan's (First Earl of Stockton's) real first name?

20 Salvias are members of which family of plants?

Answers to QUIZ 445 – Pot Luck

1	Argus	11	Freedom Food
2	Nervous system	12	Black Rod
3	North Yorkshire	13	Skeleton watch
4	Kevin Bacon	14	Spain
5	Sia	15	Carol Smillie
6	Kansas	16	Gardening
7	Mile post	17	Port Sunlight
8	Pelham Grenville	18	Rugby League
9	18th century	19	Dame Emma Thompson
10	Dick Francis	20	China

Easy

Medium

Hard

1. What is the English translation of Richard Wagner's opera *Götterdämmerung*?
2. Who painted the canvases for the ceilings in London's Banqueting House?
3. Whose Symphony No. 7 is known as the *Leningrad Symphony*?
4. Produced in Paris in 1911, who wrote the opera *The Spanish Hour*?
5. In which century was the artist Francis Bacon born?
6. What type of animal was Salvador Dali's pet, Babou?
7. Which composer wrote a symphony known as *The Clock*?
8. What was the nationality of the composer Gustav Holst?
9. The 1880s painting *A Sunday Afternoon on the Island of La Grande Jatte* was by which artist?
10. Who wrote the *War Requiem* for the consecration of Coventry Cathedral in 1962?

11. Which vocal range might be described as a coloratura?
12. The 1942 work *Nighthawks* is a painting by which artist...?
13. ...and what was his nationality?
14. Who wrote the 1962 opera *King Priam*?
15. Which pop artist designed the cover of *Sergeant Pepper's Lonely Hearts Club Band*?
16. What was the name of Wagner's second wife, whom he married in 1870?
17. For what type of painting was John Singer Sargent best known?
18. If a musical piece is written in the key of E, how many sharps does it have as its key signature?
19. The composer Puccini died in which century?
20. Which device on a pipe organ produces a wobbling effect to the note?

Answers to QUIZ 446 – Team Sports

1	Curling	11	Manchester United FC
2	90 feet	12	Bangladesh
3	Ten feet	13	Sir Donald Bradman
4	Brazil	14	Wigan Warriors
5	Gaelic football (Ireland)	15	Table tennis
6	Wembley Stadium	16	Wheelchair Rugby
7	The Oval	17	Chelsea
8	Supersoft	18	Polo
9	William Gilbert	19	Brian Whittle
10	Ice hockey	20	2000

QUIZ 449 – Pot Luck

1 If you were visiting the historic Alamo fort, in which town would you be?

2 Which 1996 action thriller starred John Travolta and Christian Slater?

3 What type of creature is a Camberwell Beauty?

4 As what did Melita Norwood achieve notoriety in 1999?

5 How many miles long is the M25 motorway?

6 Which ex-*TOWIE* sisters were the subject of the series *The Mummy Diaries*?

7 Who wrote the 1980 novel *Sins of the Fathers*?

8 Who sang the 1964 hit *My Boy Lollipop*?

9 *Chapter One* was whose debut album in October 2014?

10 The Schneider Trophy name was revived in 1981, but which type of craft competed for it between 1913 and 1931?

11 Who, in Greek mythology, married Andromeda?

12 Maria Fitzherbert was the secret wife of which king?

13 In Shakespeare's *The Merchant of Venice*, which character puts on boy's clothes to elope with Lorenzo?

14 The mouth of the Potomac River overlooks which bay?

15 In which 1959 film did Laurence Harvey star as Joe Lampton?

16 The 2005 novel *No Country for Old Men* was written by which author?

17 Which journalist and author wrote *The Tipping Point* (2000) and *Blink* (2005)?

18 Which planet has an outer ring, an inner ring and a "crepe" ring?

19 In Salford, which sport was played at The Willows?

20 How is the shrub family *Lonicera* more commonly known?

Answers to QUIZ 447 – Pot Luck

1	The Silent Child	11	Woking
2	Dennis Potter	12	Ice hockey
3	Rosemary Shrager	13	Shingle
4	New Zealand	14	1999
5	Concorde	15	Four (one was a dog)
6	Duck	16	Broad gauge
7	Helena	17	Liquified Petroleum Gas
8	Sir Henry Cooper	18	Porphyria
9	Soft	19	Maurice
10	Pacific Ocean	20	Mint

1 Which item kept in the home was named after the Roman goddess of hearths and fires?

2 The butler's sink has two different styles, named after which two cities?

3 In which decade was the distinctive Trimphone designed?

4 In which town did IKEA open its first British store?

5 What was the original full name of the former company known as MFI?

6 On a VOC rating on paint or chemicals, what does VOC stand for?

7 Gustav Dalen, winner of the Nobel Prize in Physics in 1912, invented which brand of cooker?

8 Where in the home would you find a TRV?

9 Which company manufactured the first fully automatic kettle?

10 In relation to lighting, what is a CFL?

11 What would a member of APDO help you do?

12 What general term is given to water that has already been used in the home, such as for a bath or in the washing machine?

13 In Roman villas, what did a hypocaust do?

14 Which branded cleaner derives its name from sodium perborate and sodium silicate, two of its original ingredients?

15 The 1901 "Puffing Billy" was an early version of which household item?

16 Microwave energy was originally developed for use with what piece of equipment during WWII...?

17 ...and in what year did the microwave oven first go on sale?

18 The Red House in Kent was designed and built by Philip Webb in collaboration with which designer?

19 What is the French term for the dining room?

20 The word "sofa" derives from the word *suffah* in which language?

Answers to QUIZ 448 – Art and Music

1	*Twilight of the Gods*	11	Soprano
2	Peter Paul Rubens	12	Edward Hopper
3	Shostakovich	13	American
4	Maurice Ravel	14	Sir Michael Tippett
5	20th century	15	Sir Peter Blake
6	Ocelot	16	Cosima
7	Haydn	17	Portrait
8	British	18	Four
9	Georges Seurat	19	20th century
10	Benjamin Britten (Baron Britten)	20	Tremulant

1 Bettany Hughes is a presenter of what type of programme?

2 What is the traditional bingo call for the number 73?

3 How is the London landmark of BAPS Shri Swaminarayan Mandir more commonly referred to?

4 NP is the postcode area code for which town?

5 Who was Hera's Roman equivalent?

6 Which mathematician and philosopher (d.1978) was known for his Incompleteness Theorem?

7 Tanzania, Uganda, South Sudan, Ethiopia, and Somalia all border which other country?

8 How long is the Epsom Derby?

9 Who succeeded Cecil Parkinson and preceded Norman Tebbit (Baron Tebbit) as Chairman of the Conservative party, serving from 1983 to 1985?

10 What is the code for O'Hare international airport, located in Chicago, Illinois?

11 According to legend, which children's toy was used by Filipino hunters as a method of catching animals?

12 What is a phalarope?

13 Who was the mother of Henry VII?

14 In 1997, who became President of the Republic of Ireland?

15 Corbetts, Grahams and Nuttalls are all types of what?

16 Which Briton became men's figure skating world champion in 1976?

17 Who starred in the 2008 film adaptation of *Max Payne*?

18 In 1987, who sang about the capital of Catalonia?

19 Who wrote the 1991 family history *Wild Swans...*?

20 ...and collaborated with Jon Halliday on a 2005 biography of which leader?

Easy

Medium

Hard

Answers to QUIZ 449 – Pot Luck

1	San Antonio	11	Perseus
2	*Broken Arrow*	12	George IV
3	Butterfly	13	Jessica
4	A spy	14	Chesapeake
5	117 miles	15	*Room at the Top*
6	Sam and Billie Faiers	16	Cormac McCarthy
7	Susan Howatch	17	Malcolm Gladwell
8	Millie	18	Saturn
9	Ella Henderson	19	Rugby League
10	Seaplanes	20	Honeysuckle

Easy

1 Which group released the 1997 single *Brimful of Asha*?

2 What was the title of Gary Barlow's second solo single?

3 Tori Amos was given which first name at birth?

4 *The Shoop Shoop Song (It's in His Kiss)* was remade for which 1990 film starring Cher?

5 In 1997, Jon Bon Jovi sang about *Midnight* in which area of London?

6 The Spice Girls released *Who Do You Think You Are* as a double A-side single with which other song?

7 In his guise as The Fresh Prince, with whom did Will Smith have the no.1 hit *Boom! Shake the Room*?

8 *Talk on Corners* was a 1997 album by which group?

9 What was the title of U2's 1991 album?

10 How many consecutive weeks did Bryan Adams' *(Everything I Do) I Do it for You* spend at the top of the UK charts?

11 Which TV theme tune did Mark Snow take into the charts in 1996?

12 What was the name of Whitney Houston's character in *The Bodyguard*, who sang *I Will Always Love You*?

Medium

13 Richard and Fred Fairbrass founded which 1990s trio?

14 "City dweller, successful fella thought to himself Oops I've got a lot of money" were the opening lyrics from which song?

15 In which year did Take That top the charts with *Back for Good*?

16 Which group's version of *Young at Heart* was used to advertise Volkswagen cars in the 1990s?

17 Which duo sang *Would I Lie To You* in 1992?

18 In which year did Sir Elton John have his first no.1 single with *Sacrifice/Healing Hands*?

19 What was the title of the 1991 novelty record released by Hale and Pace to raise funds for Comic Relief?

20 In which country were the group Ace of Base formed?

Hard

Answers to QUIZ 450 – Around the House

1	The vesta match	11	Declutter and organise
2	London and Belfast	12	Greywater
3	1960s	13	Provide heating
4	Warrington, Cheshire	14	Persil
5	Mullard Furniture Industries	15	Vacuum cleaner
6	Volatile organic compound	16	Radar
7	Aga	17	1947
8	On a radiator (thermostatic radiator valve)	18	William Morris
9	Russell Hobbs (1955)	19	*La salle à manger*
10	Compact fluorescent lamp	20	Arabic

QUIZ 453 – Pot Luck

1. What nationality are former tennis players Kim Clijsters and Justin Henin?

2. Which London Underground District Line stop is the closest to Stamford Bridge, home of Chelsea Football Club?

3. The folk duo First Aid Kit come from which country?

4. Who was UK Prime Minister from 1770 to 1787?

5. How is the shrub *Pyracantha* better known?

6. What is the state capital of Virginia, USA?

7. What is the first country reached on travelling directly north from Tokyo?

8. Margaret of Anjou was married to which English king?

9. Mr Tumnus is a character created by which author?

10. Of what is oneirology the study?

11. Who wrote the 1999 book *Galileo's Daughter*?

12. *Mirror in the Bathroom* was a 1980 single by which band?

13. Who rode Troy, Henbit, Nashwan and Erhaab to Derby victories in 1979, 1980, 1989 and 1994 respectively?

14. Which actor starred in the film *The Secret of My Success*?

15. Who designed Queen Mary's Dolls House, on display in Windsor Castle?

16. In the TV series *Friday Night Dinner*, who plays Martin?

17. What was the first name of Saga's detective partner in the third and fourth series of *The Bridge*?

18. In the novel and film *The Girl with All the Gifts*, what is the name of the girl?

19. What type of creature is a marmoset?

20. In which National Park is the Valley of the Rocks?

Answers to QUIZ 451 – Pot Luck

1. History
2. Queen B
3. Neasden Temple
4. Newport
5. Juno
6. Kurt Gödel
7. Kenya
8. 1 mile 4 furlongs
9. John Selwyn Gummer (Baron Deben)
10. ORD
11. The yo-yo
12. Bird
13. Lady Margaret Beaufort
14. Mary McAleese
15. Mountains
16. John Curry
17. Mark Wahlberg
18. Montserrat Caballé and Freddie Mercury
19. Jung Chang
20. Chairman Mao

1 What is the YHA?

2 What would you make with tesserae?

3 Which pastime involves a mixture of map reading and cross country running...?

4 ...and which other outdoor pursuit involves using a GPS or mobile phone to locate hidden objects?

5 Which playing card is known as the "Curse of Scotland"?

6 How many counters are on a backgammon board at start of play?

7 In knitting, which yarn is thicker, double knitting or four-ply?

8 In which year was Trivial Pursuit™ commercially released?

9 Crimps and calottes are used in which craft pursuit?

10 Which pastime is named after the tool used to create it?

11 Which card game is based round dealing on the stock market?

12 What is a cruciverbalist keen on?

13 How many squares on a Rubik's Cube™ never move?

14 Which table-top game derives its name from the Latin name of a bird of prey?

15 Origami involves paper-folding, but what is kirigami?

16 What does a player have to do in the game of Pelmanism?

17 A Canopy Relative Work (CReW) manoeuvre would be carried out in which pursuit?

18 What is the American term for abseiling?

19 What game is the card game Mhing based on?

20 On an Ordnance Survey map, what is indicated by a blue footprint symbol?

Answers to QUIZ 452 – 1990s Music

1	Cornershop	11	*The X-Files*
2	*Love Won't Wait*	12	Rachel Marron
3	Myra	13	Right Said Fred
4	*Mermaids*	14	*Country House* (Blur)
5	Chelsea	15	1995
6	*Mama*	16	The Bluebells
7	Jazzy Jeff	17	Charles & Eddie
8	The Corrs	18	1990
9	*Achtung Baby*	19	*The Stonk*
10	16	20	Sweden

QUIZ 455 – Pot Luck

ANSWERS ON PAGE 457

1 What colour stripe indicates a hypersoft tyre in Formula 1?

2 In which decade of the 20th century was George Best (d.2005) born?

3 Which prince led the Russian forces at the 1854 Battle of Alma?

4 Published in 1975, what was the title of the second part of actor David Niven's autobiography?

5 Which museum is located at Singleton, West Sussex?

6 Hughenden Manor in Buckinghamshire was the country home of which Prime Minister?

7 The colobus monkey is native to which continent?

8 What colour is the second-highest belt to the black belt in judo?

9 Of which US state is Montpelier the capital?

10 Which group had a hit with *The Power* in 1990?

11 What was a troubadour's medieval poem or song that had either ten or 13 lines?

12 In the USA, what type of furniture was a Davenport?

13 Which king was nicknamed "Silly Billy"?

14 In greyhound racing, what does GBGB stand for?

15 Which inventor, born in County Waterford in 1627, is often regarded as the first modern chemist?

16 What was the name of Gandalf's white stallion in *The Lord of the Rings*?

17 Epsilon occupies which place in the Greek alphabet?

18 In which year in the 1990s did the Conservative party win their fourth General Election in a row?

19 Which TV series based in the hip-hop music industry follows the fortunes of the Lyon family?

20 The city of Palo Alto is in which US state?

Easy

Medium

Hard

Answers to QUIZ 453 – Pot Luck

1	Belgian	11	Dava Sobel
2	Fulham Broadway	12	The Beat
3	Sweden	13	Willie Carson
4	Lord Frederick North	14	Michael J Fox
5	Firethorn	15	Sir Edwin Lutyens
6	Richmond	16	Paul Ritter
7	Russia	17	Henrik
8	Henry VI	18	Melanie
9	CS Lewis	19	Monkey or primate
10	Dreams	20	Exmoor

ANSWERS ON PAGE 458

Easy

1 In the title of the Shakespeare play, who is Cymbeline?

2 Who opened the recreated Globe Theatre in 1997?

3 How is the National Theatre of Ireland better known?

4 In ballet, what is the name of a jump where the feet are crossed and uncrossed?

5 Which Sir Tom Stoppard play opens with the two title characters betting on the outcome of tossing a coin?

6 Who wrote the 1612 play *The White Devil*?

7 Which musical was billed as "Shakespeare's forgotten rock and roll masterpiece"?

8 What does "coryphée" indicate against a ballet dancer's name?

9 Which Russian playwright wrote *Summerfolk*, first published in 1905?

10 In which branch of the arts did Dame Joan Sutherland achieve fame?

Medium

11 Which perfoming arts venue has the postcode WC2E 9DD?

12 The characters Brick and Maggie appear in which Tennessee Williams play?

13 In opera or ballet, what does a répétiteur do?

14 Which songwriting team wrote the music and lyrics to *Les Misérables*?

15 The award winning play *Humble Boy*, which premiered at the National Theatre in 2001, was written by which playwright?

16 Performance poet Benjamin Zephaniah appears in the TV series *Peaky Blinders* as which character?

17 Choreographer and dancer Crystal Pite was born in which country?

18 What is traditional Japanese masked drama called?

19 What is the Latin phrase for the list of characters given at the beginning of a play's script?

20 Originally called the Royal Coburg Theatre, which theatre was first opened in 1818 during the Regency period and is the only theatre in London from that time still in business?

Hard

Answers to QUIZ 454 – Leisure

1	Youth Hostels Association	11	Pit
2	A mosaic	12	Crossword puzzles
3	Orienteering	13	Six
4	Geocaching	14	Subbuteo (*Falco subbuteo*)
5	Nine of diamonds	15	Paper cutting
6	Thirty	16	Find matching pairs of cards
7	Double knitting	17	Parachuting
8	1981	18	Rapelling
9	Jewellery-making	19	Mah jong
10	Jigsaw	20	Nature trails or walks

ANSWERS ON PAGE 459

1   In which mythology did the character of Prometheus occur?

2   Which car company manufactures the Galaxy?

3   Who co-starred with Michelle Pfeiffer in the 1982 film *Grease 2*?

4   In which decade did the first launderette open in the UK?

5   Silverstone Racetrack is in which county?

6   On which continent did hammocks originate?

7   Which political leader adopted the name "Conservative" for what was at the time called the Tory party?

8   Which concert venue has the postcode SW7 2AP?

9   "Tweak of the thumb" is the traditional bingo call for which number?

10 What type of material is fuller's earth?

11 What relation was Richard III to Edward IV?

12 In which decade of the 20th century was Brigitte Bardot born?

13 What is the state capital of Minnesota?

14 Who wrote about *The Secret Life of Walter Mitty*?

15 On which racecourse is The Cesarewitch Handicap run?

16 What is the name of Ruby O'Donnell's character in the TV series *Hollyoaks*?

17 What soft white mineral is used to make plaster of Paris?

18 What is a protea?

19 In which 1945 allegorical novel do pigs take over from humans?

20 *Sette* is the Italian word for which number?

Easy

Medium

Hard

Answers to QUIZ 455 – Pot Luck

1	Pink	11	Rondeau
2	1940s	12	Sofa
3	Prince Alexander Menshikov	13	William IV
4	*Bring On the Empty Horses*	14	Greyhound Board of Great Britain
5	Weald and Downland Living Museum	15	Robert Boyle
6	Benjamin Disraeli (First Earl of Beaconsfield)	16	Shadowfax
7	Africa	17	Fifth
8	Brown	18	1992
9	Vermont	19	*Empire*
10	Snap	20	California

1 *A Is for Alibi* is the first in which series by Sue Grafton?

2 What is the name of *The Island* in Victoria Hislop's novel?

3 Winner of the 2018 Costa Debut Novel award, who wrote *Eleanor Oliphant Is Completely Fine*?

4 What is Matthew Shardlake's profession in the novels by CJ Sansom?

5 What is the name of Nanny Ogg's cat in the *Discworld* series?

6 Which fictional character employed Della Street as his secretary?

7 John and Isabella Thorpe are characters in which Jane Austen novel?

8 How many books by Patricia Highsmith feature Tom Ripley?

9 The 2017 novel *Midnight Line* was the 22nd to feature which character?

10 What was the title of Jessie Burton's 2014 debut novel?

11 The Crime Writer's Association make various awards annually. By what name are these awards known?

12 Who wrote the fantasy series *The Belgariad* and *The Malloreon*?

13 Who wrote the 1961 sci-fi novel *Stranger in a Strange Land*?

14 In which century was Geoffrey Chaucer born?

15 What completes this quotation from Sherlock Holmes to Doctor Watson, "You see but you do not ___"?

16 In the novels by Michael Connelly, what is the real first name of Harry Bosch?

17 *The Duchess* is a 2017 novel by which author, whose first novel *Going Home* was published in 1973?

18 Who wrote the 2001 novel *American Gods*, which was adapted for TV in 2017?

19 Which Ian McEwan novel features Edward Mayhew and Florence Ponting?

20 In *The Lord of the Rings*, who or what is Glamdring?

Answers to QUIZ 456 – Performing Arts

1 King of England
2 Queen Elizabeth II and Prince Philip
3 Abbey Theatre
4 Entrechat
5 *Rosencrantz and Guildernstern Are Dead*
6 John Webster
7 *Return to the Forbidden Planet*
8 Principal dancer
9 Maxim Gorky
10 Opera
11 Royal Opera House
12 *Cat on a Hot Tin Roof*
13 Coaches the singers or dancers
14 Claude-Michel Schönberg and Alain Boublil
15 Charlotte Jones
16 Jeremiah (Jimmy) Jesus
17 Canada
18 Noh
19 *Dramatis personae*
20 The Old Vic

ANSWERS ON PAGE 461

1   Which US state is nicknamed the "Volunteer State"?

2   The Grand Palace is in which Asian capital city?

3   For what reason did physician Dr Neil Arnott (b.1788) invent the waterbed?

4   In which country would you find airports with the codes PVG, CAN and CTU?

5   What term was given to those responsible for maintaining law and order in England's royal forests?

6   Which 2012 film about a financial fraud starred Richard Gere and Tim Roth?

7   Who plays George Warleggan in the revived series of *Poldark*?

8   What was the first British solo top ten hit for Roger Daltrey?

9   *Chanson D'Amour* was a hit for which group in 1977?

10 Which king was on the throne of England at the start of the Hundred Years' War?

11 The cashew nut is native to which country?

12 What is a wherry?

13 Which couple feature on Channel 4's *Escape to the Château*?

14 Who said "When choosing between two evils, I always try to pick the one I have never tried before"?

15 In which century was author JM Barrie born?

16 Which is the home country of model Rachel Hunter?

17 Who was the first British Formula 1 World Champion?

18 What nickname is given to the town of Kirkcaldy?

19 Kombucha is a variety of which drink?

20 Which form of transport was reintroduced in Manchester in 1992?

Easy

Medium

Hard

Answers to QUIZ 457 – Pot Luck

1	Greek	11	Brother
2	Ford	12	1930s
3	Maxwell Caulfield	13	St Paul
4	1940s (1949)	14	James Thurber
5	Northampton	15	Newmarket
6	South America	16	Peri Lomax
7	Sir Robert Peel	17	Gypsum
8	Royal Albert Hall	18	A plant
9	51	19	*Animal Farm*
10	Clay	20	Seven

Easy

1   What is a vetch?

2   What shape are beech nuts?

3   The FSC endorsement is awarded by which body?

4   Camphor oil is obtained from which tree?

5   How is a measure of two on the Beaufort scale described?

6   Which natural feature, declared a national monument, is located in the Tularosa Basin of New Mexico?

7   What term is given to the naturally occurring fuels formed by decaying organisms?

8   Which public body issues flood warnings in England and Wales?

9   Which is the shallowest of the Great Lakes on the US-Canada border?

10 In which part of the UK was the Centre for Alternative Technology founded in the 1970s?

Medium

11 Sandstone is what type of rock?

12 What is the main pollutant that causes acid rain?

13 In which year did David Attenborough present the original *Planet Earth* series?

14 In terms of oceans, what is a gyre?

15 The Bonneville Salt Flats are in which US state?

16 If a tree's leaves are described as "pinnate", what do they resemble?

17 What name is given to the region of County Clare that is famous for its limestone pavement?

18 Which British research station sits on the Brunt Ice Shelf?

19 Known as the river Donau in German, what is its English name?

20 What is another name for the wattle tree?

Hard

Answers to QUIZ 458 – Fiction

1	The *Alphabet* series	11	Daggers
2	Spinalonga	12	David Eddings
3	Gail Honeyman	13	Robert A Heinlein
4	Lawyer	14	14th century
5	Greebo	15	Observe
6	Perry Mason	16	Hieronymus
7	*Northanger Abbey*	17	Danielle Steel
8	Five	18	Neil Gaiman
9	Jack Reacher	19	*On Chesil Beach*
10	*The Miniaturist*	20	A sword

1   As well as Jean Plaidy and Philippa Carr, under what other name did novelist Eleanor Hibbert write?

2   Who wrote the 1974 play *Travesties*?

3   What do the hormones endorphins do in the body?

4   In relation to flights, for what do the initials ATOL stand?

5   Which Turkish mountain is said to be the resting place of Noah's Ark after the flood?

6   Which horse won the Cheltenham Gold Cup from 1964 to 1966?

7   In the title of a Shakespeare play, who was the beloved of Troilus?

8   Who played the title roles in the 2012 film *Arthur and Mike*?

9   Which TV presenter has had *Great Escapes* to Applecross in Scotland and Connemara in Ireland, amongst others?

10 Ian and Janette Tough created which TV and stage duo?

11 Which castle is close to the town of Ravenglass in Cumbria?

12 What was the first UK top ten hit for Canned Heat?

13 Lambda occupies which place in the Greek alphabet?

14 In which year did only six cars take part in the US Grand Prix due to a dispute about tyres?

15 What type of car is the Toyota Prius?

16 What was the informal first name of jazz singer and bandleader Calloway?

17 Which US state lies east of Kansas?

18 Who provides the voice of Gru in the *Despicable Me* films?

19 The water chestnut is not a nut: what part of the plant it it?

20 In which county is the town of Leatherhead?

Easy

Medium

Hard

Answers to QUIZ 459 – Pot Luck

1	Tennessee	11	Brazil
2	Bangkok	12	A boat
3	To prevent his patients getting bedsores	13	Dick Strawbridge and Angel Adoree
4	China	14	Mae West
5	Verderer	15	19th century
6	*Arbitrage*	16	New Zealand
7	Jack Farthing	17	Mike Hawthorn (1958)
8	*Giving It All Away*	18	The Lang Toun (Long town)
9	The Manhattan Transfer	19	Tea
10	Edward III	20	Tram

Easy

1 In which castle can you see the Fairy Flag, an heirloom of the clan MacLeod?

2 The Gulf (or Strait) of Corryvreckan is noted for which natural phenomenon?

3 Which gardens created by Osgood Mackenzie on the west coast of Scotland benefit from the Gulf Stream?

4 Shown on TV's *The Biggest Little Railway in the World*, what was the final destination of the temporary model railway that began at Corpach near Fort William?

5 Loch Sween is located in which region of Scotland?

6 What type of constructions are Dun Telve and Dun Troddan?

7 Which castle is the family seat of the Earl of Sutherland?

8 Access was restricted to which island from the 1940s until 1990 because of fears over contamination from biological weapons testing?

9 Which Highland town on Loch Broom was founded in 1788 by the Fisheries Industry as a base for the herring industry?

10 A cub from which species of animal was born at the Highland Wildlife Park in 2018, and named Hamish after a public vote?

11 What is the Lairig Ghru?

Medium

12 Which Scottish author and naturalist wrote *Ring of Bright Water* (1960)

13 What is the name of the much-photographed castle at the meeting point of Loch Duich, Loch Alsh and Loch Long?

14 A feature on the Caledonian Canal, what is Neptune's Staircase?

15 The home of which famous Scot is in Alloway in Ayrshire?

16 What is the title of the head of the Church of Scotland?

17 Who or what is the Old Man of Hoy?

18 Who was king of Scotland from 1513 to 1542?

19 Papa Stour and Muckle Roe are part of which island group?

20 What is the official residence of the monarchy in Scotland?

Hard

Answers to QUIZ 460 – Planet Earth

1	A wild flower	11	Sedimentary
2	Triangular	12	Sulphur dioxide
3	Forest Stewardship Council	13	2006
4	Laurel	14	A system of circulating currents
5	Light breeze	15	Utah
6	White Sands	16	Feather
7	Fossil fuels	17	The Burren
8	Environment Agency	18	Halley Research Station
9	Erie	19	Danube
10	Wales	20	Acacia

1   On what date did the Battle of the Somme commence?

2   Tom Bell played which London gangland character in the film *The Krays*?

3   Which Beatle recorded an album called *Liverpool 8*, in tribute to his childhood postcode?

4   What type of creature is a waterbuck?

5   Eta occupies which place in the Greek alphabet?

6   In which century was Lord Byron born?

7   Which renowned New York jazz venue was the setting for a 1984 Francis Ford Coppola film?

8   In the novel by Philippa Gregory, who was *The White Princess*?

9   Which composer, mentioned in the song *Walking in Memphis*, became known as the Father of the Blues?

10 Author Simon Barnes writes about wildlife and which other subject?

11 In legend, what would a mandrake plant do when pulled up?

12 What was the name of William Wordsworth's sister?

13 Turban and pattypan are varieties of which fruit, used as a vegetable?

14 Hvar and Vis are islands belonging to which country?

15 Animals at the top of the food chain are referred to by what two-word term?

16 What spiked helmet was adopted by the Prussian army in the early 1840s?

17 Who had a hit in 1981 with *Japanese Boy*?

18 The head of which vegetable is known as a "curd"?

19 Which National Trust property in Surrey suffered major damage after a fire in 2015?

20 What caused the formation of Africa's Ngorongoro Crater?

Answers to QUIZ 461 – Pot Luck

1	Victoria Holt	11	Muncaster Castle
2	Sir Tom Stoppard	12	*On The Road Again*
3	Suppress pain	13	11th
4	Air Travel Organiser's Licensing	14	2005
5	Ararat	15	Hybrid
6	Arkle	16	Cab
7	Cressida	17	Missouri
8	Colin Firth and Emily Blunt	18	Steve Carell
9	Monty Halls	19	Part of the stem (tuber)
10	The Krankies	20	Surrey

1   Which former wife of King Henry VIII is said to haunt the corridors of Hampton Court Palace?

2   Whom did Henry VIII consider his "true wife"?

3   Where is Henry VIII's last suit of armour displayed?

4   Where did Katherine Parr reside after King Henry VIII died?

5   What position did Anne Boleyn first hold at court?

6   Katherine Howard was related to which other of King Henry VIII's wives?

7   Where did Elizabeth I spend her childhood?

8   Where was Anne of Cleves laid to rest when she died?

9   Where was Catherine of Aragon buried?

10 Aragon is a region of which country?

11 In which building is King Henry VIII buried...?

12 ...and who is buried with him?

13 Which wife did Henry VIII marry at Hampton Court Palace?

14 Which is the only other Tudor Palace that King Henry VIII lived in that has survived?

15 Anne Boleyn lived in which stately home during her childhood?

16 Which of King Henry VIII's wives only reigned for six months?

17 Who was the youngest of King Henry VIII's wives?

18 Who was Catherine of Aragon married to before King Henry VIII?

19 Which of King Henry VIII's former wives was married four times?

20 Elizabeth I bestowed what title on Robert Dudley?

1	Dunvegan Castle	11	A mountain pass
2	Whirlpool	12	Gavin Maxwell
3	Inverewe Gardens	13	Eilean Donan
4	Inverness	14	A series of locks
5	Argyll and Bute	15	Robert Burns
6	Iron-age brochs	16	Moderator
7	Dunrobin Castle	17	A rock stack
8	Cleves	18	James V
9	Ullapool	19	Shetland Islands
10	Polar bear	20	Palace of Holyrood House

1   Which broadcaster has presented series including *The Men Who Made Us Fat* and *The Men Who Made Us Thin*?

2   The secretary bird is native to which continent?

3   In 2001, who released the album *No Angel*?

4   Which jazz double-bass player composed the tune *Goodbye Pork Pie Hat*?

5   Who wrote the short story *The Curious Case of Benjamin Button...*?

6   ...and who directed the 2008 film adaptation?

7   Which is America's "Constitution State"?

8   Who was the first Hollywood star to sign a $1m per annum contract?

9   In which Scottish council area is Pitlochry?

10   What Latin phrase means "thank the Lord"?

11   In what environment would a siphonophore be found?

12   Which TV series stars Olivia Colman and Julian Barratt as Deborah and Maurice?

13   What is a tatami, found in Japanese houses?

14   Which official US state song contains the lyrics "Just an old sweet song keeps..."?

15   George Segal plays "Pops" in which TV series?

16   Which car company manufactures the Pulsar?

17   Brantwood in the Lake District is a museum dedicated to which art critic, one of its previous owners?

18   Which 19th-century British monarch was known as the "Sailor King"?

19   Fynbos is a type of vegetation found in which country?

20   Located in California, what is General Sherman?

Easy

Medium

Hard

Answers to QUIZ 463 – Pot Luck

1	July 1, 1916	11	Scream
2	Jack "The Hat" McVitie	12	Dorothy
3	Ringo Starr	13	Squash
4	Antelope	14	Croatia
5	Seventh	15	Apex predators
6	18th century	16	Pickelhaube
7	*The Cotton Club*	17	Aneka
8	Elizabeth of York	18	Cauliflower
9	WC Handy	19	Clandon Park
10	Sport	20	The collapse of a volcano

Easy

1   How many Tests usually make up an Ashes series?

2   Harold Larwood is associated with which controversial bowling style?

3   On August 31, 1968, what did Sir Garry Sobers become the first to do?

4   Who was the first batsman to score a double century in a One Day International?

5   Which former international cricketer went on to found the Tehreek-e-Insaf political party in Pakistan?

6   For which football team did Sir Ian Botham play professionally?

7   Eden Park is a cricket ground in which country?

8   Who captained the West Indies between 1984 and 1991?

9   In which year did Darren Gough win *Strictly Come Dancing*?

10   Who, in 1963, became the first cricketer to reach 200 wickets and 2000 runs in Test cricket?

11   Which country, along with Afghanistan, was awarded Test status on 22nd June 2017?

12   *I'm A Celebrity…Get Me Out of Here!* was won by which retired cricketer in 2003?

13   How many ways can you be given out in cricket?

14   What does an umpire holding out one arm to the side at shoulder height indicate?

Medium

15   Which former captain of the England women's cricket team was ennobled to sit in the House of Lords in 2010 (d.2017)?

16   Which almanack is known colloquially as "the Bible of Cricket"?

17   Who succeeded Charlotte Edwards as England women's captain in 2016?

18   Bankstown Oval is a stadium in which city?

19   What fielding position is set to catch edged balls that are beyond the wicket-keeper's reach?

20   Where is the home ground of the Sussex Cricket Club?

Hard

Answers to QUIZ 464 – The Tudors

1	Katherine Howard	11	St George's Chapel, Windsor
2	Jane Seymour	12	Jane Seymour and Edward VI
3	Windsor Castle	13	Katherine Parr
4	Sudeley Castle, Gloucestershire	14	St James' Palace, London
5	Maid of Honour to Catherine of Aragon	15	Hever Castle, Kent
6	Anne Boleyn. She was her first cousin	16	Anne of Cleves
7	Hatfield House	17	Katherine Howard (1521-42)
8	Westminster Abbey	18	His brother, Arthur
9	Peterborough Cathedral	19	Katherine Parr (two before Henry and one after he died)
10	Spain	20	Earl of Leicester

1   *The Architect* is a 2018 album by which artist?

2   The quokka, native to Australia, is a species of which animal?

3   "Doctor's Orders" is the traditional bingo call for which number?

4   Who wrote the 1926 novel *The Sun Also Rises*?

5   In which country is the Tarangire National Park?

6   In boxing, what is the lowest weight category?

7   In which country is the volcano Kilauea?

8   What is the part of a horse between its shoulder blades?

9   On an Ordnance Survey map, what is indicated by the abbreviation CH?

10 In the 2018 film *Book Club*, what book is being read?

11 What is the term for encouraging potatoes to sprout before planting?

12 Which Shakespeare play shares its name with a Dire Straits hit?

13 Which 1982 song written by Elvis Costello and Clive Langer was inspired by the Falklands War?

14 Which film character had a cat called Mr Bigglesworth?

15 Metrophobia is the fear of what?

16 What is a cardoon?

17 In WWI, what was known as "Big Bertha"?

18 Who had a 1968 hit with *I've Gotta Get A Message To You*?

19 Who won motorsport's "Triple Crown" of the Indianapolis 500, Le Mans 24 Hour and the Monaco Grand Prix between 1962 and 1972?

20 Who was TV's *Hotel Inspector* when the series started in 2005?

Easy

Medium

Hard

Answers to QUIZ 465 – Pot Luck

1   Jacques Peretti

2   Africa

3   Dido

4   Charles Mingus

5   F Scott Fitzgerald

6   David Fincher

7   Connecticut

8   Mary Pickford

9   Perth and Kinross

10 *Deo gratias*

11 A marine environment

12 *Flowers*

13 A mat

14 *Georgia on my Mind*

15 *The Goldbergs*

16 Nissan

17 John Ruskin

18 William IV

19 South Africa

20 A giant sequoia

Easy

1   What was the name of Frank Zappa's band?

2   With which band did Rick Allen continue to play after losing an arm in a car crash?

3   *Electric Light* (2018) was the second album released by which English singer/songwriter?

4   Who was the bass player with The Who?

5   The rock band Nickelback come from which country?

6   Why did the Foo Fighters cancel their headline act at Glastonbury in 2015?

7   Which supergroup released a song in 1988 titled *Handle With Care*?

8   What was the name of Led Zeppelin's bass player?

9   Who was the lead guitarist with The Shadows...?

10 ...and what was the title of their 1963 instrumental, which reached no.1 in the UK charts?

11 Who was the front man of Humble Pie?

12 What is the title of the fifth Led Zeppelin studio album, recorded in 1973?

13 James Dean Bradfield is the lead singer and guitarist for which band?

14 Which band does Matthew Bellamy front?

Medium

15 Sir Elton John has collaborated with which songwriter (b.1950) on many of his songs, including those on the 2016 album *Wonderful Crazy Night*?

16 Who was the frontman of the band Jethro Tull?

17 Who was the drummer with The Jimi Hendrix Experience?

18 The Silver Bullet Band backed which singer?

19 The Stereophonics were formed in which country?

20 In which year did Adele release the album 25?

Hard

Answers to QUIZ 466 – Cricket

1	Five	11	Ireland
2	Bodyline	12	Phil Tufnell
3	Hit six sixes off one over	13	Nine
4	Sachin Tendulkar	14	No ball
5	Imran Khan	15	Rachael Heyhoe Flint (Baroness Heyhoe Flint)
6	Scunthorpe United	16	*Wisden*
7	New Zealand	17	Heather Knight
8	Sir Viv Richards	18	Sydney, Australia
9	2005	19	Slips
10	Richie Benaud	20	Hove

ANSWERS ON PAGE **471**

1 Striding Edge is a ridge on the approach to which English mountain?

2 Which duo sang about LS Lowry in 1978's *Matchstalk Men and Matchstalk Cats and Dogs*?

3 Which US state is nicknamed the "Beaver State"?

4 How is the heartsease also known?

5 Which actress played housekeeper Aggie in the 1950s sitcom *Life with the Lyons*?

6 What term is given to the rate at which the body uses energy when at rest?

7 John Stuart, the Third Earl of Bute, was the UK Prime Minister during which century?

8 What is the world's largest species of seal?

9 Coquet Island is off the coast of which county?

10 Which US singer had a hit in 1958 with *Stupid Cupid*?

11 In which Australian state is Kangaroo Island?

12 At which Kansas army post was wheeler-dealer Sergeant Bilko based?

13 *The Story of My Experiments with Truth* is an autobiography by which activist?

14 Who played the title role in the 2010 film *The Ghost Writer*?

15 What is the name of the ancient Greek god of war?

16 Who *Holler*-ed their way to no.1 in 2000?

17 What is mooli?

18 Rosalind and Celia appear in which of Shakespeare's plays?

19 In which decade of the 20th century was Bob Dylan born?

20 How is the Decalogue more usually referred to?

Easy

Medium

Hard

Answers to QUIZ 467 – Pot Luck

1	Paloma Faith	11	Chitting
2	Wallaby	12	*Romeo and Juliet*
3	Nine	13	*Shipbuilding*
4	Ernest Hemingway	14	Dr Evil (Austin Powers)
5	Tanzania	15	Poetry
6	Minimumweight	16	Vegetable
7	USA (Hawaii)	17	A howitzer
8	Withers	18	The Bee Gees
9	Clubhouse	19	Graham Hill
10	*50 Shades of Grey*	20	Ruth Watson

Easy

1   Which writing implement lends its name to the censoring of a work?

2   "Whitsun" is a short form of which two words?

3   The word "window" derives from the words "wind" and "eye" in which language?

4   What is the name for a sculptor's preliminary sketch or model?

5   Found outdoors, what is an Adirondack?

6   What is the meaning of the word "cenotaph"?

7   What term is given to saying the same thing twice in a sentence?

8   Which vegetable's name is taken from the Italian for "little sprouts"?

9   Of what is odontophobia a fear?

10 The word "yoghurt" originates from which language?

11 "All that glitters is not gold" is an often quoted Shakespearean line, but it is not correct. What is the actual line?

Medium

12 What does "Sputnik" mean in English?

13 "Paschal" relates to which religious festival?

14 What is dendrochronology the study of?

15 What name was given to the system of society where people gained land and protection from those for whom they worked?

16 The word "hinterland" comes from which language?

17 Which word for a large lorry is derived from the name of an Indian deity?

18 What is the opposite of "orthodox"?

19 In decorative glassware, what is the literal translation of *millefiori*?

20 What is the meaning of the word "Neolithic"?

Hard

Answers to QUIZ 468 – Musicians and Songwriters

1	The Mothers of Invention	11	Steve Marriott
2	Def Leppard	12	*Houses of the Holy*
3	James Bay	13	The Manic Street Preachers
4	John Entwistle	14	Muse
5	Canada	15	Bernie Taupin
6	Dave Grohl broke his leg prior to the festival	16	Ian Anderson
7	The Traveling Wilburys	17	Mitch Mitchell
8	John Paul Jones	18	Bob Seger
9	Hank Marvin	19	Wales
10	*Foot Tapper*	20	2015

1   What is the last stage of an Act of Parliament before it becomes law?

2   What is a dormant asparagus plant called when planted?

3   What does "chi" mean, in traditional Chinese medicine?

4   In which city was Royal Doulton pottery first produced?

5   In the animal world, what is a wryneck?

6   Who co-starred as Sid James' wife in the 1970s sitcom *Bless This House*?

7   What is an empanada?

8   Which sporting body was founded by Baron Pierre de Coubertin (b.1863)?

9   Who said "I married beneath me. All women do"?

10   What was the title of the first book to be published in Bernard Cornwell's *Sharpe* series?

11   In the 1999 film *The Mummy*, which actor co-starred with Rachel Weisz?

12   Which Shakespeare play did Ralph Fiennes bring to cinemas in 2011?

13   What was the name of Brian Poole's backing group?

14   What does the Latin word *ubique* translate to?

15   What is the Sabin vaccine used to prevent?

16   What is the term for banishment to the countryside?

17   El Capitan is a peak in which US National Park?

18   In which decade of the 20th century was Sir Ian Botham born?

19   The Liberty Bell was the first form of which machine?

20   In *The Lord of the Rings*, what creature caused Gandalf to fall into the chasm at Khazad Dum?

Answers to QUIZ 469 – Pot Luck

1	Helvellyn	11	South Australia
2	Brian and Michael	12	Fort Baxter
3	Oregon	13	Gandhi
4	Wild pansy	14	Ewan McGregor
5	Molly Weir	15	Ares
6	Basal metabolic rate	16	The Spice Girls
7	18th century	17	Radish
8	Southern elephant seal	18	*As You Like It*
9	Northumberland	19	1940s
10	Connie Francis	20	The Ten Commandments

Easy

1 Which European city did George Bernard Shaw describe as *"The Pearl of the Adriatic"*?

2 Hallgrímskirkja (a church designed like an erupting volcano) affords spectacular views over what city?

3 Where is the UNESCO Heritage town of Sintra located?

4 The Chain Bridge spans which famous river in Europe?

5 The Shard and The Walkie-Talkie dominate the skyline of which city?

6 In which country is the famous "Charles Bridge"?

7 Who designed the Chicago sculpture entitled *Cloud Gate*, popularly known as "the Bean"?

8 Which is the largest central European lake and is known as the "Hungarian Sea"?

9 In which European city can the medieval "Astronomical Clock" be found?

10 Where can you still visit "Schindler's Factory"?

Medium

11 "Juliet's Balcony" is a famous tourist site in Verona, but what actually is it?

12 In which archipelago are the Green and Blue Twin Lakes situated?

13 In which country is the town of Rovinj, popularly known as "Little Venice", where the buildings appear to drop into the sea?

14 On which Greek island was *Captain Corelli's Mandolin* filmed?

15 The ancient site of Skara Brae is located in which group of islands?

16 Which mountain of eastern Turkey is of symbolic importance to Armenians?

17 Claiming to be one of Britain's oldest pubs, in which city is *Ye Olde Trip to Jerusalem*?

18 Which sculptures, unveiled in 2013, have been described as "equitecture"?

19 In which South American country has the Coffee Cultural Landscape been declared a World Heritage Site?

20 A statue of which duke sits on Ben Bhraggie, overlooking the town of Golspie?

Hard

Answers to QUIZ 470 – Words

1	Blue pencil	11	All that glisters
2	White Sunday	12	Fellow traveller
3	Old Norse	13	Easter
4	Maquette	14	Annual tree growth rings
5	A simple wooden chair	15	Feudalism
6	Empty tomb	16	German
7	Tautology	17	Juggernaut
8	Broccoli	18	Heterodox
9	Teeth	19	Thousand flowers
10	Turkish	20	New Stone Age

QUIZ 473 – Pot Luck

ANSWERS ON PAGE 475

1   Who wrote the 1966 non-fiction book *In Cold Blood*?

2   "When the night has come And the land is dark, And the moon is the only light we'll see" is the opening line to which song?

3   In which decade was the Rugby Football Union created?

4   Which was the first film to gross $1 billion?

5   What is a mesclun?

6   *Let Them Talk* (2011) was the debut studio album of blues classics by which British actor?

7   How old was Britain's "Youngest Soldier" in WWI?

8   What is the term for a plant that lives for two years?

9   Which US State is nicknamed "The Garden State"?

10 Who invented vulcanised rubber?

11 Which substance did Joseph Lister (First Baron Lister) champion the use of as an antiseptic?

12 In which century was William Cavendish, the Fourth Duke of Devonshire, UK Prime Minister?

13 BH is the postcode area code for which town?

14 Which musician starred in the 1988 film *Buster*?

15 Which group had a hit in 2005 with *Push the Button*?

16 Haystacks is a hill next to which Cumbrian lake?

17 What is the traditional bingo call for the number 86?

18 How many pieces are there in a tangram puzzle...?

19 ...and in which country did it originate?

20 The fictional detective Jemima Shore was created by which author?

1   Xhosa is an ethnic group and language from which country?

2   *Yerma* was a 1934 play by which author?

3   Zug is a region of which country?

4   Xenon has what atomic number?

5   *Young Frankenstein* (1974) starred which British comedian as Igor?

6   Zsa Zsa Gabor was born in which country?

7   Xerxes was an ancient king of which country?

8   *You're the Top* is a song from which musical?

9   Zaragoza is the capital of which Spanish region?

10 Xanthe Mallett co-presented the Australian version of which BBC series that celebrates the outdoors?

11 Yugoslavia was in existence between which years?

12 Zac Efron played Logan in which 2012 film?

13 Xenophiles are fond of what?

14 Yul Brynner was born in which city?

15 Zainab in EastEnders was played by which actress?

16 *Xanadu* (1980) was inspired by which 1947 film?

17 Ytterbium is a metallic element in which series?

18 Ziti is what type of foodstuff?

19 Xanthus was the immortal horse of which legendary figure?

20 Yonkers is a city in which US state?

Answers to QUIZ 472 – Landmarks

1	Dubrovnik	11	A sarcophagus
2	Reykjavik	12	Azores (Sao Miguel)
3	Portugal	13	Croatia
4	Danube	14	Kefalonia
5	London	15	Orkney Islands
6	Czech Republic	16	Ararat
7	Sir Anish Kapoor	17	Nottingham
8	Lake Balaton	18	The Kelpies (Falkirk)
9	Prague	19	Colombia
10	Krakow	20	First Duke of Sutherland

ANSWERS ON PAGE 477

1 Which of Isambard Kingdom Brunel's ships was completed in 1838?

2 Which US star played Miles Davis in the 2015 biopic *Miles Ahead*?

3 In the 2010 film *Shutter Island*, who played Chuck Aule?

4 What type of creature is a grysbok?

5 Which American actor played the hapless father in the 1960s sitcom *My Three Sons*?

6 Which 1999 thriller starred Denzel Washington and Angelina Jolie?

7 Which racecourse is known as the "home of British flat racing"?

8 The saguaro cactus is the state plant of which US state?

9 Which DJ was a judge on *Britain's Got Talent* for the 2015 series?

10 Which New Testament apostle is said to have been crucified on a diagonal cross?

11 Salamanca is a city in which European country?

12 What was the nickname of John le Carré's Russian master spy Karla?

13 What is kept in a scabbard?

14 In which country did the Schnauzer originate?

15 What is secreted by the sebaceous gland?

16 What type of fabric is seersucker?

17 In 1847, which act introduced a maximum ten-hour working day?

18 The Isle of Sheppey is off the coast of which county?

19 What does the Latin phrase *Sic transit gloria mundi* mean?

20 What is the American word for "cutlery"?

Answers to QUIZ 473 – Pot Luck

1	Truman Capote	11	Carbolic acid
2	*Stand By Me* (Ben E King)	12	18th century
3	1870s (1871)	13	Bournemouth
4	*Jurassic Park* (1993)	14	Phil Collins
5	A green salad made from young leaves and shoots	15	The Sugababes
6	Hugh Laurie	16	Buttermere
7	12 years old	17	Between the sticks
8	Biennial	18	Seven
9	New Jersey	19	China
10	Charles Goodyear	20	Lady Antonia Fraser

1   Which creature can turn its stomach inside out?

2   An electric ray can inflict what strength of shock?

3   What is a smolt?

4   What type of bird is a bobwhite?

5   The galago has what more common name?

6   Which tree has the Latin name *Fagus sylvatica*?

7   Which cloud type takes its name from the Latin for a curl of hair?

8   What is the common name of the Mexican tree *Abies religiosa*?

9   *Bellis perennis* is a common species of which flower?

10   Whereabouts on a whale are its flukes?

11   What colour is a chow chow's tongue?

12   Apricot queen, Dorcas and flameburst are varieties of which flower?

13   What, in Australia, is a tammar?

14   What is the common name for the tree *Salix babylonica*?

15   Of which US state is the Syringa the state flower?

16   In which country could you photograph the Pingualuit crater?

17   What is the common name for a tree of the *Ulmus* genus?

18   What is a sea fan?

19   A lobster's blood is what colour when exposed to air?

20   What type of creature is a galah?

Answers to QUIZ 474 – XYZ

1	South Africa	11	1918-92
2	Federico García Lorca	12	*The Lucky One*
3	Switzerland	13	Foreign things
4	54	14	Vladivostok
5	Marty Feldman	15	Nina Wadia
6	Hungary	16	*Down to Earth*
7	Persia	17	Lanthanides
8	*Anything Goes*, Cole Porter	18	Pasta
9	Aragon	19	Achilles
10	*Coast*	20	New York

1   At what age did Shostakovich write his *Symphony No. 1*?

2   Which British swimmer won a gold medal in breaststroke at the 1980 Olympics?

3   What form of writing is named after its wedge-shaped characters?

4   Of what is dromophobia is a fear?

5   What was the nationality of the composer Zoltán Kodály?

6   Who created the character Mrs Doasyouwouldbedoneby?

7   When did dressage first become an Olympic event?

8   In which country are the city and province of Mendoza?

9   How were Gary Leeds, John Maus and Scott Engel collectively known?

10   When was the First French Republic proclaimed?

11   In which year were the lions added to the base of Nelson's Column?

12   Where did Mario Frick become youngest head of government in 1993?

13   At which school for girls did Miss Jean Brodie work?

14   Which organisation maintains the UK's Heritage Seed Library?

15   Which poet wrote *The Garden*, written around 1652?

16   Ahmed Sukarno was elected the first President of which country in 1949?

17   The River Pediaíos or Kanlı Dere flows through which capital city?

18   Which Algerian seaport is the setting of Camus' novel *The Plague*?

19   Of which South American country is Paramaribo the capital?

20   Whom did Charles II appoint Master Carver in Wood to the Crown?

Answers to QUIZ 475 – Pot Luck

1	SS *Great Western*	11	Spain
2	Don Cheadle	12	Sandman
3	Mark Ruffalo	13	A sword
4	Antelope	14	Germany
5	Fred MacMurray	15	Sebum
6	*The Bone Collector*	16	Cotton
7	Newmarket	17	The Factories Act
8	Arizona	18	Kent
9	Nick Grimshaw	19	Thus passes the glory of the world
10	St Andrew	20	Silverware

1 What surname connects an early English composer with an Antarctic aviator?

2 Who was Ruth's mother-in-law in the Old Testament?

3 Which American rapper was born Calvin Cordozar Broadus Jr?

4 In *Thunderball* what was the name of Emilio Largo's yacht?

5 By what name are Pluto platters now known?

6 Which Stevenson was US ambassador to the United Nations in the 1960s?

7 What is the name of Don Quixote's horse?

8 Don Diego de la Vega is better known as which fictional hero?

9 What was the name of the dog owned by Enid Blyton's Secret Seven?

10 Laurence Olivier took the title Baron Olivier of where?

11 Nicholas Blake was the pseudonym of which Poet Laureate?

12 By what name is author Lady Mallowan better known?

13 What was the name of the giant cannon in Jules Verne's *From the Earth to the Moon*?

14 Singer Conway Twitty had what real name?

15 What are Sebou, Ogooue and Cuanza names of?

16 What is the name of the strait in the Caribbean between Haiti and Cuba?

17 How is Patrick Chukwuemeka Okogwu better known?

18 How was Frederick V of Bohemia known?

19 What was the surname of the first PM of Australia?

20 Alvin Stardust had more than one stage name, but what was his birth name?

Answers to QUIZ 476 – Natural World

1	Starfish	11	Dark blue
2	200 volts	12	Rose
3	A young salmon or trout	13	A wallaby
4	Quail (North American)	14	Weeping willow
5	Bushbaby	15	Idaho
6	The beech (European)	16	Canada
7	Cirrus	17	Elm
8	Sacred fir	18	Coral
9	Daisy	19	Blue
10	On its tail	20	Cockatoo

1   In which country did Peter Mutharika become president in 2014?

2   Who sang *Let's Go to San Francisco* in 1967?

3   Which sport was originally called mintonette?

4   What is the baggage and equipment carried by an army called?

5   Which eastern European capital lies at the mouth of the River Daugava?

6   Hesperus and Phosphorus are ancient names for which planet?

7   Which musical was suggested by Ingmar Bergman's film *Smiles of a Summer Night*?

8   How many Grammy awards did Eric Clapton win for his 1993 work *Unplugged*?

9   Who directed and starred in the film *One-Eyed Jacks*?

10 What is the fastest-swimming shark in the ocean?

11 How many individual bets make up a Yankee?

12 In which Dickens novel will you find the character of Polly Toodle?

13 In which country can the Nazca Lines be found?

14 What is the name of the German cosmographer who is responsible for producing the oldest surviving globe?

15 Of which country is N'Djamena the capital?

16 In which year was George Washington elected to a second term as US president?

17 Who wrote of her childhood in Africa in the novel *The Flame Trees of Thika*?

18 A chrysophilist is someone who loves what?

19 In James Hilton's novel *Goodbye, Mr Chips*, who does Mr Chipping get married to in 1896?

20 In which country are Kannada, Oriya and Malayalam spoken?

Easy

Medium

Hard

Answers to QUIZ 477 – Pot Luck

1	19	11	1867
2	Duncan Goodhew	12	Liechtenstein
3	Cuneiform	13	Marcia Blane
4	Crossing streets	14	Garden Organic
5	Hungarian	15	Andrew Marvell
6	Charles Kingsley	16	Indonesia
7	1912	17	Nicosia (Cyprus)
8	Argentina	18	Oran
9	Walker Brothers	19	Suriname
10	1792	20	Grinling Gibbons

1   What is the main ingredient of pizzaiola sauce?

2   What is Morven?

3   Of what is cibol a variety?

4   Bunny chow is an African food dish in which a hollowed out part loaf of bread is filled with which type of food?

5   Which chicken dish was named after a Napoleonic battle of June 1800?

6   What, added before compression, affects the hardness and the depth of the rind on cheese?

7   From which country does the fish pie coulibiac originate?

8   Which magazine popularised the phrase "nouvelle cuisine" in 1975?

9   The Black Swan at Oldstead, winner of the Trip Advisor Traveller's Choice Award for Best Restaurant in 2017, is run by which chef?

10 Salmagundi is a salad of chopped meat, eggs, and onions, often arranged in rows on lettuce and served with vinegar and oil. Which fish, a relative of the herring family, is also used in the making of this dish?

11 A Sachertorte is a type of gateau with what flavour jam filling?

12 Kleftiko is a Greek dish with what main ingredient?

13 What do the initials in HJ Heinz Co stand for?

14 Merton Glory and Napoleon Bigarreau are types of which fruit?

15 Trinity cream is another name for which dessert?

16 What is the Reinheitsgebot?

17 The seeds of which common garden flower can be pickled to make poor man's capers?

18 Barsac is a sweet white wine from which area of France?

19 Timperley Early and Cawood Castle are types of what?

20 With what is food described as "veronique" served?

Answers to QUIZ 478 – Names

1	Byrd	11	Cecil Day-Lewis
2	Naomi	12	Dame Agatha Christie
3	Snoop Dogg	13	Columbiad
4	*Disco Volante*	14	Harold Lloyd Jenkins
5	Frisbees	15	Rivers
6	Adlai	16	Windward Passage
7	Rocinante	17	Tinie Tempah
8	Zorro	18	The Winter King
9	Scamper	19	Barton
10	Brighton	20	Bernard Jewry

1 Which ancient civilisation produced the *Book of the Dead*?

2 The play *The Ghost Train* was written by which member of the cast of *Dad's Army*?

3 Who composed the 1911 opera *Bluebeard's Castle*?

4 Who won a Pulitzer prize in 1976 for his novel *Humboldt's Gift*?

5 Which musician released the 2015 album *Everything Is 4*?

6 What is the proper term for flying dinosaurs, commonly called pterodactyls?

7 In which country were banknotes first used?

8 Who was the first woman to walk in space?

9 What was the title of the first Spice Girls single that did not reach no.1 in the UK charts?

10 Edward Whymper was the first person to climb which mountain in 1865?

11 Which US actor played the role of Colonel Strickland in the 2017 film *The Shape of Water*?

12 What was the bird that brought back an olive leaf to Noah's Ark?

13 What was the Roman name for the river Severn?

14 How many feet are there in a nautical mile?

15 The city of Quebec lies on the banks of which river?

16 Which dramatist wrote *Juno and the Paycock*?

17 What is the name of the Norwegian parliament?

18 The Andaman and Nicobar Islands belong mostly to which country?

19 On which river are the Angel Falls?

20 Which former UK Prime Minister wrote the novels *Coningsby* and *Sybil*?

Easy

Medium

Hard

Answers to QUIZ 479 – Pot Luck

1	Malawi	11	11
2	The Flowerpot Men	12	*Dombey and Son*
3	Volleyball	13	Peru
4	Impedimenta	14	Martin Behaim
5	Riga	15	Chad
6	Venus	16	1792
7	*A Little Night Music*	17	Elspeth Huxley
8	Six	18	Gold
9	Marlon Brando	19	Katherine Bridges
10	Mako shark	20	India

1. What is the name of the schoolmaster in Shakespeare's *Comedy of Errors*?

2. What do the initials AJ stand for in AJ Cronin's name?

3. Who wrote *The Agony and the Ecstasy*, a 1961 biographical novel about Michelangelo?

4. In the play *The Importance of Being Earnest*, who leaves a manuscript at a railway station?

5. What was the name of the deserted village in Oliver Goldsmith's poem of the same name?

6. In *Fahrenheit 451*, what is the name of the character whose job it is to burn books but finds it difficult not to read them?

7. Who published his *Mother Goose's Fairy Tales* in 1695?

8. A young man called Psmith appeared in novels by which author?

9. In the Erskine Caldwell novel *Tobacco Road*, what was the name of the sharecropper married to Ada?

10. Which Graham Greene novel features the character Pinkie?

11. Who wrote the 1855 novel *The Warden*?

12. Who wrote *The Last of the Mohicans*?

13. Who won the Nobel Prize in Literature in 1907?

14. Sydney Carton appears in which Charles Dickens novel?

15. *Incident at West Egg* was the working title of which famous novel?

16. Which philosopher wrote the 1977 book *Causing Death and Saving Lives*?

17. *The Amateur Cracksman* (1899) saw the first appearance of which literary character?

18. Which of Dame Iris Murdoch's novels is centred on an Anglican religious community in Gloucestershire?

19. Who wrote the *Earthsea* series of fantasy stories for children?

20. Which French author wrote *The Thief's Journal* (1949)?

Answers to QUIZ 480 – Food and Drink

1	Tomatoes	11	Apricot
2	Scottish cheese	12	Lamb
3	Onion	13	Henry John
4	Curry	14	Cherry
5	Chicken Marengo	15	Crème brûlée
6	Salt	16	German regulations governing the ingredients in beer
7	Russia	17	The nasturtium
8	*Harpers & Queen*	18	The Gironde
9	Tommy Banks	19	Rhubarb
10	Anchovies	20	Grapes

1   Which country's flag shows a green star on a red background?

2   Who discovered the neutron?

3   Who is the St Leger named after?

4   In 1968, which ecologist wrote of "the tragedy of the commons"?

5   Moose Jaw and Prince Albert are in which Canadian province?

6   What is the name of the small Scottish town, on the south-eastern tip of Loch Shin, associated with sheep auctions?

7   Who, in Greek mythology, was the mother of Perseus?

8   In which country is the cricket ground of Eden Gardens?

9   What was the title of the 2011 Sherlock Holmes novel by Anthony Horowitz?

10 Who wrote the song *Amazing Grace*?

11 Which boxer was known as "Will o' the Wisp"?

12 Who defeated Douglas Alexander to become the youngest MP elected in the 2015 UK general election?

13 In which country did the card game of contract bridge originate?

14 Where is Britain's Royal Mint situated?

15 Which Spanish writer died on the same date as William Shakespeare, on 23 April 1616?

16 At what height does a pony become a horse?

17 What is the full name of the capital of Colombia?

18 Who played Will Humphries in the series *W1A*?

19 With which band did Midge Ure have a 1976 UK hit with *Forever and Ever*?

20 What is the nickname for Haydn's *Symphony No. 83*?

Answers to QUIZ 481 – Pot Luck

1	Egyptian	11	Michael Shannon
2	Arnold Ridley	12	A dove
3	Béla Bartók	13	Sabrina
4	Saul Bellow	14	6076
5	Jason Derulo	15	St Lawrence
6	Pterosaurs	16	Sean O'Casey
7	Sweden	17	Storting
8	Svetlana Savitskaya	18	India (some belong to Myanmar)
9	*Stop*	19	The Churún river
10	Matterhorn	20	Benjamin Disraeli (First Earl of Beaconsfield)

ANSWERS ON PAGE 486

Easy

1 Which film concerns an alien's search for water on Earth for his dying planet?

2 Which actress was the elder sister of Joan Fontaine?

3 Which singer starred in a series of spoof spy films featuring the character of Matt Helm?

4 In the TV series *The Growing Pains of PC Penrose*, who played the title role?

5 Who directed *Ben-Hur*, *Mrs Miniver* and *Funny Girl*?

6 In which Scottish village was the 1990s TV series *Hamish Macbeth* filmed?

7 Which Tennessee Williams play was turned into a 1959 film starring Elizabeth Taylor and Katherine Hepburn?

8 Who played Clarke Kent/Superman in the TV series *Smallville*?

9 In *2001: A Space Odyssey*, what song does HAL sing repeatedly?

10 Which song is played at the end of *Dr Strangelove* after Slim Pickens rides the atomic bomb like a rodeo horse?

Medium

11 Who starred as the police officer in the 1973 film *The Wicker Man*?

12 Who directed the 1960 film *The Magnificent Seven*?

13 In the 1965 film *The Family Jewels*, which actor played seven roles?

14 Which actor starred in *Laws of Attraction* (2004)?

15 In the 1999 film *Rogue Trader*, who was Ewan McGregor's co-star?

16 Which 1975 documentary depicted the lives of two reclusive relatives of Jackie Kennedy?

17 Who won the Best Actress Oscar for her role in the 1965 film *Darling*?

18 Who directed the film *Picnic at Hanging Rock* (1975)?

19 Who directed the 1992 film *A Few Good Men*?

20 In the classic film *Casablanca*, who played Captain Louis Renault?

Hard

Answers to QUIZ 482 – Literature

1	Pinch	11	Anthony Trollope
2	Archibald Joseph	12	James Fenimore Cooper
3	Irving Stone	13	Rudyard Kipling
4	Miss Prism	14	*A Tale of Two Cities*
5	Auburn	15	*The Great Gatsby*
6	Guy Montag	16	Jonathan Glover
7	Charles Perrault	17	Raffles
8	PG Wodehouse	18	*The Bell*
9	Jeeter Lester	19	Ursula LeGuin
10	*Brighton Rock*	20	Jean Genet

1   What was the name of Frank Sinatra's original backing group?

2   Who wrote the book *Clayhanger*?

3   In which country is Lake Nakuru?

4   What nickname is given to Mozart's *Symphony No. 31 in D*, 1778?

5   In which year did Mussolini become Prime Minister of Italy?

6   What is the capital of East Timor?

7   How is James Dixon referred to in the title of a novel in which he features?

8   Who wrote *Hyperion* (1839), in which the heroine is based on his wife, Frances?

9   "News from St Stephen's" is a phrase used to describe events in which UK institution?

10   Which textile fibre is derived from the plant *Gossypium*?

11   Which poet referred to himself as "Merlin" in a summing-up of his poetical career?

12   From which country does the folk dance the Springar originate?

13   What was the name of the blustering sheriff who featured in *Live and Let Die* and *The Man with the Golden Gun*?

14   In 2014, who won the Masters Golf at Augusta?

15   Which photographer was awarded a Pulitzer Prize for his 1945 photograph of US troops raising a flag?

16   George and Weedon Grossmith wrote about the life of whom in *Diary of a Nobody*?

17   Which Dutch Caribbean island, off the coast of Venezuela, has Oranjestad as its capital?

18   In which country did 48 years of dictatorship end with the election of General Antonio Eanes in 1976?

19   Who composed the symphonic poem *The Swan of Tuonela*?

20   Which band name did The Spectres and Traffic Jam eventually adopt?

Answers to QUIZ 483 – Pot Luck

1	Morocco	11	Willie Pep
2	Sir James Chadwick	12	Mhairi Black
3	Lt Col Anthony St Leger	13	USA
4	Garrett Hardin	14	Llantrisant, Wales
5	Saskatchewan	15	Miguel Cervantes
6	Lairg	16	14.2 hands and over
7	Danae	17	Santa Fé de Bogotà
8	India	18	Hugh Skinner
9	*The House of Silk*	19	Slik
10	John Newton	20	*Hen*

Easy

1 In which country is the ski resort of Kronplatz?

2 Which former region of central France has the chief city Clermont-Ferrand?

3 In 1959, Wallis and Futuna Islands in the South Pacific voted to become an overseas territory of which country?

4 Which river was explored by Mungo Park in 1796?

5 In which country is Malbork Castle, the largest castle in the world by land area?

6 There is a town called Lansing in New York, but which state's capital city is named Lansing?

7 From which country do the Jewish Falashas originate?

8 On which island is the Foreign Legion base of Camp Raffalli?

9 What is the name of the only surviving Wonder of the Ancient World?

10 Which capital is on the slopes of the volcano Pichincha?

11 The island of Gotland is surrounded by which body of water?

Medium

12 What is the name of the Ancient Greek thinker who coined the term "geography"?

13 In which range of mountains is the Kali Gandaki Gorge?

14 What is the Isle of Wight's main river?

15 In which country is the port of Piraeus?

16 What is the capital of Kazakhstan?

17 Rosedale Abbey lies in which National Park?

18 If it is ten o'clock on a July morning in the UK, what time is it in Nairobi, Kenya?

19 How is the Bay of Gibraltar also known?

20 What is the currency of South Korea?

Hard

ANSWERS ON PAGE 489

1   The active volcano Mount Redoubt, located in the Lake Clark National Park and Preserve, is in which US state?

2   Who reached the top of the UK singles charts in 2015 with *Fight Song*?

3   Who was the Greek goddess of mischief?

4   What was the first dinosaur to be formally named?

5   In Sheridan's *School for Scandal*, in whose London home do the women meet to invent and spread malicious gossip?

6   Galileo was born in which Italian city?

7   What was the pre-1980 name for Pacific republic Vanuatu?

8   What nationality was the theatrical director and producer Erwin Piscator?

9   In which organ is the medulla oblongata to be found?

10 Dom Mintoff became the first Prime Minister of which republic in 1971?

11 Who wrote the novel *QBVII* (1970)?

12 Which American's 1953 autobiography was entitled *Call Me Lucky*?

13 Who was backed on *Disco Duck (Part One)* by his Cast of Idiots?

14 In the film *Jaws*, who plays Roy Scheider's wife?

15 Which Old Testament book precedes Jeremiah?

16 In which sport would you abide by the Cartwright Rules?

17 Who wrote the best-selling book *Men are from Mars, Women are from Venus*?

18 What is the name of the remains of an ancient crater left by a meteor?

19 Whose first opera, in 1833, was entitled *Die Feen*?

20 Which patrol group keeps track of all icebergs?

Easy

Medium

Hard

Answers to QUIZ 485 – Pot Luck

1	The Hoboken Four	11	Alfred, Lord Tennyson
2	Arnold Bennett	12	Norway
3	Kenya	13	JW Pepper
4	*Paris*	14	Bubba Watson
5	1922	15	Joe Rosenthal
6	Dili	16	Charles Pooter
7	Lucky Jim	17	Aruba
8	Henry Wadsworth Longfellow	18	Portugal
9	The House of Commons	19	Sibelius
10	Cotton	20	Status Quo

Easy

1 Which dog breed's name means "swift" in Russian?

2 Which gemstone takes its name from the Greek word for "unbreakable"?

3 What does the name Genghis Khan mean?

4 Which language is known to its speakers as Euskara?

5 Which game takes its name from the Chinese for "sparrow"?

6 The Native American language Cree belongs to which family of languages?

7 Which name means "bringer of joy" in Latin?

8 From which language does the word "cargo" originate?

9 The word comet comes from the Greek word "kometes", meaning what?

10 What did the ancient Persians call the Sun?

Medium

11 What is another name for a natatorium?

12 What Zulu word denotes a body of people, especially warriors?

13 What is the 19th letter of the Greek alphabet?

14 What does "minacious" mean?

15 In Peru, what is an arpillera?

16 How many letters are in the Hawaiian alphabet?

17 Plankton derives its name from a Greek word with what meaning?

18 What was a sepoy?

19 What is the official language of San Marino?

20 The word eclipse comes from the Greek word "ekleipsis", meaning what?

Hard

Answers to QUIZ 486 – Geography

1	Italy	11	The Baltic Sea
2	Auvergne	12	Eratosthenes
3	France	13	Himalaya
4	Niger	14	Medina
5	Poland	15	Greece
6	Michigan	16	Astana
7	Ethiopia	17	North York Moors
8	Corsica	18	Midday
9	The Great Pyramid of Giza	19	Bay of Algeciras
10	Quito (Ecuador)	20	Won

QUIZ 489 – Pot Luck

ANSWERS ON PAGE **491**

1 The Iroquois Cup is which sport's best known trophy, contested annually by English club sides?

2 What is another name for the Beluga whale?

3 In which decade was the first colour photograph taken?

4 *Ship of Fools* (1965) was the last film starring which actress?

5 Who wrote the 1997 novel *Toward the End of Time*?

6 Born in St Malo in 1491, who was the first European to map the St Lawrence area of Canada?

7 Archibald Philip Primrose was prime minister of which country from 1894 to 1895?

8 A Spinone is what type of animal?

9 What was the title of the Police's third studio album?

10 "Christmas won't be Christmas without any presents" is the opening line from which famous book?

11 Philippa of Hainault was the wife of which British monarch?

12 Which game was formerly known as Gossima™?

13 Gresty Road is the home ground of which soccer club?

14 Which former Spice Girl issued an album entitled *Free Me*?

15 In which year did Italy abolish its monarchy?

16 Who wrote *Help Me Make It Through the Night*?

17 What is the male component of the female personality, according to Jung?

18 Carl Hiaasen's novels are generally set in which state of America?

19 What colour was Red Rum?

20 Which is Britain's largest wild mammal?

Easy / Medium / Hard

Answers to QUIZ 487 – Pot Luck

1	Alaska	11	Leon Uris
2	Rachel Platten	12	Bing Crosby
3	Ate	13	Rick Dees
4	Megalosaurus	14	Lorraine Gary
5	Lady Sneerwell	15	Isaiah
6	Pisa	16	Baseball
7	New Hebrides	17	John Gray
8	German	18	Astrobleme
9	Brain	19	Richard Wagner
10	Malta	20	The International Ice Patrol

1   Which singer was Mayor of Palm Springs from 1988 to 1992?

2   How is the rock guitarist William Perks better known?

3   The tomb of which composer can be seen in the church of St Thomas in Leipzig?

4   Which 1785 Schiller poem was set to music by Beethoven?

5   Who wrote the music for the ballet *The Spider's Banquet*?

6   What is the stage name of singer/songwriter Michael David Rosenberg?

7   For which instrument was Handel's *Harmonious Blacksmith* written?

8   What was the title of the only opera written by Debussy?

9   Which Bellini opera includes the aria *Casta Diva*?

10 What was Bob Marley's middle name?

11 What is the nickname of Haydn's *String Quartet in D Minor*?

12 In which year was Strauss's opera *Die Fledermaus* first performed?

13 Which French composer, who taught at the Ecole Niedermeyer from 1861 to 1865, co-founded the Société Nationale de Musique in 1871?

14 Which was the first single and album with the same title to top the UK and US charts simultaneously?

15 What song was a no.1 hit for the singer and actor John Leyton?

16 The Shadows had a 1961 hit which referenced which famous expedition?

17 Which soprano attained world fame in 1959 in *Lucia di Lammermoor*?

18 Who was known as the "Red Priest"?

19 Which band's first top 10 UK hit was in 1996 with *Give It Away*?

20 Who wrote the music for the 1956 musical *The Most Happy Fella*?

Answers to QUIZ 488 – Language

1	Borzoi	11	A swimming pool
2	Diamond	12	Impi
3	Universal ruler	13	Tau
4	Basque	14	Threatening
5	Mahjong	15	A wall-hanging
6	Algonquian	16	13
7	Beatrice	17	Wandering
8	Spanish	18	Indian soldier
9	Hairy	19	Italian
10	Mithras	20	Failing to appear

1   What is a caladium?

2   Who founded the Hellfire Club, that held meetings at Medmenham Abbey in the 18th century?

3   In which decade was the International Date Line established?

4   Who won the Men's World Squash Championships six times in the 1980s?

5   By what other name is the Karelian dog known?

6   Under what name did Stanley Burrell achieve success as a rapper?

7   Which James Patterson novel introduced Alex Cross, the Washington-based homicide detective with a PhD in psychology?

8   In which US city was the first large, free public, tax-supported library opened in 1854?

9   The character of Louis Mazzini featured in which film?

10 Which environmentalist wrote the 1949 book *A Sand County Almanac*?

11 Which probe was the first to land on Saturn's moon Titan?

12 If you were listening to traditional Fado folk music, in which country would you be?

13 Which river of SW Germany is a major tributary of the Moselle?

14 Who wrote 94 novels under the title *La Comédie Humaine*?

15 Mount Kosciuszko is the highest peak in which country?

16 How old was Lester Piggott when he returned to racing in 1990?

17 Which work by Mussorgsky provided the title of a hit for Emerson, Lake and Palmer?

18 What was the title of Philip Pullman's 2008 novella, a prequel to the *His Dark Materials* trilogy?

19 What is the name of the European Union's global navigation satellite system?

20 Whom did Ruth Davidson replace as leader of the Scottish Conservative Party in 2011?

Answers to QUIZ 489 – Pot Luck

1	Lacrosse	11	Edward III
2	Sea canary	12	Table tennis
3	1860s	13	Crewe Alexandra
4	Vivien Leigh	14	Emma Bunton
5	John Updike	15	1946
6	Jacques Cartier	16	Kris Kristofferson
7	UK	17	Animus
8	Dog	18	Florida
9	*Zenyattà Mondatta*	19	Bay
10	*Little Women*	20	Grey seal

1   Which type of transport did John Outram invent in 1775?

2   What musical invention was developed by David Rockola?

3   Lucien B Smith patented what deterrent in 1867?

4   Who invented the car speedometer?

5   Which company developed the first electronic pocket calculator?

6   Kirkpatrick Macmillan (b.1812) was involved in the development of which form of transport?

7   Alphonse Bertillon and Sir Francis Galton were involved in the development of which aid to criminal detection?

8   Which mechanical engineer standardized screw threads?

9   Edwin Budding and John Ferrabee developed what outdoor item in 1830?

10 What did Harry Beck create the original design for, in 1931?

11 US businessman Edwin Holmes and his son, Edwin T Holmes, were involved in the development of which device?

12 Which two separate companies invented and promoted the CD-ROM?

13 How long did the Wright brothers' first sustained flight last, covering a distance of 120 feet?

14 Who invented the microwave oven?

15 What was the name of the world's first weather satellite?

16 In 1775, who was the first person to be granted a patent for a flushing toilet?

17 How many letters are used to describe the human genome?

18 Basketball and volleyball were invented by people who worked for which organisation?

19 As what did the inventors of Worcestershire sauce, John Lee and William Perrins, originally work?

20 Which type of fastening was first used on snow boots?

Answers to QUIZ 490 – Music

1	Sonny Bono	11	*Sunrise*
2	Bill Wyman	12	1874
3	Johann Sebastian Bach	13	Camille Saint-Saëns
4	*Ode to Joy*	14	*Bridge over Troubled Water*
5	Albert Roussel	15	*Johnny Remember Me*
6	Passenger	16	*Kon-Tiki*
7	Harpsichord	17	Dame Joan Sutherland
8	*Pelléas and Mélisande*	18	Antonio Vivaldi
9	*Norma*	19	Red Hot Chili Peppers
10	Nesta	20	Frank Loesser

Easy

Medium

Hard

1 What is chaetophobia the fear of?

2 In China, which number is considered unlucky?

3 What was the name of the first species of dinosaur to have its skeleton mounted for display?

4 Who starred as Mrs Lucy Muir in the 1947 film *The Ghost and Mrs Muir*?

5 In Australia, what does the acronym ARIA stand for in a musical context?

6 What was the name of the bull-headed Ancient Egyptian god?

7 Which American photographer (b.1902) is best known for his black and white prints?

8 *Yellow River* was a 1970 hit for which band?

9 What was the title of Stephen King's 2013 sequel to *The Shining*?

10 Who directed the 2017 film *Star Wars: The Last Jedi*?

11 Which video game, released in 1997, was the first sequel to *Myst*?

12 What is the (imperial) weight of one pint of water?

13 Who was the first trainer to turn out winners of more than £1 million in one flat racing season in Britain in 1985?

14 In yachting, what is a metal mike?

15 Which nation is credited with the introduction of zero into the number system?

16 Which play by JM Synge provoked a week of rioting in the Abbey Theatre in Dublin when first performed there?

17 Who was the first woman to receive a degree in civil engineering from Cornell University in 1905?

18 In which hospital was *Dr Kildare* set?

19 Which philosopher wrote the 1781 *Critique of Pure Reason*?

20 What does the "L" stand for in URL, the address of a World Wide Web page?

Easy

Medium

Hard

Answers to QUIZ 491 – Pot Luck

1	A plant	11	Huygens
2	Sir Francis Dashwood	12	Portugal
3	1880s (1884)	13	Saar
4	Jahangir Khan	14	Honoré de Balzac
5	Bear Dog	15	Australia
6	MC Hammer	16	54
7	*Along Came a Spider*	17	*Pictures at an Exhibition*
8	Boston	18	*Once Upon a Time in the North*
9	*Kind Hearts and Coronets*	19	Galileo
10	Aldo Leopold	20	Annabel Goldie

Easy

1   How old was George Foreman when he became the oldest heavyweight champion in history?

2   Which tennis trophy was donated by Hazel Hotchkiss?

3   Which jockey won the Prix de l'Arc de Triomphe from 1985 to 1987 on three different horses?

4   In which year did basketball become an Olympic sport?

5   Which sport awards the Harmsworth Trophy?

6   Which former England cricket captain's autobiography was entitled *I Don't Bruise Easily*?

7   In which decade did Lester Piggott first win the Derby?

8   In which year did Cyril Lowe make his debut appearance for the England rugby team?

9   Which football team plays at Boundary Park?

10 The sport of speed skating originates from which country ?

11 Billy Hamill and Greg Hancock have been world champions for the USA in which sport?

12 In which sport might you adopt the "egg position"?

Medium

13 Who won the BDO Women's World Championship every year from 2001 to 2007?

14 Which football team played at Saltergate from 1871 to 2010?

15 What is the traditional name for a number two wooden golf club?

16 Which world championship was Michael Brisping (b.1979) the first British competitor to win?

17 Elvis Stojko (b.1972) is a three-times World Champion in which sport?

18 Which league club did Sir Bobby Charlton manage from 1973 to 1975?

19 Which stadium hosted the 1992 Ruby League World Cup final?

20 Sean Kerly (b.1960) played which team sport for Great Britain?

Hard

Answers to QUIZ 492 – Innovations

1	Tram	11	Burglar alarm
2	The jukebox	12	Philips invented, Sony promoted
3	Barbed wire	13	12 seconds
4	Josip Belušić	14	Percy Spencer
5	Texas Instruments	15	Tiros I
6	Bicycle	16	Alexander Cumming
7	Fingerprints	17	Four (A, C, G and T)
8	Sir Joseph Whitworth	18	YMCA
9	Lawnmower	19	Chemists
10	London Underground map	20	Zip

1. Who played Minnesota Fats in film *The Hustler* (1961)?

2. What is the name of the non-existent dog belonging to *The A-Team*'s Murdock?

3. Which supermodel released an album entitled *Babywoman*?

4. Which English cartographer produced the first county maps of England and Wales?

5. Situated on the island of Viti Levu, what is the capital of Fiji?

6. What make were the three biplanes known as Faith, Hope and Charity which defended Malta during WWII?

7. The *Lewis Trilogy* was written by which author?

8. Who sang *She Wears My Ring* in 1968?

9. What is the title of Antonio Vivaldi's only oratorio known to have survived?

10. UK singer Elaine Bookbinder adopted which stage name?

11. How are Dmitri, Alyosha and Ivan collectively known?

12. In the Grand National, how many of the fences are jumped twice?

13. For which game did Harold Vanderbilt devise a scoring table?

14. Who wrote the opera *Simon Boccanegra* (1857)?

15. Approximately how many millions of years ago did the mass extinction of the dinosaurs take place?

16. The composer Percy Grainger came from which country?

17. What was the title of the rulers of Hyderabad?

18. In what activity would you make a banjo cable or a leaf rib?

19. What is the largest desert lake in the world, located in Kenya's Great Rift Valley?

20. Which implement, together with wooden sticks, formed the ancient Roman symbol of authority, the fasces?

Easy

Medium

Hard

Answers to QUIZ 493 – Pot Luck

1	Hair	11	*Riven*
2	Four	12	1 lb 4 oz
3	Hadrosaurus	13	Sir Henry Cecil
4	Gene Tierney	14	Automatic helmsman/autopilot
5	Australian Recording Industry Association	15	India
6	Apis	16	*The Playboy of the Western World*
7	Ansel Adams	17	Nora Stanton Blatch
8	Christie	18	Blair General Hospital
9	*Doctor Sleep*	19	Immanuel Kant
10	Rian Johnson	20	Locator

Easy

1   Which 16th-century artist painted *The Burial of Count Orgaz*?

2   Who painted *Boy with a Pipe*, which sold for a record sum in May 2004?

3   Which work by Leonardo da Vinci was stolen from Drumlanrig Castle, home of the Duke of Buccleuch, in 2003?

4   A group of 20th-century young artists adopted what French phrase, meaning "wild beasts" as their collective name?

5   Who was painted by both Antony Williams and Susan Ryder?

6   Which brothers painted the altarpiece known as *The Adoration of the Mystic Lamb*, which included a panel entitled *The Just Judges*?

7   *Jason and Medea*, *Orpheus* and *Hesiod and the Muse* are paintings by which symbolist (b.1826)?

8   Which of Andy Warhol's paintings was sold for more than $17m at a Sotheby's auction in New York in 1998?

9   Sculptress Elizabeth Frink is famous for using what metal?

10 Which art museum group has sites at Bilbao, Venice and New York?

11 Which artist achieved fame and renown for his spatial illusions, impossible buildings and repeating geometric patterns; his works include *Belvedere* and *Drawing Hands*?

12 Whose portrait subjects included Mrs Siddons and Dr Johnson?

13 The 1760s painting *Whistlejacket* was by which artist?

14 Who painted the 16th century works *Rest on the Flight into Egypt* and *Supper at Emmaus*?

15 Who sculpted the marble statue of disabled artist, Alison Lapper, showing her naked and heavily pregnant?

16 In which US state was the Taos art colony founded?

17 Which Russian-born French painter (b. 1887) was famous for his dreamlike images?

18 Which gallery first opened in 1985 in a disused paint factory in St John's Wood?

19 The sculpture museums Museo Chiaramonti and Museo Pio-Clementino are part of which larger museum?

20 The first portrait gallery in the world opened in 1856 in which city?

Answers to QUIZ 494 – Sport

1	45	11	Speedway
2	The Wightman Cup (she became Mrs Wightman)	12	Skiing
3	Pat Eddery	13	Trina Gulliver
4	1936	14	Chesterfield
5	Powerboat racing	15	Brassie
6	Brian Close	16	UFC (Ultimate Fighting Championship)
7	1950s (1954)	17	Figure skating
8	1913	18	Preston North End
9	Oldham Athletic	19	Wembley
10	Netherlands	20	Field hockey

1   Who wrote the comic opera *The World of the Moon* in 1777?

2   DJ Tony Blackburn had two hit records: which word features in both titles?

3   Where is the Happy Valley racecourse?

4   How is *schaum torte* better known?

5   What was the nationality of the composer Carl Nielsen?

6   What was the adopted name of Josip Broz?

7   James Grieve and Lord Lambourne are types of what?

8   In which ocean is the island of New Providence?

9   Whose mistress was Claretta Petacci?

10 In the travel-related company P&O, for what do the initials stand?

11 What is Tasmania's highest peak?

12 The 2003 thriller *Avenger* was written by which author?

13 Which early Bertholdt Brecht play is also the name of a Phoenician god?

14 What does Algol stand for?

15 Who plays the cop on the trail of Michael Douglas' character in the film *Falling Down*?

16 Whose works are catalogued under BWV numbers?

17 Mike Flowers covered which Oasis hit in 1996?

18 An algophobic is fearful of what?

19 Who is the father of Zeus in Greek mythology?

20 In which year did trampolining become an Olympic event?

Easy

Medium

Hard

Answers to QUIZ 495 – Pot Luck

1	Jackie Gleason	11	The Brothers Karamazov
2	Billy	12	14
3	Naomi Campbell	13	Bridge (contract)
4	Christopher Saxton	14	Giuseppi Verdi
5	Suva	15	66 million
6	Gloster Gladiators	16	Australia
7	Peter May	17	The Nizam
8	Solomon King	18	Knitting
9	*Juditha Triumphans*	19	Turkana
10	Elkie Brooks	20	Axe

Easy

1 In which year was the annual Oxford & Cambridge Boat Race first held?

2 Which decade saw the opening of the world's first supermarket?

3 Which country fought against Greece from 499 to 449BC?

4 What was the *Titanic*'s final port of call in Ireland before heading into the Atlantic?

5 In 1973, Mrs Susan Shaw became the first woman to set foot where?

6 Who was assassinated by Leon Czolgosz in 1901?

7 Which city did El Cid conquer and rule in 1094?

8 The Confederate Army surrendered in Appomattox, Virginia, ending the American Civil War – in which year?

9 Which geological period immediately preceded the Devonian period?

10 In which decade was *The Star-Spangled Banner* adopted as the US national anthem?

11 Who was the wife of King Prasutagus?

Medium

12 Who was the king of Libya from 1951 to 1969?

13 Which 1967 film was released in America under the title *Five Million Years to Earth*?

14 In 1940, King Carol abdicated from the throne of which country?

15 In which year was the Citizen's Advice Bureau set up?

16 In which country did the Battle of the Plains of Abraham take place?

17 Which Roman road ran between London and Lincoln?

18 In which decade did Guinness start to publish their *Book of Records* annually?

19 Who was the father of Edward VII's consort Alexandra?

20 Which French explorer founded the city of Quebec?

Hard

Answers to QUIZ 496 – The Arts

1	El Greco	11	Maurits Cornelius Escher
2	Picasso	12	Gainsborough
3	*Madonna with the Yarnwinder*	13	George Stubbs
4	Les Fauves	14	Michelangelo Mersi da Caravaggio
5	Queen Elizabeth II	15	Marc Quinn
6	Van Eyck (Hubert and Jan)	16	New Mexico
7	Gustave Moreau	17	Marc Chagall
8	*Orange Marilyn*	18	Saatchi Gallery
9	Bronze	19	Vatican museums
10	Guggenheim	20	London

1. What is the first name of Mr Bounderby in Charles Dickens' *Hard Times*?

2. The 1936 novel *Eyeless in Gaza* was written by which author?

3. Who wrote the comic opera *The Silken Ladder*?

4. Which island's capital is Flying Fish Cove?

5. In the context of food, what is cullis?

6. The Japanese dish tonkatsu is based on which meat?

7. The ariary is the standard unit of currency of which country?

8. The Sangiovese grape derives its name from which god?

9. Apart from the joker, what other playing card is "wild" in canasta?

10. Which showjumper won the Hickstead Derby in three successive years: 1987, 1988 and 1989?

11. Tony Awards are given out by which organisation?

12. Which year saw the death of Gustav Mahler?

13. Where is Randwick racecourse situated?

14. *There's Nothing Holdin' Me Back* was a 2016 single by which singer?

15. Who wrote the 1847 novel *The Children of the New Forest*?

16. The last example of which extinct animal died on 12 August 1883 in Amsterdam Zoo?

17. Which musical features J Pierrepont Finch as an ambitious window washer?

18. Whch liqueur is flavoured with caraway seed, cumin and fennel?

19. A monitor lizard is believed to give a warning of the presence of what type of creature?

20. Cape Breton Island is part of which country?

Easy

Medium

Hard

Answers to QUIZ 497 – Pot Luck

1	Haydn	11	Mount Ossa
2	Love (*So Much Love* and *It's Only Love*)	12	Frederick Forsyth
3	Hong Kong	13	*Baal*
4	Pavlova	14	Algorithmic Language
5	Danish	15	Robert Duvall
6	Tito	16	JS Bach
7	Apple	17	*Wonderwall*
8	Atlantic	18	Pain
9	Benito Mussolini	19	Cronus
10	Peninsular & Oriental	20	2000

1   Along with Terence Donovan and David Bailey, who was the third 1960s photographer to make up the "Black Trinity", also referred to as the "Terrible Trio"?

2   Who invented the digital camera?

3   In what decade was the first partially successful photograph taken?

4   Which photographer took the photograph *Identical Twins, in Roselle, New Jersey in 1967*?

5   What was the name of the French inventor of photography?

6   In which decade was the earliest known surviving photograph taken?

7   For what do the initials EXIF stand in relation to digital photography?

8   Sergio Tapiro Velasco won the 2017 National Geographic Travel Photographer of the Year contest with a photograph of a volcano in which country?

9   Shugborough Hall in Staffordshire was the family home of which photographer?

10 Which photograph of 1932 showed construction workers sitting on a girder of New York's Rockefeller Centre?

11 Where were George Mendosa and Greta Zimmer Friedman in an iconic photograph taken on VJ Day in 1945?

12 In which year was the Brownie camera introduced?

13 What is the name of the female photographer who photographed John Lennon on the day of his assassination?

14 What is the real name of rapper and photographer Normski?

15 In 2017, which guitarist published a collection of stereoscopic photos of his band?

16 The photography museum Musée de l'Élysée opened in which European city in 1985?

17 To what do the initials DIN stand for in relation to film speed?

18 Who wrote the music and lyrics to the song *Flash, Bang, Wallop!*?

19 What are the names of the two founders of Instagram™?

20 Who wrote the 1998 novel *Caught in the Light* featuring the fictional photographer Ian Jarrett?

Answers to QUIZ 498 – History

1	1829	11	Boudicca
2	1910s (1916)	12	Idris
3	Persia	13	*Quatermass and the Pit*
4	Cobh	14	Romania
5	The floor of the London Stock Exchange	15	1939
6	US President William McKinley	16	Canada
7	Valencia	17	Ermine Street
8	1865	18	1950s
9	Silurian	19	Christian IX of Denmark
10	1930s	20	Samuel de Champlain